W9-CQN-671

Profiles in Children's Literature

Discussions with Authors, Artists, and Editors

Jaqueline Shachter Weiss

The Scarecrow Press, Inc.
Lanham, Maryland, and London
2001

SCARECROW PRESS, INC.

Published in the United States of America
by Scarecrow Press, Inc.
4720 Boston Way
Lanham, Maryland 20706
www.scarecrowpress.com

4 Pleydell Gardens, Folkestone
Kent CT20 2DN, England

British Library Cataloguing in Publication Information Available

Library of Congress Cataloging-in-Publication Data

Weiss, Jaqueline Shachter.
    Profiles in children's literature : discussions with authors, artists, and editors / Jaqueline Weiss ; foreword by Carolyn W. Field.   p.   cm.
    Includes index.
    ISBN 0-8108-3787-0 (alk. paper)
    1. Children's literature, American—History and criticism—Theory, etc. 2. Authors, American—20th century—Interviews. 3. Illustrators—United States—Interviews. 4. Editors—United States—Interviews. 5. Children's literature—Illustrations. 6. Children's literature—Authorship. 7. Children's literature—Publishing. I. Title.
    PS490   .W45   2001
    028.5—dc21   00-069826

∞™ The paper used in this publication meets the minimum requirements of American National Standard for Information Sciences—Permanence of Paper for Printed Library Materials, ANSI/NISO Z39.48–1992.
Manufactured in the United States of America.

To my wonderful husband, George H. Weiss, M.D.,
and our grandchildren, Sophie and Arianna Kandell,
Naomi and Simon Shachter, and Julian Weiss,
who know the joy of reading.

From Scott O'Dell's *Island of the Blue Dolphins*.

Contents

Foreword

This book is intended for children's literature fans, including parents and grandparents; pre- and in-service teachers and librarians; university students in children's literature classes; and bright students in grade 6 and beyond. It offers readers a chance to learn about some of the twentieth century's finest creators of children's books!

In 1969, Dr. Jaqueline Shachter Weiss began professional videos of authors, illustrators, and editors in the children's literature field who met with some of her Temple University classes to discuss their work. She invited local librarians and teachers to join her in interviewing guests. The result was a collection of copyrighted videos, *Profiles in Literature*, that are both popular and of archival value. Though some guests have since died, their books are still treasured.

Profiles in Literature is known internationally. I once stopped in Singapore and met a state librarian. She was pleased to see me since her *Profiles in Literature* order had just arrived that very day.

All guests are highly celebrated. They include winners (or honor book recipients) of Caldecott, Newbery, Coretta Scott King, Pura Belpré, Regina, and Hans Christian Andersen medals, as well as Christopher, Wilder, and other awards.

This book summarizes and quotes extensively from the personal interviews in the video series and also expands/updates guests' background data. The heading of each chapter gives the interview's production year. "Update" may appear at the end of a chapter so a guest's recent achievements can be cited.

—Carolyn Wicker Field,
coordinator emerita of children's work for the Free Library
of Philadelphia; former USBBY president; recipient of the
Distinguished Service Award of the Association of Library
Service to Children; honored by the Children's Services
Division of the Pennsylvania Library Association
with the annual Carolyn W. Field Award.

Acknowledgments

With gratitude, I acknowledge Carolyn W. Field, coordinator emerita of children's work for the Free Library of Philadelphia, my literary friend for over thirty years. She was the first critic of this book after my husband, George H. Weiss, M.D.

Assistance from Montgomery County–Norristown Library came from Laurie Tynan, director; Mary Maguire, district consultant; Nancy Mack, public relations; Loretta Righter, head of reference services, and her staff (Eileen Davenport, Larry Forry, Sonja Karpow, Patricia Kelly-Evans, Mary Ann Kurcik, and Rae Rondeau Weeks); Margo Locke, district children's consultant and head of children's services; Sue Wilding, children's librarian, and the children's department staff (Ilona Halasz, Susan King, Barbara Makar, Mary Catherine McGarvey, and Moi Tan); and Eileen McNamara in the Bookmobile.

Assistance from the Free Library of Philadelphia came from Hedra Peterman, head of the office of public service support; Kit Breckenridge, retired head of children's material selection; DianeJude McDowell, children's literature research, and the following employees in the children's department: Irene Wright, head; Lois Hartman, assistant head, and Connie Deasy, staff member.

I am also grateful to George McCullough and his Drexel University television staff for technical expertise in *Profiles in Literature* productions since 1990. Also acknowledged are James Holton, Joseph Jalloway, Ross Shachter, Gary Smith, Gregg Szczepanek, and Steven Weiss for technical support.

Due to recent mergers, publishers may be listed by first owner's surname. Gale Research Corporation's *Something about the Author* was helpful in research.

Lloyd Alexander, author (1924–)

Evaline Ness, illustrator (1911–1986)

Ann Durell, editor (1930–)

1973 Interview

LLOYD ALEXANDER

Today, author Lloyd Alexander, an award-winning children's author, is best known for his work in children's fantasy and as a creator of imaginary lands. One is the kingdom of Prydain, the setting for five books published by Holt. But success was not overnight. With illustrator Evaline Ness and editor Ann Durell beside him, Alexander recalled his struggle to be published:

> I wrote for seven long years and never got published. I got up at 4 A.M. to write and then went to work. If I got tired, it was on company time. I don't know why the terrible compulsion to be a writer. It's almost worse *not* to write!

1

Lloyd Alexander was born in Philadelphia on January 30, 1934, just four years after the 1929 stock market crash bankrupted his father, a stockbroker. At the age of three, Alexander taught himself to read. He always had his nose in a book, feasting on mythology and *David Copperfield*. He said that his relatives could have been characters from a Dickens novel, adding that the lodgers in his grandmother's rooming house were "pure Dickens."

After Alexander finished high school, he became a bank messenger and, using his savings, enrolled at West Chester State Teachers College. Sensing that the courses were not helping his writing, he left college and joined the U.S. Army in 1943, during World War II. He had mastered French in high school, and so applied for special duty. The army sent him to Lafayette College in Easton, Pennsylvania, where he studied French and Spanish. His next stop was in Wales, for military intelligence work. There he discovered "a magical kingdom" that heavily influenced his writing.

When the war ended in 1945, Alexander, now working in counter-intelligence for the army, was sent to Paris. He loved the city, and there met Janine Denni, a Parisian whom he married in early 1946 and whose daughter, Madeleine, or "Mado," he adopted.

Before his army discharge came through, Janine and Mado moved to the United States and lived with his parents in the Philadelphia suburb of Drexel Hill. Alexander recalled, "I remained in Paris to study at the Sorbonne even after my army discharge. In an unusual arrangement, the French Foreign Ministry gave me an allowance to encourage my French translations."

Alexander wanted to be closer to his roots to write, so he returned to Drexel Hill, and settled with his family in an attic apartment at his parents' home. He said that the atmosphere resembled his grandmother's rooming house, with many people and lots of activity. His aunt lived there, as did his older sister, Florence, her husband, and their infant.

For seven years Alexander translated French books and supported his small family as a cartoonist, copywriter, and associate editor of an industrial magazine. His earliest published novel, *And Let the Credit Go* (Crowell, 1955), about being a struggling writer, was the first of a group of published adult biographies.

When he could afford it, Alexander moved his family to their own house. He studied the piano, violin, and guitar, becoming "first fiddler" in an only-on-Sunday string quartet that he recruited. From his experiences he created Sebastian, the fiddler in his children's story *The Marvelous Misadventures of Sebastian*. The book features a fiddle that allows its players to perform at their best (perhaps wishful thinking for Alexander's solos).

After ten years of working as a writer, Alexander realized, "I could write about a fantasy world as easily as my real one, and I could offer it to boys and girls. Writing for children was the most liberating and creative experience of my life."

Alexander's first children's fantasy was *Time Cat: The Remarkable Journeys of Jason and Gareth* (Holt, 1963). He traced a magical black cat through various historical periods in many lands. He had planned to include an episode in Wales but changed it to Ireland, saving his Welsh research for his series about that ancient imaginary land, Prydain. First in the "Prydain Chronicles" series was *The Book of Three* (1964), in which Alexander introduced an original character named Gurgi: "I could not continue this volume until I heard the whining, self-pitying voice of Gurgi, asking, 'Crunching and munching?' That character is someone with whom I have definite intimate connections."

Alexander published the other "Prydain Chronicles" books a year apart, beginning with *The Black Cauldron* in 1965, which was a 1965 Newbery Honor Book, and continuing with *The Castle of Llyr, Taran Wanderer,* and *The High King.* The fifth volume brought him the 1969 Newbery Medal. The series tells the adventures of a young hero, Assistant Pig-Keeper Taran. By the final book, Taran conquers the Death-Lord, becomes High King, and with his beloved Eilonwy starts to rebuild the land. Though *The High King* alone won the Newbery Medal, that award could easily have recognized the entire series.

According to Alexander, children cope just fine with Welsh names in his series:

Children are better than grown-ups in handling my Welsh names. An example is the bard, Fflewddur Fflam. Boys and girls are more likely to say double letters as if they were single. They'll take chances and not worry about scholarly pronunciation. The names are authentic, taken from ancient Welsh mythology.

Alexander wrote two early picture storybooks for Holt about Prydain, *Coll and His White Pig* (1965) and *The Truthful Harp* (1967). The model for that harp, bought from a violinmaker, rests on the author's mantel, and he noted that it sometimes hums late at night. Alexander added *The Fondling and Other Tales of Prydain* (Holt, 1999) with Margot Zemach's art; *The King's Fountain* (Dutton, 1971), illustrated by Ezra Jack Keats; and *The Four Donkeys* (Holt, 1972) with Lester Abrams's drawings. Another of his children's books, *The Marvelous Misadventures of Sebastian* (Dutton, 1970), won a 1971 National Book Award.

Ann Durell, an editor and fellow cat lover, published his books for Holt in the 1960s. When she went to Dutton, he followed her.

EVALINE NESS

Evaline Ness, a former model, illustrated Alexander's picture books of the 1960s, including book jackets for the "Prydain Chronicles," and *Time Cat.* She was industrious, illustrating sixty picture books and writing sixteen of them herself. She illustrated three Caldecott Honor Books: *All in the Morning Early* (Holt, 1963) by Sorche Nic Leodhas; *A Pocketful of Cricket* (Holt, 1964) by Rebecca Caudill; and *Tom Tit Tot: An English Folk Tale* (Scribner, 1965) by Virginia Haviland. She wrote and illustrated *Sam, Bangs, and Moonshine* (Holt, 1966), a 1967 Caldecott Medal winner.

Of her artistic techniques, she said:

> In every book, I used a different technique. It's so boring to do the same thing over and over. For example, in *Mr. Miacca* [Holt, 1967], a book that I wrote and illustrated, I used monotypes by pressing absorbent paper atop an oil painting and making a single print of it.
>
> Alexander's *Coll and His White Pig* gave me an unusual opportunity. Always before, publishers saved money by having me do color-separated art. I learned to overcome problems with overlays. Now *Coll* was my first chance to illustrate with full color, a luxury, and I went wild with color splurges. Only when I chose a color scheme did I give the book unity.

Ness enjoyed Alexander's compliments about her art, especially her illustration on the seventh page of *Coll and His White Pig.* She depicted Arawn, a cruel warrior, with heraldry insignias on his sleeve. Alexander said, "She's combined male and female symbols with runic death and life emblems in the sleeve treatment. What she intuitively put together is powerful!"

Ness designed jewelry and tapestries, but neither luxury item was part of her childhood. She was born on April 24, 1911, the youngest of four children, in Pontiac, Michigan, where her father worked on the Pontiac automobile assembly line. Her mother stayed at home, cooking, washing, ironing, and cleaning one bathroom for six people—not a lifestyle that her daughter wanted to copy.

For Ness, art was an escape to a better life. She attended the Chicago Art Institute for two years, supporting herself by drawing women's clothes in a fashion studio.

The first of Ness's two long-term marriages was to detective Eliot Ness (the very same Ness who was the hero of "The Untouchables"). The couple moved to Washington, D.C., where he worked for the Federal Security Agency. There she attended the Corcoran Gallery of Art. Her talent developed under the guidance of her teacher, Richard Lahey. Eventually she entered and won Corcoran's painting competition.

When Ness and her husband separated, she moved to New York and divorced him. There she illustrated stories for *Seventeen* and was art director for Saks Fifth Avenue. She left New York for Rome to study at the Academia di Belle Arti.

Ness returned to New York and later married, settling in Philadelphia with Arnold Bayard, a successful mechanical engineer. They were married for twenty-seven years.

By the 1960s, children's book editors were clamoring for Ness's art. Her first book as author/illustrator was *Josefina February* (Scribner, 1963), "inspired by large woodcuts I had made during a year in Haiti," she said.

Prodded by editor Ann Durell, Ness wrote and illustrated *Sam, Bangs, and Moonshine,* about a fisherman's lonely daughter, Samantha or "Sam." Her mother is dead, but she draws comfort from her cat, Bangs, and likes to "moonshine," or lie. This stark Caldecott winner, available in six languages, features dramatic line and wash compositions in pale green, tan, and black.

Ness found it difficult to illustrate her own tales. "After I've worked on a story, I'm rather finished. I don't think about it visually as I type it. Later, when I've done the art, I'm glad my reluctance doesn't show."

Each year from 1964 to 1967, Ness illustrated either a Caldecott winner or Honor Book. She confessed, "I still think of myself primarily as an illustrator. I typewrite only two double-spaced pages when I provide text for a picture book."

ANN DURELL

"Authors and illustrators do all the conceiving and labor. I call myself a midwife," joked Ann Durell, Dutton's editor of children's books. She explained:

> The editor stands between the author and the artist and serves as a neutral, facing what can be two hostile powers. Alexander and Ness are in harmony, but this isn't always the case. Most writers want to control the artist and say, "I don't picture the girl looking like that." Next, they may add, "I believe I'd draw that scene, not this one."

Durell, who was born on September 30, 1930, in Belleplain, New Jersey, brings a sense of humor to her task. She studied at Mount Holyoke College in Massachusetts and at the University of St. Andrews in Scotland, but her experience as a manuscript editor (from 1960 to the present) was more effective than courses.

Durell understands a writer's problems, as she has worn an author's hat herself. Doubleday published three of her children's books: *Holly River Secret* (1956), *My Heart's in the Highlands* (1958), and *Lost Bea* (1959).

In 1960 Durell made the move from writing to editing, working for the Junior Literary Guild as editor in chief for two years. During the seven years that followed, she was the children's book editor for Holt, Rinehart, and Winston, during which time she met Alexander and Ness. In 1969, she became Dutton's editor. She spoke about her role as vice president for eighteen years of Dutton's children's books:

> I'm responsible for the children's books in my department, selecting what will be published and marketing them. It's like a little publishing house within a larger one. I have an art director who's also a designer, an assistant editor, and a production manager. I work with the authors and help them do their best possible work, such as strengthening a weak character. It has to be the way the writer sees it, not the editor. An author once told me, "If I could put my manuscript away for five years, I wouldn't need you."

Alexander disagreed: "Five years wouldn't do it for me. I'd still be immersed in my own work, and I'd get used to my mistakes. You're more objective than I."

Since middle school students are the main target of the "Prydain Chronicles," Durell conceived the idea of creating picture books about this imaginary land. She wanted younger and less experienced readers to have fun with the fantasy and the "Prydain" theme: good overcomes evil.

Durell said, "A picture book is the hardest form to write. Some authors are so detailed, they don't give an illustrator leeway."

Durell appeared to be a "mother hen" of the picture-book team she had assembled. The threesome—editor, author, and illustrator—clearly enjoyed their friendship.

UPDATES

In 1991, Alexander and his wife suffered the death of their only child, Mado. "Fortunately, she left us with five grandchildren. Three are lawyers. We're delighted that we now have great-granddaughter Zoe!" he reported during his 1992 interview (see next chapter).

Unfortunately, Ness died of a heart attack on August 12, 1986. The gifted artist was seventy-five years old when she passed away in Kingston, New York.

Durell, a Children's Book Council past president, continues to edit for Alexander. In 1982, she married James McCrory, now a retired businessman and a recognized pianist. Five years later she became Dutton's editor at large, a position she continues to hold.

Lloyd Alexander, author (1924–)

Trina Schart Hyman, illustrator–author (1939–)

1992 Interview

LLOYD ALEXANDER

Twenty years after his first interview, Alexander's reiterated goals are unchanged: "I write fantasies for young people since they suit my personality, and I can express myself more openly than in the real world."

His books about newly fantasized lands include *Westmark* (1981), for which he won an American Book Award. He also received the 1986 Regina Medal from the Catholic Library Association and the 1991 Lifetime Achievement Award from the Pennsylvania Center for the Book. The "Westmark" trilogy includes *The Kestrel* (1982) and *The Beggar Queen* (1984).

Alexander often writes books in a series. *Westmark*, the first book in the trilogy, describes an imagined kingdom that is a bit like both colonial America and parts of feudal Europe. Alexander's World War II experiences in France and Germany influenced this setting.

Alexander's next five books, in the "Vesper Holly Adventures" series, featured a red-headed, teenage heroine who has "a goat's digestion and a chess master's mind." She travels to imaginary Illyria, El Dorado, Drackenberg, and Jedera before returning to Philadelphia.

Alexander explained his strategy: "I set these books in the 1870s when the characters wouldn't have too many resources. If they could make phone

7

calls, my series would be over." In *The Jedera Adventure* (1989), Vesper goes to a Mediterranean land to return a library book that is fifteen years overdue.

The Remarkable Journey of Prince Jen (1990) received the 1991 Pennsylvania Young Readers' Award. The book is about a prince who travels in ancient China to learn from his people how to serve them. The elderly characters with rhyming names, Wu, Fu, Shu, and Chu, "are the same person: mysterious, elusive, Zen, Buddhistic, Daoistic," Alexander explained.

Always appreciative of his teammates, Alexander relaxed with Trina Schart Hyman, illustrator of his book jackets for *The Jedera Adventure* and *The Philadelphia Adventure* (1990). She recently painted his portrait, which hangs in his home. Her illustrations and his text created a magnificent picture storybook, *The Fortune-Tellers* (Dutton, 1992).

TRINA SCHART HYMAN

Trina Schart Hyman is herself a star, with two Holiday House self-illustrated picture books that were Caldecott Honor Books in 1984 and 1986. Hyman retold the first one, *Little Red Riding Hood* (1983). The second was Eric Kimmel's *Hershel and the Hanukkah Goblins*. In 1985, her illustrations for Margaret Hodges's *Saint George and the Dragon* (Little, 1984) brought her the Caldecott Medal, her crowning glory. In accepting her Caldecott Medal, Hyman asserted that books and illustrations are "not just what I do; they're what I am."

She flashed an easy smile as she talked about illustrating Alexander's book, *The Fortune-Tellers*:

> I waited over twenty years to illustrate one of Alexander's picture books. When the chance came, I knew I could not draw one more story in medieval England, Germany, Italy, or France. I had just completed my twenty-seventh such tale.
>
> I showed the manuscript to my daughter, Katrin, a Peace Corps volunteer in French-speaking Cameroon for four years. She said, "This reads like a Sufi tale from Northwest Africa." I wasted no time in calling Lloyd to ask if we could set the story in Cameroon, and Lloyd was willing. I had been to Cameroon twice. The first time was when my daughter wrote that she had met a man she might marry. I went to meet him. The second time was when I attended their wedding.
>
> I did worry about one thing. I was concerned since Alexander and I were two white book creators trying to interpret the black experience, and the entire cast of characters was African. Fortunately, book reviewers have been positive.

Alexander's sense of humor contributes to the charm of *The Fortune-Tellers*. On the fifth page, he describes a con artist who forecasts for patrons, "Rich you will surely be. On one condition: that you earn large sums of money."

"You can't deny it!" Alexander said with a laugh.

Hyman has a small companion in her book jacket photograph. "He's my grandson, Michou Tchana. Both Lloyd and I dedicated the book to him." The book turned into a family affair of sorts:

> I've drawn a picture [on the ninth page] of Michou; his mother, Katrin; and at a background table, Lloyd Alexander. I've depicted my son-in-law throughout as the man who became the new fortune teller. I've also shown his parents and sister.

Hyman used real people again to illustrate the back cover of Margaret Hodges's *Saint George and the Dragon*.

> The drawing shows the author and her husband, Margaret and Fletcher Hodges, dressed in the period of King Arthur, approaching my home. I look like a scribe and am sitting at my medieval drawing board. They visited me at my request, and we agreed on a pre-Arthurian time period for the book.
>
> It was the beginning of a wonderful friendship, so I felt free to phone Margaret later and tell her that I can't show Saint George thrusting his sword through the dragon's mouth, piercing his brain. She calmly suggested showing the dragon after it's killed. What a fine solution!

Hyman directed attention to another cherished book:

> *Little Red Riding Hood*, a 1984 Caldecott Honor Book, is a story with my own words and illustrations. This tale was very important to me because at age four, when my mother was reading the story to me, I began to read. What's more, I actually became Little Red Riding Hood that year!
>
> My mother sewed a red satin hooded cape that I wore every day, and she'd give me a "basket of goodies." My dog, Tippy, was the wolf that I confronted. I'd travel around the backyard going to Grandmother's and greet my father, the woodsman, when he came home from work each day. Little Red Riding Hood suited me. She was so dumb!

Hyman was born in Cheltenham, Pennsylvania, on April 8, 1939. She was a bright girl, skipping first grade when she started school. Hyman shared her world with a younger sister, Karleen, for whom she made two fairy dolls. On the dolls' backs, she glued wings from several dead monarch butterflies. The two dolls became so important, Karleen later put them on her wedding cake. Unfortunately, Karleen died early of leukemia.

Hyman's life changed when she went to art school in Philadelphia. She felt as if she had "come home." She married a mechanical engineer, Harris

Hyman, and moved with him to Boston. "I drew Harris in the background on the eighth page of *The Fortune-Tellers*," she said.

Hyman attended the Boston Museum School of the Arts and the Swedish State Art School in Stockholm. In Sweden, Astrid Lindgren, an editor and author of *Pippi Longstocking,* hired her to illustrate a book.

Once the couple returned to Boston, Helen Jones, Little, Brown's book editor for children, gave Hyman books to illustrate. The artist gave birth to a daughter, Katrin, and used her as a model in Norma Farber's *How Does It Feel to Be Old?* (Dutton, 1988). "Here I drew reality in black and white, and memories in brown and white, helped by my own old family photos," she said. "I cry when I see that moving book!"

Trina and Harris divorced in 1968, and she moved to Lyme, New Hampshire:

> I now have a farmhouse with two to five cats, two dogs, and four sheep in the barn. I've also had a pony, a horse, and a goat. I described my drawing-board animal companions in a 1981 Addison-Wesley book that I both wrote and illustrated, *Self Portrait: Trina Schart Hyman.*

She then became art director for the children's magazine *Cricket.* "I recruited *Cricket* artists and invented the cartoon characters that ran around its borders: Cricket, Lady Bug, Sluggo, Marty the Worm, and others." Hyman is no longer the art director, but she and Lloyd Alexander are still on the magazine's executive board.

Because of her work as an illustrator and at the magazine, Hyman receives fan mail from children. One letter, which she put on the door of her studio, reads:

> Dear Mrs. Hyman:
> You work very hard. You are very beautiful.
> Love, Charles

UPDATE

Alexander continued to write epic adventures. In 1995, Dutton released his book, *The Arkadians,* the story of a young man, a poet-turned-jackass, and a girl with mystical powers who oppose a king's wicked soothsayer. In 1997, the author offered *The Iron King,* which describes King Tamar's perilous journey. In 1996, the U.S. Committee of the International Board on Books for Young People (IBBY) nominated Alexander for the Hans Christian Andersen medal.

Hyman illustrated two more Margaret Hodges books, both for Holiday House, *The Kitchen Knight* (1992) and a tale of an evil magician, *Comus* (1996). She also did the art for Howard Pyle's *The Bearskin* (Morrow, 1997). In 2000, she received a Caldecott Honor Award for illustrating John Updike's *Child's Calendar* (1999), a Holiday House book of poems for each month. Hyman continues to draw in magnificent detail, and has illustrated more than 200 books.

Aliki, illustrator–author (1929–)

1995 Interview

Aliki, whose single name is well known in the world of children's literature, was born into a Greek-speaking family on Labor Day, September 3, 1929, while her family was vacationing in Wildwood Crest, New Jersey. Both her heritage and her love of drawing have influenced her life and work.

She grew up in Philadelphia and in suburban Yeadon, Pennsylvania, where she attended public school. "My name . . . doesn't have an English equivalent, but they called me Alice in kindergarten," she recalled. She also attended Saturday art classes, and drew constantly. "My kindergarten teacher encouraged me to draw. She saw my pictures of Peter Rabbit with his siblings and my drawings of my own family. Both have three girls and Peter." Her brother is Peter Liacouras, former law professor and past president of Temple University in Philadelphia.

After graduating from the Philadelphia Museum College of Art in 1951, Aliki became a freelance artist. She painted murals, taught art, and sold self-drawn greeting cards for seven years.

In 1956, Aliki spent six months traveling and painting in Europe, and she learned about her heritage in Greece. While in Florence, Italy, she met Franz Brandenberg in the printing shop where he worked and where she had gone to purchase a dictionary. A year later, they married and moved to his native Switzerland. While there, she created her first book, *The Story of William Tell* (Faber & Faber, 1960), inspired by a Swiss legend.

In 1960, the Brandenbergs moved to New York City. Aliki illustrated other authors' books before beginning to write and illustrate her own. Later, her husband became her agent. In 1964, Prentice-Hall issued *The Story of William Penn*, a Junior Literary Guild Book. Aliki explained why she had chosen ink line and watercolor to illustrate it:

> Illustrations in the *Penn* book look like old-fashioned woodcuts. In fact, I try to make my art in all books tune in to the subject. I'll tell you why I did that book: I used to live close to Philadelphia's City Hall with Penn's statue atop it.

Next, Aliki created *A Weed Is a Flower: The Life of George Washington Carver* (Prentice-Hall, 1964), illustrated in gouache. She said, "The book was reissued. I've been lucky since children are still interested in my topics."

Aliki writes biographies of people who challenge and fascinate her. She does her research carefully, writing in a simple way for children about her chosen personalities. For *The Many Lives of Benjamin Franklin* (Prentice-Hall, 1977), Aliki especially enjoyed writing the dedication:

> I dedicated this book to the one and only Carolyn Field, who, as the Philadelphia public librarian in charge of children's work, has done so much for young people. On the dedication page, I drew the Free Library of Philadelphia, not only because of its role in the book world, but because it's where I first heard chamber music.

Another biography, *The King's Day, Louis XIV of France* (Crowell, 1989) required her extensive effort:

> For my research, I went to all the paintings I could muster and all the written work I could read. For three years, I worked on that book, drawing Louis XIV with all his courtiers. It took a lot of time under the magnifying glass. If I were a person who gives up easily, which I'm not, that was one book I would not have finished.

Hosting royalty is her subject for a Reading Rainbow Book, *A Medieval Feast* (Harper, 1983). In this nonfiction work Aliki shows stages from planting/gathering food to preparing/presenting it, and entertaining dining courtesans. She dedicated her book to family members, "remembering the annual feast. . . . My mother made a party every year for my father's Name Day. Greeks celebrate Name Days more than birthdays."

Stressing her Greek heritage, Aliki retold a Greek folk tale, *Three Gold Pieces* (Pantheon, 1967). She also created *Diogenes, the Story of the Greek*

Philosopher (Prentice-Hall, 1969). Her pastel illustrations of Greek friezes enriched this tale of a humble man who was respected by Alexander the Great. Aliki's *The Gods and Goddesses of Olympus* (Harper, 1994) interprets myths of fifteen of the mightiest Mount Olympus deities. She used still another method to paint them: "I colored my illustrations with multiple layers of watercolor on board."

In 1969, Dr. Franklyn M. Branley, editor of the Let's-Read-and-Find-Out Science Books, guided Aliki into a popular topic for young children: dinosaurs. She reported, "My research was so complex, I had to do four books for Crowell: *My Visit to the Dinosaurs* [1969], *Digging Up Dinosaurs* [1981], *Dinosaurs Are Different* [1985], and *Dinosaur Bones* [1988]."

In 1992, the illustrator–author created a game for Harper called *Aliki's Dinosaur Dig: A Book and Card Game.* Aliki wrote two other science books for middle-grade elementary pupils, *Fossils Tell of Long Ago* (Harper, 1972) and *Corn Is Maize: The Gift of the Indians* (Crowell, 1976). When her 1976 book won recognition, Aliki admitted, "The award thrilled me. Since I'm a Virgo, I like to be correct."

A 1981 prizewinner for older children is *Mummies Made in Egypt* (Crowell, 1979). Aliki, who acknowledged help from an Egyptian Art specialist at New York University, also did research at the British Museum.

The Brandenbergs moved to London in 1977 when their children, Jason and Alexa Demetria, were teenagers. Aliki described how she often used her children as models for her illustrations: "I drew pictures of my children in my books, sometimes as field mice or cats and sometimes as themselves." A perfectionist, Aliki works twelve to fifteen hours a day, sometimes on six books at a time, all in different stages. She does not consider isolation in her small, fifth-floor London studio to be solitary confinement. Instead, she sees it through the eyes of friends who dub it affectionately as "Aliki's Heaven."

In addition to nonfiction, Aliki creates fiction, mainly for Greenwillow:

> I am a combination of information and curiosity. Fiction is true and comes from deep inside me. For Greenwillow, I did a trilogy: *Feelings* [1984], *Manners* [1990], and *Communications* [1993]. . . . The other two books are an extension of *Feelings.*

One book she described as emotionally satisfying is her *The Two of Them* (Greenwillow, 1979), a Reading Rainbow book adapted as a Weston Woods filmstrip. Aliki explained the book's characters:

> The grandfather is actually my father, who was a hard-working Philadelphia grocer. I wrote this about him after his death. The little girl is partly me and

partly my daughter, Alexa, as she related to her grandfather. I illustrated the book in pencil crayon because he had a moving face, not the watercolor type.

Aliki is also known for *The Story of Johnny Appleseed* (Greenwillow, 1979), a Junior Literary Guild selection. The legend, reprinted in Silver Burdett & Ginn's *World of Reading* basals, won a readers-choice award and also became a Weston Woods filmstrip.

In addition to illustrating more than fifty of her own books, Aliki has illustrated 150 books by other writers. This includes more than twenty picture books that were written by her husband, Franz Brandenberg, whose "Aunt Nina" series is well known. His books were published by Aliki's editor, Susan Hirschman, at Macmillan, and then by Greenwillow, when Hirschman moved to that company. The couple's daughter, Alexa, is also a book illustrator. She did the art for Brandenberg's book *A Fun Weekend* (Mulberry, 1991), as well as her self-written study, *I Am Me!* (Harcourt, 1996). The couple's creative son, Jason, is a film producer.

The future will bring many more award-winning books by Aliki. When a child asked her, "What will happen when you run out of ideas?" Aliki replied, "I'll be dead."

AWARDS

In 1991, Aliki won the Drexel Citation from Drexel University and the Free Library of Philadelphia. Among her other book prizes are the Boys' Club of America Junior Book Award for *Three Gold Pieces* (Pantheon, 1967); the New York Academy Children's Science Book Award for *Corn Is Maize: The Gift of the Indians* (Crowell, 1976); the Garden State Children's Choice and Dutch Children's Book Council Silver Slate Pencil awards for *Mummies Made in Egypt* (Crowell, 1979); and the 1987 *Prix du Livre pour Enfants* in Geneva for *Feelings*. She also received an award from the Youth Services Division of the Pennsylvania Library Association in recognition of her outstanding literary contributions.

Avi, author (1937–)

1993 Interviews

Avi (standing) and Jaqueline Weiss

> People are always asking me about my name. My name was given to me by my twin sister, Emily, when we were infants. I use no family name because my family was annoyed at my becoming a writer. That's why I decided not to put their name on my books.

This is how children's author Avi introduced himself to his audience in 1993. By now his family is probably not as annoyed at his chosen profession. Among Avi's prizewinning children's books are *Encounter at Easton* (Pantheon, 1980), recipient of the 1980 Christopher Award, and *The Fighting Ground* (Lippincott, 1984), which won the 1984 Scott O'Dell Historical Fiction Award. Four Avi books, including *Something Upstairs: A Tale of Ghosts* (Orchard, 1988), were nominated for the Mystery Writers of America Edgar Awards. Orchard published his two Newbery Honor Books: *The True Confessions of Charlotte Doyle* (1990) and *Nothing but the Truth* (1991).

Avi was born in New York City on December 23, 1937. His father was a psychiatrist, and his mother was a social worker. His older brother, Henry Wortis, is an immunologist. Avi discussed his career choice:

> I made up my mind to become a writer when I was in high school. My twin sister, Emily Leider, is a writer, poet, critic, and biographer. My grandmother was a writer and so were her two great-grandfathers.

16

My problem was that I flunked out of one high school. In the second high school, I was allowed to come back only because I had tutoring to help my inadequate writing. Still, I stubbornly wanted this career.

I was so traumatized by high school English teachers that in college, I took English only one semester. I majored in theater and history at the University of Wisconsin.

Eventually, Avi became a librarian:

The crude truth is that I had to find a way to make a living beyond carpentry and hamburger making. My writing in those days was for the theater. I got a job as a clerk in the theater collection of the New York Public Library, doing nothing but filing. I discovered that, within a few years, this collection would move to Lincoln Center and [they would] expand their staff. I immediately enrolled in Columbia University Library School at night. In 1964, I became a librarian instead of a clerk and served as such for twelve years.

During 1968, Avi was an exchange librarian in London. He made the move from theatrical writing to composing for young people with the birth of his sons, Shaun and Kevin. When Avi read his stories to his boys and they asked for more, he knew he was on to something. Both sons are now rock musicians who write their own lyrics. Shaun is also a Boston library clerk, and Kevin manages San Francisco bands.

Avi often writes with a gentleman cat, Felix, perched atop his computer monitor: "Felix, cherishing the warmth there, stares down, and goes to sleep as my prose gets more lush."

The British Book Council named Avi's second children's book, *Snail Tale: The Adventures of a Rather Small Snail* (Pantheon, 1972), as one of the best books of 1973. Editor Fabio Coen earned Avi's respect by saying that "eight words" would strengthen the book. Coen really meant that improving an aspect of one character would help. Out of appreciation, Avi honored him in the dedication of another work, *Shadrach's Crossing* (Pantheon, 1983).

When Avi tours, he shows particular interest in special education students to whom he reveals his own spelling problems. He wrote *Man from the Sky* (Knopf, 1980) with the hero being a nonreader who leads state troopers to a sky-diving robber. With large type and only 117 pages, this book has special appeal for remedial readers. It earned a 1980 Children's Choice Award from the International Reading Association.

From 1970 to 1986 Avi was assistant professor and humanities librarian at Trenton State University. While there, he won writing grants from the New Jersey State Council on the Arts. He shared why he particularly enjoyed writing historical fiction:

I was raised in an environment where history was considered important. I often referred to Butterfield's illustrated interpretation of American history. Remember that history is a story.

Because of my background as a librarian, research is not difficult. I tend to write my historical novels where I'm living. In a general sense, I'm interested in how people lived, not in historical events or minutiae, so I write with more freedom.

Avi's first historical fiction, set in 1783, was *Captain Grey* (Pantheon, 1977). The author explained unusual circumstances when he wrote the book, which creates some empathy for a pirate:

I started to write a funny book about a pirate, but dismal conditions around me began to take over. What were the conditions? The faculty at Trenton State College was among the first in higher education to go on strike. On the first day, there was much solidarity, but the second day was sad. I didn't know what to do with myself until I said, "You're an idiot! You can write all day." I had never been able to do that before, but what I wrote wasn't humorous at all.

Two years after *Captain Grey* was published, Pantheon issued *Night Journeys* (1979), about two indentured servants, and a year later, published its sensitive sequel, *Encounter at Easton* (1980). Avi tied these three books together with a change in the second edition reprint of *Encounter at Easton* when the tavern owner, Mr. Grey, adopts Robert Linnly. This boy is mentioned briefly in *Night Journeys* and is dominant in *Encounter at Easton.* Robert becomes Captain Grey and creates a Free Nation for his crew on the wild, uninhabited New Jersey coast in 1783. Avi has outlined two more books to continue the saga.

At one point, the author thought *Captain Grey* might inspire a five-part television contract, possibly with John Wayne in the title role. No contract followed, but Avi did get ideas for two more sequential books, *Night Journeys* and *The Fighting Ground* (Lippincott, 1984). *School Library Journal* rated *Night Journeys* as one of the best books of 1980. Avi made his young protagonist, Peter York, less appealing than the boy's conscience-stricken guardian, the Quaker farmer, Everett Shinn, whom Peter resents until the story's end. Avi, aware that Peter York is a "know it all," commented:

I used to know it all. Incidentally, Everett Shinn was the name of a famous New Jersey illustrator a century later. He could have been my character's "descendant."

I rewrite all my stories, like *Night Journeys,* forty or fifty times. It's not that I'm a perfectionist, but I'm trying to get to know the people I'm writing about.

The Fighting Ground was Avi's next historical novel. This book received a citation in the *Bulletin of the Center for Children's Books* and in 1984 it was listed among ALA's best books for young adults. The story traces an event-filled day during the Revolutionary War, during which a colonial corporal kills the parents of a young French boy:

> The corporal was similar to Ollie North [the military man involved in the Iran-contra scandal during the Reagan administration], contradicting the very values he espouses. As the writer, I understand what this character would do.
>
> In *The Fighting Ground*, I deliberately didn't translate Hessian words within chapters, just at the end, as a way of showing that colonists' inability to understand German helped separate sides.

Avi discussed eerie aspects of his *Something Upstairs: A Tale of Ghosts* (Orchard, 1988), named a best 1989 book by the Library of Congress:

> The *something upstairs* is a murdered slave, Caleb, whose spirit haunted my eighteenth-century house. Every year, the local historical society brought about five thousand people to my door. I lost the privacy of address, a big mistake.
>
> A fan wrote me that he is not allowed to read horror stories by Christopher Pike or Stein, but he is permitted to read *Something Upstairs*. He "complimented" me by writing, "Your book is just as horrible as theirs."

Avi's *The Man Who Was Poe* (Orchard, 1989) was a Library of Congress Best Book of the Year in 1990. The story is about eleven-year-old Edmund who turns to Edgar Allan Poe to solve the mysterious disappearances of his twin sister and aunt. Avi found that Poe in Providence "was complicated, disturbed, and an alcoholic genius."

The biggest prizewinner for Avi was *The True Confessions of Charlotte Doyle*. A Newbery Honor Book, it received the *Boston Globe-Horn Book* 1991 Award, a Golden Kite Award, and a citation from the Society of Children's Book Writers. *School Library Journal* listed it among the best books of 1990. The story, which has a surprise ending, traces thirteen-year-old Charlotte Doyle's unusual 1832 *Seahawk* voyage with a dozen rough crewmen. Avi likes to tell sea stories: "I've lived near the sea, on both the East and West coasts. It has a romantic appeal for me." One reader's mother wrote Avi that her daughter has read *The True Confessions of Charlotte Doyle* sixteen times.

A year after receiving his first Newbery Honor Medal, Avi's *Nothing but the Truth* (Orchard, 1991) became a Newbery and *Boston Globe-Horn Book* Honor Book. Avi paid tribute to his Orchard editor:

> I started with Richard Jackson as my editor at Bradbury and followed him when he moved to Orchard. If Richard Jackson moves tomorrow, I hope he'll take me along.
>
> At one point, I was thinking of calling *Nothing but the Truth* "Discovery," because its structural idea is information discovered about a crime. It's like a

mystery: not *who did it* but *what happened.* Truth is so complex, the only way
to get at it is to invent it.

   Nothing but the Truth presents the illusion that I, as the narrator, am neutral.
The response of characters is what makes the book interesting.

   Philip Malloy, the protagonist, is not the most admirable character. He is un-
encumbered by adults. He voluntarily reads S. E. Hinton's *The Outsiders,* which
shows he is not a nonreader. He had an objection to one teacher and a traditional tale with which he could not relate.

According to librarians who conducted a Connecticut Young Critics Club,
Avi's book touched a nerve:

> Never have we seen a book evoke such passion as *Nothing but the Truth.* It was
> clear that the readers (in grades 5 through 8) were loving the book at the same
> time they were hating it. Sometimes they gave the book four stars (the highest
> rating) while hurling it on the floor. . . . He said something important that
> needed saying in a compelling and infuriating way. (*Journal of Youth Services
> in Libraries,* spring 1993, p. 255)

UPDATE

In the mid-1990s, Avi moved to Denver, Colorado. There he has created
chapter books about adventures of country mice. The prequel is listed first:
Ragweed (Avon, 1999), *Poppy* (Orchard, 1995), and *Poppy and Rye* (Orchard, 1998). Another chapter book is *Tom, Babette, and Simon* (Macmillan,
1995), three original stories in which a boy and cat change places.

   In 1996, Orchard released a two-volume story, *Beyond the Western Sea,*
about three teenagers who go from an Irish village to the New World together. In 1999, HarperCollins published Avi's easily read book, *Abigail
Takes the Wheel,* about a captain's daughter who learns to steer a ship up the
Hudson River.

   Avi has led workshops in thirty-eight states. Not unexpectedly, young people have nominated his books to win U.S. readers' choice awards in at least
eighteen states. It is an amazing record for a writer of varied genres whose
books don't always have happy endings.

Natalie Babbitt, author–illustrator (1932–)

1990 Interview

Natalie Babbitt, who creates young people's fantasy and fiction, shielded her brown eyes behind horn-rimmed glasses as she commented:

> I think limiting vocabulary is a poor idea. After all, we read difficult words in Kipling's children's books. In general, young people are hopeful, and the best-remembered stories for them turn in the end toward expectation rather than resignation.

Hopeful endings characterize Babbitt's prizewinners. They include *Kneeknock Rise* (1970), a 1971 Newbery Honor Book, and *Tuck Everlasting* (1975), a 1975 Honor Book of the International Board on Books for Young People (IBBY), and a 1976 Christopher Award winner. Of course, the devil is often the loser in *The Devil's Storybook* (1974), her humorous 1974 National Book Award nominee. Farrar, Straus & Giroux published her self-authored books until 1994 when her editor, Michael di Capua, joined Harper-Collins, and she followed him.

Natalie Zane Moore was born in Dayton, Ohio, on July 28, 1932. Her family is from early-settler stock. One ancestor, kidnapped by Wyandot Indians, was raised near what is now Detroit and helped to keep Wyandots loyal to the colonists during the Revolutionary War. Another ancestor, Zebulon Pike, discovered Pike's Peak, but, she revealed, "he was later a traitor in cahoots with Aaron Burr."

The author's father, Ralph Zane Moore, worked in industrial relations. He shared with Babbitt and her older sister, Diane, a sense of humor and an interest in word puzzles. From her mother, Genevieve Converse Moore, a painter, Natalie developed artistic ability. At age nine, after receiving *Alice in Wonderland* with John Tenniel's art, Babbitt decided to become a children's book illustrator. She revealed, "Being left-handed does not present the same problems in drawing that arise in writing." Her mother's reading of books influenced Natalie as a writer, and so did her father's inventive use of language. She illustrated six books by poet Valerie Worth as well as her own books.

The Depression destroyed any expectations Babbitt's mother had for affluence, which her father never took seriously. Babbitt recalled moving many times, including to the shores of Lake Erie, which she recorded in her book, *The Eyes of the Amaryllis* (1977).

After attending Laurel, a private girls' high school near Cleveland, Babbitt went to Smith College in Northampton, Massachusetts, where she majored in art. Following graduation, she married Samuel Fisher Babbitt, who is a vice president at Brown University in Providence, Rhode Island. The couple had three children, who now pursue distinct careers: Chris is a clinical psychologist; Tom is a Boston rock guitarist; and Lucy Fraterroli, who writes young-adult fantasies, is the mother of Peter and Maggie.

In 1966, the Babbitts collaborated on a book titled *The Forty-Ninth Magician*. Samuel wrote the book in only two hours, and Natalie illustrated it with india ink. Michael di Capua published it for Pantheon. After di Capua moved to Farrar, Straus & Giroux, Natalie Babbitt gave him her first book, *Dick Foote and the Shark* (1967), which she wrote (in verse) and drew (in black, white, and bayberry green). The book, a Junior Literary Guild selection, poked fun at nineteenth-century Cape Cod inhabitants.

Babbitt showed appreciation for her editor:

> He never messes with ideas, but is fussy about repetition of words. I admit that he has rejected two of my complete books, but from one chapter, I got the idea to do *The Devil's Storybook*. I did the first and second *Devil* books over twelve years apart, the second suggested by my editor because the first sold so well.

The Devil's Storybook (1974) won a *Horn Book* Honor citation. It contains ten comic stories about a middle-aged, petty devil who, although he connives, is frequently outsmarted as he tries to increase his southern population in hell. *The Devil's Other Storybook* (1987) is distinct.

Babbitt's last book in verse was *Phoebe's Revolt* (1968). It depicts a New York City child, Phoebe, in 1904 who protests wearing Victorian frocks with uncomfortable frills. Babbitt switched to prose when she wrote *The Search for Delicious* (1969). In this modern fairy tale, an orphan boy, twelve-year-old Gaylen, the prime minister's special assistant, tries to end a dispute by searching for what is most delicious. *The New York Times* called this the best book of 1969 for children aged nine to twelve.

Goody Hall (1971), a Gothic story, is set in an English country mansion, Goody Hall. The heir, Willet Goody, solves the mystery of his father's disappearance with help from his Shakespeare-misquoting tutor. Babbitt discussed this Book World Spring Festival Honor Book:

> *Goody Hall* is my favorite of my children's books but one of the slowest sellers. Mrs. Goody is a little like my mother was in terms of being ambitious for position in the world. In this book, I feel like I'm having the conversation I would have had with my mother had she not died when I was only twenty-four. The book may be appreciated most by British children who know about Shakespeare and are advanced readers.

Babbitt is best known for two books. One, *Kneeknock Rise*, is a *Horn Book* Honor Book and a 1971 Newbery Honor Book. Babbitt dedicated it to her fat mutt, Alice, who was the model for the book's dog, Annabelle. In this prizewinner, Insteppers refuse to relinquish their mythical Megrimum, believed to be a mysterious "beast" on a mountain peak. A lad, Egan, climbs to the peak and discovers a scientific source of moaning sounds attributed to Megrimum, but the villagers don't believe him. Babbitt compared Insteppers with herself: "I was angry when my sister told me there was no Santa Claus. *Kneeknock Rise* and *Tuck Everlasting* inspire children to think for themselves."

Tuck Everlasting, a major literary contribution, has the artist's sketch of Babbitt's Pond on its cover but no illustrations inside. Among other citations, this classic was a *Horn Book* Honor Book and was on the International Reading Association choices list.

Tuck Everlasting is a timeless story about the pioneering Tuck family who, in the 1880s, along with their horse, drank water from a spring that gives them eternal life. (An old meaning of *tuck* is "life.") The family—Angus and Mae Tuck, their older son, Miles, a carpenter, and their younger son, Jesse—all remain at the same age they were when they drank the water. This, of course, brings about many problems. Also, the spring doesn't remain a secret. Ten-year-old Winnie Foster discovers the spring on her family's property and goes home with the Tucks. A mysterious man in a yellow suit overhears Ma's explanation about the spring to Winnie. The man ends up dead and Winnie ends up in jail. Before the Tuck family moves on, Jesse gives Winnie some of the water and tells her to drink it when she's seventeen.

Does she drink it? And what happens to the spring? Read the book for answers.

Not all readers like all parts of the book, Babbitt has found. Referring to the storm in *Tuck Everlasting,* the author said, "I thought everyone knew that lightning is the symbolic weapon of the hand of God. It's not important to the story, but it has peaked children's curiosity."

Babbitt referred to fan mail:

> An eleven-year-old girl expressed extreme anger about the ending of *Tuck.* I wrote back, saying it was just a story and inviting her to write me when she was seventeen. To my surprise, I got a response from her six years later. No longer angry, the girl had come to better terms with mortality.

In 1989, Anita Silvey, head of ALA's Wilder Award selection committee, said, "If I were forced to choose one book from the past twenty years to take to a desert island, it would be *Tuck Everlasting,* a novel that seems to improve every time I read it."

Tuck Everlasting and *The Eyes of the Amaryllis* were both made into Disney movies. "Both films had the same director, but I made no input for *Tuck* and was disappointed with results," Babbitt said. "I took an interest in *The Eyes of the Amaryllis,* which is a better film with professional actors and a higher budget."

In 1989, Babbitt did a full-color picture book, *Nellie, a Cat on Her Own* (Farrar, Straus & Giroux).

> I carved a marionette cat from balsa wood as easy as carving butter. I also used broom straw and yarn. In the story, the marionette mixes with real cats. I changed my cast, originally having a girl as my protagonist and a mixture of animals.

In her self-drawn, full-color picture book, *Bub or the Very Best Thing* (HarperCollins, 1994), Babbitt drew those who are dear to her:

> My dog, Rosie, a golden retriever, modeled for the book. She likes to pose but hates the minstrel's bells on her hat. The book involves a king and queen who search for the best thing they can give their son, the prince. The model for the prince is my grandson, Michael. I am painting all my family members' portraits and even that of my editor, using a magnifying glass. My editor approved the book based on a complete dummy.

Babbitt was a U.S. nominee in 1981 for the international Hans Christian Andersen Medal. A perfectionist, she strives to offer children "a Thanksgiving feast of good literature, rather than a mid-morning snack."

UPDATE

Babbitt continued to illustrate her own work until 1998. She preferred not to illustrate her 1999 ALA Notable Children's Book, *Ouch! A Tale from Grimm* (HarperCollins, 1998). The book has full-color pictures by Fred Marcellino. In Babbitt's version of the Grimm tale, Young Marco, who is nobody special, fulfills an errand in Hell, helped by the devil's grandmother, and then he becomes a king.

Pura Belpré, translator–author (1899–1982)

1971 Interview

Pura Belpré's career as an author started when, as a puppeteer, she couldn't find enough Puerto Rican-based folk tales to perform. In fact, her first book, *Perez and Martina* (Frederick Warne, 1932 in English and 1966 in Spanish), started out as a story she performed at library school. Since then, she said, the story "has become a classic." She recalled:

> I sent it [the book] to publisher Frederick Warne without an agent. Warne and I like the colorful illustrations of Carlos Sanchez. Warne would publish more of my stories if Sanchez could illustrate them. I don't know where he is. I hope he's still alive!

Pura Belpré was born in Cidra, Puerto Rico, on February 2, 1899, and was educated there in her father's language, French, as well as in English and Spanish. After coming to the U.S. mainland, she attended the New York Public Library School, becoming the first Latina librarian in the New York Public Library's Office of Children's Services in 1921. Later, she was a Columbia University student of Latin American literature, Portuguese, and puppetry.

In library school, students had to write a story to be shared in class. Belpré chose to record her storytelling grandmother's favorite folk tale, *Perez and Martina,* which may have originated in Persia. Belpré did a puppet presentation of the story's Puerto Rican variant with Martina as a cockroach in a black *mantilla* and Perez as an elegant mouse. In the story, Martina picks Perez as her suitor. The romance is cut short, however, when Perez tries to sample sweetened rice cooking for Christmas. While reaching for an almond, he falls into the hot pot and dies. Martina mourns on her balcony, singing and strumming a guitar.

Belpré performed *Perez and Martina* on a Spanish-language television station with help from the South Bronx Library Project staff. Nationally, she accepted many puppeteering and storytelling invitations.

Since Belpré found no Puerto Rican folk tales on library shelves when she became a librarian, she wrote some. Frederick Warne published four of her books. They were *Juan Bobo and the Queen's Necklace*, illustrated by Christine Price (1962), about a country lad who finds jewels no one else could locate; *Dance of the Animals*, illustrated by Paul Galdone (1965), excerpted from *The Tiger and the Rabbit, and Other Tales*; and collective legends, *Once in Puerto Rico,* again illustrated by Christine Price (1973). Pantheon issued *Ote: A Puerto Rican Folk Tale*, illustrated by Paul Galdone (1969), about a peasant's encounter with the devil.

Belpré's first original story, *Santiago*, resulted from a personal experience. On a wintry February morning, the author was walking with her husband, Clarence Cameron White, a concert violinist, conductor, and composer, on a New York street when she was almost tripped by a white hen. That white hen became the heroine of *Santiago* (Frederick Warne, 1969 in Spanish, and 1971 in English). This is a tender story of a young student, Santiago Román, who brings vivid memories of his pet hen, Selina, with him to New York City after moving from Puerto Rico. Symeon Shimin's magnificent illustrations help this book come alive. In 1973, *Santiago* brought the author the Brooklyn Art Books for Children citation.

In addition to writing seven children's books about her culture, Belpré has translated filmstrips, records, and at least fourteen well-known children's books into Spanish. Of her translation work, she said:

> I had nothing to do with the selections. They're requests from publishers based on book popularity. Publishers translate books that have sold and are still selling well because they don't want to lose money.
>
> My first assignment in 1962 was from Viking for a Spanish record of Munro Leaf's *The Story of Ferdinand*. To be from Cidra, a little Puerto Rican town, and do that book was exciting! I'm sorry they "went to town" with sound effects because that caused the New York Public Library not to buy my translation.
>
> I had the good luck of being asked to translate six of the "I Can Read" books for Harper and Row in 1969, including *Little Bear* by Else Holmelund Minarik. Next, I translated Jane Thayer's book that was very popular in the New York Public Library, *The Puppy Who Wanted a Boy*, published by Morrow in 1958.

> Grosset and Dunlap had me translate six head-start books sold at grocery stores. They are fine and inexpensive. I want my books to be accessible since I remember author–illustrator John Steptoe once told me, "I wrote a book that's too costly for my people to buy."
> My Spanish translations include filmstrips for Weston Woods, such as Ezra Jack Keats's *The Snowy Day* and *Whistle for Willie.*

The author–translator confessed that she does not always experience "smooth sailing." While attending a Washington, D.C., library convention to speak about her work, she met a friend, Margaret Bates, who was returning from Brazil. Bates handed her some Brazilian stories and told her, "Do what you want with them." After Belpré rewrote the stories, the Consul General of Brazil asked her, "Please, do me the honor of letting me read your copy. I'm glad children in the U.S. will get to know Brazilian stories." Later, this woman complained that the content concerned struggling jungle animals. Belpré, who was not able to find a publisher, lamented that too many folk tales revolve around royalty only.

Belpré said she has learned to cope with failure as well as success in finding publishers. However, as a librarian, she had few setbacks. She organized puppetry clubs and started a folkloric celebration of "The Three Kings' Day" on January 6. She resigned from the library in 1945 to travel and write, but returned to work from 1961 to 1968, after her husband's death.

Belpré said she treasured her 1970 Special Award from *El Instituto de Puerto Rico* in New York City. It recognized her contribution in bringing to the United States an appreciation of Puerto Rican culture.

UPDATE

Belpré died in 1982. In 1996, the Association for Library Services to Children (ALSC) and National Association to Promote Library Services to the Spanish Speaking (REFORMA), an ALA affiliate, started biennial Pura Belpré Awards. One is for Latino writers and a second for Latino illustrators whose work best exemplifies authentic Hispanic cultural experiences in children's literature. (See Pura Belpré Awards in Appendix.)

Jeanne Bendick, author–illustrator (1919–)

Robert Bendick, author (1917–)

1973 Interview

"Science isn't something in a corner but is related to everything that happens each day," said Jeanne Bendick, a prolific author–illustrator of children's informational books dating from 1937 to the computer age. In her opinion, "The greatest gift to children is to develop their curiosity, for questions are more important than answers."

Jeanne Garfunkel was born on February 15, 1919, and grew up with her younger sister, Bobby, in Manhattan. Her ability and love of writing stemmed from her father, Lou, a Columbia Journalism School graduate. Lou had promised his father, Max, that if he didn't become a successful writer within a year after college, he would join Max's Busy Bee luncheonette chain. The time was too short to test his writing skills, so during the Depression Lou served paying customers inside a luncheonette and later his own private bread line behind it. Lou was proud of his older daughter's writing success. Jeanne Bendick's maternal grandfather, Charley Hess, developed her interest in science by taking her to the American Museum of Natural History. He also encouraged her as an artist, urging persistence until she got drawings just right.

In Manhattan, Bendick attended what later became the High School of Music and Arts with the sister of Duke Ellington, who volunteered his band for their prom. After high school, she went to Parsons School of Design, earning part of her tuition by teaching a Saturday children's art class and illustrating for a children's magazine, *Jack and Jill*. She graduated in 1939 with a coveted Parsons scholarship to study for a year in Paris. She turned down the scholarship because of the spread of Nazism in Europe and because she was engaged to Robert "Bob" Bendick, whom she married in 1940.

During World War II, Bob enlisted in the Air Force, and Jeanne and her formerly stay-at-home mother, Dot, joined the American Women's Voluntary Services. Her family called Dot "the General" since she became assistant to General Drum, New York Port Commandant of troop movements.

Jeanne was illustrating *What Makes It Tick?* (Houghton, 1943) when the Japanese attacked Pearl Harbor. A children's science book was a novelty then. In *Electronics for Boys and Girls* (McGraw, 1944), Jeanne tried to clarify RADAR (Radio Detecting and Ranging). She included a section on atomic energy, so after the atomic bomb's explosion in Japan, she was often interviewed. After the war ended and her husband returned in 1945, the couple began their family. Jeanne gave birth to Bob Jr. and two years later, to Karen.

On the heels of *What Makes It Tick?* was a Franklin Watts series of "First" books that Jeanne began as illustrator, but soon became author–illustrator. Jeanne is first to admit that she is not trained as a scientist. She merely likes to break down complex scientific concepts into parts and share findings with young people. Fred Hofkins, who was the Philadelphia School District science director in 1973, told Jeanne how much his own children learned from her series starter, *The First Flying Book* (1943). She explained:

> *The First Flying Book* is a rebus with pictures taking the place of some of the words, but this awkward format was later discontinued. The book's new title is *The First Book of Airplanes.*
>
> Each of the "First" books is written differently. *The First Book of Airplanes* appeals to a young child. *The First Book of Space Travel* is for older children. I always try to use appropriate language for the intended reader's level. I encourage thinking.

As an author of science books, Jeanne often tests ideas before writing about them. For *The First Book of Automobiles* (1955), her family helped her make a soapbox car, and all four of them coasted down a street in wooden boxes atop old wheels. "A science writer also must update books," Jeanne said, adding that she rewrote *The First Book of Space Travel* (Franklin Watts, 1953) at least six times. It won a New York Academy of Sciences Award. When she initially submitted the book, no one had orbited Earth. Her book, *Electronics for Boys and Girls* (McGraw, 1944), has been revised at least six times and has been translated into more than twenty languages. It is in heavy demand, not only by juveniles but also by adults who want basic understanding. If she were to rewrite her book *The Wind* (Rand McNally, 1964), which was intended for young children, "I'd write it in a different way now with many more activities," she explained.

Jeanne said she learns a lot when she illustrates books by other science authors, such as Nina and Herman Schneider, who made technology comprehensible, and Glenn Blough, the elementary education specialist in the U.S Education Office who exposed some natural world mysteries. She applies knowledge from scientists to books for children, starting with *All Around You: A First Look at the World* (McGraw, 1951). From that old title may have come the name, *The First Look,* a yearlong NBC children's television program based on Jeanne's "First Book" series. While Bob Bendick was director–producer, Jeanne wrote some of the scripts and edited all of them. The cast included folksinger Oscar Brand.

After the television program aired, one of Jeanne Bendick's friends, Myron Atkin, a dean at Illinois University, invited Jeanne to join a new science textbook writing team at Ginn and Co. The offer allowed her to write three volumes for the kindergarten/lower elementary grades without restrictions. Her teammates, composing for grades four through seven, were Isaac Asimov and Roy Gallant. She analyzed what made the company consider the team's writing to be literary:

> Writing style makes the books be considered literature. It's significant that the company hired known authors, not teachers. When teachers complained about difficulty, we assigned materials to one grade above. My kindergarten program went to first grade, and I wrote anew for kindergarten.
>
> The focus in almost every picture is a person of the reader's intended age handling something related to the topic. When I did my units on comparisons, children saw pictures and spoke about what's alike and what's different. Then they heard recordings of Oscar Brand singing his own music and my lyrics for "Comparing." It begins, "Comparing's what you do to see how things are alike and how they're different too." The recordings give children a chance to move, acting out "bigger and smaller" and other comparisons.

One of the author–illustrator's favorite self-written books is *Names, Sets, and Numbers* (Franklin Watts, 1971). "It makes me think my work is going somewhere," she said.

Jeanne has operated independently for the most part, though she has had joint books/endeavors with her husband. Both enjoy sailing and are environmentalists.

ROBERT BENDICK

Book collaborator and television producer–director Bob Bendick was born on February 8, 1917. He attended Manhattan's New York University and completed his studies at Clarence White School of Photography. He moved into film when he was hired as a motion picture cameraman for a Canadian publicity film, not knowing anything about that profession. Bob rented a movie camera, practiced for a week, and was successful on the job, later becoming one of CBS's first three television cameramen. Soon after that, Jeanne and Bob married.

Bob was part of a combat camera unit for the Air Force in China-Burma-India. During this time, when Jeanne was also working on her early science books, the couple worked—via the mail—on a joint project, a book based on Bob's U.S. film experiences. The finished book was entitled *Making the Movies* (McGraw, 1945), and was revised as *Filming Works Like This* (1970). It cites various styles of films, from documentaries to animations. The Bendicks's second book, *Television Works Like This* (McGraw, 1959) has been revised four times due to public interest.

When Bob became director of CBS-TV News, Sports, and Special Events in 1945, the Bendicks moved to Fresh Meadows, New York. Bob worked with Edward R. Murrow. Soon, Lowell Thomas coaxed Bob from CBS to direct a wide-screen movie called *Cinerama Holiday*. Bob directed *Cinerama Holiday* in 1955. He traveled coast to coast doing movies and television. He produced NBC's *Today* show for three years, during which time he won the Albert Lasker and Critics' awards. He produced *The Great American Dream Machine*, which won Emmy Awards for two years, and was producer-director of *Wide, Wide World*. As his own company's president, he produced daily programs of the Olympics in Mexico City for Latin American television.

Bob joined Jeanne in the Ginn multimedia science project, driving across the United States for six weeks to take photographs of children for use in textbooks and other media. Bob stressed a role for films in helping poor readers learn:

> Film strips should have no sound tracks in kindergarten, so pupils can verbalize, and sound tracks should be optional in high school. The multimedia approach is wise since it reinforces learning with films, games, slides, recordings, charts, and books.

After this project, Bob and Jeanne did two one-hour public television documentaries that explored the reasons for hunger in Europe, Africa, Asia, and Latin America. Bob was producer–director and Jeanne was writer and unit manager.

Bob and Jeanne said that they relish their rare chances to collaborate on books and projects.

UPDATE

At the American Museum of Natural History in 1985, Jeanne Bendick won the American Nature Study Society's Eva L. Gordon Award. She wrote and illustrated *Tombs of the Ancient Americas* (Franklin Watts, 1993), dedicating it to her daughter, Karen, an artist who married a physicist, Peter Holton. In the 1993 book, Jeanne shared unsolved mysteries in Peruvian, Guatemalan, and Mexican pyramids, as well as in U.S. cliff cities and mound sites.

For Henry Holt, Jeanne wrote two books that Todd Telander illustrated, *Exploring an Ocean Tide Pool* (1992) and *Caves! Underground Worlds* (1995). The first book ends with a plea to keep oceans clean for healthy air, water, and food, and is dedicated to her son, Bob, who is director of the Rhode Island Environmental Management Department. He and his wife, Jill, are parents of the Bendick grandchildren, Rob, Rebecca, and Eric.

In *Caves! Underground Worlds*, Jeanne's exciting view of Cro-Magnon cave art, she discusses sites in Spain, Algeria, Peru, and France. Animal drawings of penguins are in a Marseilles cave, far from penguin habitats today. On page 60, Jeanne shows Stephen Bishop, a slave who mapped Kentucky's Mammoth Cave in 1842 after teaching himself to read, so he could learn more about caves.

Stan Berenstain, illustrator–author (1923–)

Jan Berenstain, illustrator–author (1923–)

Michael Berenstain, illustrator–author (1951–)

1979 Interview

STAN AND JAN BERENSTAIN

One common rule of thumb is that married couples should avoid working together, unless they enjoy extra stress. But the "mom and pop" team of author–illustrators Stan and Jan Berenstain, who often work seven-day weeks, say that they never have disagreements, only violent agreements. Stan's jutting chin made his explanation seem authoritative:

That's not as facetious as it sounds. We may be both getting at the same thing from different directions. Usually there's a correct solution to a storytelling problem. We have a United Nations rule: each reserves a veto right—at least until the next day. That's worked out well because it's much easier to react to something than to create it. If I came up with an idea and Jan said, "I don't think that works," I believe her, because why should she lie? The reverse is also true.

A second common rule of thumb is that family members should avoid working together. Again, the Berenstains have proven the rule-makers wrong. The two are proud of their talented sons, Leo and Michael, who now work with them. Stan, Jan, and their sons have created more than 175 Berenstain Bears children's books. "More than 240 million copies have been sold internationally in at least fourteen languages and braille!" Stan stated.

Jan and Stan were both born in Philadelphia in 1923—she, on July 26 and he, on September 29. She was named for Janice Meredith, a children's book heroine and artist who traveled with George Washington. Jan's father worked as a carpenter/builder, and was also an amateur artist who, for eight years, attended night classes at the same art school where Stan and Jan later met.

At school, Jan was considered the "class artist." Asked her favorite book as a child, she replied, "It was *A Child's Garden of Verses* illustrated by Jessie Wilcox Smith, who drew little roses with faces inside them." Stan said, "My reading list included *The Bobbsey Twins* and *Tom Swift*. I joined the public library when I was eleven and read adult books."

At age five, Stan began to draw wherever he could. He was living with his parents behind and above a run-down clothing store that his mother tended. She was preoccupied when he entered a newly papered upstairs room and crayoned what he thought was a vast prizefighting mural, really a red scrawl, on its pristine surface. His Popeye drawings were more recognizable.

Destined to be an artist, Stan went to the Philadelphia Museum School of Art, later called the Philadelphia College of Art, where he met Jan in 1941. He commented, "I was impressed with Jan's art and liked everything about her."

He was drafted into the U.S. Army during World War II. For three years, while they were apart, the couple exchanged letters, often illustrating them. Stan's war task was at Indiana's Wakeman Army Hospital where Major Truman Blocker, a plastic surgeon, saw Stan's hospital ward sketches and chose him as medical artist. Stan remembered, "I scrubbed, entered the operating room, and sketched facial reconstructive surgery." His work was included with patients' medical records.

After the war, the surgeon offered to help Stan start a medical art service, but Stan had other plans. In the service, he had sold four original cartoons to Norman Cousins of the *Saturday Review of Literature*, and he wanted a cartoonist's career.

Two weeks after his 1946 discharge, Stan married Jan, who had done war work in an aircraft factory. While Stan attended the Pennsylvania Academy of the Fine Arts on the GI Bill, Jan taught at the Philadelphia College of Art and also painted giftware.

Working as a freelance cartooning team, the couple sold a cartoon to *Collier's*, which established them with major magazines. In time, they built a small house in Cheltenham, Pennsylvania, and welcomed their first son, Leo, a source of cartoon humor about childhood. Macmillan recognized their talent and published two of their adult cartoon books: *The Berenstains' Baby Book* (1951) and *Baby Makes Four* (1956). The latter focused on arrival of a second son, Michael.

Another windfall came in 1955 when *McCall's* magazine enlisted them to do a cartoon feature, "It's All in the Family," which they published for fourteen years. *Good Housekeeping* magazine picked up the series and published it for nine years: "We did cartoons with a Christmas theme twenty-three times, always with jargon changes." They created black-and-white cartoons for Hallmark greeting cards, and they did twenty *Collier's* colored covers of panoramic scenes, like family zoo visits, company picnics, and dancing school.

"In those days, there weren't many picture books about family life," Stan commented. "Theodor Seuss Geisel, better known as Dr. Seuss, had started Beginner Books after his success with *The Cat in the Hat* (1957). He called us to his Random House office and, as editor, inspired us to perfect our first bear book, *The Big Honey Hunt*."

Jan added:

Geisel gave us a restricted word list for that book. We rhymed whenever we could because we know rhyming is a reading aid. At times, we thought of a rhyme scheme or idea in the middle of the night. Geisel was editor for our first seventeen books.

The Big Honey Hunt was published in 1962, after almost two years of work and five revisions. To satisfy Geisel, the couple had to do simple illustrations with nothing in the background, so children could tie pictures with words. They had hoped the first book would start a series, but Geisel urged them to do something else. After *Honey Hunt*'s success, Geisel decided to continue bear tales. It was Geisel who named the series when he announced the second book, *The Bike Lesson* (1964), as "Another Adventure of the Berenstain Bears." In this story, Papa Bear teaches Small Bear to ride a two-wheeler.

"We've done books for children from two to ten years of age," Jan said. "In the past, we did Bright and Early concept books for toddlers, Beginner

Books to encourage reading with laughter as a reward, and the Bear Facts Library for instruction. A book in the last category is *The Berenstain Bears' Science Fair"* (1977).

Stan added:

> *Science Fair* was a difficult project. My first instinct was to explain relativity, which I don't understand. I guess the bear theory of relativity is that all bears are relatives. I always assumed that a simple science book for young readers had been done before our publication in 1977, but now I know why few have tried it.

"We did three revisions of *Science Fair*," Jan reported. "We decided to introduce only terms that we could illustrate simply and avoid abstractions." For example, the cover shows Mama Bear with a pulley, Sister Bear with a lever, Small Bear with a wedge, and Papa Bear testing jet propulsion.

Stan and Jan are equal writing and drawing partners. A text results from much thinking over two or three workweeks. The person with an idea may write a two- or three-page story summary and expand it into a tale, perhaps with twice the needed 1,100 words. The partner condenses it into a workable manuscript.

Illustrations begin with Stan doing a rough layout. Jan offers a perfect pencil version, which Stan inks. Both paint equal amounts, using bottled transparent watercolors. Then Random House gets the manuscript by Federal Express.

The Berenstain animals don't look like real bears or teddy bears; they act exactly like people, have facial expressions, and wear human clothing. Papa Bear has bib overalls and Mama Bear wears a blue, polka-dotted dress, but they are barefoot.

As if having to incorporate a limited vocabulary into a book isn't challenging enough, "Random House also gave us fragrance labels to use in special books," Jan said. "I discovered that the labels included the ingredients used in pizza, so that's the origin of our scratch-and-smell effort, *Papa's Pizza: A Berenstain Bear Sniff Book*" (1978).

The couple's books are often egalitarian. Jan said, "Our books, like *He Bear, She Bear* (1974) show a female doctor, carpenter, and truck driver." In an effort to avoid sexual stereotyping in his own home, Stan said that he occasionally attempts to cook. "I'm a good cook when it comes to boiling spaghetti," he said. "Fortunately, I like spaghetti."

MICHAEL BERENSTAIN

"I wouldn't eat Dad's cooking," Michael quipped without bragging about his own culinary expertise.

Michael, born on December 21, 1951, described his childhood reading: "My reading ranged from *Gulliver's Travels* to *Mad* magazine. There weren't enough funny books when I was young."

Michael's early interest was in art. He loved art history and valued books with reproductions of old masters' paintings. Butterflies in his collection served as drawing models. His father offered encouragement by giving him a cast of a Roman woman's head, which Michael often drew.

After graduating from high school, Michael considered becoming an entomologist but decided on an art career instead:

> I attended the Philadelphia College of Art and studied painting at the Pennsylvania Academy of the Fine Arts. I even did a political cartoon in art school. There's a false idea there that cartooning, where no live models are used, is inferior to drawing.

After college, Michael got a job in New York as Random House's art director of children's books. If an artist missed a printer's deadline, Michael would copy the artist's style and do needed book drawings.

But Michael also has his own style. He prepared historical reference books for schools and libraries for his publisher, David McKay. He exhibited craftsman's accuracy in taking youngsters on guided tours with cutaways in *The Castle Book* (1977), *The Ship Book* (1978), *The Lighthouse Book* (1979), and *The Armor Book* (1979). The books have full-color covers and pencil drawings inside.

Michael released books of fantasy for his new publisher, Random House, beginning with *The Troll Book* (1980). *Time* magazine put *The Sorcerer's Scrapbook* (1981) on its annual list of the ten best children's books. *The Creature Catalog* (1982) was another Random House humorous spoof. Bantam published two of his fantasies about possumlike animals, *The Dwarks* (1981) and *The Dwark Meets the Trash Monster* (1984). Michael has also illustrated books by other authors.

UPDATE

Leo, a trained scientist, is now a full-time writer. He published *The Wind Monkey and Other Stories* (1992), a Random House adult book.

In the mid-1980s, Stan and Jan heard from children who had grown up with Berenstain Bear picture books and now wanted chapter books in which the text dominated, not pictures. Stan and Jan were busy with First-Time Books, eight-inch square paperbacks that do not teach reading but are read aloud to children, aged three to seven. They welcomed Michael and Leo voluntarily becoming full-time teammates. With parental collaboration, Leo has written many Big Chapter Books published by Scholastic, and Michael has illustrated them. Among their titles are *The Berenstain Bears and the Drug Free Zone* (1993), *The Berenstain Bears' Media Madness* (1995), and *The Berenstain Bears and the Big Date* (1998).

In 1982, Stan and Jan received the Drexel University/Free Library of Philadelphia Citation. They also extended into the adult market with *What Your Parents Never Told You About Being a Mom or Dad* (Crown, 1995).

The popularity of Berenstain Bear books has increased through fan clubs, television specials, and the distribution of toys, puzzles, watches, T-shirts, chocolates, filmstrips, cassettes, and a CD. For those who can't get enough of the friendly animal family, the Allentown, Pennsylvania, Dorney Park theme section is devoted to the Berenstain Bears.

Photograph by George Cooper

Judy Blume, author (1938–)

1973 Interview

Author Judy Blume is a voice for young people in the world of children's literature, tackling such issues as menstruation, sex, envy, and wet dreams—topics that interest preteenagers but are rarely discussed in books written especially for them. Blume knows just how to write to this vast group of eager readers:

> I become whoever I'm writing about. I think it has something to do with having a great memory of how I felt and putting myself in someone else's shoes. I cry and laugh as I read my own manuscripts. I'm very emotional.

Blume was born on February 12, 1938, in Elizabeth, New Jersey, and was especially close to her father, Rudolph Sussman, a dentist. She was more entertaining than her quiet, mechanically talented brother, who was four years older and the rebel in the family. Fond of dancing, she was afraid of thunderstorms, dogs, and darkness. She was just as curious about sex as are her characters. In 1959 she married attorney John Blume and had two children: a daughter, Randy, in 1961 and a son, Larry, two years later. The couple divorced in 1975.

Blume's first efforts as a children's writer began in the late 1960s. She recalled:

> I read books to Randy and Larry. When they were aged six and four, I started to write for children. I began with imitation Dr. Seuss, mailed booklets, and got rejection letters.

Since I was a graduate of New York University, I got a notice of their course in writing for children. I took the course twice and wrote a chapter a week of *Iggie's House.* . . . I even received professional encouragement.

Blume's first picture book, *The One in the Middle Is the Green Kangaroo,* was published in 1969 by Reilly and Lee. The story focuses on Freddy Dissal, a middle child, who blossoms when cast as a green kangaroo in a school play. Her next book went to Bradbury, a publishing house she felt she "discovered":

I read that Bradbury was looking for realistic fiction, so I sent *Iggie's House* to them. I talked with them for many hours and then went home and rewrote the book, though they did not promise to publish it.

In 1970, Bradbury issued *Iggie's House,* a book about the integration of a residential block populated by white families. When Iggie moves, an African-American family, the Garbers, occupy her former house, and a neighbor, Winnie Barringer, becomes their new friend. Though thirty other neighbors sign anti-Garber petitions, the Garbers courageously remain.

In 1970, Bradbury published Blume's most popular book, *Are You There God? It's Me, Margaret,* which *The New York Times* called "outstanding." The story is about a sixth-grade girl named Margaret whose parents practice different religions and let Margaret choose her own affiliation. The book, written in first person, discusses a girl's physical changes. The author shared book contents with her daughter during the writing stages:

When I was writing *Are You There God? It's Me, Margaret,* my daughter, Randy, was eight years old, which is younger than its intended audience. She's read everything I've ever written. She came home from school and ripped my copy out of the typewriter. She's a wonderful junior editor. She read that book throughout rewrites, galleys, hardback, and softback editions.

In writing the book, Blume remembered her own life as a sixth-grade girl:

There's a lot of me in *Are You There God? It's Me, Margaret.* I acted and thought as Margaret did. There's always a "first time" for every event, which experienced people think is "old hat."

Ninety percent of my fan mail comes from girls, aged ten to thirteen. They write me about *Are You There God? It's Me, Margaret.* Many want another book about Margaret, but I will not do one. Instead, I'll write more books like it. . . .

When I'm talking about *Are You There God? It's Me, Margaret,* I always bring the hardback and softback covers. Children seem to prefer the softback edition's

front cover, which I can't stand. It shows Margaret as a blonde with long, flow-
ing hair. Margaret in the hardback cover is the way I picture her, as a day-
dreaming preteen brunette.

Blume's next controversial book was *Then Again, Maybe I Won't* (Bradbury,
1971), in which she mentioned wet dreams:

> While I was waiting to hear if the publisher would accept the book about Mar-
> garet, I was nervous, so to keep myself from worrying, I began another book. It
> was *Then Again, Maybe I Won't,* material I was warned not to write.

This book is about thirteen-year-old Tony Miglione. He lives next-door to
sixteen-year-old Lisa, who undresses nightly without lowering her window
shades. Tony copes with his sexual arousal and other problems faced by
boys his age, problems that are never easily resolved. Blume recalled that
one mother commented on this book at a party.

> A mother of a twelve-year-old boy told me, "I snipped out two pages of *Then
> Again, Maybe I Won't.* When my son complained, I said, 'That happens all the
> time. When they're binding books, they make mistakes.'"
> I asked the mother if she would clip out pages on menstruation.
> She said, "No, because that's normal. I don't think at age twelve my son is
> ready to read about wet dreams."

Blume disagrees: "The book gives a parent the perfect excuse to sit down
and answer a child's spontaneous questions."
Also in 1971, Blume published *Freckle Juice,* an easy-to-read Four Winds
tale. It relates how Andrew Marcus envies a freckled classmate, Nicky Lane.
Andrew thinks he could avoid washing neck dirt with freckles as camouflage. For fifty cents, he buys a recipe that claims to induce freckles. Blume
dedicated the book, "For Randy, favorite freckle face."
In 1972, Dutton issued Blume's *Otherwise Known as Sheila the Great* and
the "Fudge" trilogy with *Tales of a Fourth-Grade Nothing,* followed by *Su-
perfudge* (1980), and *Fudge-a-mania* (1990). The series focuses on various
aspects of family love and sibling rivalry. Aside from her Dutton series,
Blume continued individual Bradbury Press novels, including *It's Not the
End of the World* (1972), about a young girl's effort to prevent her parents'
divorce, followed by *Deenie* (1973), about a seventh-grader with scoliosis.
Blume researched material for *Deenie* at the New Jersey Orthopedic Hospital, where she saw how the molding of braces is done and learned that this
spinal curvature is reparable. The book stirred controversy because it raised

the issue of masturbation; the young protagonist learns from a gym teacher that such stroking is harmless.

Blume's *Forever* . . . (Bradbury, 1975) was published as a novel for young adults. Librarians often place *Forever* . . . in the adult collection, even though its protagonist, Katherine Danziger, is a senior in high school. Blume revealed in 1973, "My daughter wants a book about older girls, about sex and romance, so *Forever* . . . was the book, and I dedicated it: 'For Randy as promised . . . with love.' "

Forever . . . deals with Katherine's loss of virginity when dating seventeen-year-old Michael Wagner. On her eighteenth birthday, he gives her a silver pendant with her name on one side and the word, "Forever," on the other side. Four days after making love to Michael, Katherine begins work as a tennis assistant at a Maine summer camp and becomes attracted to Theo, the head tennis counselor. She finds she no longer enjoys intercourse with Michael when he visits, and she decides, "I think it's just that I'm not ready for forever."

UPDATE

Blume has continued to write on controversial subjects. Her book *Blubber* (Bradbury, 1977) is one example: "It's about fifth graders and the cruel way they treat each other at age ten." The book includes the use of "four-letter words," for which Blume was criticized. Another 1977 Bradbury Press book, *Starring Sally J. Freedman as Herself,* concerns a ten-year-old girl who worries about a new school and about death of a relative in a Nazi concentration camp. Sally dreams of working to get Hitler arrested and helping to end the war.

Other books Blume has written since 1973 include *The Pain and the Great One* (Bradbury Press, 1984), a picture book dealing with sibling rivalry; and *Just as Long as We're Together* (Orchard, 1987) and its sequel, *Here's to You, Rachel Robinson* (Orchard, 1993), depicting three girls' long-term friendship.

Blume received a 1984 Carl Sandburg Freedom-to-Read Award as well as a 1986 American Civil Liberties Award. The popular nonconformist has sold over sixty-five million copies of her books!

In 1988, the author and her son, Lawrence Blume, produced a Barr Films screenplay that she adapted from her novel, *Otherwise Known as Sheila the Great.* Blume also wrote a television adaptation for her *Tiger Eyes* (Bradbury, 1981), about a family dealing with the death of a father and husband. This book stemmed from the author's grief over her own father's death and her mother's refusal to discuss his demise.

Blume's latest books include adult fiction, *Summer Sisters* (Delacorte, 1998). She also has created adult nonfiction, *Letters to Judy: What Your Kids Wish They Could Tell You* (Putnam, 1986). It includes letters Blume has received from young people. She uses royalties from sales of that book and *The Judy Blume Diary* to endow her KIDS Fund, which she began in 1981. The fund helps nonprofit groups that promote parent/child communication. She has declined offers to sell Judy Blume bras, jeans, T-shirts, and board games.

Blume has homes both in Manhattan and Santa Fe. She is now married to another writer, George Cooper. Having long fought book censorship, she has received tributes for her courageous honesty. Best of all, young people have showered her with over forty-five U.S. readers-choice awards.

Arna Bontemps, poet–author (1902–1973)

1971 Interview

Arna Bontemps advised would-be writers that "Patience is the greatest attribute. Many have talent but few have patience." After years of practicing such patience, Arna Bontemps became an author known for talent, knowledge, and pride in his African-American culture. His talent was reflected in *Story of the Negro* (Knopf, 1948), a 1949 Newbery Honor Book and a 1956 Jane Addams Children's Book Award recipient. His knowledge and pride led to such publications as *Golden Slippers: An Anthology of Negro Poetry for Children* (Harper, 1941), the first collection of African-American poetry for children.

George Bontemps was born in Alexandria, Louisiana on October 13, 1902. His father, Paul, was a brick mason, as his grandfather and great-grandfather had been. His mother, Marie, was a teacher. As a boy, Bontemps preferred "Arna," his grandmother's nickname for him, rather than his given name.

After an altercation with some drunken white men late one night, Arna's father, who was also a musician, decided to move his family—wife, son, and daughter—to a Los Angeles neighborhood populated mostly by white, but friendly, families. He continued as a mason and became a part-time preacher for the Seventh-day Adventist Church. Bontemps's grandmother arrived later to take care of the family when Arna's mother became ill. Her younger brother, whom Bontemps called "Uncle Buddy," soon joined the family.

Uncle Buddy introduced Arna, then eleven years old, to an African-American culture that his school history books did not cover, including how

45

U.S. and Caribbean slaves fought for their freedom. Unlike his father, who wanted a clean break with the past, Arna read extensively about his heritage. After Arna's mother died, his father, trying to end Uncle Buddy's influence, sent his son to San Fernando Academy, a white boarding school. The father cautioned, "Now don't go up there acting colored," Bontemps remembered.

After graduating from high school, Bontemps entered Pacific Union College. He was aware of only one African-American poet, Paul Lawrence Dunbar, but knew there must be more. Following his college graduation, he went to New York City to find other writers and intellectuals and to learn more about his culture. Once in New York, Bontemps's world opened up. He began teaching at Harlem Academy, an Adventist high school. Bontemps met Alberta Johnson, who had moved to New York from Georgia; they married in 1926 and eventually had six children. Then Bontemps began to receive writing awards. In 1926 and again in 1927, Bontemps won the Alexander Pushkin Poetry Prize. In 1927, he also won first prize in a poetry contest sponsored by *Crisis*, magazine of the National Association for the Advancement of Colored People (NAACP).

Bontemps drew inspiration from New York's Harlem Renaissance, a time in the 1920s when Harlem attracted gifted, creative African Americans from all over the country, including, Countee Cullen, Aaron Douglas, W. E. B. DuBois, Jessie Fauset, Lorenz Graham, W. C. Handy, Du Bose Heyward, Langston Hughes, Zora Neale Hurston, Charles S. Johnson, James Weldon Johnson, Nella Larsen, Alain Locke, Claude McKay, "Jellyroll" Morton, Louise Thompson Patterson, Bessie Smith, Jean Toomer, and Dorothy West. Through poet Countee Cullen, Bontemps met writer Langston Hughes, who became a close friend and, at times, a coauthor.

Bontemps observed that some whites also joined in the Renaissance movement:

> One was composer George Gershwin who, influenced by the Harlem beat, wrote "Rhapsody in Blue." Another was author Carl Van Vechten who, helped by his publishing contacts, issued a novel about the Harlem Renaissance in 1926. Since Van Vechten's book won public attention early, less-experienced African-American authors could not sell their work on the same subject.

It was during this time that Bontemps wrote "A Black Man Talks of Reaping," a poem published in a book that he edited, *American Negro Poetry* (Hill and Wang, 1963, pp. 75–76). The poet said, "I was originally paid only ten dollars for it by a New York magazine, but each reprint in school textbooks brought me about thirty-five or forty dollars."

Though exploitation is obvious in the poem's conclusion, Bontemps referred to the exploiters as "my brother's sons" with this rationale: "We are all brothers, all Americans, though some enjoy advantages that others don't have. When I wrote the poem, I was thinking of the Harlem Renaissance, and the word 'brother' was in the front of my consciousness."

One insider who eventually profited from the Renaissance was musician W. C. Handy. Bontemps, who wrote Handy's biography, *Father of the Blues* (Macmillan, 1941), remembered: "Handy sold 'Memphis Blues' for fifty dollars but came back with 'Saint Louis Blues' and didn't give that one away. He lived solvently for the rest of his life."

Bontemps's first adult novel, *God Sends Sunday,* was issued in 1931 by Harcourt. His publisher, Alfred Harcourt, was also his editor since publishers were among those who suffered during the Depression. Countee Cullen helped Bontemps later adapt his book for the stage as "St. Louis Woman," which starred Pearl Bailey in her first Broadway musical. Metro-Goldwyn-Mayer planned a movie version that was eventually abandoned.

During his early years of success, Bontemps was reluctant to use an agent. He said:

> I got my first book contract without the benefit of an agent. A lot of people would like to be your agent, but they'll charge you. The only agent that's worthwhile is the one who pays you. At times, it's harder to get a good agent than a publisher.

The release of *God Sends Sunday* did not bring economic security to Bontemps and his family. When the Depression hit New York, many Renaissance artists left to take any jobs they could find. In 1931, Bontemps went to teach near Decatur, Alabama, close to Scottsboro, where nine African-American young men, the "Scottsboro Nine," had been charged and were being tried in the rape of two white girls. The case became a national scandal, and eventually the nine males were freed. Bontemps remembered the case:

> The boys had been riding empty boxcars and, unfortunately, were joined by two unknown white girls in overalls. The boys were charged with rape. Guilty was the usual finding for such suspects [black males who were charged with raping white women], and death, the usual penalty.

In an atmosphere that promoted racial injustice, Bontemps used his pen to let the world know about the plight of his people. In the fall of 1931, Bontemps saw a newspaper clipping that inspired his "A Summer Tragedy," which John Henrik Clarke included in *American Negro Short Stories* (Hill and Wang, 1956, pp. 54–63). The short story reflects the dignity of an elderly, devoted African-American couple, Jeff and Jennie Patton. "The story won a contest prize and now appears in twenty-odd books. That's what I like!" the author said with pride.

Bontemps felt it was dangerous for him and his family to stay in Alabama, so he took a teaching job in Chicago. There he began writing books that his four daughters and two sons could read. First, he collaborated with Langston Hughes on an upbeat tale, *Popo and Fifina: Children of Haiti* (Macmillan, 1932). The two men later collaborated on a monumental adult collection, *The Book of Negro Folklore* (Dodd, 1958).

Trying to eliminate negative generalizations about African Americans, Bontemps created more children's works. Ilse Bischoff's unfortunate stereotypical illustrations almost ruined his study of an African-American farm boy, *You Can't Pet a Possum* (Morrow, 1934). More somber is *Sad-Faced Boy* (Houghton, 1937), a tale about three Alabama boys visiting an uncle, a Harlem apartment house custodian. Similar in tone is *Lonesome Boy* (Houghton, 1955), a poignant account of a New Orleans trumpet player.

Houghton published three humorous children's tall tales that Bontemps wrote with Jack Conroy, his Chicago colleague on the Works Progress Administration (WPA) Federal Writers' Project. Typical was *The Fast Sooner Hound* (1942), whose animal hero would "sooner run than eat." The dog follows his master, Boomer, a train fireman, running beside the locomotive. Finally, the hound gets permission to stay by Boomer's side in the cab. Virginia Lee Burton's lively illustrations for this book began her successful career.

Bontemps's compilation, *Golden Slippers: An Anthology of Negro Poetry for Children* (Harper, 1941), reflected his belief, "The best contribution to American literature comes from the simple lyrical verses of my people." Twenty-eight years after *Golden Slippers*, he edited the poetry anthology, *Hold Fast to Dreams* (Follett, 1969). It contains his old and new favorite poems.

Bontemps took graduate English courses and earned a master's degree in library science from the University of Chicago in 1943. Though he felt a bond to fellow writers in the "Windy City," he could not accustom himself to Chicago's ghetto life. After burglars ransacked his apartment twice, he realized that he had fled lawless Alabama's Scottsboro/Decatur environs to lawless Chicago's crime-ridden South Side. That made Bontemps move his family for the last time, in 1943, choosing Nashville, Tennessee, a smaller and safer city. The writer began a twenty-two-year stint as head librarian and later, as public relations director at Fisk University. He and his wife often hosted students at their home, helping to create the warm, intellectual atmosphere identified with Fisk. His volunteer activities included serving on the Nashville School Board. In Nashville, Bontemps also wrote steadily. One of his first works for juveniles was a prizewinning exposé of slavery, *Story of the Negro* (Knopf, 1948). Fisk's Jubilee Singers, who introduced spirituals to the musical world, inspired Bontemps to write *Chariot in the Sky* (Winston, 1951).

Among Bontemps's collective biographies are *Famous Negro Athletes* (Dodd, 1964) and *We Have Tomorrow* (Houghton, 1945). The latter encouraged unusual careers by showing twelve young, successful African Americans in challenging occupations, such as Dean Dixon, a symphony orchestra conductor.

Bontemps's individual biographies, intended for students in third grade and beyond, include *The Story of George Washington Carver* (Grosset, 1954) and *Frederick Douglass: Slave-Fighter-Freeman* (Knopf, 1959). Douglass's abolitionist role was the focus of Bontemps's book for teenagers and adults, *Free at Last: The Life of Frederick Douglass* (Dodd, 1971). Two of Bontemps's poems, "Close Your Eyes" and "The Daybreakers," appeared in *The Poetry of the Negro, 1746–1970*, edited by Langston Hughes and Arna Bontemps (Doubleday, 1970).

The prolific poet and writer said he never suffered from writer's block. "I never have to worry about ideas. My problem is finding enough time to write them down."

All-embracing Bontemps spoke in 1971 as a visiting professor and the curator of the James Weldon Johnson Collection at Yale University. In 1972–1973, he became a writer-in-residence at Fisk University and worked on his autobiography, declaring, "I've already shared autobiographical information when I've written book introductions."

UPDATE

Bontemps died on June 4, 1973, after suffering a heart attack and before he completed the story of his life as a versatile poet, novelist, anthologist, biographer, critic, playwright, librarian, educator, husband, and father.

Eleanor Cameron, author (1912–1996)

1972 Interview

All authors have fans, but few probably have the kind of young admirer Eleanor Cameron described:

> Steve Kuehler has been writing me ever since he was nine. He wrote me three-and four-page, single-spaced letters, eighty of them by the time he was fifteen. He drew a cover design for my book, *A Spell Is Cast*, and he knows children's literature. I think he's a genius! He's always making thunderous discoveries. He came from Texas to spend his fifteenth birthday with me.
>
> He is now thirty-two, and we are still close and treasured friends. Can it be because of our friendship that, after a start in another direction, he has decided at last to become a librarian?

Not many authors have nurtured a friendship of such duration. Cameron was such a caring individual, she connected with soul mates of any age.

Cameron's fantasy, *The Wonderful Flight to the Mushroom Planet* (Little, Brown, 1954), won the 1960 Hawaiian Nene Award, which is chosen by children. In 1965, she received the Mystery Writers of America Edgar Award and the Commonwealth Award for *A Spell Is Cast* (Little, Brown, 1964). *A Room Made of Windows* (Little, Brown, 1971), which is largely autobiographical, won the 1971 *Boston Globe-Horn Book* Award.

Cameron was born in Winnipeg, Canada, on March 23, 1912, a chilly day that registered a temperature of forty degrees below zero, according to her mother. When Cameron was three years old, her family moved to a small, failing farm in Ohio. To help make ends meet, her mother, Florence Butler, who was from England, worked from 6 A.M. until late at night as housekeeper of the Houston Inn in South Charleston, keeping her daughter with her.

The family's next move was to Berkeley, California, when Cameron was six years old. They lived in a small, brown-shingled bungalow. Cameron remembered her father as being stern with both her and her mother. Her only positive memory of him was when she was eight or nine, and he built her a desk. She later described the desk in *A Room Made of Windows*. Cameron's father died in solitude, many years after her mother divorced him.

After the divorce, Cameron and her mother moved into a small two-story apartment where the child had her own small "room made of windows" and an opening into an attic space where someone was moving on the other side of a wall. That someone was Daddy Chandler, whom the child came to love like a grandfather in *A Room Made of Windows*. On her side of the wall, the young Cameron began to write:

> I was Julia in *A Room Made of Windows*. At the age of eleven, I knew I wanted to be a writer. At twelve, the "Berkeley Young Author's Page" of the *Berkeley Daily Gazette* began to publish my stories and poems.

As the only child of a single parent, Cameron felt a strong attachment to her mother. "I looked upon my mother as my own property," she recalled. "I hadn't seen my father in a long time. I set up impediments to Mother's remarriage. My reaction to Uncle Phil was as I wrote it." She explained:

> In *A Room Made of Windows,* a character, Riannon Moore, in a dressing gown and with her hair hanging down, came from the next-door red house and told Julia, "Your mother wants the love of a man."
>
> There never was an actual neighbor like Moore. She came to me as a hypnagogic experience while I was half-sleeping, half-waking. Moore said, "I have a son named Oramore, and he is a great pianist." Moore almost becomes the center of the book.

A Room Made of Windows introduces Gregg as Julia's older brother. Cameron never had a brother, but the author used her son, David, as Gregg's model. The author said that Trina Schart Hyman, the book's illustrator, captured Gregg's reading posture perfectly. David gave permission to be included in the book and allowed his mother to say that he had a messy room, "but don't go further."

After Cameron's mother remarried, the new family moved to a hilltop house that had a view of Berkeley and Marin County woods. They vacationed together in the redwoods and Yosemite. At the age of fifteen, Cameron got her first job as a Berkeley library clerk after school and on Saturdays.

When the Depression hit, Julia's folks lost their beautiful home because they gave it as security for a loan to save their employer's doomed business. Los Angeles was the only place where they could find jobs, so the three moved there. After graduating from high school, Cameron took a Los Angeles library-training course and got a part-time library job in the afternoons and evenings. She studied at the University of California, Los Angeles, in the mornings for two years. For another year, she took morning art classes, planning to illustrate her own books.

At the Los Angeles Library, two memorable events occurred. One was a frightening earthquake. Another was meeting an attractive young man, whom her mother recommended. He was Ian Cameron from Scotland, a graphic arts consultant. His nickname for Eleanor was *Speug* (pronounced spee-ug), the Scottish word for sparrow. In 1933, four years after the couple met, they married.

Cameron worked for six years as a Los Angeles Library clerk. She then worked for six more years as a Los Angeles School District library clerk. No elementary school libraries existed, so she gave elementary teachers book bundles. A highlight for her was meeting book creators, such as Leo Politi and Munro Leaf.

When her husband entered the U.S. Army in 1942, Cameron left library work to begin her adult book, *The Unheard Music* (1950), a stream-of-consciousness novel. She finished it after Ian's discharge and after the birth of their only child, David. The boy was seven years old when Cameron, upset from her second adult book's rejection, considered her son's request for a children's book about him and his friend, Chuckie. In the story, the two would build a small spaceship and fly to an unknown planet, "just the right size to explore in a day or two." Cameron told her reaction:

> The next morning, I discovered that overnight the personality of the slight, quick, wise, little man, whose name I found later to be Tyco Mycetes Bass, had taken shape in my imagination as well as the central idea of *The Wonderful Flight to the Mushroom Planet.*

Cameron's 1954 book, like all of Little, Brown's "Mushroom Planet" books, was a Junior Literary Guild selection. David wanted the series to continue, so Cameron wrote *Stowaway to the Mushroom Planet* (1956), *Mr. Bass's Planetoid* (1958), *A Mystery for Mr. Bass* (1960), and *Time and Mr. Bass* (1967). In 1964, Cameron discovered the importance of setting when she wrote *A Spell Is Cast*, illustrated by Joe and Beth Krush. In the book, Cory, a preteen girl, visits in the California home of Uncle Dirk and his reserved mother, Mrs. van Heusen. They are the brother and mother of the actress who has cared for Cory since the death of the child's parents. After Uncle Dirk meets and marries Laurel, a weaver, the couple decides to adopt Cory.

In 1969, Cameron won the Commonwealth Award for Literature for *The Green and Burning Tree: On the Writing and Enjoyment of Children's Books* (Little, Brown, 1969). This adult book of literary criticism offers essays about genres of children's literature. Picture books are omitted.

Long before she wrote *A Room Made of Windows*, Cameron saw a room in the Los Angeles County Art Museum in which items from a chateau in France had been reassembled in minute detail. Cameron also saw a bedroom and dining room of similar style at the Metropolitan Museum in New York City, and these rooms inspired her first time fantasy, *The Court of the Stone Children* (Dutton, 1973). (She said she had originally thought of naming it after Chagall's painting, *Time Is a River Without Banks*.)

The Court of the Stone Children is set in San Francisco, where a secondary student, Nina, visits the French Museum. There she finds statues in a courtyard and a painting of Dominique ("Domi"). The museum also has a replica of the chateau's interior where Domi had lived during Napoleon's reign. Domi, a ghostly apparition, talks only with Nina. She gets Nina to prove that her father, accused of murder, was innocent. Nina reports her findings to the French Museum employee who is writing a biography of Domi's father and clears his name.

Cameron spoke about the importance of a writer's style:

> Style is the sound of self. I did not get a style of my own for a long time. In *The Unheard Music*, I imitated Virginia Wolfe. I certainly wasn't going to write the Mushroom Planet books in the style of Virginia Wolfe. *A Spell Is Cast* enabled me to be myself. Everything since *The Green and Burning Tree* has been more reflective.
>
> In my books for children, my instinctive desire seems always to instill in them, if not outright magic, then the feeling of magic.

UPDATE

Eleanor Cameron continued to win awards during her long career. Her fantasy, *The Court of the Stone Children* received the 1973 National Book Award, and her realistic fiction, *To the Green Mountains* (Dutton, 1979), was a 1979 National Book Award semifinalist.

After *A Room Made of Windows*, Cameron wrote four more books about Julia Redford, going back in time to the early part of her sixth year and forward to her fifteenth year. These four books, published by Dutton, are *Julia and the Hand of God* (1977), *That Julia Redfern* (1982), *Julia's Magic* (1984), and *The Private Worlds of Julia Redfern* (1988).

Cameron died on October 11, 1996, at Hospice House in her beloved Monterey, California. She was eighty-four years old.

John Ciardi, poet–critic (1916–1986)

1976 Interview

John Ciardi (pronounced CHAR-dee) was a member of the American Academy of Arts and Letters whose work includes a translation of Dante's *Divine Comedy* for adults. He was also a children's poet, offering such pieces as *The Man Who Sang the Sillies* (Lippincott, 1961), winner of the 1963 Junior Book Award of the Boys' Club of America. In Ciardi's opinion, "Children's poems are *eternal*; adult poems are *mortal*."

The poet offered a humorous reason as to why he wrote largely funny poems for boys and girls: "My wife got busy and filled the house full of kids. It seemed the best way of playing with them." He practiced first on nieces and nephews when he and his wife lived at his sister's New Jersey home.

Ciardi was born on June 13, 1916, the fourth child and only son of Italian immigrants, Carminantonia Ciardi, a Metropolitan Life Insurance agent, and his wife, Concetta. They lived in Boston's "Little Italy" section and spoke Italian at home. Later, the family moved to nearby Medford, Massachusetts. In his book *In Fact* (Rutgers University Press, 1962), Ciardi included his poem, "Heritage," which memorializes his father, who was killed in an automobile accident when Ciardi was three. The poet said it was from his father that he inherited his sense of humor.

Following Italian custom, his mother treated her son as the "man of the family" after his father's death, elevating him to what his sisters might have called "stellar brathood." His mother could not read, so he became her bridge to English. He learned early that one culture existed in the home and one existed outside. His bilingual upbringing made him aware not only of the two languages, but also "the differences between them."

Ciardi remembered always loving words and books. He was an eclectic reader and a good student, worked part time at odd jobs, and was a Boy Scout. He stayed an extra year in high school, trying to save college money. Teachers recommended Bates College, a poor academic choice, but he stayed for three semesters before transferring to Tufts University.

At Tufts, he took a writing class taught by John Holmes, who became a father figure and mentor, guiding the fledgling poet. Ciardi wanted to earn enough for basic needs and to give his mother money, but still to "live for poetry!" Holmes arranged for Ciardi's graduate study at the University of Michigan, where he received a scholarship and met his second mentor, Roy W. Cowden. In 1939 at Michigan, Ciardi received a master of arts degree and won a coveted Avery Hopwood Award of $1,000 for his poetry. Ciardi repaid debts, gave his mother some money, and toured the country. *Poetry* magazine bought one of his poems and Henry Holt published his revised Hopwood prized poems.

From 1940 to 1942 he was a guest lecturer at the University of Kansas City, earning $900 per semester. In 1942, Ciardi feared he would be drafted into the infantry, so he enlisted, becoming a gunner on noncombat aerial missions. Once officers discovered his writing skills, they made him handle awards and write condolence letters to families who lost a son, brother, or husband in the war.

When peace was restored, Ciardi returned to teaching in Kansas City before accepting a position at Harvard in 1946. He was thirty years old, and sensing security with that position, married Judith Hostetter. He continued to advance professionally during the next year or two. *The New Yorker* began buying his poems, and in 1947, Atlantic Monthly Press and Little, Brown published *Other Skies*.

Ciardi taught English at Rutgers University in the 1950s. It was then that he translated Dante's *Divine Comedy* from fourteenth-century Italian into English. He said, "The Dante book is approaching two million in sales since it's used as a textbook. I also wrote several poetry books whose total sales have been three copies in the United States alone." Ciardi stopped teaching when he "found his own papers more interesting to work on than those of students."

Ciardi's greatest claims to popular fame were at the juvenile level. In a distinctive, resonant voice, he read aloud the title poem from his earliest children's book, *The Reason for the Pelican* (Lippincott, 1959), before he commented, "I got a letter from a bird curator at a California nature museum, asking for my pelican reference. My poetry is humorous, not erudite." The book, based on a game he played with nieces and nephews, goes beyond pelicans, offering: "Why Nobody Pets the Lion at the Zoo" and "The Principal Part of a Python."

Ciardi was motivated to write juvenile poetry by his own three children: daughter Myra, a musician, and sons Jonnell, a lawyer, and Benn, an aspiring musician.

After *Scrappy the Pup* (Lippincott, 1960), Ciardi released his favorite book, *I Met a Man* (Houghton, 1961):

> I had just written a 1960 adult textbook, *How Does a Poem Mean?* My Houghton editor gave me a first-grade vocabulary list of 420 words, saying, "I think you can take this list and make something more interesting than "Look, Dick, Look." I cherish the *Saturday Review* reader who wrote that backwards it is "Kool, Kid, Kool." The kids can spell "detergent" before they spell "cat." They've been studying in front of the tube.
>
> My daughter was in kindergarten, and I wanted to write the first book that she read all the way through. It was *I Met a Man*. She drew bad pictures for it, but she learned to read from it. When she went into first grade, the teacher scolded me for accelerating her. I said, "You're being paid. I have problems with her without being paid."

Another 1961 Ciardi book was Lippincott's *The Man Who Sang the Sillies*, written in Edward Lear's style. Children enjoy its twenty-four nonsense poems whose topics include lobsters, time, summer, and children of various sizes.

Ciardi's *John J. Plenty and Fiddler Dan: A New Fable of the Grasshopper and the Ant* (Lippincott, 1963) has Madeleine Gekiere's prizewinning illustrations. Ciardi's hero is not an industrious ant, too frugal to eat gatherings, but a grasshopper whose fiddle fills the air with song, inspiring his praise of musicians:

> This is my testimonial to the musicians' union. My daughter is a musician, and my youngest son wants to be one. I don't know what keeps musicians alive. I guess their father does.
>
> I'm working from my side of the street. I count it among my blessings after apprenticeship and indenture to mundane jobs, I can now make a living doing what I like.

Ciardi enjoyed poetical spoofing in *You Know Who* (Lippincott, 1964), which includes "Sit Up When You Sit Down" and an account of cookie jar robbers:

> Childhood is a time of enormous emotional violence. Children have surcharges of emotion. They often overdo and have to learn when to stop. If one can take

some of that violence and wrap their feelings into a dance or a poem, it has to be therapeutic. I don't know what you got out of the genetic grab bag. Maybe you got angel fluff. I got savages.

Ciardi proceeded to paint poetically the savage family of his son, Jonnell, in "John the First (A Bedtime Story for Monsters)" from *The Monster Den; or Look What Happened at My House—and to It* (Lippincott, 1963). John marries a sow who puts grease in his stew, content that fascinated his children:

> I could not keep my interest and that of my children in goody, goody material. I dislike most poems I see because they seem like sponges dipped in warm milk and sprinkled with sugar. All bad poems are terribly decent. More poems die of decency than anything else.

Ciardi voluntarily read a not-too-decent poem, "And on Some Days I Might Take Less," from *Fast and Slow: Poems for Advanced Children and Beginning Parents* (Houghton, 1975). He called it "a little revenge poem after raising three teenagers together." The poems in this collection show caustic wit for older, sophisticated children.

On *Fast and Slow's* cover, Becky Gaber drew the old crow to resemble Ciardi with horn-rimmed eyeglasses. He said, "The picture looks a little like me and not by accident. The artist has her own sense of humor." The title of the poem was partially autobiographical.

Ciardi told about a National Council of Teachers of English (NCTE) poetry reading preference survey, whose findings were issued in 1974 by C. A. Terry. She found the most popular poem among 422 children in grades 4–6 was Ciardi's "Mommy Slept Late and Daddy Fixed Breakfast" from *You Read to Me, I'll Read to You* (Lippincott, 1962). Ciardi commented:

> The poem makes Daddy look ridiculous. My editor said children won't understand "bituminous" and "anthracite." Votes showed enough comprehension. It's no high-water mark in English literature, but it's the happiest award I ever received because *you cannot fix that jury!*

The poet was host of "Accent," a CBS television show; poetry editor for *Saturday Review* with 600,000 readers; and director of Vermont's Bread Loaf Writers' Conference. He recorded literature, had a weekly National Public Radio series, lectured, and visited schools.

He had no grandiose adventures as background for his writing, declaring, "This isn't necessary. Ask Emily Dickinson!" In describing his habits, he said, "I am a night person. I can't manage to spit before 12:00 noon, and for the next hour or so, my total vocabulary consists of grunts."

Ciardi found that bright third graders are the least inhibited in enjoying verse. "Why is it," he questioned, "that every American child delivered to the school system starts as a natural audience for poetry and almost everyone who leaves hates it?" Ciardi showed that a really good poet could satisfy children, offering them a fun-filled dance on the ever-playing instrument of language.

UPDATE

Consistent with his interest in etymology, Ciardi's last project was *A Second Browser's Dictionary and Native's Guide to the Unknown American Language* (Harper, 1980): "I sometimes spend two pages discussing a single word," he said while working on it. "This is more than is in most dictionaries, so I have to limit the number of entries." Harper published the second volume in 1987.

In 1982, the National Council of Teachers of English (NCTE) sponsored an award for Excellence in Poetry, given to a living American poet in recognition of an aggregate body of work for children aged three to thirteen. Ciardi was the 1982 winner!

In 1986, Houghton published *Doodle Soup* with verses like "Why Pigs Cannot Write Poems" and "The Dangers of Taking Baths."

Ciardi died of a heart attack on Easter Sunday 1986. Publishers issued twelve of his children's books during his lifetime and a number posthumously, including two published by Houghton, *The Hopeful Trout and Other Limericks* (1989) and *Mummy Took Cooking Lessons* (1990).

Beverly Cleary, author (1916–)

1979 Interview

Author Beverly Cleary's prodigious memory and gentle humor has helped create books that children love to read. This same humor helps when naming her characters (including a grumpy man, Mr. Grumbie; a cat, Socks; and a lean dog, Ribsy). She describes her name search:

> Some funny names just spring forth. I'm a great reader of telephone books in every city where I've spent the night. I read obituaries when I'm searching for a name. The name has to feel right or the character won't come alive. Some actual names of places are also funny, like Klickitat Street in the neighborhood where I grew up.
>
> You want to know where I got the idea for Beezus' younger sister, Ramona? She appears almost by accident. I needed an explanation for an unusual nickname for Beatrice. When I was six, I met two girls. One called her older sister, Beezus. The little sister was licking a stick of butter as if it were an ice cream cone.

Cleary's sense of humor and talent have benefited Morrow, her book publisher for young people. The company is proud of her awards, which include a 1984 Newbery Medal and Newbery Honor Books in 1978 and 1982.

Cleary's long-term memory goes back over many decades. She was born on April 12, 1916 in McMinnville, Oregon, and was an only child on a Willamette Valley farm at nearby Yamhill (another funny actual name). During her second year, church bells rang to announce the end of World War I.

Until she was six, Beverly lived in an eleven-room farmhouse with a tin roof. The fine house had belonged to her paternal grandfather who had installed in it one of only two bathrooms in the whole county. Her father farmed his eighty-two acres, but her mother, a former teacher, was ill suited for farm chores. Instead, she organized a popular county public library.

Financial losses caused Beverly's father to lease his property and move his family to Portland, Oregon. There he became a night guard at the Federal Reserve Bank. His daughter was happy to have neighborhood friends with whom she could skate and clunk on stilts made with two-pound coffee cans and twine. Alan Tiegreen illustrated such stilts in Cleary's book, *Ramona and Her Father* (Morrow, 1977).

Beverly was disappointed in her initial school days: "I had such a terrible time learning to read when I was in first grade. I suffered so much being in the low reading group with unhappy little boys." Her group, disgraced Blackbirds, was in sharp contrast with successful Bluebirds and average Redbirds. Not until she was in third grade did she brighten a rainy Sunday by suddenly reading Lucy Fitch Perkins's *The Dutch Twins* and *The Swiss Twins*. From then on, she made frequent trips to the library.

When Cleary was in seventh grade at Fernwood School, a librarian/English teacher, Miss Smith, had students write a letter as if they had lived in George Washington's day. Cleary, a former nonreader, wrote an imaginary cousin about sacrificing a pet chicken for Washington's hungry Valley Forge troops, a paper that earned her teacher's praise.

The next assignment was an essay about a favorite book character. Cleary submitted "Journey through Bookland," describing a girl's dream of conversing with book characters. She wrote during a rainstorm, weather that stimulates her creativity even today, and remembered, "My teacher complimented me."

Miss Smith, the teacher, also suggested that Cleary become a writer. She told her mother, who confessed that she had wanted the same career, but she advised her daughter to find a way to earn a living. Beverly decided early to become a librarian. She praised her mother for helping her read:

> I owe a lot to Mother. When I was resisting reading, she kept a changing supply of library books at our house that were at my reading level. She also had a sneaky habit of reading aloud the first chapter of such books and never had time to finish them. Eventually, I read them myself.

As an adult, the author has returned to Fernwood, where she attended grades one through eight. "I visited Fernwood School when I was in Portland and was astonished at how little it has changed in the fifty years since I grew up. I think it's an amazingly stable neighborhood."

Nearby, in northeast Portland's Grant Park, is Beverly Cleary Sculpture Garden for Children with a fountain on which cluster bronze statues of some book characters: Ramona, Henry, and his dog, Ribsy. The park is just four blocks from her Klickitat Street neighborhood.

By the time Beverly graduated from Grant High School, she had managed to elude a sexually aggressive uncle. She realized that the parent with whom she related most was not her dictatorial mother but her quieter father. The nearest her mother came to discussing sex with her was to advise, "Don't play leapfrog with boys. They might look up." The daughter felt empathy for her father who suffered from unemployment during the Depression. Because money was limited, the would-be writer was not sure if she could afford college. It was her father who realized she needed independence and arranged for her to go by bus to southern California to stay with relatives and attend a free junior college. At the bus station, he was the one who kissed her farewell.

Unlike friends, Beverly did not go to college to "catch" a husband. However, she met her future mate, Clarence T. Cleary, now a retired accountant, while in college and married him in 1940. She attended Chaffee Junior College in Ontario, California, and received a bachelor's degree from the University of California in Berkeley.

The writer also got a bachelor's degree in library science from Seattle's University of Washington in 1939 and worked as a librarian for six years, beginning as a children's librarian in Yakima, Washington. There she learned that her young patrons did not want to read about royalty, preferring funny books about "real people." Neither she nor her patrons wanted didactic material:

> I don't try to instruct children. I would like to think that I instruct some adults on children's points of view. I feel boys and girls should be allowed to select books freely. Parents should turn off the television and set an example by being readers themselves.

Cleary enjoys reading in her comfortable home. She discusses life in her ranch house on California's Monterrey Peninsula:

> San Francisco is 130 miles north and Los Angeles, 300 miles south. Above the living room sofa is my needlepoint tapestry, which depicts my family life. There's an apple tree, which really is in our backyard. I'm shown chasing a butterfly, a symbol of ideas.
>
> Another interior view is of my daughter, Marianne, a cellist studying for a master's degree in music at Stanford. Behind me is an open door, which leads to my small study.
>
> Marianne has a twin brother, Malcolm, shown in a British Amateur Athletic Meet in London. He sells sporting goods to support himself as a world-class run-

ner. The boy is outgoing while the girl is introspective. When they were in nursery school, they inspired my picture book, *The Real Hole* [1960].

Later, the twins prompted me to do *Mitch and Amy*. Its theme is rivalry, going beyond sibling rivalry. I'm not sure you can separate theme from subject matter in all my books. I do spread peanut butter on pinecones as bird feeders, but I'm not as nearsighted as the twins' mother in that book.

When the twins were in fourth grade, my son was disgusted with books and reading. I asked them what kind of story they'd like. Malcolm requested one about a motorcycle, and my daughter said, "One about a nice little animal." That's why I wrote my first fantasy, *The Mouse and the Motorcycle*. I wrote *Runaway Ralph* after my son was feverish one vacation night, and I wished I had Ralph to bring an aspirin.

The Mouse and the Motorcycle (1965) evokes grins as readers envision a mouse on a toy motorcycle with half a Ping-Pong ball as a crash helmet. *Runaway Ralph* (1970) is a sequel.

Cleary's first book, *Henry Huggins* (1950), is not fantasy but fiction. While it is generally hard for an unknown writer to get published, Cleary's initial book was accepted by Morrow, the first publisher to receive it. It is still in print. She originally titled it *Spareribs and Henry*. Since she began that book on January 2, she likes to start other books on that date. She works on weekday mornings, writing on a legal pad first. She talked about her first book's main character:

Of course, I thought my first novel would be about a sensitive girl. Incidents in *Henry Huggins* were what I had observed over the years. I looked up Gesell's interpretation of eight-year-olds and found that Henry was psychologically sound.

The character, Henry Huggins, was featured in a television series for a year in Japan. In the Scandinavian countries, he was in a four-part series. *Henry Huggins* has been translated into fourteen foreign languages.

An early companion to *Henry Huggins* is *Henry and Ribsy* (1954), which introduces a mongrel. Henry finds it fitting to have his two loose canine teeth pulled by a dog and thereafter, he can "spit double." Henry and two boyfriends wear sailor hats with brims turned down after their mothers give them home haircuts, resulting in "chewed" hair.

Humor abounds in Cleary books. In *Henry and Beezus* (1952), Henry wins $50 in beauty shop treatments and then eats dog food to prove his masculinity. In *Mitch and Amy* (1967), Amy wants the U.S. president to abolish her nemesis: multiplication tables. *Ramona the Pest* (1968) shows Ramona waiting for a gift since her kindergarten teacher told her where to sit for the present. Cleary thought about *Ramona the Pest* for fifteen years before writing it. Ramona is her most-developed character.

The author cited a favorite incident from *Ramona the Brave* (1975):

> In *Ramona the Brave* I enjoy a touch of satire when Ramona and Beezus are examining their school progress reports. Beezus is a little smug about hers. Of course, Ramona can't stand any type of criticism and explodes into the bad word, "Guts!"
>
> Some high school girls asked me to write humorous books for their ages, so I did *Fifteen*. I liked the change of pace.
>
> I enjoy writing all my books or I tear up what I'm writing and throw it away. I begin with a character or an incident. The joy of writing is seeing what I can do with that incident. I've never had a course in writing though a course on the English novel was helpful. I don't have a book previewer, but my husband and daughter read everything I've written.
>
> My editor at Morrow never pressures me and publishes my books as I write them. For twenty years, Louis Darling was my illustrator, and now I'm just as delighted with Alan Tiegreen.

In 1978, Cleary's *Ramona and Her Father*, which discusses an unemployed father's demoralization, was a *Boston Globe-Horn Book* Honor Book. In 1975, the American Library Association gave Cleary the Laura Ingalls Wilder Award, now presented every three years, for her contributions to children's literature. The author showed a congratulatory valentine from students at Juan Cabrillo School in Seaside, California.

Cleary's books are so popular around the world that she and her husband sometimes travel to meet fans. In Hawaii, wearing carnation leis, she addressed children on four islands. In Invercargill, New Zealand, the mayor and several hundred children surprised her by greeting her with paper butterflies, since she lives where Monarch butterflies spend the winter.

Her books do not involve racial or ethnic integration because she says that she is recalling her own childhood. She advised would-be writers, "Observe, listen, read, and write. Hear the way people actually talk."

She added, "Children tell me they like my books because they understand what is funny and sad, and lately they've added that my books show caring for others!"

UPDATE

Winner of the 1980 Regina Medal and 1982 University of Southern Mississippi Medallion, Beverly Cleary has written more than forty-three books for two generations of young people and short stories for periodicals, such as

Women's Day. She has won more than twenty-five awards from children or librarians. Her two grandchildren now have joined her numerous readers.

In 1980, *Ramona and Her Father,* a Newbery Honor Book, was named an Honor Book of the International Board on Books for Young People (IBBY). In 1982, her *Ramona Quimby, Age 8,* was again a Newbery Honor Book and was nominated for an American Book Award. In 1984, she won the Newbery Medal and Christopher Award for *Dear Mr. Henshaw,* a tale of a sixth-grade boy, Leigh Botts, who suffers from parental divorce and weak ties to his father. Cleary continues Leigh's story in *Strider* (1991), which depicts a dog he holds in "joint custody" with his friend, Barry.

In 1982, *Ralph S. Mouse* joined *The Mouse and the Motorcycle* and *Runaway Ralph* to form the mouse trilogy. Joining the Ramona books were *Ramona Quimby, Age 8* (1981), *Ramona Forever* (1984), and *Ramona's World* (1999). In 1988, Cleary published *A Girl from Yamhill,* an autobiography of her growing-up years.

When she accepted the Newbery Medal in 1984 for *Dear Mr. Henshaw,* Cleary revealed that her mother was happiest teaching in one-room schoolhouses, but laws forbade her to teach after marriage. Beverly, her mother's one continuous student, benefited from maternal writing advice:

"Write something funny. People always enjoy reading something that makes them laugh."

Karen Cushman, author (1941–)
Dinah Stevenson, editor

1996 Interview

KAREN CUSHMAN

For most authors, writing is a rather solitary endeavor. But when it comes to mulling over ideas, sharing thoughts aloud with those closest to you can lead to getting a story on paper, as author Karen Cushman discovered:

> *Catherine, Called Birdy* was my first book. Over the years, I've had lots of book ideas. I'd tell my husband and that would be that. This time when I said, "Listen, I have this great idea for a book," he refused to listen. He muttered, "Don't tell me. Write it down." So I did, and the rest is history.
>
> Now I use this story as a metaphor for living when I speak to school classes: It's not enough to have an idea. You have to make a commitment, take a stand, write it down.

She accepted his advice, and results were exciting. Her first book, *Catherine, Called Birdy* (Clarion, 1994) was the only 1995 Newbery Honor Book. The next year Cushman's *The Midwife's Apprentice* (Clarion, 1995) rose to the top, earning the 1996 Newbery Medal. Clarion is the author's only publisher.

Cushman was born to Arthur and Loretta Lipski in Chicago on October 4, 1941. As a child, she used to check out about ten books a week at the library. The books inspired her to write poems, short stories, and even a multicultural play, "Jingle Bagels." Her published novels, with their historical themes, are a natural outgrowth of her academic training; she majored in both Greek and English as an undergraduate student at Stanford University.

After graduating from Stanford, she got an administrative job at Hebrew Union College in Los Angeles. There she met Philip Cushman, a rabbinical student. He later become a psychologist. The couple married in 1969 and moved to Oregon, where Philip worked at a small college for two years. Karen Cushman's life was pretty relaxed during this time. She recalled: "I wove, made blackberry jam, and had a daughter, Leah." The couple built a big dining room table with hardwoods from around the globe.

The family—and the table—moved to Oakland, California, where Philip has a private practice. He also is an associate professor at the California School of Professional Psychology in Alameda, and writes about psychotherapy.

Karen Cushman went on to get her master's degree in museum studies at John F. Kennedy University in Orinda, Calif. She also taught at that university, edited their *Museum Studies Journal,* and coordinated masters' projects. Today, she writes and travels as a speaker. She spoke about her easier lifestyle before becoming a published author: "I used to spend more time in the shaded backyard of our Oakland home."

Cushman's love of reading and libraries continues today. Library books by Sue Townsend, such as *The Adrian Mole Diaries* (Grove, 1985), inspired Cushman to use a journal format for her *Catherine, Called Birdy.* She felt a diary made her story intimate, immediate, and youthful: "There's humor in Birdy interpreting her world through her own eyes rather than those of readers. She's like me: a 'wise guy.'"

Cushman's books are set in the Middle Ages. She said that she enjoys researching that early period that moved into the Renaissance, "like a child growing into adolescence." Museum holdings that date from the Middle Ages are limited, and items that belonged to commoners are rare, as they did not seem worthy of preservation. Also missing are items and memoirs concerning children from that era:

There are no first-person diaries from children of that period, only from important adults. Children had few books or toys. Researchers have found leather balls. On sticks are dancing dolls or knights.

I was drawn to the Middle Ages, not only because I liked the music and tapestries of that period, but because I wanted to expose the poor treatment of girls. A girl in England in 1290–1291 would have no power or value except as a marriage pawn. Much of the book is based on careful research about beekeeping, sheep shearing, ointments and remedies, superstitions and fears, clothing, language, table manners, recipes, bathing habits, and privies.

Beyond items from that time period, I investigated attitudes, values, and expectations. Many readers feel Birdy's father was mean to marry off his daughter, not for romance, but to acquire power, property, or further family fortunes. It was not the father, only Birdy, who was working against public expectation.

In staying true to the historical time period, Cushman had to write about actions and events that wouldn't be popular if they happened today.

> Some say that I used dirty words, but I wrote common terms used for bodily functions at that time. It was not enough for me to mention eating eel pie and drinking ale for breakfast. I had to cite people enjoying bearbaiting or watching public executions. Imagine, they took picnic lunches to watch someone being hanged! I knew if I didn't get attitudes right, repeating, "Corpus bones!" wouldn't make my novels historically accurate.

It took Cushman three years to complete *Catherine, Called Birdy*. Afterward, she benefited from the criticism of Sandy Boucher, a published author who lives in Oakland. During the editing stage, Cushman deleted forty pages of her original work. She took her manuscript to an agent who promotes her husband's psychology books. The agent accepted her material and so did Clarion, the company that has published all her books to date.

The popular illustrator, Trina Schart Hyman, was assigned to draw the jacket for *Catherine, Called Birdy*. Cushman's first reaction to the finished cover was not positive:

> My immediate reaction was that it's not what I anticipated. I thought it was too dark. The book is light-hearted, and I expected the humorous aspect to be emphasized. Now that I've lived with it, Trina's drawing has become Birdy to me. It's so beautiful that I couldn't help but love it. I appreciate how authentic her garb is and how her dark room contrasts with the light outside.

Hyman's treatment for the back cover shows five birds in their cages painted on the dark bedroom wall by the girl whose preferred name, Birdy, seems appropriate. A flying devil is attacking one cage with one claw and holding an ale stein with the other. He has cloven back hooves, a looped tail, and a pointed red hat on his human head. During Cushman's visit to a school, she remembered, a child asked about that odd back cover. Not waiting for Cushman's explanation, another student replied, "Remember when Birdy paints a mural on her wall, and the devil has her father's face?"

Catherine, Called Birdy won the 1994 Carl Sandburg Award for Children's Literature, Golden Kite Award, *Publishers Weekly's* Cuffie Award, was on *School Library Journal's* 1994 Best Books List, and was a 1996 IBBY Honor Book.

Cushman's second book, *The Midwife's Apprentice*, was on *School Library Journal's* 1995 Best Books List. Hyman also did the jacket art for the hardcover edition of this book. The front pictures a girl, Alyce, with her cat, Purr. The girl is aware that the midwife, visible through an open window, is helping a new mother. Though the author always liked the cover, she valued it even more when a gold seal announced this book as the 1996 Newbery Medal winner.

Hyman seemed obsessed with devils on back covers since the second book again shows that evil character. This time, a farmer is an object of scorn by the devil. He has a human face with an animal's two legs and tail. The scene refers to Alyce's outwitting superstitious villagers. She carves wooden blocks into devil's hooves before leaving earthen prints at strategic spots. After her deceit, she throws the wooden blocks into a river.

Cushman explained what inspired her second book:

> It began with the title, but it didn't come alive for me until I saw the image of a homeless girl awakening on a dung heap and arising as if she were just born. After all, we are all created homeless and nameless. How she longed for a name, a full belly, and a place in the world! I wrote the story in six months, partly because I had already completed most of the research and partly because I knew this girl.

The Midwife's Apprentice focuses on Alyce, a homeless, parentless girl, who begins to learn about delivering babies from a midwife, Jane Sharp. Alyce tries and fails to help deliver a baby, and is so ashamed that she leaves and begins work as a maid at an inn. While there, one of the guests, Magister Richard Rees, teaches her how to read. Alyce successfully assists an inn guest to give birth and then returns to work for Jane Sharp.

The author concluded, "Writing the ending for my Newbery winner was difficult." Cushman added:

> Some readers would have preferred for Alyce to marry Magister Rees and continue her education. However, at that time, magisters had to take minor Holy Orders in order to attend a university. They were lesser priests who were expected to respect celibacy.

For her third book, *The Ballad of Lucy Whipple* (1996), Cushman's setting is California during the Gold Rush. Few female-focused books have been written about this period, so Cushman created a first-person account of Lucy, a twelve-year-old girl. After Lucy's father dies of pneumonia, her mother sells their house and feed store. She takes her children to Lucky Diggins, California, a mining town, where the mother runs a boarding house in a tent.

Four years later, when fire destroys the town, the mother moves her family to the Canary Islands, but Lucy stays behind. At age sixteen, Lucy becomes librarian for the book-starved folk who rebuild Lucky Diggins.

Cushman admitted autobiographical parts of *Lucy Whipple*:

> I was playing out my move when, at age ten, I had to leave my grandparents and dog to travel with my seven-year-old brother, Arthur ["Duffy"], and my parents. We left a Chicago suburb and went to the San Fernando Valley near Los Angeles, to Tarzana. I identified with Lucy's wish to return home. My father found no promised job waiting for him in the West. Our first California Thanksgiving didn't seem right since we were wearing shorts and eating outside at a picnic table instead of being where frost was on the pumpkin.

With a tribute to nineteenth-century California completed, Cushman chose medieval England again, as the setting for her latest book, *Matilda Bone*. "It takes place in the medical quarter of a medieval town," she said. "It is gross enough—full of blood letting, leeches, and barber surgeons—to satisfy me and the average seventh-grade reader." Her young fans appreciate her work. They show their support in fan mail, their letters often beginning with an illuminated alphabet letter, imitating medieval parchments of the Middle Ages.

Cushman uses her dedications to show her appreciation for those who have helped her during her career. She credited her parents who "brought me west" in dedicating *Lucy Whipple*. When acknowledging difficulties with the second half of *The Midwife's Apprentice*, she noted, "My editor, Dinah Stevenson, helped me give birth to this book, so I named my husband, Philip, and Dinah as Alyce's midwives in the dedication."

DINAH STEVENSON

Dinah Stevenson is modest when Cushman cites how the editor helped her with the Newbery winner, *The Midwife's Apprentice*. Stevenson said:

> I gently led Cushman to discover for herself the wisdom of having Alyce return home instead of traveling and engaging in lengthy picaresque adventures. That's all in the job description of an editor. If you gave a manuscript to five editors, you'd have five different books. Each editor will influence the author in a distinct way, so the end product may vary.

Stevenson stressed her need for an editor's anonymity: "Perhaps one of the reasons I have chosen a career 'behind the scenes' is that I'm most comfortable there." She was an avid reader as a child, which influenced her literary career choice. In 1963, she received an M.A. in English literature from the University of Chicago, and has completed all doctoral requirements except the dissertation.

Since 1971, Stevenson has worked in children's book publishing with positions at J. B. Lippincott, Harper & Row, Knopf, and Lothrop, Lee & Shepard. In 1989, she became an executive editor at Clarion Books.

Stevenson spoke about her working relationship with Cushman:

We have quickly developed a mutual trust and understanding that enables us to speak in telephone shorthand. After all, we're three thousand miles apart and don't often have the luxury of looking at a manuscript side-by-side.

Marguerite de Angeli, illustrator–author (1889–1987)

1976 Interview

With a focused mind and a straight back, eighty-seven-year-old Marguerite de Angeli, an author and illustrator, exudes the warmth that earned her the title "Everybody's Grandmother." Like many grandmothers, she is willing to share her optimistic advice with others: "If you come to a stone wall and look hard enough, you'll find a way out."

This philosophy prompted her one day while she was washing dishes in her summer cottage in Toms River, New Jersey. She called out to her husband, Dai, in the next room, "You suggested a good title for my book, *The Door in the Wall.*"

He answered, "But I didn't say that."

Then she realized she had been subconsciously thinking of a name for her 1949 book. The book became a 1950 Newbery Medal winner, but it wasn't her first award-winning book. It was preceded by her self-illustrated 1945 Caldecott Honor Book, *Yonie Wondernose* (1944). She also drew a 1955 Caldecott Honor Book, *Book of Nursery and Mother Goose Rhymes* (1954). In 1957, her writing was again acknowledged as *Black Fox of Lorne* (1956) became a Newbery Honor Book. Doubleday published all her titles.

Marguerite de Angeli, who was born on March 14, 1889, in Lapeer, Michigan, said she acquired a cheerful attitude from her parents, Shadrach Lofft, an artistic photographer, and his homemaking wife, Ruby. She had an older sister, Nina, and four younger brothers: Arthur, Harry, Walter, and Dick.

When Marguerite was thirteen, her father got a job as an Eastman Kodak representative and moved his family to Philadelphia.

Marguerite was a classical student at Girls' High and hoped to attend Bryn Mawr College. She was hired as a contralto in church choirs and used her earnings to pay for voice lessons. Oscar Hammerstein I accepted her in the Metropolitan Opera chorus of "Samson and Delilah," which was heading for London. She dropped out of high school and, advised by her parents, did not go to London.

At age twenty-one, she married John Dailey (Dai) de Angeli, who had played first violin in the Symphony Society, which preceded the Philadelphia Orchestra. He was a salesman in Canada for Edison record-playing cabinets and made a good living, but she insisted that he work locally. The couple had six children, one of whom died young. Remaining were a daughter, Nina, and four sons, Jack, Arthur, Harry (Ted), and Maury.

The large de Angeli family lived across from Marguerite's parents in Collingswood, New Jersey. Their neighbor was the mother of Maurice Bower, a full-time illustrator and a protégé of Walter Everett of the Brandywine Tradition. Marguerite invited his criticism of her art. Bower encouraged de Angeli to focus on art. He taught her to emphasize the important and minimize the trivial. In 1922, after working with her for a year, he introduced her to Westminster Press. That company showed her work to the Baptist Publication Society, and both gave her illustration jobs. Bower offered to get the art ready for reproduction.

Working and taking care of five children was no easy task. The artist told how she fulfilled one particular commission:

I waited until some of my children went to school before working in my studio, which had an open door. Year-old Ted wanted to be with me, so I brought him up. He cried when I put him in the studio's playpen. Then I left him outside and went in the playpen myself with my drawing.

During the Depression, the de Angelis lost their Collingswood home and moved quite often, but the artist remained optimistic as she checked on opportunities for her sons and herself:

My two sons, Jack and Arthur, won a scholarship to a summer dramatic school in Bar Harbor, Maine, meeting people like Maude Evans and Dame Sybil Thorndike. They both earned a living by working in a hotel. The visiting mother of a school colleague, Jack Van Zanten, invited Jack's friends to be her fall housekeepers in Brooklyn. They were to buy food, cook it, and send out the laundry. During the day, they were to go to dramatic school with Jack. I went to Brooklyn to see if the Van Zantens were suitable for our boys. Mrs. Van Zanten invited me to spend the night. The boys took me to New York City the next day.

I had my fortune told the day before, and I had been told that my life was going to take a new turn. I went to the address of a publisher for whom I had never previously worked. That name was not on the directory, but I recognized Helen Ferris of Junior Literary Guild atop the directory, so I called on her. She suggested that I write a book for children to read in first grade. She said, "Take a simple subject, like going to the grocery store. I know you can do it." I knew I could too.

I had not been well, so when I boarded a return train, I was pretty well "used up," as my grandmother would have said. I went down inside myself and thought about *Ted and Nina Go to the Grocery Store*. Since I was using the names of two of my children, I later drew the body of Maury instead of Ted, so he wouldn't feel left out.

Artistic de Angeli sent a dummy copy of *Ted and Nina Go to the Grocery Store* to Ferris, who suggested more emphasis on in-store occurrences. She approved a revision and recommended sending a copy to Margaret Lesser of Doubleday. At Lesser's suggestion, de Angeli rendered the art by color-separated lithography on glass. This first book appeared in 1935 and in 1936, she did a sequel, *Ted and Nina Have a Happy Rainy Day*.

Lesser encouraged a book series on minorities, emphasizing universality despite differences, so de Angeli visited Amish homes in Morgantown, Pennsylvania, to prepare *Henner's Lydia* (1936). Her second published book about a minority was *Petite Suzanne* (1937), which concerns French Canadians. She traced Christopher Dock's Mennonite contributions in *Skippack School* (1939). *Yonie Wondernose* (1944) was written after she studied the Pennsylvania Dutch culture.

When her father died, de Angeli created *Copper-Toed Boots* (1938) about his boyhood yearning for boots and his pranks with Ash Tomlinson in Lapeer, Michigan. She discussed Quakers as a Pennsylvania minority in *Thee, Hannah!* (1940), showed Swedes in colonial Delaware in *Elin's Amerika* (1941), and Pennsylvania Poles in *Up the Hill* (1942). While promoting her books on minority groups, de Angeli bought dolls with bisque heads, and her friend, Hedwig Ryglewicz, put different wigs and attire on them. Sold as "Hedwig Dolls," they resembled the lead character in de Angeli's books.

When Doubleday approved her book on African Americans, de Angeli met with Nellie Bright, a school principal, and Jessica Cole, a scout leader. Cole's daughter was the protagonist's model in the 1946 book, *Bright April,* one of the first books to reveal childhood discrimination. Honored by the 1946 *Herald Tribune* Children's Book Festival, the book's success was the answer to charges that it would be "too controversial."

The next focus of de Angeli was on the physically challenged, influenced by a neighbor, Harmon Robinson, in Toms River, New Jersey:

I got my idea for *The Door in the Wall* from Harmon. He played viola in the quartet in which my husband was violinist. He was also a gifted cabinetmaker. Beginning at age ten, he had been in bed for three years and when he was able to get up, was frozen in a sitting position. His lower body was that of a small ten-year-old boy, but his upper body was well developed. He had to walk with his hands on his knees or with crutches to support himself. I was impressed that Harmon was often the center of attention because he was knowledgeable about so many subjects.

A youthful representation of Harmon became the lead character, Robin, in de Angeli's book about medieval England. "I did at least ten sketches of Robin on the shoulder of John Go-in-the-Wind." Doubleday supported her book idea:

My editor said, "That's a wonderful idea. You must go to England!" On the same day when I proposed the book, she went with me to the travel agent to arrange travel by ship for my husband and me.

The Doubleday representative in London took us to the Tower of London. At Windsor Castle, I entered the George Chapel and saw a two-handed sword that I thought must have belonged to Edward III. I felt, "That's the first sign for my book's time period."

Then the verger said, "This is the tomb of Edward III. It was opened during your colonial period to make sure he was inside. We found his red hair. Hair is one of the most lasting relics. I believe someone has a lock of his hair."

I thought that if I could see that hair, the whole period would come alive for me. I went back to London and on to Oxford, reporting my experiences to another houseguest, Miss Carol Herschel. She said, "You may see the lock of hair. I have it." She came back with a jewel about two inches in diameter. It was of green enamel with a crystal center covering an opal around which curled the lock of red hair.

Herschel explained that her ancestor had been the organist in George Chapel when Edward's tomb was opened. King George III gave the organist the inscribed token, but de Angeli had not read the inscription. She later learned the hair had been that of Edward IV, not Edward III, but it had served its purpose.

The Door in the Wall brought de Angeli the highest honor in the children's book world, the 1950 Newbery Medal, presented by the Medal's originator, Frederic Melcher. The book also won the Lewis Carroll Shelf Award.

After *The Door in the Wall*, de Angeli spent more than three years compiling 376 rhymes and doing more than 260 drawings for her 1954 publication, *Book of Nursery and Mother Goose Rhymes*, a 1955 Caldecott Honor Book. Her mother is featured in some illustrations. Many readers concur that this book contains the artist's best pictures.

A taste of triumph was still pending for de Angeli: in 1957, her historical fiction, *Black Fox of Lorne*, was a Newbery Honor Book. It features twin Norse boys in tenth-century Scotland who save themselves by deceiving their captors. They find their mother and search for their father's murderer.

One of de Angeli's last major research projects was *The Old Testament* (1960). To do its original art, she went to the Near East with her daughter, Nina. The two barely exited from Israel during a war alert. Since she had chosen her book's text before leaving, de Angeli, once home, began the art, using University of Pennsylvania Museum amulets to decorate chapters. She identified one model:

> When I came to the story of Esther, I wanted her in rich clothing, so I bought red brocade and had Arthur's wife, Nina, pose with the drapery just as she had posed as Robin's mother in *The Door in the Wall*.

As author–illustrator of thirty books and illustrator for other authors, she discussed her writing and art:

> I make an outline as a rule. I have a beginning and sort of know how it will end. At first, I wrote by hand. I have learned to type with two fingers now. I revise a lot. . . .
>
> I visualize the pictures first before the text and tend to draw larger than book size. In my last years, I used a brush with Weber's watercolors from England, favoring lemon yellow, vermilion, and permanent blue.

In 1969, de Angeli was the first recipient of the Drexel University/Free Library of Philadelphia Citation. That year, she finished *Marguerite de Angeli's Book of Favorite Hymns,* and the next year, retold *The Goose Girl.*

Honors multiplied. In 1968, she received the Regina Medal from the Catholic Library Association. Lehigh University made her an honorary Doctor of Letters, and Girl Scouts gave her the Juliette Low Award.

The award recipient also wrote an autobiography geared for adult readers: *Butter at the Old Price* (1971). When finalizing her manuscript, she consulted interviewer Jaqueline Weiss about that odd title before giving Doubleday her book. The title goes back to de Angeli's birthplace, Lapeer, where a farm woman, Ella Tuttle, got top price for her clean butter, but another woman, Mrs. Desireau, got the old price, due to an impure product. This case inspired a family expression of consolation for imperfection, "butter at the old price."

UPDATE

In 1977, de Angeli offered *Whistle for the Crossing*, her illustrated story about a boy whose father drove the first steam engine from Philadelphia to Pittsburgh on the Pennsylvania line. She wrote and did black-and-white illustrations for *Fiddlestrings* (1981), a book about Dai's childhood. (Dai died in 1969 after the couple had been married for almost sixty years.) When she was ninety-two years old, she issued her last book, *Friendship & Other Poems* (1981).

Marguerite de Angeli died on June 30, 1987, at the age of ninety-eight, mourned by her children, grandchildren, and great-grandchildren. She would have appreciated Doubleday's annual Marguerite de Angeli Prize. Begun in 1992, it encourages exemplary fiction for readers who are seven to ten years old.

Tomie dePaola between Carolyn Field and Jacqueline Weiss

Tomie dePaola, illustrator–author (1934–)

1984 Interview

When Tomie dePaola was six years old, he experienced a sense of frustration in first grade. The art teacher had given students only one sheet of paper and insisted that they copy her Pilgrim drawing, using the school's crayons that came in only eight colors. The teacher finally got reluctant dePaola to draw the Pilgrim by giving him another sheet and permission to use his own set of sixty-four crayons.

That scene was one of many in dePaola's childhood that portended his future as a famous illustrator. His offerings in classical fantasy include *Strega Nona: An Old Tale* (Prentice-Hall, 1975), winner of the 1976 Caldecott Honor Medal and the 1978 Nakamore Prize in Japan: "I retold a classical tale about the porridge pot, using the Italian ingredient, spaghetti. I thought I invented *Strega Nona,* but I'm not sure."

Thomas Anthony dePaola was born on September 15, 1934, in Meriden, Connecticut. At home was an older brother, Bobby. Later, two sisters, Maureen and Judie, joined the family. Their quiet father was a barber who became a salesman.

Tomie dePaola traced his childhood memories back to when he was three years old: "I sang my first church solo, 'On the Good Ship, Lollipop,' complete with Shirley Temple gestures. I was lucky that the church organist knew the music."

The artist has written about his nonconformist childhood in *Oliver Button Is a Sissy* (Harcourt Brace, 1979). His father would have preferred if his son played outdoor sports. However, like Oliver Button, dePaola enjoyed dressing in costumes and playing with paper dolls. "By age four, I knew I wanted to write, draw, and tap dance," said dePaola, who studied tap dancing for fourteen years. When dePaola's father built him a sandbox, his son dumped the sand and turned the box over as a stage. Later, the boy made puppets and a puppet theater in his attic. His parents were as supportive as those of his book character, Oliver Button: "They were similar in taking me for pizza after I was in a show."

September 1952 marked an exciting time for dePaola. Armed with his high school's Maloney Scholarship, he began four years of art study at Pratt Institute in Brooklyn, New York. There he worked intensively, always carrying a sketchbook to practice drawing what he observed. He was also interested in dramatics, and told about joining the Institute's theater group, Playshop: "I went to school with [illustrator] Arnold Lobel, who was one year ahead of me, and [illustrator] Anita Lobel, who was a year behind. She and I were often cast in plays as husband and wife, though she's taller than I."

At Pratt, dePaola developed his own simplified artistic style, influenced by folk art. His drawings have a childlike appeal though some of his characters look similar. He is allergic to turpentine's smell, so he uses a tempera-watercolor-acrylic combination, sometimes with colored pencils.

After he received his bachelor's degree in fine arts from Pratt, dePaola's parents sent him to Europe where he could appreciate art masterpieces in person. On his return voyage, he was off the Massachusetts coast on July 26, 1956, when his ship, *Andrea Doria*, and the *Stockholm* collided. The *Doria* sank, but he reached New York on another boat. Divers recovered *Doria's* safe and inside was a dePaola traveler's check that he had signed in India ink. After the accident, the check was shown on television.

DePaola entered a Benedictine monastery many times to become a monk, but always left to pursue art: "I supported myself for twenty years by teaching art." He earned a master's degree at California College of Arts and Crafts in Oakland and did doctoral-equivalency work at San Francisco's Lone Mountain College. Feeling a need for guidance, dePaola consulted a therapist, and he paid her with a drawing for each session. After a while, she displayed all of his art, noting that each showed a child trying to escape. "From then on, I've tried to discover my childhood in fantasies and dreams, not just memories."

In a 1973 Putnam release and a 1974 Prentice-Hall book, the artist-writer showed the success of his new approach:

> In 1973, I published my first self-written book, *Nana Downstairs and Nana Upstairs*. It's about the special relationship between the very old and the very young. When I was four years old, my ninety-four-year-old great-grandmother was my very best friend. My book is a celebration of this Irish woman who taught me how to read tea leaves.
>
> I dreamt that my Italian grandmother stood on the porch and asked, "How come you no write a book about me?" That's why, a year later, I did *Watch Out for the Chicken Feet in Your Soup*.

In New York, dePaola met two people who would influence his life. One was artist Ben Shahn, his mentor. The other was Florence Alexander, who became his agent. With her promotional skill, he has found demand for his work and has illustrated more than 220 books, about seventy of which he also wrote. Publishers in at least twenty countries have issued his books: "My three main U.S. publishers are Putnam; Holiday House; and Harcourt, Brace, Jovanovich. I'm a juggler with special projects for each house, so they respect me and each other." He used to worry that he would run out of ideas for these publishers. Now he prevents that sinking feeling by starting a new project before finishing his current one, and he concerns himself with details:

> In writing, I give a lot of attention to the sounds of words. I was lucky because my mother spent long hours reading aloud to her family. Of course, I loved Beatrix Potter's work. In addition to folk and fairy tales, I read the encyclopedia. Maybe that's why I like doing informational books.

One of dePaola's most appreciated books is *The Clown of God* (Harcourt, 1978), which has been translated into thirteen languages. Successfully adapted for the stage from an old French tale, the story traces an orphan beggar from childhood to old age.

More celebrated is dePaola's *Strega Nona*:

> It was my first full-color book. I used transparent watercolors and inks because that media reproduces well. Always before, I had to economize by doing pre-separated art. Now I'm putting a colophon, which describes my media and the printer's type, in all my books where there's room.
>
> Occasionally, I've chosen to do limited color, as in *Now One Foot, Now Another*. Full color is expensive, and I felt my choice was appropriate for that book.

Now One Foot, Now Another (Putnam, 1981) tells how a grandfather teaches his grandson, Bobby, to walk. After the grandfather's stroke, Bobby uses the same watchwords to help the elderly man walk.

Strega Nona is now a talking book, and a Braille edition is available of an informational dePaola book, *Charlie Needs a Cloak* (Prentice-Hall, 1973), about a shepherd who sews a coat after shearing sheep, spinning and weaving wool (which dePaola has done), and dyeing the cloth red.

The artist introduced another popular book, *Helga's Dowry: A Troll Love Story* (Harcourt, 1977):

> Each Scandinavian country seems to have a distinct troll. Helga is Norwegian. *Helga's Dowry* is original, written like a folk tale. It is a reverse *Cinderella* story. Cinderella sits around and waits for her Fairy Godmother to make magic. Helga is in charge and makes her own magic.
>
> Incidentally, in the Italian *Cenerentola*, which may predate *Cinderella*, the heroine removes her own glass slipper and leaves it for the prince to find, so she helps determine her fate.

The pages of *Helga's Dowry* feature a gingerbread border. Designs from dePaola's own quilt collection are in his page borders for Clement Moore's *The Night Before Christmas* (Holiday House, 1980). In *Fin M'Coul, the Giant of Knockmany Hill* (Holiday House, 1981), the artist's page border shows Irish jewelry and metalwork patterns. The jewelry suggests dePaola's artistic interests beyond illustrations. Some of his ventures include designs for music boxes, glasses, towels, washcloths, even Japanese futon covers. He has prepared posters, greeting cards, magazine covers, and the outside of Neiman Marcus's *Christmas Book*. He has also participated in art exhibitions. In order to do so much, the self-proclaimed "workaholic" seldom takes vacations.

A task dePaola has undertaken with pleasure is to create an annual Christmas book, reporting: "My editors noticed how exciting my Christmas books are and have encouraged me. I do have a special feeling for the holiday and enjoy decorating my house." He set a precedent in 1971 when he did a puppet ballet, "A Rainbow Christmas."

The artist–author lives in New Hampshire, a setting with few distractions:

> I now live on a fifteen-acre farm in New London. My back meadow will be the eventual site of a swimming pool if my work keeps going so well. The shed may become my permanent studio, though I like my present studio's garret window. The farm has room for pets, like my fourteen-year-old Abyssinian cat, Satie, and Baby Bingle, an Airedale puppy. Some New Yorkers are betting when Baby Bingle will appear in a book.

I set the dining room table with antique dishes from my grandmother. I love to cook and entertain. Because of my Italian heritage, I've learned to fix pretty good homemade pasta primavera or pasta with veal and marsala wine.

In my living room is a pillow of Strega Nona that I designed, but I treasure the needlepoint done by Carolyn Field. She gave it to me when I won the Regina Medal.

DePaola won the 1981 Kerlan Award from the University of Minnesota and in 1983, became the youngest person yet to receive the coveted Regina Medal. The Catholic Library Association presents it in honor of the body of literary work done by a recipient.

The artist told about one fan, who did not understand the Regina Medal's purpose. She looked dePaola over carefully before questioning, "For *your* body?"

UPDATE

Instead of a 1985 Christmas story, Putnam issued *Tomie dePaola's Mother Goose.* This began a series of anthologies, including nursery tales, poems, Bible stories, and Christmas carols.

In *The Art Lesson* (Putnam, 1989), dePaola tells how he convinced his first-grade teacher to let him use his own sixty-four crayons, rather than the school's eight-color box, for his Pilgrim drawing.

In 1990 dePaola was nominated for the Hans Christian Andersen Award, and in 1995 he received the University of Southern Mississippi Medallion. He has continued illustrating books by other writers, including Tony Johnston's *The Quilt Story* (Putnam, 1985) and Jane Yolen's *Hark! A Christmas Sampler* (Putnam, 1991).

In 2000, dePaola's first chapter book, *26 Fairmount Avenue* (Putnam, 1999), became a Newbery Honor Book, enriched by his black-and-white illustrations. He tells a warm autobiographical account of events when he was five years old, and his parents were building their first house. The story ends just as the family moves to 26 Fairmount Avenue. The author promises to continue his life story, so readers look forward to more.

Eleanor Estes, author–illustrator (1906–1988)

Margaret K. McElderry, editor (1912–)

1975 Interview

ELEANOR ESTES

"I never say, 'I'm going to write with humor.' It just happens!" said Eleanor Estes, referring to her work for children. "I remember my husband coming home from work and enjoying my chapter of the day. When he read the lamb chop episode from *The Middle Moffat* (1942), he laughed so hard, he had an asthma attack."

Estes won the 1952 Newbery Medal for her self-illustrated *Ginger Pye* (Harcourt, 1951) with Margaret McElderry as her editor. Three of her books were named Newbery Honor Books in the following years: *The Middle Moffat*

(1943), *Rufus M.* (1944), and *The Hundred Dresses* (1945). Harcourt published all of Estes's books.

Estes was born on May 9, 1906, in West Haven, Connecticut, daughter of book-loving Louis and Caroline Rosenfeld. Her books take place in her own childhood setting: "I've given my hometown the fictitious name, Cranberry, placed my Moffat and Pye imaginary families there, and made them acquainted with each other."

Estes's mother had wanted to be a writer and often quoted from Tennyson and Shakespeare. She was a dramatic storyteller as she prepared dinners: "The way Mama could peel apples!" were the beginning words in Estes's first book, *The Moffats* (1941). The author drew on memories of her own mother as she wrote about a widow, short on material things but long on family warmth.

In their little parlor, Estes said that her mother gave adults dancing lessons, was a dressmaker, and sewed costumes for town hall plays. A black trunk held all the costumes except the brown flannel ones for the three bears. She and her brothers slept in them during cold winters, an experience that prompted her to write the three bears chapter in *The Middle Moffat.*

The first three "Moffat" books take place during World War I and trace episodes in the life of the books' widow and her children. The older, responsible siblings are Sylvie and Joey, but more humorous are younger Rufus and Jane, introduced at ages five and eight respectively.

Estes has a small sculpture that depicts a rear view of Jane looking upward between her legs:

> Jane finds the world looks clearer and brighter upside down. The idea may be based on pictures I drew upside down for my only child, Helena, while she faced me in a highchair. My pictures kept her interest long enough for her to finish eating.

In *The Moffats*, Jane is kind when Joey loses his way while steering a horse and Salvation Army wagon. Jane tells him, "Well, things look different behind a horse." In a simple way, Estes demonstrated ability to capture a child's observation and speech.

Estes traced the inspiration for the beginning of her third "Moffat" book, *Rufus M.*, in which Rufus learns to spell his name for a library card: "This incident was based on five-year-old Barbara Cooney who filed a library application, climbing the big stairs of New Haven's George Bruce Branch Library where I worked."

Estes's library memories are drawn from her years at the New Haven and New York public libraries. She won a scholarship to study at Pratt Institute Library School in Brooklyn. There she met a fellow student, Rice Estes, and married him. He later became a library science professor at Pratt.

The cruel effects of poverty are apparent in *The Hundred Dresses*. Translated into many languages, *The Hundred Dresses* is slight in length (only eighty pages) but deep in multicultural significance. It is the story of fourth-grade girls who taunt a poor classmate, Wanda Petronski. The leading snob is rich Peggy; her "sidekick" is Maddie, a captive since she receives Peggy's hand-me-downs.

According to Estes, the protagonist in *The Hundred Dresses* is passive Maddie, not Wanda, the motherless Polish girl who always wears the same faded blue dress each day. Spurred by jealousy of classmates' finer clothes, Wanda claims to own a hundred frocks, and she draws them for an art contest. Wanda's father takes her and his son, Jake, to a big city where people would less likely belittle their surname. The book takes on new meaning when Maddie is interpreted as the main character. Maddie knows that abusing Wanda is wrong, but she is afraid to act independently and incur Peggy's scorn.

"I want to move my readers emotionally," Estes said in explaining why she wrote the book. "I didn't create a happy ending by having Wanda return. You have one opportunity to follow the Golden Rule and treat others the way you want to be treated. The theme is there's no second chance to say, 'I'm sorry.'"

Estes's thematic interpretation was more penetrating than that of most critics. It has modern relevance because many who witness injustice today cowardly refuse to get involved.

Estes said that it took her six months to write *The Hundred Dresses,* but "my whole life actually went into writing that book." She had the rare privilege of choosing an illustrator of *The Hundred Dresses* and the first three "Moffat" books:

> My initial Harcourt editor was Elizabeth Hamilton, who presented me with finished drawings on heavy cardboard for *The Moffats*. I rejected the illustrations after my husband and the famous sculptor, Louis Slobodkin, agreed they couldn't be improved. All I wanted were pen and ink drawings. My Harcourt editor let me pick my own illustrator, telling me the book's printing would be delayed if the publisher did not like the results. In 1941, I engaged Slobodkin to do his first book illustrations. He started on *The Moffats* and began a whole new career.

Previously, Slobodkin was known only for his sculpture. His eight-foot bronze Lincoln representation is in the federal capital's Department of Interior building. By contrast, his illustrations were often small sketches that, contrary to fact, seemed casually done. They extend significant textual thoughts. Only three years after Estes commissioned him, he won the 1944 Caldecott Medal for his illustrations in James Thurber's *Many Moons* (Harcourt, 1943).

Estes considered Slobodkin to be a dynamo:

> Maybe it's because his grandfather was a Ukrainian cowboy, and the steppes' wild wind is in his blood. He influenced my art. Slobodkin guessed how an old motorcycle looked when he drew pictures for *The Middle Moffat,* so I drew an antique Ford based on my imagination when I illustrated *Ginger Pye.*

Estes based many of her characters on people she knew. Mr. Pye was much like her husband. Mrs. Pye resembled Estes's mother, sister, and even herself. Ginger is the only real name in any of her books. He was the family pet who was lost on Thanksgiving Day as a puppy, and in May reentered their lives as a grown dog. In the book, Ginger appears in the window of an ivy-covered brick school, like one Estes attended in fifth grade and beyond. He has a pencil in his mouth, so his nickname becomes "intellectual dog."

Another animal, a black kitten with a raspberry tongue, was the subject of Estes's sequel, *Pinky Pye* (1958).

Estes praised her editor, Margaret McElderry:

> She makes me laugh. Sometimes I've laughed so hard, tears are running down my cheeks. Besides, we're both frank and trust each other. I've even phoned her from Rome about galley proofs. I paid the bill too.

MARGARET K. MCELDERRY

Margaret McElderry was the Harcourt children's book editor who helped Estes with her Newbery winner, *Ginger Pye.* The editor moved to Atheneum where, in 1971, she began issuing Margaret K. McElderry Books.

McElderry was born in Pittsburgh, Pennsylvania, on July 10, 1912, and graduated from Mount Holyoke College in Massachusetts before earning a library science degree at Carnegie Institute of Technology. Her first job was in the New York Public Library's children's division under Anne Carroll Moore.

> During World War II, I took a leave of absence from the New York Public Library and worked with the Office of War Information in London and Brussels. I had just returned to New York and met Mabel Williams, head of Work with Young People at the New York Public Library. After I left, she was at a traffic light when she saw Frederic G. Melcher. [R. R. Bowker Company's president, publisher of *Publishers Weekly,* and initiator of Newbery and Caldecott Medals.] He said, "There's a Harcourt job open for a children's editor, but the only person for it is overseas."
>
> When Melcher learned I was back, I got the job and the chance to work with Estes on *Ginger Pye.* She took great care in her writing. By the time she sub-

mitted something, it was basically finished. I made tucks to shorten it a little, but nothing major. Of course, her main interest was not plot but people.

In 1952, Melcher brought me the news in person that, for the first time, the same publisher had won both the Newbery and Caldecott Medals: Eleanor Estes, the Newbery for *Ginger Pye*, and Nicolas Mordvinoff, the Caldecott for his illustrations in Will Lipkind's *Finders Keepers* [Harcourt, 1951].

McElderry offered a funny story about Estes's introduction at the medal-accepting banquet. The star was wearing a strapless white tulle gown with a bouffant, long skirt. Lipkind, seated next to her, had pushed his chair when she rose, and the chair leg had caught on her skirt. She got up partially and then went down.

McElderry thought the author had fainted, but after Lipkind moved his chair leg, Estes got up, laughing, and told the audience, "All my life since I knew I wanted to be a writer, I've dreamed of winning this award. And what do I do? I fall flat on the floor." The audience of a thousand laughed with her.

Joking was obvious in McElderry's relationship with Estes: "Eleanor and I spent a lot of time laughing. I think we got along because of her sense of humor. We seemed to be on the same wave length."

A seasoned traveler, McElderry has shown an interest in her Northern Irish parentage and in international affairs. She is a former president of the U.S. Board on Books for Young People (USBBY). McElderry has been prophetic about a need for quality children's books in a computer age. She early predicted in *Publishers Weekly* (February 26, 1973, p. 65), "If books died out, someone would have to invent them again."

UPDATE

The Moffat Museum (1984) was a fourth book that completed the "Moffat" series, forty-one years after a preceding book. This last work discussed Sylvie's wedding and Joey's first job after he had to quit school to help earn money for his family.

Estes died of stroke complications on July 15, 1988, in West Haven. The author would have welcomed being remembered as a permanent source of laughter in her nineteen children's books.

McElderry is now vice president and publisher of books bearing her name in Simon & Schuster's Children's Publishing Division of Maxwell-Macmillan International. Carol Fenner's *Yolonda's Genius* (Simon & Schuster, 1995), a McElderry title, was a 1996 Newbery Honor Book.

Tom Feelings, illustrator–author (1933–)

Muriel L. Feelings, author (1938–)

1972 Interview

TOM FEELINGS

The worlds of African and African-American culture were brought to the forefront in children's literature by Tom Feelings, the first African American to be named a Caldecott illustrator. He received that honor in 1972 for *Moja Means One: Swahili Counting Book* (Dial, 1971), written by his first wife, Muriel L. Feelings.

Tom was born on May 19, 1933, in Brooklyn's Brownsville, and he grew up in Brooklyn's Bedford-Stuyvesant section. In kindergarten, a teacher praised his art and showed it to other classes. Tom's mother, a factory worker, encouraged Tom's artistry by stitching folded paper on her sewing machine and asking him to draw a book. His father, who lived nearby, worried about his son's job chances, and told Tom, "Maybe if you can get into college, you can teach or something."

As a boy, Tom enjoyed such neighborhood resources as a local library's adult African-American collection containing Langston Hughes's poetry. He learned artistic skills after school at a Police Athletic League (PAL) Center. The center was in gang territory, but another art student convinced fellow gang members to leave him alone, stating, "He's *our* artist."

A Creole teacher, Mr. Thipadeaux, showed confidence in Tom, who went on to win citywide competitions and had television exposure on "Teen Canteen." The artist recalled that Thipadeaux's successor, Mr. Bilah, a quiet African American, taught him that kindness was not weakness.

As junior high ended, Tom won a medal for best artist in his 1947 class. He became an art student at George Westinghouse Vocational High School, where he learned lettering and silk-screen printing. A teacher, Mr. Shulman, told him about a post-high school scholarship to Cartoonists' and Illustrators' School. When Tom did not apply, the teacher acted on his student's behalf, and in 1951, Tom won a three-year scholarship.

Art studies included life drawing and comics. *The New York Age*, a Harlem newspaper, had already published Tom's historical comics, "Tommy Traveler in the World of Negro History." Now Tom's story-development teacher led him from comics to book illustration where Tom found that he "projected more content and personal feeling."

After illustrating for four years in the U.S. Air Force, Tom enrolled in New York City's School of Visual Arts to become an artist. "For the first time, I started drawing from life in my own community, all the places and the people I had not put down on paper before. I took my drawing pad and pencil everywhere." Tom was troubled when neighborhood children cautioned, "Don't make our lips too large!" In lands of black majority he expected more self-respect, less self-disparagement.

From 1964 to 1966, Tom worked as an illustrator in Africa for the Ghanaian Government Publishing House, near Accra. President Kwame Nkrumah, who brought Ghana to independence in 1957, welcomed African Americans, and Tom was attracted by the land's large printing press. He illustrated the magazine, *African Review*, while also preparing visual materials for Ghanaian television and the country's airport. He realized in Africa his drawings were "more vivid and alive, as though they had light radiating from within." Before his job ended and Tom left Ghana, he met the American poet, Maya Angelou, a three-year professor there.

With views of Africans in his portfolio, Tom returned to New York in 1966 when publishing doors, once closed, were opening. *Look* and *Freedomways* were among magazines commissioning him now. He illustrated his first children's book, Letta Schatz's *Bola and the Oba's Drummer* (McGraw-Hill, 1967) and thought he was effective by limiting colors, "pulling my audience in quietly."

Tom could sense a difference in the work he did in the United States, when compared to that done in Africa. In explanation, he recited Ruth Duckett Gibbs's poem, "Afro-American Child's Lament," from a book he illustrated, *Black Is the Color* (Center for Media Development, 1973). The poem indicates that skin color is not among African boys' problems.

In New York Tom renewed friendship with Muriel L. Gray, and they married on February 8, 1968. Their sons have Swahili names: Zamani, which means "First One," and Kamili, which means "Perfect."

In 1968, Tom illustrated *To Be a Slave* (Dial, 1968), a Newbery Honor Book edited by Julius Lester. "To do that book, I had to experience slavery!" Tom said. "Also, after illustrating at least ten books, mainly about Africa, this was the first book by an African-American for a major publisher that I was asked to do."

Muriel explained Tom's perfectionist approach:

> He has respected Julius Lester's leadership since childhood, so he didn't feel anything he drew was good enough. It wasn't until Julius Lester phoned and told him that he appreciated the illustrations that Tom could put his mind at ease.

Tom also writes children's books, such as *Black Pilgrimage* (Lothrop, Lee & Shepard, 1972). He said, "The text adds to my drawings during a ten-year period in Brooklyn, North and South Carolina, Louisiana, and Ghana." He added on the jacket, "My heart is with the Black people of America, but my soul is in Africa." For emphasis, the vigorous man wore a *fulana,* or African shirt.

At the end of 1970, the Feelings family left for small, independent Guyana, invited by the government of the only English-speaking country in South America. Tom, appointed to head a children's book project, announced, "I plan to develop the talent of native illustrators."

In Guyana, Tom, who was limited to two-color jobs on small printing presses, said, "I experimented by printing on tone or mottled paper, trying to get the mood of full color. . . . I rediscovered the lesson of my ancestors—improvising within a restrictive form."

MURIEL L. FEELINGS

Muriel Feelings was born on July 31, 1938, in Philadelphia, where she lived among books and artists. Great-grandmother Lavinia Harris, a Philadelphia elementary school teacher, drew children's portraits published by the American Dairy Council. Lavinia's brother, Rev. Robert Harris, attended the Philadelphia Museum School of Art and was a muralist, later also an Episcopalian priest. The priest's younger brother, John T. Harris, was founder and head of Cheney University's art department. He encouraged Muriel and her brother, Lawrence, to attend Saturday art classes at what is now the University of the Arts.

Muriel studied art at Germantown High School, but she also had a flair for writing. An English teacher there was convinced that Muriel had plagiarized an essay on Ernest Hemingway because it was so perceptive. Muriel protested, and eventually the teacher, unwilling to apologize, did acknowledge, "You have remarkable insight."

After high school graduation in 1956, Muriel worked and studied part-time at Philadelphia Museum School of Art, hoping to teach art. She moved to Los Angeles, where her aunt lived, and attended Los Angeles City College. When she transferred to State University at Los Angeles, she met Maulama Karenga, founder of an African-based cultural festival, Kwanzaa. The civil rights movement inspired Muriel to help emerging independent African nations.

After graduating from college in 1963, Muriel eventually moved to New York. She joined Malcolm X's Organization of Afro-American Unity and witnessed Malcolm's shocking assassination. In 1966, she went to Kampala, Uganda's capital, to teach art. She described being the first African-American female teacher at Kitante Hill Senior Secondary School, which attracted local students and those from remote areas who boarded at state-run hostels:

> At the boy's high, I had to spell "color" with a "u" to follow King's English. I taught all week and had a Saturday Creative Arts Workshop. Among other activities, we built a stone sculpture garden and prepared a televised puppet show.
>
> Under the Cambridge educational system, the boys had to pass a difficult high school leaving exam equivalent to an American junior college level. I doubt that I could have passed it. This system may change because of the new East African Examining Board. When I arrived, the country had been independent from Great Britain only for four years. The government made education a priority, building schools and dorms.

The Apondos, parents of medical students her mother had entertained in Philadelphia, hosted Muriel for a month in a Kenyan village. She reported, "As a visitor, I was given the best of everything, food and folk tales. While English was Uganda's official language, Swahili was Kenya's main tongue."

After two years in warm Africa, Muriel returned to cold New York. She enjoyed reunions with friends, one of whom was Tom Feelings, another Pan-Africanist and a former sweetheart. They married and settled in Brooklyn, where Muriel taught for the Ocean Hill-Brownsville Experimental School District.

Muriel used her older son's name, Zamani, in writing her initial picture book, *Zamani Goes to Market* (Seabury Press, 1969). She said:

> In fiction I tried to depict African respect for elders and division of labor (mothers with daughters and fathers with sons). I also showed the elders' confidence in Zamani when he came of age to lead an animal to market.

To share other aspects of East African life, Muriel wrote and Tom illustrated a second book, *Moja Means One: A Swahili Counting Book*. As an example, Muriel depicted "one" with Mount Kilimanjaro; "six" with six styles of East African clothes; and "nine" with nine performers on different musical instruments. Muriel's introduction informs readers that, though there are eight hundred African languages, Swahili is used in the largest land area and could be the common tongue to help unify the continent's population.

In 1970, Muriel, Tom, and Zamani went to South America, to Guyana, which means "Land of Many Waters." The first year, Muriel was a teacher and teacher-trainer at two high schools, doing rural village workshops for women in textile dyeing and design. Using local materials, she guided students to make items, such as tie-dyed and batik garments that they sold. In her second year in Guyana, Muriel joined the Materials Production Unit as an editor and writer.

Muriel returned to Philadelphia in 1972 for the birth of her second son, Kamili. While raising her sons in Philadelphia, Muriel spent four years training field staff and writing publications for Opportunities Industrialization Center (OIC) International. During the next five years, she was director of education at the Afro-American Historical and Cultural Museum. She also pursued her main skill, writing books. Her next picture book was *Jambo Means Hello: A Swahili Alphabet Book*. Tom again provided double-page illustrations. Since "Q" and "X" are not in the Swahili alphabet, Muriel dealt with twenty-four letters, supplying for each a key word and definition. She began with the key word, *arusi* (wedding), and ended with *zeze* (a musical instrument).

The couple's work promoted African roots and African-American life in children's books. Muriel said, "Prior to 1965, black children were largely invisible in U.S. children's literature."

When asked if the children were invisible since there were no black artists to illustrate them, Tom protested: "From 1960 to 1964, I walked around to every New York publisher with a portfolio of drawings of black children, and I wasn't given a job. The same publishers are hiring me today."

UPDATE

After returning to the United States in 1974, Tom and Muriel divorced. Tom now lives with his second wife, Dr. Dianne Johnson Feelings, and their daughter, Niani Sekai. (In Zimbabwi's Zezuru culture, their daughter's middle name means "laugh.") Tom, who sculpts as well as illustrates, is an art professor at the University of South Carolina at Columbia, where his wife is an English professor.

Jambo Means Hello: A Swahili Alphabet Book, a 1974 release, received the 1975 Caldecott Medal for illustrations. On *Jambo's* last page, Tom cites his art methods, involving use of tissue paper, a method he originated in art school when his funds were limited. Tom combines two imprints of his drawing, a complete one in black ink and a second one in ochre that is not obvious. Results retain the original art's warmth.

Tom has won many Coretta Scott King Awards for illustrations: 1979 winner for Nikki Grimes's *Something on My Mind*; 1982 runner-up for Eloise Greenfield's *Daydreamers*; 1994 winner for his own book, *Soul Looks Back in Wonder* (1993); and 1996 winner for his own book, *The Middle Passage: White Ships, Black Cargo* (1995).

In *Soul Looks Back in Wonder,* his first anthology, Tom showed his collages, each of which inspired a poem printed on the same double-page spread. The thirteen poets include Maya Angelou, Lucille Clifton, Walter Dean Myers, and Margaret Walker. For the first time, Tom used his drawing and a poem Langston Hughes wrote about it. Stylized end papers show a rainbow of African Liberation Movement colors—red, black, and green—descending from a youth's head.

In 1996, ALA gave Tom a Special Black Illustrators Award for *The Middle Passage: White Ships, Black Cargo.* Tom tells his story with sixty-four illustrations in somber chiaroscuro tones that show tightly packed ship captives and the crew's cruelty. The most effective original art are figureheads on a boat's prow that seem to scream in open-mouthed terror.

Tom collaborated with Maya Angelou on *Now Sheba Sings the Song* (Plume-Penguin, 1994). In the book's introduction, Tom tells about being at a bus stop in Ghana with a woman who balanced wares on her head. The middle-aged woman, glowing with a dark purple hue, smiled at him, and he knew what he "had been taught in America about Black being ugly—was a lie. . . . I was looking at the most beautiful sight my eyes had ever seen."

Among his other awards, Tom received a grant in 1996 from The National Endowment for the Arts.

In 1984, the Pennsylvania School Librarians' Association named Muriel L. Feelings an Outstanding Pennsylvania author. She also won the Drexel Citation in 1985 from Drexel University and the Free Library of Philadelphia.

In 1990, Muriel's *Zamani Goes to Market* was reissued by Africa World Press in Lawrenceville, New Jersey. The book, which Tom illustrated, won a Junior Literary Guild citation.

Since 1986, Muriel has been director of Temple University's Pan-African Studies Community Education Program. Her workshops for parents, teachers, and students often discuss African-American literature.

The Feelings' sons, Zamani and Kamili, are now six-footers. Zamani, a trumpet jazz enthusiast, helps students as a staff member of Philadelphia's Concerned Black Men. Kamili, a Temple University honors graduate, is writing and acting in Trustus Theater productions in Columbia, South Carolina.

Jane Flory (Freedman), author–illustrator (1917–)

1978 Interview

With Houghton Mifflin as her publisher, Jane Flory has written and illustrated eleven long fictional books for children who are eight to eleven years old, and has created more than twenty-five picture books. Her book about the California Gold Rush, *The Golden Adventure* (1976), became a French Notable Book of the Year.

Jane Trescott was born on June 29, 1917, in Wilkes-Barre, Pennsylvania, to a family of storytellers. "My ancestors just missed the *Mayflower*, and they claim they've been 'missing the boat' ever since. . . . In the 1700s, the New Englanders who came down to Pennsylvania were great tellers of stories and anecdotes. That's been much of my material," she said.

Flory, who also makes quilts and weaves, casts the image of a wholesome, enterprising pioneer. She reminisced about her childhood in Woodbury, New Jersey:

> I began to write and draw for children as soon as I could hold a pencil. From the start, I folded my work into books. My father wrote very well and had a lot of articles published. We were all readers. We thought of the town library as a house annex.

Flory's writing career was delayed until she learned to spell at age five. After high school, she set goals: "My only ambition was to write and illustrate for

children who are more impressionable than adults." To learn more about illustrating, she went to the School of Industrial Arts, now the Philadelphia
College of Art. She graduated in 1939 and, two years later, married Arthur
Flory, a fellow student who became known nationally and abroad for his
paintings and prints. The couple lived across from Tyler School of Fine Arts,
where Arthur Flory taught. Here she helped raise three daughters, Cynthia
(now Jessamyn), Christine, and Erica, and was a freelance writer and illustrator. Her daughters were her first book critics. She said, "They assumed the
role naturally as though everybody's mother were a writer." Jessamyn now
owns a children's bookstore in Toronto and is a reader for Canada's Book of
the Year for Children. Erica is a children's sweater designer and knitter, and
Christine, a painter and printmaker.

When her husband had multiple sclerosis, Flory worked for sixteen years
as director of the evening division of the Philadelphia College of Art. After
her husband's death in 1972, she resigned to create more books. She remembered a high point in her husband's career and in her life:

> Arthur Flory won a Rockefeller Grant to start a lithography workshop in
> Tokyo. When the girls and I went over, all sorts of exciting things happened,
> and I kept thinking: *This is wonderful material for a book.* Almost the last
> night there, on New Year's Eve, we went to a temple to hear the traditional
> 108 bells.

The title of Flory's book set in Tokyo is *One Hundred and Eight Bells* (1963).
The Japanese story's protagonist, Setsuko Sagawa, who is about twelve years
old, wants to be an artist like her father. Her mother gradually accepts Setsuko's career aspirations. The book ends on New Year's Eve at a temple
where the family hears 108 bells.

Flory writes a lot of Pennsylvania historical fiction:

> My roots are deep in Pennsylvania history, and that is the source of most of
> my book ideas spring from. Mother remembered clearly life on her grand-
> mother's little farm and was a wellspring of wonderful, funny, human stories.
>
> My great-grandmother became a widow on a farm with eight small girls to
> raise. The youngest was only two years old. Stories about the widow depict the
> theme: courage in the face of difficulties. Her children turned out to be very in-
> teresting people.

Peddler's Summer (1960) tells how Pa Scoville, who valued an education for
his daughters, dies of a sudden fever one autumn in about 1880. Uncle Boli-

var threatens to remove the oldest girls from school and have them work. He wants to divide the family so they can survive the winter. Resisting, Ma supports her eight daughters. They refute Uncle Bolivar's claim that they are "nine helpless females."

The sequel to *Peddler's Summer* is *Mist on the Mountain* (1966). It begins a year after Pa's death and celebrates Ma's spirit. The family survives by selling homemade cider and apple butter. Amanda's earnings from demonstrating a new invention, a sewing machine, buy horseshoes and girl shoes, schoolbooks, and lamp oil. Ma becomes the "birthing woman."

"I like to write about strong women," Flory said. Another of her books built on that theme is *The Liberation of Clementine Tipton* (1974). It takes place in 1876 when Philadelphia was celebrating its centennial and experiencing a growing women's movement. Ten-year-old Clementine, raised in a wealthy home, benefits from the arrival of her new governess, Miss Lamb, who attends women's rights meetings. Clementine cuts her tangled, ginger-colored hair and announces (p. 213):

> I've a brain, a good smart brain, and I'm going to fill it with all the things Miss Lamb can teach me, whether they're boys' studies or not. I'll grow up to be a woman, and I'll vote, too, just you wait, and I'll do all the exciting things women are going to do!

Flory switched from a female to a male protagonist in *It Was a Pretty Good Year* (1977). The book, which is set in 1910–1911, is based on the childhood experiences of Barney Freedman, whom Flory married in 1980. The period piece mentions an iron kitchen stove that had to be blacked to prevent rusting. Blacking was a punishment for whichever son misbehaved and was caught.

Some of Flory's long books have been translated into French and German, and a picture book is in Turkish. *The Liberation of Clementine Tipton* appears in England with a British cover. Flory also produced *Ramshackle Roost* (1972), a long book, and two picture books, *We'll Have a Friend for Lunch* (1974) and *The Unexpected Grandchildren* (1977), both illustrated by her friend, Carolyn Croll. Having grandchildren motivated Flory to consider doing picture books again. If she is illustrating her own picture books, Flory admitted, "I'm thinking pictorially as I write."

Forever creative, Flory now devotes the third floor of her home to making family quilts. Previously, she revealed, "I was a dollhouse freak. I've got five of them, and one is Victorian. This hobby parallels writing. I have my own miniature world that I control."

UPDATE

Flory illustrated her own picture book, *The Lost and Found Princess* (1979), but in 1980, Carolyn Croll's art was featured in Flory's *The Bear on the Mountain*. The author's final long book, *Miss Plunckett to the Rescue* (1983), is a spy story about a teacher whose mission in another land, Tiltweg, is to rescue a secret apple muffin recipe.

Paula Fox, author (1923–)

1987 Interview

Author Paula Fox won't soon forget the ceremony at which she received the 1978 Hans Christian Andersen Award for her collective children's books—the first U.S. woman author to win the prestigious honor:

> I received it in a wonderful building called the Residence in Würzburg, Germany, about eighty miles from Frankfurt. Although Würzburg had been bombed, the Residence survived. It was an extraordinary place with paintings by Tiepolo on almost all the ceilings. The old building had no heat, so it was like the frozen north that fall. We listened to speeches from the Andersen Committee. I think everyone became utterly frozen. There was hardly any sign of life. Then onto the stage came a group of young musicians, about twelve to fifteen years old, who played Mozart in this marvelous room. I gave a short thank-you speech, because I think people would have left if it had been longer than a page.

Fox wasn't new to the award scene, however. Her *Blowfish Live in the Sea* (Macmillan, 1970) was a 1971 National Book Award Finalist. *The Slave Dancer* (Bradbury, 1973) won the 1974 Newbery Medal. *A Place Apart* (Farrar, Straus, 1980) got the 1983 American Book Award for a Children's Fiction Paperback. *One-Eyed Cat* (Bradbury, 1984) was a 1985 Newbery Honor Book, and both it and *The Slave Dancer* were inscribed in Andersen Honor Lists.

Fox was born on April 22, 1923 in New York City. Her father, Paul Hervey Fox, was also a writer:

> He was a playwright who became a play fixer, trying to get plays by others ready for Broadway. He went to Hollywood with my mother and became a screenwriter for Metro-Goldwyn-Mayer. When he was about forty, he settled in England and wrote novels that were not too successful.

Unfortunately, Fox's Irish-English father was alcoholic, which prompted her to include alcoholic characters in some of her children's books, including *Blowfish Live in the Sea* and *The Moonlight Man* (Bradbury, 1986). Fox spent only a short time with her father and with her Spanish mother, Elsie de Sola.

For her first six years, the author lived with a Congregational minister and his wheelchair-bound mother in a Victorian house overlooking the Hudson River. During electric storms, the three sat near the entrance so they could escape if lightning struck, and he told her stories. The minister, who was also a writer, taught her to read and inspired her to become a writer. Once her parents removed her from this home, her life lost its stability:

> After I lived with the minister in the Hudson Valley, I was taken to California for a couple of years. When I was eight, my grandmother and I lived on my great-aunt's sugar plantation in Cuba. There was a small revolution during Batista's time when President Machado was killed. We left before Castro. I moved around a great deal, uneasy about where I would be next.

By the time the author was twelve, she had gone to nine schools, including a one-room school in Cuba where she learned Spanish. She stayed with relatives and rarely saw her parents. Public libraries offered her joy and a refuge.

When she was seventeen, she began to support herself. She was a Bethlehem Steel machinist and a reader for a movie production company. She described other jobs:

> I punctuated fifteenth-century Italian madrigals. I was a reporter, a "stringer," for a small British news agency in Poland. I taught children with severe learning problems. I also taught English as a second language to doctors and nurses of foreign patients.

In New York, Fox married in 1948 and had two sons, Adam and Gabriel. Fox's older son is now an energy expert. The younger one, a high-tech welder, speaks Chinese, is a linguist, and is interested in his mother's books.

After her divorce in 1954, Fox studied at Columbia University and began college teaching. She remarried in 1962 and now lives in Brooklyn with her husband, Martin Greenberg, a literature professor, critic, author, and former *Commentary* editor.

Fox's first book for children, *Maurice's Room* (Macmillan, 1966), is a humorous tale of eight-year-old Maurice and his friend, Jacob, who fill their bedrooms with "junk" collections. When Maurice moves to the country, he starts a new collection.

How Many Miles to Babylon? (David White, 1967; Bradbury, 1980) expresses tension in its very title. "The line following the title in the nursery rhyme is, 'Can I get there and back again?'" she said. In the story, ten-year-old James Douglas, an African-American child, lives in Brooklyn with his three aunts. His father deserted his mother, and she is hospitalized with depression. James escapes from young dog thieves who seize pets and return them to owners for rewards. He goes home to find his mother there, a "light" in this novel of despair.

Portrait of Ivan (Bradbury, 1969) was a Child Study Association of America Children's Book of 1969. In it, a withdrawn father hires Matt Muztazza to paint a portrait of his eleven-year-old son, Ivan. His mother had drowned during the boy's infancy, and thereafter, his father had cloistered him. Matt drives Ivan and the boy's elderly companion to Florida to meet twelve-year-old Geneva, a girl who enjoys freedom.

Blowfish Live in the Sea shows a relationship between twelve-year-old Carrie and eighteen-year-old Ben, her half brother who has a ponytail, uses pot, and rejects college. Carrie's father is a New York physician. After her birth, Ben's father, Donald, sent him a blowfish "from the Amazon River." Ben writes, "Blowfish live in the sea," exposing Donald's lies. Curious about Donald, Ben and Carrie search for him and find him, a drunk running a seedy Boston hotel. Ben stays to sober Donald up and fix the hotel while Carrie returns home.

One-Eyed Cat, supported by a 1984 Rockefeller Grant, won the 1985 Christopher Award. Reverend Wallis in the tale reminded Fox "of the minister I knew in my childhood." The reverend forbids his eleven-year-old son, Ned, to accept an air rifle as a birthday gift and hides it in the attic. Ned finds it and fires a shot outdoors. A one-eyed cat appears, and Ned thinks his shot blinded the creature in the other eye.

Fox is no stranger to controversy when it comes to writing. *The Slave Dancer* begins when a white, thirteen-year-old street musician, Jessie, is kidnapped in 1840 in New Orleans to work on a slave ship. He travels to Africa, and when slaves are forced aboard, he plays his fife to "dance" them, keeping them healthy and profitable. Six months later, off the Cuban coast, the captain sees an American ship and drowns ninety-seven slaves to avoid being caught with contraband. (The United States had already outlawed the slave trade.) Jessie, the only surviving crew member, saves one African boy, Ras, and the two dogpaddle to shore. Ras heads north and Jessie returns to New Orleans. However, Jessie can no longer listen to music, since it is too painful a reminder of slave dancing.

Fox said, "*The Slave Dancer* took a year to write and was not casually penned." She described the book's background:

> I was lured by a footnote from *The Middle Passage* by a man named Mannix. Even though slavery had been outlawed from Benin to the Caribbean to the Georgia coast, it continued. The footnote said that ship captains would often kidnap children, waifs who had been abandoned in London or any large city. While these children begged, they played an instrument, like a fife or drum. Such children were kidnapped or shanghaied and used as cabin boys or to exercise the slaves.
>
> During the latter eighteenth century, sea captains discovered that . . . if they exercised the slaves, they would be in better condition and bring more money. They certainly didn't do it out of kindness.
>
> Musicians were valuable. They were called slave dancers. They were kidnapped in England, so I had a boy kidnapped in New Orleans. I had lived in New Orleans but don't know if anyone was actually kidnapped there.

A second experience also motivated Fox to write the book:

> On television news, I saw an indignant elderly woman picketing over cheap housing for black families. She said, "They *chose* to come over here in ships, just as my grandfather and grandmother did." It seemed to me incredible that she had lived here all her life without ever absorbing the information that Africans had not *chosen* to come here.

Fox told why *The Slave Dancer* will remain her only historical novel: "The history was difficult. I had read for a year, and was so filled with facts, I was repressed by history. It was difficult to be free in my writing."

In *The Slave Dancer*, Fox described vividly a storm at sea similar to one she had experienced:

> In 1945 . . . I was indeed in a bad storm at sea in a small frigate. One puts these things together out of one's own life, which sets off imaginative possibilities, even with historical lives. The Irish writer, J. Farrell, said, "The bricks are real, but the architecture is invented."

Fox defended her work against claims that a white person cannot write about slavery because he or she doesn't have the experiential background:

Do only those who died in the war have the experiential background to write about dying in the war? Women can write about men. If not, poor George Eliot wouldn't have had a chance, would she? It has nothing to do with imaginative fiction. It has to do with propaganda. That is ideological and political. . . . *The Slave Dancer* showed how stricken I was with the whole notion of slavery.

Fox will never forget when she was told she had won the Newbery Medal for *The Slave Dancer*:

The phone call came at 3 A.M. I said, "Wha?" because I was too sleepy to say, "What?" We all got up and had tea and toast.

I was to leave that same morning for Chicago and didn't have a proper dress. On the way from the Chicago airport, I stopped at Saks Department Store. They had this very large black dress, which I bought. When I came to the hotel, no one would speak to me, because I wasn't supposed to know [about the award]. It was like a Japanese Noh play.

I went into a small room, got into the black dress, and entered a large ball-room. Again, people would not speak to me except for John Donovan of the Children's Book Council. When it was announced that I had won the Newbery, everyone looked at me. I was then received into human society.

After the awards ceremony, Fox resumed her college work. A fellow professor reacted to a review of her book, but not the award:

I was teaching at Stonybrook at the time. When I went in, a colleague said, "I see you had a very poor review in the *New York Times* for *The Slave Dancer*." You know how some colleagues are! The review was late for the *Times*. I had just won the Newbery. It didn't seem to make much difference. Then I went back to work because the excitement of winning the prize is over quickly, sometimes quicker than the sting of a poor review.

Among other honors, Fox won the 1972 National Institute of Arts and Letters' Award, a 1972 Guggenheim Fellowship, and a 1987 Silver Medallion from the University of Southern Mississippi.

Fox, who has also written five books for adults, considers the story to be critical for her and hints that her tales, often socially conscious, begin with a character. Fortunately, she understands a child's viewpoint. She carefully plots, explaining the denouement of *The Village by the Sea* (Orchard, 1988) with an adage: "Envy's a coal comes hissing hot from hell." Praised for her writing style and originality, she feels that is ephemeral but concludes that composing is "unremitting labor."

UPDATE

Fox has continued to produce award-winning books tackling controversial issues. *The Village by the Sea* won a 1989 *Boston Globe-Horn Book* Fiction Award. It also includes an alcoholic character, this time a woman, the lead character's aunt. In *Monkey Island* (Orchard, 1991), eleven-year-old Clay is homeless after his father loses his job and deserts both him and his pregnant mother. Overwhelmed, she moves them to a welfare hotel and leaves him. In a park, he meets an African-American youth, Buddy, and an elderly alcoholic, Calvin, who become his family. *The Eagle Kite* (Orchard, 1995) discusses AIDS. Liam's father has the disease, and his family cannot talk about it until Liam reveals a secret: he has seen his father embracing another man at the beach.

Russell Freedman, author (1929–)

1989 Interview

Photography has long been one of Russell Freedman's hobbies, so it's no wonder that his books are filled with photographs instead of drawings. "One of my motivations for writing children's books was to illustrate them with photographs," he said. "I wanted to have control over the design of a book, its rhythm and flow. I discovered that photographs had more dramatic impact and seemed more credible than illustrations."

Freedman was born on October 11, 1929, in San Francisco, California, one of two children. His father, Louis, a Macmillan publisher's representative, filled their home with books. His mother, Irene, prepared leg of lamb for such guests as John Masefield, William Saroyan, and John Steinbeck. Freedman enjoyed meeting his family's literary dinner companions and relished reading. His favorite fiction was Robert Louis Stevenson's *Treasure Island,* and Ernest Thompson Seton's *Wild Animals I Have Known* was his favorite nonfiction.

In 1951, after earning a bachelor's degree from the University of California in Berkeley, he went to Korea for two years of service with the U.S. Army's counterintelligence corps. After his discharge he wrote for the Associated Press news agency and, later, for an advertising company as a television program publicist. From 1969 to 1986 he taught writing workshops at the New School for Social Research in New York and prepared encyclopedias.

Freedman was moved to write for young people after reading in *The New York Times* about a sixteen-year-old blind boy who developed a braille typewriter. He realized that Louis Braille was only fifteen when he devised the braille alphabet. After researching other young pacesetters, he wrote his first book, *Teenagers Who Made History* (Holiday House, 1961).

He followed that with *Two Thousand Years of Space Travel* (Holiday House, 1963): "It was about the history of the idea of space travel and had a chapter on Jules Verne," he said. Verne stirred his interest, and for his third book, *Jules Verne: Portrait of a Prophet* (Holiday House, 1965), he explained, "I went to Europe, visiting Verne's birthplace and Brittany, where he spent much of his life. Of course, I read all of his books, including some at the Library of Congress."

Freedman next began work on more than twenty books about animal behavior, collaborating on some with James E. Morriss. One intriguing title is *Can Bears Predict Earthquakes? Unsolved Mysteries of Animal Behavior* (Holiday House, 1982). He did more than twenty drafts of a book for second graders about how animals survive snowy days, *When Winter Comes* (Holiday House, 1981). Beginning in 1977, he used photographs to illustrate his Holiday House animal books.

> In *Hanging On: How Animals Carry Their Young*, I wrote a series of short essays and showed with photographs how lions carry their cubs, beavers carry beaver kits as they swim, and bats fly with their young clinging to fur on their bellies. I learned if I got my own photographs and coordinated them with the text, I would have organic control over the wholeness of a book.

One of Freedman's friends suggested that the author view an exhibit titled "New York Street Kids." The photos had been taken in the nineteenth century by the Children's Aid Society. The exhibit inspired Freedman:

> I saw a close-up of a ten-year-old newsboy and newsgirl whose clothing was from a hundred years ago as was the architecture of the buildings and the horses and carriages passing in the street. I realized that the children had grown up and were dead and gone, but the expressions on their faces were timeless as they smiled at me from the past. That resulted in a book called *Immigrant Kids* [Dutton, 1980].
>
> I conceived the idea for *Children of the Wild West* the same day as *Immigrant Kids*. However, finding its photos was much more difficult. There's no such category in libraries. You have to sift through a lot. Also, in *Children of the Wild West*, I found the photographs first, laid them all out on the living room floor, and spent weeks moving them around before I wrote the manuscript.

Clarion issued *Children of the Wild West* in 1983, and the following year it won the Western Heritage Award of the National Cowboy Hall of Fame. Freedman's *Cowboys of the Wild West* (Clarion, 1985) won a Western Writers of America Award. Authentic photographs in *Cowboys of the Wild West* helped break the stereotype of movie cowboys as white only:

> One out of every three authentic cowboys were black, Native American, or Hispanic. There were a number of ranches in which all the hired hands were American Indians. There were American Indian-owned ranches.
>
> The cowboys originated after the Civil War. There were a lot of black cowboys who, as slaves, had been trained to work with cattle on plantations. After the Civil War, they were liberated and became ideal cowboys, especially on ranches in Texas, a former slave-holding state. They were much in demand.

In most people's minds, cowboys are often paired with American Indians. Freedman's next western project was *Indian Chiefs* (Holiday House, 1987), which was named as a Jefferson Cup Award Honor Book. He found it difficult to write about the six leaders featured in that book:

> *Indian Chiefs* deals with diverse individuals who spoke different languages, came from different cultures, and each fought a different war with the U.S. Cavalry. They faced complex, controversial issues that were difficult to simplify. Many strands had to be tied together.

In *Buffalo Hunt* (Holiday House, 1988), Freedman looked at the animal that gave meat, hide, and bones to the Indians of the Great Plains. Illustrations consist of art that Freedman selected, by George Catlin, Karl Bodmer, Albert Bierstadt, and other artist-adventurers of the 1800s. The book shows how white hunters' greed for buffalo hides severely depleted the buffalo herds and left Indians to starve. *Buffalo Hunt* was named "among the best books of the year" by *School Library Journal,* ALA's *Booklist, Parents* and *Parenting* magazines, and the Library of Congress.

Freedman used archival photographs in *Lincoln, a Photobiography* (Clarion, 1987), which won the 1988 Newbery Medal. He was the first person in thirty-two years to win that medal for a work of nonfiction.

> I didn't realize nonfiction was eligible, though I knew that Hendrik Van Loon's *The Story of Mankind* won the first Newbery Medal in 1922. With this exception, all six nonfiction winners, including mine, have been biographies. Nonfiction has been dwelling in the servants' quarters.

Freedman highlighted differences between modern and past biographies written for children:

> Previously biographical subjects were sanitized and idealized. Thanks to Jean Fritz and Milton Meltzer, biographers today are more honest, treating their subjects with respect without being reverential.
>
> As a child, I wasn't interested in Lincoln. Later, I read an essay by Mary McCarthy who said that she admired Lincoln because of his intellect and melancholy. I didn't know he was melancholic. Then I read in *The New York Times* an article about the contents of Lincoln's pockets the morning after his assassination. Before my eyes, he was stepping down from the Lincoln Monument statue, changing from marble to a flesh-and-blood human being.
>
> When Clarion asked if I wanted to do a presidential biography, I thought of Lincoln because I wanted to learn more about him. It's my main reason for writing about any subject.

Lincoln's flaws were a Freedman concern:

> I didn't consider melancholy as a weakness. It was an affliction perhaps. He was depressed a lot. He was painfully shy, indecisive, insecure, and was a crybaby. He walked around feeling sorry for himself. A fascination of his life story was watching him overcome his weaknesses and mature into a remarkable being.

Freedman discovered that Lincoln learned to joke even about being homely. A political rival called him "two-faced," so Lincoln quipped, "If I had another face, do you think I'd wear this one?"

He also discovered that Lincoln didn't like to be called "Abe" in person:

> Lincoln spent a good part of his life trying to overcome his log-cabin origins. He was self-educated. It was hard to do. He was proud of himself. He rose from dirt-farm poverty into considerable affluence as an attorney. At the time he was elected president, he was quite a wealthy man because of his law practice and his extensive investments in railroads and real estate. There was a humble side of Lincoln, but he also respected his achievements.
>
> Lincoln couldn't stand the nickname, "Abe." No one who knew him well would dare call him that to his face. It was either "Lincoln" or "Mr. Lincoln." His own wife called him, "Mr. Lincoln."

Lincoln clearly cherished his dignity. Less certain was his initial goal in fighting the Southern states' attempt to withdraw from the Union, which led to the U.S. Civil War. Freedman gave his interpretation:

His goal wasn't emancipation. Lincoln's initial goal was to save the union. He said quite explicitly that his purpose was not to extinguish or continue slavery. He suffered personally from the war's death toll. He began to think the Civil War was some sort of retribution against slavery. He had always been against slavery, but he became passionately against it as the war with all its bloodshed progressed.

Lincoln's advisers told him that under his executive powers and emergency war powers, he could issue an Emancipation Proclamation. He did so partly as a moral imperative and partly to speed the end of the war.

While working on his Lincoln biography, Freedman visited a number of places, including Lincoln's birthplace in Kentucky, his boyhood home in Indiana, where Lincoln became a well-known lawyer in Illinois, and historic sites in Washington, D.C. "I tried to visit every significant Lincoln historic spot," he said. "I think that added a lot" to the book.

Just as extensive was Freedman's library research:

> I used library resources in many places, but I spent considerable time at the Illinois State Historical Library. In some cases, I wanted the "feel" of the original documents more than to learn their contents, which I already knew from published books. Tom Schwartz, curator of the Lincoln collection, asked, "Would you like to enter the vault?"
>
> It was an enormous bank vault. He twisted the combination and said, "Let's step inside." It was a quiet, cool, temperature-controlled vault. He began to show me scraps of paper where Lincoln had doodled or made some notes in the courtroom; a letter to his wife; and an original draft of the Emancipation Proclamation. He explained that the paper had been especially treated to remove acid from it. He held up a note with Lincoln's scrawled doodles and said, "This will last a thousand years."

Freedman's next step was integrating the Lincoln manuscript and photographs:

> I did about six drafts of *Lincoln, a Photobiography*, but that's standard. After I completed the writing, I went out and spent considerable time finding photographs. In *Lincoln*, the photograph has to appear on the same double-page spread where reference is made to it, and the caption beneath the photo has to supply ideally information not found in the text.

Ninety photographs and drawings in the book included the only house Lincoln ever owned, Civil War battlefields with dead Federal and Confederate soldiers lying side by side, Lincoln's family members at various stages of life, and John Wilkes Booth, Lincoln's assassin.

Never one to sit still, the author was working on two other books:

> I'm finishing a biography of Franklin Roosevelt to be published by Clarion. I'm also beginning a description for Holiday House of the work of the Wright brothers. It's not a biography but deals with how the brothers conceived, built, launched, and flew the world's first airplane. I've read excerpts from their journals and looked at their own glass negative photographs.

UPDATE

In 1991, Freedman's *Franklin Delano Roosevelt* (1990) won the following awards: Orbis Pictus, National Council of Teachers of English, Golden Kite, and Jefferson Cup awards.

Freedman's *The Wright Brothers: How They Invented the Airplane* (Holiday House, 1991) was named a Newbery Honor Book in 1992. It also won the 1992 Golden Kite and Jefferson Cup Awards and a *Washington Post/* Children's Book Guild Nonfiction Award.

Finally, Freedman won the Regina Medal in 1996 and the Laura Ingalls Wilder Award in 1998 for all his books.

Jean Fritz, author
(1915–)

1974 Interview

Although Jean Fritz was born and lived overseas, she has never considered herself to be anything but American. Growing up in China, where her parents were missionaries, gave her much to consider later while writing historical fiction and short, unconventional American biographies for children. It also helped to foster an avid interest in her country's past.

> My folks were missionaries in China, working for the YMCA. It's perhaps *because* I was born in Hankow, China, and went only to a British School that I felt *very* American, alienated from other Americans. One Scottish boy at recess would say nasty things to me about America, and I felt I had to defend it. I've been fighting the Revolutionary War for a long time!

Students at the British school were all expected to sing "God Save the King." Jean didn't want to sing that anthem, so her father told her to mouth "America," while the other students sang. It worked enough to pacify a young Scottish patriot, Ian Forbes, who treated her like an outsider.

Fritz was born on November 16, 1915, in Hankow (now called Wuhan), an industrial city on the Yangtze River. Her parents, Arthur and Myrtle Guttery, had been living in China for two years. "I spoke Chinese before English. I can understand Chinese today if I'm conversing with someone who speaks slowly and doesn't use political terms."

111

Her family's early years in China were peaceful. They took pleasant vacations at Peitaiho, a Pacific Ocean resort north of the capital, Peking (now called Beijing). Near the resort, they enjoyed picnics where the Great Wall meets the sea, and she could look out at Mongolia. She recalled:

> I read and wrote a lot as a child. My mother loved reading. I envied *The Bobbsey Twins,* inseparable children, who went camping and did all the things I wanted to do. I read *The Secret Garden,* a book of Indian legends, and Hawthorne's stories. When I was eight, *St. Nicholas* magazine published something I wrote.

The author described life between her tenth and thirteenth years in China, 1925–1928, in *Homesick: My Own Story* (Putnam, 1982). She wrote it after her father died, when she felt she must record her childhood. The book tells of a child's bonds with her Chinese *amah,* or caregiver, Lin Nai-Nai.

Life in China didn't remain peaceful, however. The British School closed during riots against Westerners and greedy Chinese landlords. The democratic leader of the Nationalist Party, Sun Yat-sen, died in 1925. His successor, Chiang Kaishek, subdued warlords, but he supported conservatives. After fighting *with* Communists against Japan from 1937 to 1945, he led the nation's military against them in a civil war that lasted until 1949. Chiang Kaishek fled to Taiwan when Communists won the war, led by Mao Zedong.

During her last years in China, Jean witnessed much upheaval. Rioters made it into her family's living room, and a shell fell in their yard. Her family barely escaped, sailing from Shanghai on April 26, 1928, aboard the *President Taft.* The trip to San Francisco took twenty-eight days.

Once in California, her father bought a new Dodge and drove his family to his folks' home in Washington, Pennsylvania. Jean attended a local public school and protested when a student ridiculed the Chinese by calling them "Chink, Chink Chinaman." School gave her less joy than sharing a home with loving paternal grandparents and her aunt Margaret.

After a year in Pennsylvania, her father got a YMCA job in Hartford, Connecticut, and moved his family there. In 1937, Fritz graduated from Wheaton College in Norton, Massachusetts. Her parents were then living in Manhattan, so she joined them, doing textbook research at Silver, Burdett, and taking a children's literature course at Columbia University.

Jean married Michael Fritz in 1941. The couple lived on the West Coast, when he was an army officer during World War II, and they had two children, David and Andrea. In 1951, the family settled in Dobbs Ferry, New York, where Michael became a laboratory assistant for Columbia University.

The Dobbs Ferry Library had no children's room and few children's books, so Jean volunteered to conduct a weekly story hour under "The Magic Umbrella." It was so popular, she was hired as a children's librarian.

After reading many children's books, Fritz felt she knew what appealed to young readers. In 1954, Alice Torrey, an editor for Coward, accepted Fritz's first full-length picture book about a cat, *Fish Head*, and engaged Marc Simont as illustrator. Fritz recalled:

> The idea came from an oceanographer friend who had gone on an experimental ocean trip near Bermuda and one or two days out, found a cat had climbed on board. It's a funny story about a cat stowaway on a fishing boat who has to find his sea legs. I wrote this when my own children were quite small, and I was tied down at home. Maybe I would have liked to have gone to sea!

Fritz's first historical fiction, *The Cabin Faced West* (Coward, 1958), featured a protagonist named Ann Hamilton. The book brought back childhood memories:

> I felt lonely as an only child in China. My book that comes closest to expressing my loneliness was *The Cabin Faced West*. I thought I was writing a fictional story about my grandmother's grandmother, but actually, I was writing about myself. The loneliness of Ann, a pioneer in western Pennsylvania in the 1790s, is really my loneliness.
>
> There was an actual Ann Hamilton. She was out picking cherries one day when a gentleman on horseback stopped her and asked, "Little girl, what are you having for supper tonight?" After she told him, he said, "Go tell your mother that General Washington would like to have supper with you." He *bated* at her house.

Bate is an old-fashioned word for a person having dinner and his horse getting hay. George Washington's diary on September 18, 1784, lists that he "bated at the Hamiltons" when he was traveling west to inspect land that he owned. Beyond this fact, Fritz's book details are fictional. For Washington's visit in the book, Ann's mother used lavender flowered plates and a linen tablecloth. Peas, potatoes, corn bread, and pumpkin pie were probably on the menu.

The author did visit Hamilton Hill with her father and sat on the one remaining original bench from Ann Hamilton's church. Authenticity was always Fritz's goal.

The Cabin Faced West "hooked" the writer on historical research. She again used a western Pennsylvania setting for *Brady* (1960), which takes place in pre–Civil War days. She referred to this book, the first of her three historical novels published by Coward:

> Half the population of western Pennsylvania were southerners, like Brady's mother, and half were northerners, like Brady's father, a preacher. The underground railroad ran right through their home. Brady's problem was that he usually couldn't keep secrets. He found a runaway slave on their property and did keep the secret. At the book's end, an illustration shows Brady holding a candle beside his father's bed, and his father recognizes him as a man, the book's denouement.

Brady and its companion novel, *Early Thunder* (1967), benefit from the illustrations of graphic artist Lynd Ward. The book about Brady Minton takes place at a later time than *Early Thunder*, which is set in Salem, Massachusetts in 1775, just before the Revolutionary War. Fritz explained:

> In *Early Thunder*, I wanted to get into the years preceding the Revolution. I called my book *Early Thunder* before the Revolution's *big* thunder. I gave a boy a Loyalist father in Salem with problems of his own. Then I found an incident in Salem research.

Fritz shares this incident for the first time in children's fiction and puts fourteen-year-old Daniel West at the site. The British attacked Salem on a Sunday when civilians were in church. In the book, Daniel joins community defenders who try to defeat the British. His father eventually supports his efforts. "For *Early Thunder*, I had a beginning and an ending but had to explore the middle," Fritz explained. "There aren't just two sides in a political skirmish. At times there are five or six sides, and people may be too extreme."

The third novel, *I, Adam* (1963), takes place when Adam Crane had finished school in 1850. His father returns home after losing a leg on his last trip as captain of a whaling vessel. Adam feels pressure to manage the farm that his father bought for retirement, but the youth would rather become a schoolmaster and scholar. When he courageously announces his preference, his parents accept his choice:

> Adam had such a tremendous sense of responsibility to his family. The place, the coastal part of New England, started me on that book. *I, Adam* points out the importance of schooling. The early days of teaching in our country were tough times. Some pranks of students in the past would be considered delinquent today. Common in the eighteenth century was smoking out the teacher and students from the classroom.

To Fritz, her three historical novels featuring teenage protagonists are related: "I dealt with great moments in American history and put a youth right square in the middle where he himself had to make a decision."

Fritz has also written short biographies for children that are humorous, readable, and accurate, with verifying book endnotes. She always travels to do research, reading old newspapers, books, and correspondence. For her biography on King George III, she got permission to work in the Royal London Archives.

Investigating the historical figure's childhood is important because problems in early years seem to plague persons throughout their lives, Fritz said:

> I like to see the human side of great historical figures and make them come alive without being too irreverent. I was motivated by the [U.S.] bicentennial celebration to do some of my children's biographies. They are at a slightly older reading level than *George Washington's Breakfast* and should be read aloud in grades four, five, and six.

Coward published the Fritz book, *George Washington's Breakfast* (1969), in which young George has hoecakes (cornmeal pancakes) and tea for breakfast. Coward also gave young readers seven biographies by Fritz (about Samuel Adams, Christopher Columbus, Benjamin Franklin, King George III, John Hancock, Patrick Henry, and Paul Revere). Each title asks a question, like *And Then What Happened, Paul Revere?* (1973). In that book, Fritz tells how silversmith Revere had eleven children. To support them, he sold many items, including false teeth that he whittled from hippopotamus tusks. When it was time to ride from Boston to alert Lexington and Concord residents of the impending British attack, Revere found that his spurs were at home. He tied a note to his wife around his dog's neck and sent him home. The dog returned with spurs attached to his collar.

For young adults, Putnam published Fritz's biographies on Benedict Arnold, Harriet Beecher Stowe, Sam Houston, Stonewall Jackson, James Madison, Pocahontas, and Teddy Roosevelt.

No matter what she writes, Fritz has her own style:

> If I do two pages at the typewriter in eight hours, I'm lucky. I'm slow and compulsive. I'm not disciplined. It takes discipline to get me into the kitchen at all. I write first in long hand and then type at the end of the day. Each morning, I reread from the beginning. In fiction, I take bits and pieces from people I know. The hardest part of writing is when you're in bed at night, and the creative juices flow.

UPDATE

Fritz published *The Double Life of Pocahontas* in 1983. The book's critics say that it trivializes the Native American plight. Despite this, the Pocahontas story was a *Boston Globe-Horn Book* Honor Book, as were the Benedict

Arnold (1981), John Hancock (1976), Stonewall Jackson (1979), and Paul Revere (1973) biographies. Most of Fritz's historical works have been named Notable Children's Books.

Homesick: My Own Story was named a 1983 Newbery Honor Book and a *Boston Globe-Horn Book* Honor Book, winning both the American Book and Christopher Awards. The sequel, *China Homecoming* (Putnam, 1985), was named a Notable Children's Trade Book in the Field of Social Studies. *China Homecoming* includes photographs by Michael Fritz, Jeanne's husband. Fifty-five years after she left China, Fritz and her husband traveled to China, where they were able to make trips alone, not with a tour group, and were assisted by China's Foreign Affairs Bureau. Her former residence was occupied by several Chinese families, and the British School had become a geologists' rest home. The Foreign Affairs Bureau made Fritz an honorary citizen of Wuhan.

Fritz's 1988 Putnam book, *China's Long March, 6,000 Miles of Danger*, explains Mao's legendary trek in China during 1934–1935, leading the First Front Army with anywhere from 20,000 to 100,000 people. Fritz interviewed some survivors of the mainly male army. Its goal was to improve life, primarily for the peasants. After the rugged Long March came the Cultural Revolution, and Fritz discusses some of its errors.

In 1992, Owens published Fritz's autobiography for children, *Surprising Myself*. Fritz's daughter, Andrea Fritz Pfleger, was the book's photographer. One picture shows Fritz leaving a current writing project in the refrigerator before going on a trip, so it won't be destroyed in case of fire.

In addition to previously cited honors, Fritz has been recognized for all her books. She received the 1985 Regina Medal, the 1986 Laura Ingalls Wilder Award, and the 1988 University of Southern Mississippi Medallion.

Jean Craighead George, author–illustrator (1919–)

1974 Interview

"You have to live among waterfalls and streams in order to write about them," said Jean Craighead George, a sturdy explorer of nature and promoter of ecosystems. She was young when she projected a career goal: "I've wanted to write and illustrate books ever since I was in third grade." Along the way, she's received a number of awards, including the 1973 Newbery Medal for *Julie of the Wolves* (Harper, 1973), which was a National Book Award finalist. She also received a 1959 Newbery Honor Medal and a 1962 Hans Christian Andersen Award, both for *My Side of the Mountain* (Dutton, 1958).

Jean was born on July 2, 1919, in Washington, D.C. Her introduction to ecology came very early in life. Her father, Dr. Frank Craighead, was an entomologist for the U.S. Forest Service, and her mother, Mary, was an entomologist's assistant. Her father, George said, "was the first ecologist. While his emphasis was on insects, he believed you had to study also the trees and other animal life."

Her older twin brothers, Frank Jr. and John, began falconry as a U.S. sport, and in high school wrote *National Geographic* and *Saturday Evening Post* stories about it. Later, they studied endangered grizzly bears in Yellowstone National Park, putting radios on bear necks to find out where they denned. Their sister, who had to carve her own niche, said, "I was more or less a loner for an interesting reason. My brothers, who are ecologists too, are identical twins who had this great thing going between them. I was always, 'Me too, let me come along.'"

Her father did give her individualized attention:

My very first pet was a turkey vulture that my father brought from the wilderness and gave to me. It was a beautiful, white, fuzzy bird. We finally got rid of it because it would sit on the kitchen door and watch my mother cook. She couldn't abide that very long.

All our pets as children were birds. I studied about the ethology of birds at the University of Michigan. I've always identified with birds.

George showed interest in a bird of prey in *The Summer of the Falcon* (Crowell, 1962). The author said, "It's largely autobiographical. For the falcon, my mother allowed us to keep dead sparrows, wrapped in wax paper, in our ice box."

Another bird, a water ouzel, is the subject of *Dipper of Copper Creek* (Dutton, 1956). It won the American Library Association's first Aurianne Award for the best nature book of 1956. Earlier books were about a red fox, mink, raccoon, great horned owl, and pet skunk. ("My pets were really two skunks, living in the house with me. They were never descented and never sprayed.") Jean George wrote these earlier books with John George, who was then her husband.

In 1969 Paramount made her award-winning *My Side of the Mountain* into a movie, directed by James B. Clark and starring Ted Eccles with Theodore Bikel. The book drew some criticism because it tells of a youth, Sam Gribley, who runs away from his New York City home to live in the Catskill Mountains alone. Jean George explained:

> The publisher almost didn't allow the book for that very reason. My editor and I talked it over. It's better to have one run to the mountain than to the city. I didn't anticipate it, but this whole camping, outward-bound movement has evolved. Everyone goes backpacking now. I had such a good time doing it as a child that I wished other children could do it too.
>
> That's the dream world of the child: to be alone and independent of parents. I read the book to some youngsters in a school before it was published. One boy, who was terribly engrossed in it, said, "That's what I'm not. I'm not independent of my parents." This was why he loved it.
>
> The human child in its development goes through loving the mother, father, and family group. Then comes the moment of independence when they've got to be alone with themselves before they can rejoin human society. This happens to Sam, Julie, and most of my youthful characters.

George said she was not influenced by British books which often show a child surviving alone.

> What really influenced me was my parents' attitude. They would take us out along the Potomac River to a deserted island and leave us, saying, "Make a living here." We ate all those things I described in *My Side of the Mountain*, all those delicious tubers and crayfish.

Jean and John George married in 1944 and divorced almost twenty years later. The family, who lived in Chappaqua, New York, included two sons, Craig and Luke, and a daughter, Carolyn, nicknamed "Twig." "She was too small to be a branch of the family tree," George said in explaining the name.

George introduced her children to white-water canoeing, cross-country skiing, and camping. Various pets moved into their "ark," and George wrote about some in her children's books. There was a crow named New York, trained to say, "Hello!" Also included were Otus and Buho, both owls; Trinket, a cat; a boa constrictor; Sarah, a dog; and Larus, a seagull.

The gull was a reminder of visits by the writer and her family to Block Island off Rhode Island. George wrote *Gull Number 737* (Crowell, 1964) after studying efforts to prevent herring gulls from causing airplane accidents on runways. "They realized that they could control birds by imitating their own alarm cries," George said.

In addition to gulls, Jean George has studied what wolf societies had in common with human beings:

> I read an article by Ginsburg of Chicago's Brookfield Zoo on the social behavior of wolves. It intrigued me because they were so much like the human family. I followed up the research at Barrow, Alaska, talking to scientists. I then went to McKinley National Park in Alaska to watch a wild wolf pack. I identified alpha leaders and tried to decipher their language. They communicate better than most animals.

George and her son, Luke, traveled to Alaska with some support from *The Reader's Digest,* for which George has served as a staff writer and roving editor. In Barrow, she consulted the Arctic Research Laboratory, maintained by the U.S. Navy and administered by the University of Alaska.

> I have a notebook that I kept when I was in Alaska doing *Julie of the Wolves.* I sketch as I take notes because I can feel myself more on the scene. I have little drawings of the environment.
>
> These are the wolves I watched as I was lying on my stomach, looking through a spotting scope among the cold willows. These are the alpha male and alpha female. They are the leaders. These are two hunters and nine puppies.
>
> I watched them from about six o'clock in the evening when they awakened, through the summer night of 1970 because this was Alaska and the sun doesn't set until about 2 A.M. I watched them again at dawn. The notebook is full of Eskimo terms.

In 1973, George's *Julie of the Wolves,* illustrated by John Schoenherr, received a Silver Skate Award from the Netherlands, and won the German

Youth Literature Prize. The story features a thirteen-year-old Inuit girl, Miyax, who runs away from a forced marriage. The name Julie comes from Miyax's pen pal in the United States. She gets lost on the tundra but saves herself by communicating with the wolves, and they feed her. Eventually, she finds her father, Kapugen, in Kangik village and moves in with him and her step-mother, Ellen. George explained the prototype for Julie:

> Julie is patterned after an older woman who befriended me. Her husband felt that we had something in common: we were both leaders. I saw a girl going across the tundra by herself, and she inspired me to make the main character be a girl. Actually, the wolves relate to children better than adults, and I prefer to write about children.

George, who "thinks in pictures," illustrated her early books in a unique way. "I dipped watercolor paper in the bathtub to get it soaking wet," she said. "Then I used old Chinese watercolors and brushes on the wet paper, so the colors ran." She developed her artistic talent at Pennsylvania State University, which named her Woman of the Year in 1968. She worked toward a master's program in art at Louisiana State University, but left to take a job sketching in Washington, D.C., courtrooms.

The artist worked for newspapers and wanted to write as well as draw. She has achieved her goal, having created more than sixty juvenile books of fiction and nonfiction. She has two major book themes: "children's relation-ship to the earth and how they grow among plants and animals" and "young people finding themselves and becoming independent personalities."

UPDATE

George has written a number of sequels to her popular stories. *On the Far Side of the Mountain* (Dutton, 1990) continues the story of *My Side of the Mountain. Julie and the Wolves* eventually became a trilogy for Harper. The other two books are *Julie* (1994), in which Julie learns to relate to her step-mother and faces the conflict between old and new ways of survival, and *Julie's Wolf Pack* (1997), in which Julie saves two starving puppies from her old wolf pack, marries Peter Sugluk, an Inuit, and gets college funding to study wolves while living on the tundra.

George has written nonfiction, including *The Wild, Wild Cookbook: A Guide for Young Wild-Food Foragers* (Crowell, 1982) and a coast-to-coast guide to historic and natural walking trails in the United States. Her prizes for total work include the Kerlan Award from the University of Minnesota and the University of Southern Mississippi Medallion. In 1976, the Children's Literature Association listed *Julie of the Wolves* as one of the ten best American children's books in two hundred years. The novel has also recently been added to Oprah Winfrey's Book Club Kids' Reading List, and a film version is being discussed.

Lorenz Graham, author (1902–1989)

1975 Interview

After many wide cultural experiences, Lorenz Graham, author of more than a dozen books for young people, projects in his work a tone of friendship among humans, "white, black, and all shades in between," often united against hostility. He is most remembered for four books about David Williams. The first in that series, *South Town* (Follett, 1958), won a Follett Medal and cash prize, Child Study Association of America Award, and Book World's first prize.

Among those who inspired him to become a writer, he said, was his older sister, Shirley Graham DuBois, wife of African-American scholar Dr. W. E. B. DuBois. He also remembers another memorable woman he met when he was twelve years old:

> I was selling weekly newspapers for five cents. A black woman was one of my best customers. I told her about a certain story to read. She responded, "Son, I don't read."
>
> I suggested, "Get someone else to read it to you."
>
> She replied, "Don't nobody ever reads to me."
>
> I appreciated her anew because she was making only fifty or seventy-five cents a day on her job.
>
> She added, "I just does that to help you out."

Inspired by this woman who survived on faith and generosity, Graham concluded, "Today, I'll buy a paper from a little black boy, even if I've already read it."

Graham absorbed a reverend's goodwill and adjustment to new locations from his peripatetic father:

> My father was a Methodist minister, and we were moving a lot. I was born in New Orleans on January 27, 1902, and started school in Chicago. Then we moved to Tennessee and Colorado. I finished school in the state of Washington. I've also lived in Virginia, New York, and abroad. I've visited the Soviet Union, China, Israel, and Africa. My home now is in California.

Graham did not learn to read at school. His mother had designated his sister, Shirley, who was six years older, to teach him to read and write. When he was six, he entered school in second grade, following in the footsteps of his older brother, David. Lorenz, in turn, was followed by his younger brother, William.

Later, his sister introduced Lorenz Graham to his first publisher. Messner had issued her novelized biographies for young people on African-American leaders, including *Dr. George Washington Carver, Scientist* (1944) and *Paul Robeson, Citizen of the World* (1946). Her first original story, *Zulu Heart* (Okpaku Communications, 1973), is about a white man in Africa who shows an interest in Zulus after getting a Zulu's transplanted heart. Graham visited his sister in Ghana in 1964 when she was directing Ghanaian television after the death of DuBois, her second husband.

Like his sister, Graham spent time in Africa where he walked dark trails at night that were safer than lighted U.S. city streets. In 1924, he left the University of California to work in Liberia. He was a teaching missionary at Monrovia College in a building without plumbing. There he became the bishop's secretary-treasurer. His parents joined him when his father was named college president. Graham became afflicted with malaria, and his parents arranged treatment in Germany. For the next six months he had to avoid the tropics. He recuperated in France and learned the language. When he returned to Liberia, his mother turned matchmaker with Graham and Ruth Morris, an American Baptist minister's daughter who was a recruit in Liberia.

After Graham's parents returned home, he became ill with black-water fever or advanced malaria. He returned by steamer to New York where he stayed and decided to become a writer during the Harlem Renaissance. He retold the Bible tales from missionaries, using the lilting speech pattern of Liberians newly acquainted with English and reflecting Spanish influence on the African coast. In 1946, Reynal published his illustrated tales as one book, *How God Fix Jonah,* with an introduction by DuBois, with whom he worked as a research assistant for one short season. His book illustrations show biblical characters as Africans. In the 1970s, Crowell reissued the Bible tales as separate picture books: *David He No Fear* ("David and Goliath," 1971), *God*

Wash the World and Start Again ("Noah's Ark," 1971), and *Hongry Catch the Foolish Boy* ("The Prodigal Son," 1973).

Included among Bible tales was *Every Man Heart Lay Down* (1970), a title showing people at peace. In this account of Jesus' birth, the storyteller refers to infant Jesus as "Him small pican." The word "pican" derives from *pequeño niño* ("small child" in Spanish), which, in slurred form, was *pickaninny* (often a derisive term in the United States). Jesus wanted followers to be kind, so "bye-m-bye they savvy the way." ("Savvy" derives from *saber*, the Spanish infinitive, "to know.")

A Road Down in the Sea (1970), the last of the five tales, is an account of the Hebrew exodus from Egypt. Its introduction establishes that it took place long ago, "before them big tree's papa live." The tale begins, "The Egypt people hold the Hebrews tight," and proceeds to the parting of the Red Sea when the slaves crossed "and no man wet him foot."

Crowell also issued two original Graham books with African settings. Graham spoke about the name, Momolu, used in *Tales of Momolu* (Reynal, 1946) and a sequel, *I, Momolu* (Crowell, 1966):

> Momolu is one of the most used proper names. It's pronounced Mohammed in other parts of the world. Among worshippers of Islam, it's considered proper to name a son Mohammed. I know one family in East Africa who called their son Mohammed Mohammed. The publisher, who thought Momolu would replace Sambo, died and it took me twenty years to get *I, Momolu* published.

Tales of Momolu originally included "The Song of the Boat," a story told in the same language as the Bible tales. It is about a father and son who search before finding a perfect tree to carve as a canoe. In 1975, Crowell reissued *The Song of the Boat* as a separate picture book illustrated by Caldecott winners Leo and Diane Dillon.

Graham created *Tales of Momolu* because, he said, he had never read children's books about ordinary Africans. He described young Momolu in an isolated Liberian village, Lojay, among the Kewpessie people. His mother is Portee, an older sister is Sindah, and his father is Flumbo, a strong rice farmer who limps because an alligator tore his left leg.

The tale continues in *I, Momolu,* which shows the protagonist at age fourteen. In the story, the father and son go to jail because they are unable to pay the penalty for Flumbo's insult to a soldier. A friend helps them pay the penalty, and they return to their village. Flumbo decides that soldiers are brothers, and Momolu focuses on learning to read.

The two Momolu books show socially organized Africans who discuss concerns at the *palaver* house, a West African village center. ("*Palaver*" derives from the Spanish for "word," *palabra*.) "*Palaver* House" is also the title of a story Graham wrote abroad but never published, because an editor said Americans wanted books about Africans as savages.

While in New York, Graham enrolled in writers' classes at Columbia University. He supported himself as resident manager of sixteen apartments, getting a small, free basement unit for his own use. After Ruth Morris returned from Africa in 1929, Graham dated her, and they married during the Depression.

The couple settled in Virginia and had five children: Lorenz Jr., twins Jean and Joyce, Ruth, and Charlie. To support them, Graham worked as a waiter in Richmond. He earned a degree at Virginia Union University and got a job as educational adviser for the Civilian Conservation Corps, which hired unemployed young men in camps to plant trees, build dams, and fight forest fires. While working with enrollees in South Hill, Virginia, Graham came across a town of biased leaders and wrote about it in *South Town* (Follett, 1958). On the jacket, Graham stated why this book was sorely needed:

> Stories had been written about heroic Negroes and many more had been written about degenerates. . . . I had not found much written about the kind of people I most often saw. . . . The mothers and fathers are saying, "I want my young ones to have a better chance than I had." These are the people I have written about in *South Town.*

Graham's book tells the story of David Williams, a tenth-grade student at a segregated school in the South. After saving a boy from drowning, the boy's father offers him part-time work at his garage. There, David meets a kind white mechanic, Solomon Travis, whom an African-American soldier had rescued in Korea. David's father, Ed Williams, a mechanic, wants the garage owner to hire him at the same pay whites get. Instead, Williams is arrested for disturbing the peace, and vigilantes threaten his family. Church members and some white people, including Travis, help protect the family, but in the scuffle Travis is killed. Ed's family sells their home and heads north.

The series continues with *North Town* (Crowell, 1965). David enters integrated North Town Central High, insisting he is college-bound, but the school lists him as a vocational student. After police intimidation, his family moves from the ghetto. David's father undergoes brain surgery, and until he recovers, David works at night and stays in school. His father returns to work and David again becomes a full-time day student.

In *Whose Town?* (Crowell, 1969), eighteen-year-old David Williams is still living in North Town. The family faces more trouble with police, and David's father loses his job. But David graduates from high school and wins a State College scholarship.

Twelve years elapse before the period of Graham's final book in the series, *Return to South Town* (Crowell, 1976). David, at age thirty, is single and a New York physician. He returns to South Town, builds his office there, and is joined by his mother. John "Little Red" Boyd, the boy David saved from drowning as a youth in *South Town,* returns in this story.

Careful plotting is key to Graham's writing style. "I don't think of characters first but of situations with characters," he said. A number of experiences influenced this series:

> David Williams was a composite character. Some incidents are autobiographical. I remember when my sixteen-year-old son went to an integrated school for the first time. About three years ago, I rented a car in the South and saw the changes that have been made there.

Graham's books show the sacrifice David's parents made to give him and his sister a good education. Similarly, Graham moved his family from Virginia to New Jersey and New York, so his children could be in better schools; all five attended college.

Graham became a social worker in New York City, "working with delinquents and pre-delinquents." In 1957, he moved to California where he was a probation officer. To help young people who have difficulty reading, he wrote four paperback novelettes published by Houghton in 1972. Titles include *Detention Center, Carolina Cracker, Stolen Car,* and *Runaway.*

After carefully researching John Brown, Graham wrote a children's book, *John Brown's Raid, A Picture History of the Attack on Harpers Ferry, Virginia* (Scholastic, 1972). Milton Meltzer, consulting editor, made available many fine pictures for the book. Of the twenty-one in Brown's group, only five were African Americans, perhaps because Frederick Douglass opposed the raid as a "steel trap." Brown's last letter indicated he realized that dying for abolition might be more valuable than living for it.

Graham was president of the Los Angeles chapter of Poets, Essayists, and Novelists (PEN), a worldwide organization. The chapter helped to send Graham, his wife, and the author, Gloria Miklowitz, to a literary symposium in South Africa. Graham welcomed returning to the southern part of that vast continent.

UPDATE

In 1978, Graham issued *John Brown: A Cry for Freedom* (Crowell). He died of cancer on September 11, 1989, in West Covina, California, at age eighty-seven. The message that was printed on the bottom of his personalized stationery was the theme of his books on David Williams and guided much of his life: "Black and white together, we shall overcome!"

Elizabeth Janet Gray (Vining), author (1902–1999)

1969 Interview

Elizabeth Janet Gray said of her writing, "I do think if I have any gift, it is of imagining myself back in another age and feeling very much as if I had really lived then." An ability to place herself in the historical time period helped the author garner a number of awards, including the 1943 Newbery Medal for *Adam of the Road* (Viking, 1942). This fiction is set in thirteenth-century England. Along the way, she collected Newbery Honor medals for *Meggy MacIntosh* (Viking, 1930) in 1931; *Young Walter Scott* (Hale, 1935) in 1936; and *Penn* (Viking, 1938) in 1939.

Gray said she knew early in life that she wanted to become a writer. She was born on October 6, 1902, in Philadelphia. Her father was from Scotland, and her mother came from a New Jersey family. Her only sibling was a sister, Violet, who was eighteen years older than she. Gray remembers being a serious, shy child; her most memorable birthday was her third, when she got tired of all the noise and ran away with another child.

Gray went to Germantown Friends School, and at age sixteen, entered Bryn Mawr College. After graduating, she taught for a year but always wrote in her spare time. Selling a story to *Young Churchman* for two dollars confirmed her desire to become a writer. She was twenty-three years old when her first book, *Meredith's Ann* (Doubleday, 1929), a tale of a girl growing up in a New Hampshire family, was published. Gray said, "I sent my first book, *Meredith's Ann,* to one publisher who turned it down, and the second one accepted it. I've never had any trouble since that first book." Through *Meredith's Ann*, she met young May Massee, a children's book editor at Doubleday at that time. Massee later moved to Viking, as did Gray.

Gray's second book, *Tilly-Tod* (Doubleday, 1929), was about Quaker twins in western New Jersey, where her mother had spent her childhood. She dedicated her third book, *Meggy MacIntosh*, to her Scottish father since it is about a Highland girl, an eighteenth-century immigrant in the Carolina Colony. She combined fiction about Meggy with an actual historical figure, Flora Macdonald, a Jacobite leader. Marguerite de Angeli drew the cover for this prizewinner.

In 1926 Gray earned a bachelor of science degree in library science at Drexel University and went to work at the University of North Carolina library in Chapel Hill, where she researched Flora Macdonald. In Chapel Hill, she created *Tangle Garden* (Doubleday, 1932), a story about the Dales, a family whose members were happier when poor than when they acquired wealth. The author married Morgan Vining, and they had a one-story house built in an acre of woods. She combined housekeeping with writing and teaching library science during summer school at the University of North Carolina. She told how she preserved some independence:

> Before marriage, I had already published four books, so I thought I might just as well go on with my maiden name. Then I had another thought: my husband was associate director of the Extension Division of the University of North Carolina, and I was writing children's books. I thought I might write something that would embarrass that university, so I just kept Elizabeth Janet Gray on my books.

Gray used Chapel Hill as a setting in pre–Civil War days for *Jane Hope* (Viking, 1933). This is a tale of a girl whose father died and who finally accepts her mother's remarriage.

In October 1933, four years and eight months after a marriage of "blazing happiness as few people know," Morgan Vining was killed in an automobile accident. The couple had been passengers in an automobile struck by a car driven by a boy. Perhaps this tragedy prompted her to counsel: "Don't avoid sorrow. Accept it in your home as a guest who may not be there forever."

Gray returned to Philadelphia to live with her mother and sister, and found comfort in writing. She set her book *Beppy Marlowe of Charles Town* (Viking, 1936) in Carolina Colony of 1715. Beppy and her brother, Rolfe, are spoiled London youngsters, but Rolfe gets banished to Charles Town and Beppy goes with him. They stay there after Blackbeard's raid. Gray next offered *The Fair Adventure* (Viking, 1940), which features Page MacNeil, the youngest of five children in a professor's family.

Gray had planned to go to Scotland with her husband to follow the footsteps of poet/novelist Walter Scott in preparation for writing *Young Walter Scott*. Instead, she traveled alone. She thought it would be difficult in her book to make Scottish terms understood:

> I've been working on that all my life. When I wrote *Young Walter Scott*, I thought there would be a great many Scottish terms that could not be understood. I haven't any one device. After I use a word, I slip in some little phrase, so anyone who can put two and two together can figure out what I mean.

To write *Penn*, Gray traveled to London, Buckinghamshire, Oxford, Sussex, and Bristol, England. She learned why Penn and his father clashed, and she came away admiring Penn's idealism:

> The father and son were very much alike. That's why there was conflict between them. The father's last words to his son were: "Live in love." I think he had come to recognize the son's real dedication and commitment to this religion, Quakerism, which was so offensive to the father.
>
> The thing that made me want to write about William Penn was not simply my Quaker interest. It was the story I had read about Penn as a young man in the Tower of London. He was at odds with his father. His father had planned to make a great man of him. The son put all this aside to become a Quaker at a time when Quakers were totally despised.
>
> Penn had written a book about his new religion, which he omitted to have licensed by the bishop, so he landed in the Tower of London. It was not a happy place to be. He was well aware of all the people who had been beheaded there. After some months, he got word that if he would recant his book, he could come out. Otherwise, he could stay for the rest of his life.
>
> He sent back word, "My prison shall be my grave before I will budge a jot, for I owe my conscience to no mortal man." That seemed to me so utterly thrilling and magnificent that I wanted to write a book about him.

Gray did most of her extensive research at the Pennsylvania Historical Society. "I read all of Penn's books, which I must say was a challenge. A great deal was very boring. Some was beautiful and quite thrilling. There were gold nuggets here and there. What the Quaker background gave me was sympathy and interest, but the actual facts I had to dig out from secular libraries."

While in England, she also did research for her book, *Adam of the Road*, illustrated by Robert Lawson, about eleven-year-old Adam Quartermain. "I was in England in 1937 and was living on three levels. I was in modern England, the year of the coronation. I was in seventeenth-century England with *Penn*, and then in the Middle Ages for *Adam*, but I felt very much at home in all three."

Gray's original intention was not to write fiction about Adam:

> I started to make a collection of tales that minstrels told in the thirteenth century, the metrical romances of the Middle Ages, which I had studied in college. I was to make my own translations in retelling them. I was planning to mix stories within a little frame of a minstrel and his son who would go about the roads of England. They would tell one kind of story in a manor house, another kind in a castle, another kind in an inn, et cetera.
>
> Suddenly, this minstrel came into my mind so clearly that I saw his striped surcoat, his little harp on his arm, and his freckles. I saw his red hair and his dog at his heels. Then adventures simply attached themselves to him. Before long, he had taken over the book, and I never did get to write my collection of minstrel tales.

Gray clarified the theme of her book that won the Newbery Medal:

> The theme of *Adam of the Road* is that each one of us has a talent, which is ours to develop. If we don't use it, it rusts. This is borne out in Adam. In searching for his lost dog, he's separated from his father [Roger the Minstrel]. He goes down the roads of England, hunting for his father and his dog [Nick]. . . .
>
> I don't write morals in my children's books. I don't write down to children ever, and if you put in obvious morals, you are writing down to children. When a child finishes a book, if it's worthwhile, there's some residue left, something a child takes away. It might be very simple: that life is good, and one should live it to the fullest.
>
> Adam's a very appealing, attractive youngster, and many people want to help him along the way. In the act of helping him, they all try to make him be something he isn't. The parish priest wants to make him into a parish priest. Somebody else wants to make him a scholar. The farmer, with whom he stayed for some time, wants him to remain and be a farmer. In the course of the story, he discovers that what he really wants to be is a minstrel.

Gray used Shakespeare's England of 1596 as the setting for *I Will Adventure* (Viking, 1962). Here, twelve-year-old Andrew Talbot leaves simple rural life to be his uncle's London page. *Sandy* (Viking, 1945) is a World War II tale of a college student, Sandy Callam, in an English village during summer. She decides to train for a United Nations Relief and Rehabilitation Administration job. The book won the 1945 *Herald Tribune* Spring Festival Award.

While one of her books took her three years to write, most of the author's children's stories "start slowly, ending with a big burst of labor, and nine months later, I may have a book." She described her unique writing process:

I write just one book at a time. . . . I rather like to alternate factual books and fiction. . . . I don't find one more difficult to write than the other.

Some ideas come to me that can be better expressed as nonfiction rather than as fiction. . . . What people seldom realize is that after the research and plot outline comes the thinking. I mull over a book in my mind when I'm waiting for a traffic light or a train or before the theater curtain rises. I'm thinking about my characters all the time, and then the writing may go fast. . . . I do the first draft and ordinarily, there's not a great deal of rewriting. It's mostly cutting. I think anything can be improved by condensing. For one of my books, I did rewrite the first chapter six times.

Gray revealed the biggest problem in writing about the past:

What is most difficult is to capture the past climate of thought. It's easy to pick up information about people's dress, customs, and events, but individuals thought differently in the past.

It's hard to pick up past thought and make modern people accept it. An example is the poet John Donne in *Take Heed of Loving Me*. He married a lovely young girl, eloped, and was ruined as a result for many years. They had thirteen children, and she died with the thirteenth. In those days, children were God's gift. So many died that if you had thirteen, you could probably raise five or six. Modern readers have written, scolding me because he allowed his darling wife, Ann, to have so many children. Thinking is different today.

Following visits to Japan, Gray wrote a children's book, *The Cheerful Heart* (Viking, 1959), about the Tamaki family in Japan after World War II. An eleven-year-old spirited girl, Tomi, and her family return to their former home after three years in the countryside. "The theme of *The Cheerful Heart* is it's loving that makes one happy, and Tomi was a loving little girl," Gray said.

The author spent from 1946 to 1950 in Japan after the Japanese emperor selected her to tutor the crown prince in conversational English. At the time, Gray had been working at the American Friends Service Committee and had intended to resign to write a book at the MacDowell Colony, an artists' retreat in Peterborough, New Hampshire. She allowed her name to be submitted, saying, "It was an extraordinary thing after a war so bitterly fought that the emperor of Japan should want somebody from the conquering country to come over and tutor his son." Gray said that she was chosen over a long-term teacher "perhaps because, as a writer, they knew I could express rather big ideas in simple language." Gray described how she improvised as a teacher in Japan:

I can remember in one of the early lessons, there was a Japanese chamberlain present in striped pants and morning coat and a representative of the empress, a very formal grande dame. The difference between *jump* and *hop* came up. I got up and showed the difference while these dignified Japanese looked on without cracking a smile. I did a great deal with games.

Both the emperor and prime minister encouraged the author to write a book about Japan. The book's title, *Windows for the Crown Prince*, was suggested by the minister of the Imperial Household, who encouraged her to go beyond tutoring the lad in English: "We want you to open windows onto a wider world for our Crown Prince," he told her.

Gray explained why she used her married name for her byline for *Windows for the Crown Prince* (Lippincott, 1952): "When I went to Japan, of course, there wasn't a newspaper in this country and a good many other countries that didn't have Elizabeth Gray Vining splashed all over it. That naturally was the name under which I wrote *Windows for the Crown Prince*. After that, I decided I would keep my adult books under Elizabeth Gray Vining and my children's books, which numbered quite a few by that time, under Elizabeth Janet Gray."

Of all her adult books, the most popular with adolescents seems to be *Windows for the Crown Prince*. Crown Prince Akihito, to whom she dedicated the book, was young, between the ages of twelve and sixteen, so youth identified with him, and she wrote the book with popular appeal. She gave the prince a Western name, "Jimmie." Nothing like her book, giving an inside view of a royal household, exists, except perhaps Margaret Landon's *Anna and the King of Siam* (Harper, 1944).

Akihito was still a teenager in 1953 when he came to visit his former tutor at her Philadelphia home. She made two return visits to Japan, seeing him again in 1957 and 1959. The latter occasion was when she was the only non-Japanese person at his wedding to Michiko.

UPDATE

Emperor Akihito sent the author congratulations on November 8, 1990, when she received a Lifetime Achievement Award from the Free Library of Philadelphia. By then, Gray had created twenty-nine books, about half of which are for children.

At her ninety-sixth birthday celebration on October 6, 1998, Japanese Ambassador Otsuka came from New York City to deliver Emperor Akihito's birthday wishes. Otsuka entertained her on bagpipes that he learned to play in Scotland.

On November 27, 1999, Gray died in her sleep in Kendal at Longwood, a Quaker retirement home. There the new ambassador and consul general of Japan, Takekacu Kauamiura, and his wife attended the memorial Quaker meeting, held on December 18, 1999, in honor of Elizabeth Gray Vining. The Japanese government had previously awarded her the Third Order of the Sacred Crown.

Bette Greene, author (1934–)

1981 Interview

The route Bette Greene had to take to get her book *Summer of My German Soldier* published is a lesson in perseverance. After being overlooked by a writing professor and being rejected by eighteen publishers, however, Greene's story about a Jewish girl and a German POW finally found a home at Dial in 1973 and was named a 1974 National Book Award finalist.

Greene was born in Memphis, Tennessee, on June 28, 1934, and grew up in Parkin, Arkansas; she still retains a slight Southern drawl in her speech. She was nine years old when the *Memphis Commercial Appeal* published her byline atop an article on a barn fire and paid her eighteen cents for her work. After that, journalistic writing became an occupational consideration for the girl whose quiet sense of humor sustained her in difficult times. She remembers only one friendly person of authority from her childhood:

> My third-grade teacher, Miss Ada Norsworthy, was important to me. She was also the school's librarian of a minuscule collection confined to several bookshelves. She thought I was funny. That's good enough for a storyteller.

Bette said that she got only love crumbs from her parents, who gave the "cake" to her younger sister, Marcia, considered prettier and more docile. Those who cared for her were her Memphis grandparents and the African-

American housekeeper in her childhood home. She named the housekeeper, Ruth, in her largely autobiographical *Summer of My German Soldier.*

The twelve-year-old protagonist in *Summer of My German Soldier,* Patty Bergen, drew strength from an unusual source for a Jewish girl: a young German prisoner of war, Anton Reiker. She met him when soldiers escorted World War II prisoners from a nearby camp to her father's clothing store. Later, he escaped and took refuge in a hideout above her family's garage. When the soldier saw Patty's father whip her brutally, he tried to help and barely avoided revealing himself. The soldier taught Patty that she was a person of value, before he hopped a train and left Jenkinsville. (This fictitious town is modeled after the author's actual hometown, Parkin, Arkansas.)

The author wanted to record this story. She studied at Memphis State University and University of Alabama before focusing on writing courses at Columbia and Harvard universities. She said, "Columbia was supposed to be the best place to learn to be a writer. My valuable lesson there was to trust my own judgment. If I did something I liked, I guess that would be something my peers would like."

At Harvard, the professor read everyone's manuscripts aloud, except for hers. She explained that his neglect was "probably because he was afraid of its intimacy." His assistant suggested that she hire a ghostwriter.

Greene coped with other defeats. Eighteen publishers rejected the novel, basically because a twelve-year-old is the narrator. Older readers often do not want a book narrated by someone younger. She cited that *To Kill a Mockingbird* and *Member of the Wedding* are narrated by girls who are younger than twelve. They are classics, and she felt her book would be too. She was proven right when Bantam Books issued twentieth-anniversary "Classic" editions of *Summer of My German Soldier* and its sequel, *Morning Is a Long Time Coming* (Dial, 1978).

After all the rejections, Greene's agent sent Dial a fifth draft of her book, and the company agreed to publish it in 1973. At that point, Greene said, "I was knee-deep into the sixth draft. I also agreed to work as an adviser on the television movie. I saw all the drafts and worked in collaboration with a scriptwriter."

Greene agreed that the adapter, Jane Howard Hammerstein, who had "a real knack for characters," deserved her Emmy Award for the 1978 television movie. Actress Esther Rolle also merited her Emmy for depicting the family's housekeeper.

The first book and its sequel, *Morning Is a Long Time Coming,* have jacket paintings by the artist Charles Lilly.

Summer of My German Soldier was a *New York Times*'s Outstanding Children's Book of 1973 and won the Golden Kite Award as well as the

Massachusetts Children's Book Award. The honors helped justify Greene's long years of work.

After the book was finally published, the Jewish Defense League complained that Patty's father, Harry Bergen, "is so vile, he encourages anti-Semitism." Greene answered that the father is no more representative of all Jewish men than Patty is of all Jewish girls. Despite the controversy, many Holocaust libraries have the book on their shelves.

The author humorously estimated, "About 83 percent of *Summer of My German Soldier* and 78.5 percent of *Morning Is a Long Time Coming* are autobiographical. Both Ruth and Anton were people I knew whom I tried to recreate." Greene commented about writers:

> What universe do writers explore? Themselves! . . . Thoreau had never gone more than ten miles from Walden Pond. It's internal travel that counts. I begin a book when I have a story I want to tell. I've always been interested in people and the ways we defeat ourselves.

The book's sequel begins as town citizens call Patty "Jew Nazi lover!" She had returned from nine weeks in reform school because she had aided the German prisoner. She wrote a newspaper article, "Reform School Needs Reforming." Following high school graduation, Patty said good-bye to Ruth and went to Paris. Leaving home, no matter how harsh the environment, was hard for her. Green revealed:

> The sequel shows that Patty had to leave her parental home to discover that she was a person of worth. Leaving home is a bittersweet experience. It's a wrench! Incidentally, I got into trouble, but I didn't have to go to reform school. I did live in Europe for a while. In France, I was learning French. On a quest, I went to the house of Anton's mother, finding that she had died.

After two demanding novels, Greene turned to lighter material, *Philip Hall Likes Me. I Reckon Maybe* (Dial, 1974), for readers aged seven to twelve. The title was named a 1975 Newbery Honor Book. She discussed two controversial small references:

> On page four, I refer to Mama's "strong dark arms" and on page six, to Philip's "coffee-colored arms." My publisher, expecting difficulties, felt it would be better if I dropped those references entirely. People might feel I was trying to write about the black experience when I'm white.
>
> Beth Lambert and Philip Marvin Hall were black students whom I knew, and they had to be black characters. Both were from the middle class in a Southern white community, and attitudes would have been different if I took out the two references and made them white. The book jackets also showed their identity.

The most amazing thing happened. Black militant periodical reviewers saw my material and offered no criticism. They were wonderful about it!

Greene humorously tells about Philip's and Beth's rivalry. In *Philip Hall Likes Me. I Reckon Maybe*, Beth does many of Philip's farm chores until she asks, "Is Philip Hall number one only 'cause I let him be? Afraid he wouldn't like me if I were best?" Enlightened, she shows leadership in capturing her father's turkey thieves with a BB gun while Philip watches. She even wins a calf-raising contest that Philip also enters. Finally, the two compete in square dancing as a Pocohontas, Arkansas, *couple*. Young feminists identify with the story.

In the sequel, *Get on out of Here, Philip Hall* (Dial, 1981), Beth boasts so much that her Pretty Pennies Club rejects her. She resolves the conflict by moving to her grandmother's house in Walnut Ridge, Arkansas. She transfers to the local school and forms the Irritated Oysters Club. Philip attends the Oysters' successful New Year's Day town party and coaxes her to return home. In the end, she is a humbler "born leader." The Nebraska Library Association nominated the book for a Golden Sower Award.

The author dedicated *Summer of My German Soldier* to her husband, Donald S. Greene, a neurologist, with whom she lives in Brookline, Massachusetts. She dedicated her Newbery Honor Book to her children, Jordan, a medic with the New Mexico State Police, and Carla, who owns a hair salon in New Hampshire.

Greene hopes to help would-be authors with her advice: "Writers are the last of the cottage industry. Others take advantage of us. I encourage multiple submissions unless one has a contract." She suggests that writers study the sections of books by other authors that make them laugh or cry, and to try to become more emotional in their own writing. She also urges careful observation of people.

UPDATE

Greene continues to publish books for young readers. *Them That Glitter and Them That Don't* (Knopf, 1983) is about a high school senior, Carol Ann Delaney, and her parents, who live in a mobile home. Her Irish father, Charles "Painter" Delaney, a full-time drinker, used to have a job spraying the middle stripe on Arkansas highways. Her Gypsy mother, Evangelina Yergis Delaney, is a fortune-teller and con artist. Carol alone gives nourishing food to her younger siblings, Alice Faye and baby brother, Bubba Jay, who teethes on dog biscuits.

Carol, scorned by classmates as "Little Gyp," concludes that being different does not mean being bad. This was a discovery that Greene had made in her own life as a Jewish girl in a small Arkansas town populated mainly by Protestant fundamentalists.

Another small Arkansas town, Rachetville, is the setting for Greene's *The Drowning of Stephan Jones* (Bantam, 1991). The book resulted from an actual gay man's drowning perpetrated by teenagers. The novel lacks the understated emotional force of Greene's best first-person books, but it has a surprise ending. It provokes readers to think about cruel "gay-bashing," a rare topic in youth literature.

Virginia Hamilton, author (1936–)

1978 Interview

"Read widely, have open minds, and observe. Be slow to form opinions!" Virginia Hamilton advised would-be writers. For Hamilton, recognition is important since she thinks few people understand and respect children's literature. She said that she resented when people asked her if she'd ever write for adults. "It's as though they believe you're second-class because you write for children," she concluded.

In the children's book category, Hamilton was the first African American to receive the Newbery Medal, winning the 1975 prize for *M. C. Higgins, the Great* (Macmillan, 1974). She also has written Newbery Honor Books: *The Planet of Junior Brown* (Macmillan, 1971) and *In the Beginning: Creation Stories from Around the World* (Harcourt, 1988).

Hamilton was born in Yellow Springs, Ohio, on March 12, 1936, the youngest of five children. Her father, Kenneth James Hamilton, cherished her as "Dad's Baby." Hamilton's mother, Etta Belle Perry, was the oldest daughter of a fugitive slave, Levi Perry, who was born in 1855. He escaped with his mother by following the Underground Railroad, crossing the Ohio River from Virginia, a slave state, to Ohio. Aided by Native Americans and white abolitionists, about 50,000 slaves similarly emancipated themselves. After marrying, Grandfather Levi Perry made his home on Yellow Springs's rich farmland. Coaxing him to stay was abolitionist Horace Mann, then president of the community's Antioch College. Every year, Grandfather Perry told his ten children how he escaped from slavery, instilling pride in their history. The Perry clan set an example of a strong African-American family, which, Hamilton said, "I emphasize in all my stories."

Hamilton referred to her aunts, uncles, and parents:

> They're reluctant farmers but willing storytellers. My father, an outsider from Illinois and Iowa, was a great spinner of tales. Mother, too, could enlarge on family fiction, stretching the truth to produce chuckles.

Hamilton's Creole father had run gambling halls in mining towns. Her father graduated from Iowa State Business College in the early 1890s, and was a skilled mandolinist. However, he couldn't get work because the Musicians' Union did not accept African-American members. His chords on his ivory-inlaid Gibson comforted Virginia on "moonless Ohio nights that I feared." He subscribed to both *The New Yorker* and the NAACP's magazine, *Crisis*, which W. E. B. DuBois founded and edited.

Hamilton's parents encouraged her to read and, at age eight or nine, to write freely, influencing her career. As an Antioch College scholarship student, she stayed awake for thirty-six hours to write a story about an imaginary Watusi queen whose picture she saw in *Life* magazine. Hamilton left Antioch after three years and spent two years at Ohio State University. Then she settled in New York City where she was an unpublished author for eight years. There, a college friend helped to promote the story of a Watusi queen:

> My friend worked for a publisher, Macmillan, in their juvenile book department. She suggested that I adapt my paper for children. That was the story behind my first book, *Zeely*. It was my way of talking to the "black is beautiful" movement. From the beginning, I've had a great editor, Susan Hirschman.

Before publishing her first book, Hamilton experienced the joy of being on the same continent as her queenly character's ancestors. In 1960, she honeymooned in northern Africa with her husband, Arnold Adoff, a poet, anthologist, and author. For twelve years, he taught in Manhattan's upper west side and Harlem. Among Adoff's books of original poetry for children is *Black Is Brown Is Tan* (Harper, 1973), an account of his family after marriage.

Following *Zeely* (Macmillan, 1966), Hamilton wrote *The House of Dies Drear* (Macmillan, 1968) about a former Underground Railroad station. Her story's station is based on her hometown's abandoned mansion that had concealed slaves and set her imagination afire. The suspenseful mystery won the 1969 Edgar Award, named for Edgar Allan Poe.

For fifteen years, Hamilton struggled to publish material in New York City, an environment she found "too stimulating." She earned a living as an accountant, nightclub singer, and museum receptionist. After *Zeely*'s acceptance, she, her husband, and two young children moved to Ohio to be near her widowed, eighty-six-year-old mother. On her father's former farmland, next to other family members, she and Adoff built a contemporary redwood home surrounded by a two-acre "park." The couple's children, now grown, live in New York City, where Leigh is an opera singer and Jamie Levi is a computer expert and Web site developer.

Struck by the independence of young characters in her books, Temple University philosopher Monroe Beardsley interpreted self-reliance as one of her major book themes. Hamilton reacted:

I call it survival. While my characters are not based on real people, they represent something in my past. As a child living in rural Ohio, I was often on my own, made mistakes, and learned from them. I isolate my characters in a setting where they are alone, as on a mountain, so I can see them more clearly. The children must create their own play and get their own dinner. Sometimes, they must go out and hunt for it. It goes deeper than self-reliance.

The Planet of Junior Brown (Macmillan, 1971), Hamilton's first Newbery Honor Book, is a forerunner of books about homeless children. Buddy offers Junior Brown and other homeless boys a refuge, a "planet" in the basement of a condemned tenement, and buys food with his job earnings. Hamilton said of her characters:

In the beginning, children seem to me to be abundantly creative. I wish there were some way we could capture that and keep it without having it dissipate in all the rules and regulations that we make them go through. In my books, I praise creatively combating adversity. Children can do so many things, even when they work with little.

M. C. Higgins, the Great, which also won the National Book Award in the children's book category, is about an African-American family whose son, M. C., sits on a bicycle seat atop a forty-foot pole, his reward for swimming the Ohio River. He tries to protect his home on Sarah's Mountain from a downward-moving ooze caused by strip miners' environmental neglect. He finally builds a wall, hoping to stop the ooze.

Though *M. C. Higgins, the Great* is original, Hamilton incorporates many known elements. She said authors should write from their own experiences: "It's best to write about what you know."

Green tried to replicate Indian-sounding language in *Arilla Sundown* (Greenwillow, 1976), which tells the story of a combined African-American and Native American family. The author said:

> *Arilla Sundown* . . . was as close as I'll come to an interracial situation, not necessarily my own. I wanted to show the identity of characters when one child is black, and the other is certainly Native American. There are many interracial families in this country and in the world.

The author writes in various genres. Her nonfiction includes *W. E. B. DuBois, a Biography* (Crowell, 1972) and *Paul Robeson, the Life and Times of a Free Black Man* (Harper, 1974), books about two leaders respected by her family.

Hamilton shared information about her writing habits:

> I never outline and often compose between 9 A.M. and 1 P.M. I have only a general idea of my book ending and work toward it. My editor thinks my characters are my strongest feature, and I think my plot is. I try to do good writing that is smooth and almost always looks simple. My books say something original.

UPDATE

Hamilton's talent continues to attract a lot of attention. In 1995, anonymous scouts from the MacArthur Foundation chose her to receive a "genius grant" of $350,000. The press described Hamilton as "a children's writer who weaves black folk tales into her work." Her book, which the grant supported, feminizes "history" at the beginning of its title, *Her Stories: African American Folktales, Fairy Tales, and True Tales* (Scholastic, 1995). This collection, which includes supernatural and scary tales, brought Hamilton a 1996 NAACP Image Award.

Hamilton returned to the interracial theme in *Plain City* (Scholastic, 1993). Here twelve-year-old Buhlaire-Marie Sims, who is of mixed parentage, lives in an African-American home with her mother and aunts. She searches for her father and discovers that she has his same light eyes, honeyed vanilla skin color, and light hair, which she twists into dreadlocks.

At times, the author's fiction expresses humor, like *Willie Bea and the Time the Martians Landed* (Greenwillow, 1983). The tale is based on the Perry family's reaction to a 1938 Orson Welles radio broadcast of H. G. Wells's *War of the Worlds*.

Hamilton's fiction often focuses on family ties. In *A Little Love* (Berkley Books, 1985), Sheema and her boyfriend hunt for her father, a stranger to her, and she recognizes her grandparents as her true nurturers. This book won the Coretta Scott King Award in 1983. A different kind of family story, *Junius Over Far* (Harper, 1985) involves a son and grandson rescuing Grandfather Jacabo, a Caribbean island visitor who becomes disoriented. Hamilton claimed her most autobiographical work is *Cousins* (Philomel, 1990), in which she shows Cammy Coleman's ties to her relatives. The author's *Second Cousins* (Scholastic, 1998) offers more stories of family love and betrayal.

Since Hamilton's maternal grandfather had been a slave, she researched two centuries of slave narratives, recasting thirty of them in *Many Thousand Gone: African Americans from Slavery to Freedom* (Knopf, 1993). *Anthony Burns: The Defeat and Triumph of a Fugitive Slave* (Knopf, 1988) is largely nonfictional, what she called "historical reconstruction based on fact." It won the 1988 *Boston Globe-Horn Book* Award for nonfiction.

Hamilton's third Newbery Honor Book is *Sweet Whispers, Brother Rush* (Philomel, 1982). The ghost of a dead uncle, Brother Rush, tries to usher his niece into the past to help her cope with the present. *Sweet Whispers* was an American Book Award nominee, won a Coretta Scott King Award, and was named an IBBY Honor Book. Another Coretta Scott King Award winner was *The People Could Fly: American Black Folktales* (Knopf, 1985). Hamilton received the 1990 Regina Medal, the 1991 Ohioana Career Medal, and the 1995 Laura Ingalls Wilder Award for all her books.

The writer is aware that, out of five thousand children's book titles published annually, maybe forty are of African-American content. To encourage more books about African Americans, she lent her name to the Virginia Hamilton Literary Award, which is given each year at Kent State University to an American author or illustrator whose multicultural books for children and adolescents demonstrate artistic excellence. At the Virginia Hamilton Conference in 1994, the author said that her picture book, *Jaguarundi* (Scholastic, 1995), extends her liberation theme. The jaguarundi, a wild cat, is among Central American rain forest animals whose habitat is threatened by humans.

Hamilton has long been interested in ecology, as her books demonstrate. In *Drylongso* (Harcourt, 1992), a boy named Drylongso, desperate to end farmland drought, uses a dowser to try to determine the underground presence of water. In her Newbery winner, *M. C. Higgins, the Great*, a subplot involves strip-mining's effect on the environment.

In 1992 Hamilton became the first African American to win the Hans Christian Andersen Award for her writing. On learning about the award from the International Board on Books for Young People, Hamilton proclaimed:

They have affirmed their interest in multicultural concerns and their support for cultural diversity. I hope to continue writing good books for some time to come. This is a culmination of twenty-five years of my career.

While celebrating her "jubilee," Hamilton emphasized that telling a good story is her primary goal. Her books, now numbering over fifty, are released by a variety of publishers. Fulfilled in full measure is her prediction: "to write like no one else!"

Carolyn Haywood, author–illustrator (1898–1990)

1978 Interview

"I love to draw children," said Carolyn Haywood, who has written more than fifty books for seven- to ten-year-old children, most of which she illustrated with live models. *"B" Is for Betsy* (Harcourt, 1939) was her most popular book, but she also wrote for boys. *Eddie and His Big Deals* (Morrow, 1955) won the Boys' Club of America Junior Book Award.

Haywood was born on January 3, 1898, in Philadelphia. She painted as a young girl and attended Philadelphia High School for Girls, intent on art as a career. She went to Philadelphia Normal School and taught at Friends Central School for a year. Then she enrolled at the Pennsylvania Academy of the Fine Arts, where she contributed to their permanent collection. She won their Cresson European Scholarship after excelling in such courses as Henry McCarter's painting class. Beside McCarter, she had other mentors:

> I studied illustration privately with Jessie Wilcox Smith and Elizabeth Shippen Elliott. I also served as an assistant to Violet Oakley when she was doing murals at the state capitol. Since these three had worked with Howard Pyle, I called myself his "grand-pupil."

Following Oakley's tutelage, Haywood painted murals for Philadelphia banks and a public school. She also painted children's portraits and contributed to the juvenile magazine *Jack and Jill*. From her single year as a teacher, she remembered a shortage of appropriate recreational reading books for students:

> Many years ago, when I taught third grade for a short time, I found very little children's literature for that age group. I decided to illustrate children's books. I hadn't thought of writing them.
>
> Through showing my illustrations to editors, I met Elizabeth Hamilton, who worked for Harcourt. She said, "I've been trying to get someone to write a book about an American child who's six years old, has to go to school, but got some false impression and doesn't want to. Things work out for her." Hamilton gave me the whole idea.

Haywood's *"B" Is for Betsy* was an immediate success, helped by her black-and-white illustrations. A drawing that shows a boy in knickers somewhat dates the book. Haywood created her own episodes, often with light humor. Readers are anxious when Betsy begins school and loses her way.

"B" Is for Betsy has 159 pages and is longer than most of today's chapter books. Emphasis is on sharing: Betsy gives a birthday party for her friend, Ellen, whose father works at night and sleeps during the day; also first graders offer a Thanksgiving basket to Grandma Pretzie, an elderly pretzel vender and storyteller. This book began a "Betsy" series.

Beginning in 1939, Haywood published more than a book per year. She did her first eight for Harcourt, working on the last one with editor Margaret McElderry, whom she termed "a joy." Among her Harcourt books is *Primrose Day* (1942), which Haywood called "my favorite." It concerns Merry Ramsay, who leaves London during World War II and lives with relatives in the United States while attending second grade. Merry's April birthday falls on England's Primrose Day, and she celebrates it in her adopted land by picking primroses in a special garden.

Haywood explained why she started with a new publisher:

> When Elizabeth Hamilton moved to Morrow, I followed her because, after all, to the author, the editor is the most important person in the company. I once called my Spanish stucco home in Chestnut Hill "the house that Betsy built." I now call it "Good Morrow" because of long association with my publisher, Morrow.

Haywood's books maintained their popularity. For male appeal, Haywood introduced a friend on Betsy's block, seven-year-old Eddie Wilson, in *Little Eddie* (Harcourt, 1947). Eddie collects junk that he considers "valuable property." The "Eddie" series includes *Eddie and His Big Deals* (Morrow, 1955), which shows Eddie trading a doll for a printing press, so he can print his *Hot News*.

Haywood considered "one of her funniest books" to be *Eddie and Gardenia* (Morrow, 1959). After Eddie's pet goat, Gardenia, chews "a mouthful of Buick" (the canvas top of the Wilsons' new car), Uncle Ed, who lives on a Texas ranch, agrees to accept the outcast. Eddie delivers her and visits his eight-year-old cowboy cousin, Georgie. *Eddie and Gardenia* introduces fine Latino role models: Manuel, a broncobuster, and his wife, Carmencita.

The author–illustrator visited a Texas ranch before writing *Eddie and Gardenia*, rode a school bus in Maine for two days (with special permission) to prepare *Here Comes the Bus* (Morrow, 1963), and stayed with friends near England's Thames River, which resulted in *Robert Rows the River* (Morrow, 1965). Her notes and drawings confirm her conclusion, "Traveling gives me book ideas."

In 1970, Haywood was the third winner of the Drexel University/Free Library of Philadelphia Citation. The 1963 recipient, Marguerite de Angeli, praised her friend, Carolyn Haywood, for her skills, including "faithful portrayal of children in their own world."

Haywood became the favorite author to visit Blue Bell Elementary in Blue Bell, Pennsylvania, the school that inspired her book *Away Went the Balloons* (Morrow, 1973). Her book jacket appropriately shows children celebrating Balloon Day by releasing colorful balloons with tags asking the finders to send a message back to owners. Haywood recalled:

> It's wonderful to see all those balloons. Each chapter is about a different balloon and where it landed. One fell at a circus, one at a hospital, and notes came back to pupils from various places.
>
> This book's German translation was nominated as one of the Children's Books of the Year in Germany. It's also in Japanese. Two of my books are in French, and all are in the Scandinavian languages.

Blue Bell School's former librarian, Kendall Kanasky, wrote:

> Miss Haywood noticed our library's oil painting, "Balloon Girl," by a previous school art teacher, Elizabeth Wolpert, and it inspired her fictionalized treatment of Balloon Day.
>
> We got to know Miss Haywood in other ways, too. Some of our fourth graders modeled for her drawings in *Eddie's Happenings* [Morrow, 1971]. Our kindergarten teacher, Dorothy Palmer, suggested that Miss Haywood do *A Christmas Fantasy* [Morrow, 1972], and our first grade's pet rabbit, Cupcake, prompted her book, *"C" Is for Cupcake* [Morrow, 1974].
>
> In 1978, we dedicated the storytelling section of the school library as the Carolyn Haywood Storybook Center. In it are stuffed animals, all her books, and a rocker with her name on a brass plate.

A photograph shows the librarian, seated in the rocker, reading *Away Went the Balloons* to Blue Bell students.

Haywood illustrated her books until the late 1970s, when she could no longer draw because of a stroke. She carefully chose other artists to work on her books. Haywood went to London to meet Victor Ambrus, a two-time winner of the United Kingdom's Kate Greenaway Medal for outstanding children's book illustrations. He drew the pictures in Haywood's *A Christmas Fantasy* (Morrow, 1972) and *A Valentine Fantasy* (Morrow, 1976). "I had lunch with him in London after he had read the Christmas manuscript," she recalled. "He consented to illustrate it, and we dedicated the book to editor Margaret McElderry because she introduced me to him."

Haywood had a special relationship with one particular fan:

> My first child's fan letter came from Carolee. As an adult, Carolee McDougal Helmuth went to New York, looking for a job related to children's books. Within three months, she began to work at Morrow. By an odd coincidence, she helped on three of my books and was excellent!

UPDATE

Haywood and Ambrus collaborated again for *The King's Monster* (Morrow, 1980). In 1981, she received the Utah Children's Book Award for the body of her work.

Haywood, who never married, maintained an unusually youthful appearance and viewpoint. She died of a stroke in Philadelphia on January 11, 1990, at age ninety-two. Weeks before her death, she had finished writing her fifty-third book, *Eddie's Friend Boodles* (Morrow, 1991). Influenced by a circus, Boodles Carey tries to teach his dog, Poochie, tricks. Poochie's surprise is a self-instructed backward flip, rewarded not by dog biscuits but by love.

Tana Hoban, photographer–author

Susan C. Hirschman, editor

1975 Interview

Susan Hirschman (left) and Tana Hoban

TANA HOBAN

Tana Hoban, a concept book pioneer, hopes her photographic picture books will help children discover "wonder in everyday objects and often surprises."

Hoban's parents arrived in Philadelphia from Russia, where they recalled winters so cold that "birds dropped frozen from the sky." Tana was born in Philadelphia and was raised in Lansdale, Pennsylvania. Her younger brother, Russell, is also a children's author. He wrote *Bedtime for Frances,* initiating a "Frances" series among other books.

Hoban returned to Philadelphia after receiving a scholarship to the School of Design for Women (now Moore College of Art). Her last course, photography, "hooked" her. She was still in college when her father died at the age of forty-two. He did not live to see her win at her 1938 college graduation a free painting excursion to Europe.

After her trip, Hoban married photographer Edward Gallob. She specialized in photographing children, finding them less self-conscious than adults. Her photographs were displayed in the window of her mother's clothing shop for children.

Following World War II, Hoban converted a five-story Philadelphia town house into a photographic studio and dwelling. Her mother took the two upper floors, lavishing affection on the photographers' daughter, Miela, whose name means "sweet" in Russian.

Camera Arts called Hoban "the best child photographer in America today." In New York, Edward Steichen, the Museum of Modern Art's photographic chief, put her work in his great "Family of Man" exhibit. The Museum of Modern Art also has her first film, *Catsup*, only three minutes long, in its permanent collection. The film features three cats—black, orange, and striped—as they singularly emerge from a bag, chase a windup toy frog, and return inside the bag (the same footage backwards).

Hoban spoke about her film involvement:

> In the sixties, I began experimenting with film. I became a consultant to producers of television commercials, and I made short films. The first one was *Catsup*. I distributed this as an inexpensive short film with just a musical track. We had so many cats in our building, we didn't need to pay model fees.

The 1967 Venice Film Festival showed *Catsup*, winner of a Cine Golden Eagle Award in Washington, D.C. She said, "I've also done ten conceptual sound filmstrips for Scholastic, illustrating songs with my photographs, like *Ears, Nose, Fingers, and Toes*."

Hoban showed her first book, *Shapes and Things*, to Macmillan's editor, Susan Hirschman. It contained photograms or pictures that develop on chemically treated paper without a camera. She used a common comb, toothbrush, and toothpaste tube, recognizable without captions, as white shapes on a black background. Hirschman and her art director, Ava Weiss, bought *Shapes and Things* (1970) and Hoban's first peephole book, *Look Again!* (1971).

Shapes and Things inspired teachers and students at a Wilmington school to make their own photograms—five hundred of them, which they mounted on a wall.

Another Notable Children's Book is *Count and See* (1971), inspired by five city trashcans. On one page is an enlarged numeral, 100, and on the facing page, open pods with a hundred peas. Hoban's *Circles, Triangles, and Squares* (1974), which won honorable mention from New York's Academy of Sciences, stresses circles with bicycle wheels mounted atop a car, and squares with building windows of that shape.

"I cut circles and triangles from cookie dough, so at times, I contrive examples," Hoban said. "I make my own prints. My early books were black and white since that's cheaper." More recent picture and board books are in color.

Hoban noticed early that a camera made its user more appreciative of surroundings. She confirmed her notion after an experiment at New York City's

Bank Street College. Teachers asked students, "What did you see on your way to school?" Children responded with shrugs until they got cameras. Then the whole inner-city world proved inviting. Hoban also found simple urban scenes to be exciting for her, whether in Philadelphia, New York, or Paris.

Beside family members, the person who continues to play a significant role in Hoban's life is editor Susan Hirschman. In 1974, when the editor left Macmillan and became Greenwillow Books's editor in chief, Hoban's testimonial was: "I'd follow her anywhere! Now that I've known her for over thirty years, I realize how lucky I am."

SUSAN C. HIRSCHMAN

Reflecting on an editor's search for talent many years ago, Susan C. Hirschman thought that Hoban was a perfect fit: "I was looking for someone whose photos tell a story and in walked Tana Hoban!"

Hirschman was born and grew up in New York City. She graduated from Wellesley College near Boston in 1953, and until her senior year there, did not think of a career as an editor. Before college ended, she met a *Horn Book* editor displaying picture books. Hirschman's favorite was Ruth Krauss's scant text about bears. She said she admired anyone who could make a living by offering a seventeen-word book.

Pursuing her editing goal, Hirschman acquired typing and shorthand skills. She became children's book department secretary at Knopf in the mornings, and in the afternoons, worked with the company's library promotion director. In between, her bosses let her write copy and read manuscripts, a yearlong learning experience.

Hirschman's second job was as a reader of Harper's unsolicited manuscripts in the children's book department. She also saw illustrators' dummies and portfolios. Her department head, Ursula Nordstrom, promoted books with limited vocabularies. Nordstrom's guidelines were: "Remember the children!" and "The author is always right." She also requested, "Tell me if a manuscript has as much as a single good sentence, so I can write the author an encouraging letter."

Hirschman won promotion at Harper to become editorial assistant, assistant manager, associate manager, and managing editor. She stayed for ten years until Macmillan made her their children's book editor in chief:

After ten years at Macmillan, in 1974, I launched Greenwillow Books with some former Macmillan colleagues, art director Ava Weiss, and executive editor Ada Shearon. I publish books under my own imprint. By its twenty-first year, Greenwillow had two Newbery Medal winners, two Newbery Honor Books, ten Caldecott Honor Books, and more than a hundred American Library Association Notable Children's Books and Best Books for Young Adults.

Over the years, Hirschman engaged some unknown authors and illustrators who have since achieved prominence. At Harper, she got Arnold Lobel to do his initial illustration job on *Red Tag Comes Back* (1961). She had seen a picture of a grasshopper in his portfolio and wisely chanced that he could do a salmon as well. Then he began to write as well as illustrate in the same professional, perfectionistic manner in 1960. When his wife, Anita Lobel, gave Hirschman samples of fabrics she had designed, the editor hired the artist to write and illustrate her own book, *Sven's Bridge* (Harper, 1965). Both Lobels have published with her at Greenwillow. She developed a deep friendship with them and with others whom she has guided in publication, including Donald Crews, Chris Crutcher, Virginia Hamilton, Ann Jonas, Ezra Jack Keats, and Peggy Parish. "One publishes authors, not books," she said.

On a recent trip to see Hoban in Paris, Hirschman, with unwrapped, long, crusty baguette bread loaves under her arm, showed humor in her hat choice. Hoban took a rear photograph of her editor who has close-cropped brunette hair. Attached to her tam's back edge trailed an artificial, long, blonde French curl.

UPDATE

In 1983 Hoban received the Drexel Citation from Drexel University and the Free Library of Philadelphia. In 1995, when Hirschman got the same award, Hoban showed slides of her latest photographic books. The slides reviewed Hoban's children's books published first by Macmillan and, starting in the mid-1970s, by Greenwillow, always with Hirschman as editor.

Twelve years after *Shapes and Things*, Hoban published an alphabet book of photograms, *A, B, See!* (1982).

Children have imitated Hoban's peephole book, *Look Again!* It became a Notable Children's Book, so she did three more with peepholes. They were: *Take Another Look* (1981); *Look! Look! Look!* (1988), which won a 1988 *New York Times* Award for Best Illustrated Book; and *Look Book* (1997). In 1990, Hoban received the *Boston Globe-Horn Book* Award for *Shadows and Reflections*.

In *26 Letters and 99 Cents* (1987), Hoban used full color to demonstrate coin equivalences for numbers. The highest number, 99, has beside it three silver quarters, two silver dimes, and four copper pennies. She has also released a 1987 French version with French coins.

In the 1990s, Hoban photographed *Exactly the Opposite* (Mulberry/ Morrow, 1990), contrasting an open and closed gate, a filled and empty hammock, and the front and back of both a sunflower and a sheep. Afterward, she created *Spirals, Curves, Fanshapes, & Lines* (1992), using everyday objects such as a colorful string lying in the street. Her *Construction Zone* (1997) features photographs of a bulldozer, forklift crane, and cherry picker.

Hoban marks significant life changes with book dedications. She dedicated the colorful *Round&Round&Round* (1983) to her second husband, John G. Morris, a photojournalist, with whom she moved to Paris. Morris's autobiography is *Get the Picture, a Personal History of Photojournalism* (Random House, 1998). He was European correspondent for *National Geographic* and earlier, had been picture editor of *Ladies' Home Journal, The Washington Post,* and *The New York Times.*

Hoban remembered her daughter, Miela Ford, in a dedication along with son-in-law, Bob, an optometrist, and grandchildren Jeneva and Max. She dedicated *Dots, Spots, Speckles, and Stripes* (1987) to them. Miela Ford, a Philadelphia College of Art graduate, makes artificial, custom, prosthetic eyes. Of her work, she says, "This is the only art where my best compliment is for no one to notice what I have done."

Miela Ford has recently also become a photographer/writer of Greenwillow picture books, such as *Bear Play* and *Follow the Leader,* 1996 and 1997 Please Touch Museum winners. When Ford wrote *Little Elephant* (1994) with photographs by Tana Hoban, the mother felt that "collaboration with my daughter was one of the highlights of my life."

Kristin Hunter (Lattany), author (1931–)

1978 Interview

Kristin Hunter has written some of Scribner's popular juvenile books, including the award-winning *The Soul Brothers and Sister Lou* (Scribner, 1968), which is geared to adolescents. The author commented about her book, which deals with people in the popular music scene:

> Janet Loranger, Scribner's juvenile editor, invited me to write a book for children. I put the invitation aside but remembered it later when I heard a singing group below my apartment at Broad and South. I always knew it was spring when a beer bottle would be broken in the alley and then a group began to sing. I had to add a girl because I always wanted to be a singer.

Hunter described street musicians in Philadelphia, the city where she was born on September 12, 1931. George and Mabel Eggleston, her parents, named their only child for the heroine in Sigrid Undset's trilogy, *Kristin Lavransdatter*. Their daughter's literary career choice seems appropriate. She talked about her heritage:

> I am African-American for five generations on at least two sides of my family and American Indian, probably Powhatan, on at least two branches. After Haley had *Roots* published, I traced my family. It's not quite as complex as I thought in 1964, when I referred on the jacket of *God Bless the Child* to "my complex racial identity."

154

Hunter's father, George Eggleston, a New Jersey elementary school principal, was an ROTC graduate from Howard University. He was active in the National Guard and was a commanding officer at Fort Campbell, Kentucky. Her paternal grandmother, Gillie Eggleston Burgess, lived in a large house in Washington, D.C., and took in roomers. Hunter said, "She was the only older relative who gave me unconditional love, not tough love, like my family's maternal relatives and like many mother figures in my novels."

Hunter's mother, Mabel Manigault Eggleston, whom the author described as "fairest skinned of four children," spoke with a sharp tongue when her family faced prejudice, a trait imitated by her usually ladylike daughter. Her mother would leave a penny tip if she were treated unfairly at a restaurant and kept her daughter from watching blackface Mummers performers. When Hunter was ten years old, her mother took a job at Philadelphia's Frankford Arsenal. The mother urged her daughter to pursue a career, discouraging Hunter from having children.

After graduating from Haddon Heights High School in 1947, her folks insisted that she go to college. At age nineteen in 1951, precocious Kristin Hunter, always an avid reader, followed parental advice and got her education degree at the University of Pennsylvania, where she took as many English electives as possible. "I always wanted to be a writer," she recalled. "At fifteen, I was writing a column on youth for the *Pittsburgh Courier*'s Philadelphia edition. No one else in my family had been a writer, and my parents thought teaching was the only safe occupation for women of color." She pursued teaching after she graduated, but discovered it was the wrong career choice:

> I could not control thirty-eight children, aged seven to fourteen, in a third-grade Camden class at Fetters School. I didn't have a commanding personality, so I resigned.
>
> Camden schools then were 85 to 90 percent black and 10 percent white. I had one white girl who was literally insane. Her parents were bigots and told her not to associate with black children. She inspired me to write "Minority of One," a winning 1955 CBS documentary.

Convinced that she could earn her living as a writer, Hunter got a job at Lavenson Bureau of Advertising and was a copywriter for seven years. This work had a positive effect on her writing since she had to express herself with minimal words.

After leaving advertising, Hunter received a year of support from the John Hay Whitney Foundation, which offered grants to minority writers and scholars. Then she wrote news and speeches as a Philadelphia Information Officer, and was a research assistant for two University of Pennsylvania social work professors.

Hunter's marriage to journalist Joseph Hunter ended in divorce after seven years. She met her second husband, John Lattany, while demonstrating for integration at the formerly all-white Girard College in Philadelphia. He was once a merchant mariner and is now a photographer. The couple married in 1968, and Hunter helped Lattany raise his four children. They eventually moved to her parents' former home in Magnolia, New Jersey.

When she attended the University of Pennsylvania, few students were African-American. She enticed more after she joined the faculty in 1972. Her job, which she got because of her book credentials, gave her a chance to offer some exciting courses:

> At the University of Pennsylvania, I've taught a course on the background of African-American literature in which I went from folklore to modern work with five major writers and a few lesser-known ones. I've also taught a course in writing for children and a short story workshop. It was a dream come true to teach at my alma mater.

She explained her approaches to writing:

> My inner-city settings are actually in Philadelphia, but I try not to identify a city. I've received letters from children and young adults who write, "It's amazing you know Boston or Chicago or Los Angeles so well." I write about what's in any large urban area. Some of my later books are moving away from center city. I turn toward the suburbs and even to the South.
>
> When I'm writing a novel, I assign myself a quota of five legal pages a day or a chapter a week. One book, *Boss Cat*, I actually wrote in a day.

Fifty-eight-page *Boss Cat* (Scribner, 1971) is a funny tale set in the Benign Neglect apartment of the Tanner family: parents; a son, Tyrone; fat twin daughters, Puddin' and Dumplin'; and baby Jewel. The father's black cat, Pharaoh, makes up for destroying the mother's wig by capturing mice.

Humor dominates "BeeGee's Ghost," one of eleven short stories in *Guests in the Promised Land* (Scribner, 1973), an apt book title. "BeeGee's Ghost" shows how confusing black and white limitations can be when a white mortician tells young black Frederick Douglass Jackson to go to a colored pet cemetery to bury his white dog, BeeGee (Bee and Gee are the initials for Brown Girl). "Humor has helped African Americans to survive," Hunter said.

Hunter's 1968 popular children's book, *The Soul Brothers and Sister Lou*, is about Louretta Hawkins, a teenager. Her mother is raising her among eight children. The Soul Brothers are three male singers, Frank, David, and Ulysses, who join her in a quartet, rehearsing in a clubhouse, a former storefront church. The quartet uses the piano that the church left behind. Lou's older brother, William, has a printing shop on the first floor and lets the quartet use part of the building as a clubhouse. The quartet's accompanist is Blind Eddie Bell, an old street musician. At a dance to raise money for instruments, police raid the clubhouse and shoot Jethro Jackson. At his funeral, the Soul Brothers and Sister Lou sing "Lament for Jethro." The recording of this dirge sells well.

The Soul Brothers and Sister Lou won a 1967 National Council on Interracial Books for Children Award, a 1968 Sigma Delta Chi reporting award, a 1969 Mass Media Brotherhood Award from the National Conference of Christians and Jews, and a 1971 Lewis Carroll Shelf Award. Hunter's short stories, *Guests in the Promised Land*, won the 1973 Book World Children's Spring Festival first prize, was a 1974 National Book Award finalist, and won the 1975 Christopher Award.

"I think I gave false hope in my ending of *Soul Brothers*," Hunter said. "What I've learned since about the music industry made me want to do a sequel with a more realistic finale." Hunter said that she had not emphasized materialistic values excessively, for "to people who have no shoes, going barefoot isn't chic."

Readers of *The Soul Brothers and Sister Lou* are aware of rich characterizations and a hopeful spirit as the novel ends, a Hunter trait:

> I think degradation and horror have been emphasized too much. Even in inner city, there are people going to church on Sunday and getting meals on the table. I'm a hopeful optimist, and I celebrate it. I may not stay that way.
>
> I've been criticized that I have happy endings, which are no longer fashionable. I feel there are too many hopeless finales, too many characters wondering what is the meaning of life, and authors leaving readers confused.

Hunter doesn't use only her own experiences to shape her work:

> *The Soul Brothers and Sister Lou* isn't autobiographical because, while my first childhood years were spent in a row-house neighborhood, I didn't grow up in a large family. The characters occupy the foreground, but I am everywhere. . . .
>
> Obviously, I don't think authors should write just about what they've experienced since I use my imagination freely. You have to be able to empathize with others and draw an analogy to something you have gone through. You shouldn't write about what you're currently experiencing. The distant past is okay.

In addition to her children's books, Hunter has written adult novels. In 1970, United Artists made a film version of one of her adult books, *The Landlord* (Scribner, 1966), starring Pearl Bailey and Beau Bridges. Numerous magazines from *Seventeen* to *Essence* have featured her poems and short stories.

One of her articles, reprinted in *Reader's Digest*, was "Pray for Barbara's Baby." It resulted in Hunter getting real-life Barbara out of a chaotic family situation.

Hunter said there are benefits when writing for young people, rather than adults. "I like writing for children better. It's immediate, you don't have to be artificial, and the response is good."

UPDATE

Hunter's sequel to *The Soul Brothers and Sister Lou,* for teenage readers, is *Lou in the Limelight* (Scribner, 1981). In the second book Lou and other quartet members record a hit album and perform in New York clubs as well as in a Las Vegas casino. After trouble with the mob and other problems, Lou plans to get her high school diploma and accept a cousin's help to pay for her college education.

In 1996, Ballentine published Kristin Hunter Lattany's *Kinfolks.*

Hunter has been on the board of directors of the Walt Whitman Poetry Center in Camden, New Jersey. In 1981, she won the Drexel Citation from Drexel University and the Free Library of Philadelphia. In 1996, she received the Lifetime Achievement Award of the Twelfth Annual Celebration of Black Writing.

After teaching for twenty-three years at the University of Pennsylvania and being a guest lecturer at Emory University in Atlanta, Georgia, Hunter retired in 1995 to write more books.

Johanna Hurwitz,
author (1937–)

1990 Interview

As a children's librarian, Johanna Hurwitz may include her own books among others offered to patrons. However, her library work occupies only one day a week. "It's just to keep my foot in the door," she said.

She wouldn't be steering patrons wrong in suggesting her own books. A partial list of her titles that have won U.S. readers' choice awards are: *The Hot and Cold Summer* (Morrow, 1984) in Texas and Wyoming; *Class Clown* (Morrow, 1987) in Kentucky, Mississippi, and West Virginia; and *Teacher's Pet* (Morrow, 1988) in Florida and New Jersey. *Anne Frank, Life in Hiding* (Jewish Publication Society, 1988) was a Notable Children's Trade Book in the Field of Social Studies.

Hurwitz's humorous titles include *Aldo Applesauce* (Murrow, 1979), *Russell Sprouts* (Murrow, 1987), and *The Adventures of Ali Baba Bernstein* (Murrow, 1989). In the last book, David Bernstein finds too many with his same name in Manhattan's phone book, so after reading *Arabian Nights*, he changes his name to Ali Baba Bernstein. For fun, he calls his friend, Valerie Fishbone "Sheherazade" Fishbone. The writer claims to have "a British sense of humor that children understand."

Johanna Frank was born on October 9, 1937, in New York City. Her parents, Nelson and Tillie Frank, both cherished books. Her mother had been a library assistant, and her journalist father had owned a secondhand bookstore. He gave up the store, but his unsold books lined the walls of their Bronx apartment. They once caused a minor incident:

> As a child, I hurt my head and was bleeding heavily. My mother called for an ambulance. When the drivers came for me, they stared because they had never seen so many books in a home. Instead of putting me on a stretcher, they just gaped and said to Mother, "Gee, lady, you sure like to read!" My mother was trying to rush them to the hospital before I died. I still have a tiny forehead scar.

Johanna got her first card at Melrose Public Library when she was about five, knowing then how to read and sign her name with a pen. She said, "I lived in the library. It was near my home, so I went every day after school. By the age of ten, I was practically a librarian already." At age eleven, she joined a weekly Melrose literary club that heard members' stories. "Books" was an apt title for her first original poem, written when she was ten and published by *New London Way*. It made her fifty cents richer.

The author's home was near Yankee Stadium, and for twenty-five cents, she attended Ladies' Day ballgames with girlfriends. Her baseball knowledge and pride in the Baseball Hall of Fame in Cooperstown, New York, are evident in *Baseball Fever* (Morrow, 1981).

An unusual Hurwitz book, *The Rabbi's Girls* (Morrow, 1982), deals with death and anti-Semitism. It was a 1983 ALA Notable Children's Book. The author explained:

> This book is different because it's based on my mother's childhood. She was one of seven sisters, and her father was the rabbi living in a little town, Lorain, Ohio. When I finished it, the editor said, "Seven sisters in a family! It sounds unbelievable. No one is going to accept it." I made a change to six sisters. . . .
>
> The story takes place in 1923 and 1924. A tornado occurred in 1924. This wasn't something Mother had made up. It was a terrible disaster. When I read microfiche, I realized eighty people were killed, many of them young, when a movie theater's balcony was torn off by the force of the tornado.

Hurwitz wrote *The Rabbi's Girls* about her mother and traced her own growing-up years in the Bronx in *Once I Was a Plum Tree* (Morrow, 1980):

> Most of what happens is about my own childhood. I did grow up in the Bronx in that period, the late 1940s. I couldn't repeat some autobiographical things that I had already used in other books. For example, in my 1978 book, *The Law of Gravity*, Margot goes to the library every day. I couldn't say it again here.

In *Once I Was a Plum Tree,* the father is a postal worker. Hurwitz's father was a labor reporter for the now-defunct *New York World Telegram*. Pflaumenbaum (plum tree) had been her family's surname. During World War I, due to anti-German sentiment, her grandfather changed his surname to meaningless Flam.

In 1952, just before senior high began, her family moved to a semi-detached Queens home. Since her records did not reach Bryant High in time, she was not in advanced classes. For a book report, her English teacher required copying a book's paragraph. Johanna asked her, "How do you know they've read the book?" Johanna thought she was a prig, like Cricket Kaufman in *Teacher's Pet* (1988).

Hurwitz had some sad feelings about moving from the Bronx to Queens and transferred her sentiments to the main character in *Aldo Applesauce*. In this sequel to *Much Ado About Aldo* (Morrow, 1978), the Sossi family moves from New York City to Woodside, New Jersey. "I didn't have him move to Long Island, like me, because I didn't want it to look too autobiographical," she said.

At Bryant High School, Johanna began reading classics and working in the library. At age sixteen, she was a page in the New York Public Library system. She graduated from high school and Queen's College early, and attended Columbia University's library science classes until July 1, 1959. Then she was to marry a twenty-two-year-old classmate, Lincoln Reisman. Three weeks before the wedding, he died of peritonitis from a ruptured appendix. She coped with grief by staying busy.

While working as a full-time children's librarian, she took a New York University writing course. Later, classmates formed a writers' group. One member was Uri Levi Hurwitz, a doctor's son from Berlin, Germany, whose family moved to Palestine (now Israel) to escape Hitler. After studying there, he came to New York for advanced work. Uri, who was fluent in English, made her laugh. On February 19, 1962, the two writers married in Manhattan City Hall. Their daughter, Nomi, was born in 1964 and their son, Beni, in 1966.

Hurwitz discussed her family. Her husband had taught Hebrew at the City University of New York before retiring. *The Assassin*, his 1968 Doubleday novel, used Uri Levi as a byline, omitting his surname. Her daughter, Nomi, is a social worker, and her son, Beni, is studying computer science. Hurwitz said, "My son is very proud that I've reached the end of the twentieth century and am finally working on a computer."

Hurwitz's books *Busybody Nora* (Morrow, 1976) and *Superduper Teddy* (Morrow, 1980) were based on her young family's life:

> We lived in an apartment building then, very much like the one I wrote about in *Busybody Nora*. So many of the stories happened to my children or almost happened or could have happened to them.

I've written four books about Nora, and now I've written four books about Russell, who is a neighbor. Russell has a little sister, Elisa. The stories all take place in the same apartment building with the same children who are gradually getting older.

Working without an agent, Hurwitz persistently approached publishers to issue *Busybody Nora*:

I went down a list of publishers. My first book came out in 1976, but I finished writing it in 1972. I would send it out, and it would come back. I would send it out again. One day, it didn't come back. That was in 1975, and Morrow kept it.

Hurwitz always has her book characters on her mind:

I can get story ideas just from looking out the window. It's actually happened. I saw a father trying to help a six-year-old girl learn to use a two-wheel bicycle. It reminded me how I learned and taught my children to ride. I thought: *Little Russell is old enough to have a bike.*

One of the nice things about being a writer is I didn't have to go to a store to buy him a bicycle. All I had to do was go to my computer with a story.

Hurwitz is devoted to her book characters and her children. When the children were young, the Hurwitz family left the city during part of the summer to enjoy nature. They picked wild berries and made jam. After renting a house with others, they bought a home in Wilmington, Vermont, in 1992, dividing their time between New York and Vermont.

Hurwitz related some of the family's Vermont experiences in *Yellow Blue Jay* (Morrow, 1986). Jay Koota, an eight-year-old city boy, is reluctant for his family to vacation in Vermont with the Rosses, who have a twelve-year-old son, Mickey. Jay learns to capture a flying bat, swims in Snake Lake, cooks kabobs with knitting needles as skewers, and makes twig houses for "elves." He becomes Mickey's pal, not a scared "yellow blue jay."

Influenced by Vermont's greenery, the Hurwitzes moved to a home in Queens, New York. After twelve years in an apartment building, a good story source, they settled in 1974 in Great Neck, Long Island. Hurwitz could walk to the train, so she could keep her New York Public Library job. She also had her own study with proper equipment:

Nowadays, I write on a computer. I wrote my first book by hand. I couldn't write it fast enough. I had too many ideas. I decided I better teach myself to use a typewriter. My second book I did on a typewriter. Then I upgraded to an electronic typewriter, and now I actually use a computer.

Hurwitz once wrote an entire book based on a false impression. In *The Law of Gravity* (Morrow, 1978), eleven-year-old Margot Green in New York City has a summer project: get Mom downstairs. For nine years, agoraphobic Mrs. Green has not left the fourth-floor walk-up apartment with a rooftop garden. While her flutist father is on concert tour, Margo's project helper is twelve-year-old "Bernie" Bermazzoli. Margot does not get Mom downstairs but does cement ties with Bernie.

Hurwitz told her own mother that she had written about a woman in their apartment building who never left it. Her mother said, "Where'd you get that idea? You must have been at school and didn't see her." A fine book would not have been written if Hurwitz had previously known the truth.

Woodside, New Jersey is Hurwitz's setting for *The Hot and Cold Summer.* Two ten-year-old lads, Rory and Derek, discourage a visiting girl who's their age, redheaded Bolivia, from joining them. She stays with her next-door aunt while her parents are summer archaeologists in Turkey. By the end, the male twosome is a congenial threesome.

In 1986, Hurwitz went to Amsterdam to research nonfiction for the Jewish Publication Society's *Anne Frank, Life in Hiding* (Morrow, 1988). She saw where the Franks hid during World War II, but was unable to meet Miep Gies. Mrs. Gies helped the Frank family hide from the Nazis, saved Anne's diary, and, after the war, assisted Anne's father, the family's only concentration camp survivor. "She was then working on her own book," Hurwitz said of Gies.

Hurwitz compared her two biographies:

The Anne Frank story is sad because Anne didn't reach her sixteenth birthday. My other work of nonfiction was happier. It was *Astrid Lindgren, Storyteller to the World.* It was a perfect balance to the Anne Frank story.

Lindgren was eighty-one and could speak English. I visited her in her country home facing the Baltic Sea. She told me that every morning she swims in that freezing water. Perhaps because she does it daily, she has adjusted to the cold temperatures. She has a wonderful sense of humor and a very quick mind. All the things one feels when reading her books are still evident, even though she's no longer a young woman.

Astrid Lindgren, Storyteller to the World (1989) was published by Viking Kestrel. Lindgren's daughter, Karin, gave the name, Pippi Longstocking, to her mother's best-known character. In 1958, Lindgren won a Hans Christian Andersen Medal for her work. For some years, Lindgren wrote in the morning and worked for her publisher in the afternoon.

Hurwitz also expressed strong ties to her publisher:

Connie Epstein was my first editor, and we clicked perfectly. David Reuther, Connie's successor, is wonderful. He'll say, "It's your name that goes on the book, so adopt only what you think is best." Sometimes, an editor shows me that what I thought is obvious, exists only in my head.

For Connie, I sent a complete manuscript or ten book chapters before getting a contract. I still do that with David, though I suspect he wouldn't require it. I get an advance for a shorter time, but it takes pressure off me because no one is waiting for my work.

At this stage in her career, Hurwitz participates in selecting the illustrator for her books. She listed some names she has recommended: "Donald Carrick for *Yellow Blue Jay*; Diane de Groat for 'Aldo' books; Gail Owens for *Ali Baba Bernstein* and *The Hot and Cold Summer*; and Jerry Pinkney for *New Shoes for Silvia.*"

Hurwitz has visited thirty-eight states to promote her books. One incident that happened in Alaska appeared in *Class Clown*. "It could have happened anywhere," she recalled. "A boy stuck his head into the rear of a chair between the backrest and the seat. He was able to get his head out, but I could see a potential problem. It gave me the idea for Lucas Cott. . . ."

Class Clown (Morrow, 1987) concerns a bright third grader, Lucas Cott, who talks out of turn. While a mime performs in assembly, Lucas gets his head stuck in the back of a chair. He redeems himself when he substitutes for ringmaster in the class minicircus.

Hurwitz's popularity is reflected not only in readers-choice awards but also in the quantity of her fan mail:

> I get incredible amounts of mail. Some stories are sad. About two weeks ago, I got a group of letters from a class. When I replied, I wrote a single letter but I headed it, "Dear . . .," listing names of all those who had written me. One child, Avery, was crying because she didn't think her letter was good enough for me to include her name. A mother in that class phoned me, giving me a way to reach Avery. I called the child and thought afterwards: *Wouldn't it be wonderful if all the world's problems could be solved so easily?*

UPDATE

Hurwitz, who has more than forty books to her credit, departed from longer stories to write her first picture book, *New Shoes for Silvia* (Morrow, 1993), featuring Jerry Pinkney's fine watercolor illustrations. She got the idea for the book while visiting her daughter, who was in a volunteer service program in Nicaragua. The story tells about family warmth in a land with no luxuries.

Jesse Jackson, author (1908–1983)

1976 Interview

Children's libraries are filled with many books written for boys and girls that have withstood the test of time. One such book is Jesse Jackson's *Call Me Charley* (Harper, 1945), which the author cited as his best-known book. Winner of a Child Study Association Award, the book was in print for more than forty-five years in hardback or paperback editions and was read by more than a million young people. The book's sequel, *Anchor Man* (Harper, 1947), won the National Council of Christians and Jews Award.

Jackson received the Carter G. Woodson Award from the National Council for the Social Studies for *Black in America, a Fight for Freedom* (Messner, 1971) and *Make a Joyful Noise Unto the Lord! The Life of Mahalia Jackson, Queen of Gospel Singers* (Crowell, 1974). There's one long-term goal he never completed:

> My mother told me stories about my great-grandmother, who was a slave on Henry Clay's plantation in Lexington, Kentucky. When I was four or five years old, Mother told me how my great-grandmother's son, Reuben Todd, was sold by Henry Clay's overseer because he was unruly. As a young man, I promised myself that I'd write about Uncle Reuben. I've been in correspondence with the Kentucky Historical Society to find the names of the slaves for whom Henry Clay paid taxes.

165

Jackson was born on New Year's Day in 1908 in Columbus, Ohio. His mother, Mabel Rogers Jackson, was a domestic worker with a gift for story-telling. His father, Jesse Jackson Sr., tended flowers in the yard of the family's first home, a comfortable four-room house with a privy. The yard was big enough for a dog, cat, and barnyard fowl that fascinated him and his older sister. The Jacksons were the only African-American family in a German neighborhood.

The flooding Scioto River forced his family from their home and into a ghetto when Jackson was five years old. One of their houses was in an alley near a street where the wealthy lived, so the Jackson children attended an excellent school for three years until the school district rezoned, favoring segregation.

Jackson's mother, whom her family called a "church mouse," centered her life around Baptist activities. He was close to his mother's sister, Aunt Hannah, called "Aunt Hetty" in his last two books. Aunt Hetty took him to Chautauqua, New York, for a month when he was sixteen.

Jackson's father became foreman at an iron foundry though European immigrant employees objected. His father was a strict person and didn't communicate well with Jackson, whom he kept out of trouble with many odd jobs. After school, Jackson delivered his mother's laundry, mopped factory floors, and carried newspapers.

> The newspaper job introduced me to a lot of people who could help me later on during lean years. I met a judge who asked me to write speeches for him.
>
> In high school, I started to write for a newspaper. Naturally, I wanted to become a journalist. After high school, I worked on a weekly, four-page newspaper for the black community. I sold it on the streets and went out into the countryside. The only way to get money out of it was to sell advertising, which wasn't too flourishing.

Jackson continued his education at the Ohio State University School of Journalism, from 1927 to 1929, and pursued university sports. "I won a boxing tournament there, but couldn't earn a living at it. My parents objected. I learned to stay on my feet during a fight. I soon became intelligent enough to get out of the boxing ring."

The boxing coach let Jackson work in his training department as a masseur for sixty-five cents an hour. The athlete tried other jobs to support himself. "I went into construction, building streets after tearing up old ones," he recalled. "I had to load the tar and asphalt on trucks, which helped my muscles. For relaxation, I was fond of swimming and became a lifeguard."

Jackson said, "The turning point of my life occurred [in 1936] when I became a probation officer for juvenile court." There he learned the extent of poverty in Columbus. In his office one day, he found three scared boys, aged fourteen to sixteen, who had killed a restaurant owner in a robbery that gave them five dollars and resulted in a life sentence. The "inability to read made kids be truant from school and led to crime," he concluded. "I began writing stories about some of my cases."

Jackson left his probation job, choosing less emotional work at the post office. In 1938, he was a part-time Ohio State University student, had married Ann Newman Williams, put a down payment on a home, and became father of a daughter, Judith. He also tried to get published:

> I took my stories to Professor Francis Utley at Ohio State University to see if they were publishable. With his encouragement, I went to Bread Loaf Writers' Conference. A Bread Loaf teacher, Wallace Stegner, suggested that I stop in New York at Harper Brothers to talk with editor Ursula Nordstrom.

A renowned juvenile editor, Ursula Nordstrom saw Jackson's papers about probation cases before saying, "What I'm looking for is the story of a black boy growing up. Can you do it?" She previously offered the chance to Richard Wright, who turned it down. Jackson accepted the challenge.

> I said I would try to write what she wanted and went back to Columbus to work on the story that later became *Call Me Charley*. It's a book that departs from stereotypes of the *Penrod and Sam* period. Ms. Nordstrom suggested that the book take place in a Midwestern town in the late 1940s, nine years before the Supreme Court's school desegregation decision.

After Jackson finished about eight chapters, he sent them to Ursula Nordstrom. She wanted him to come to New York to complete *Call Me Charley*. He went, leaving his family behind, and found the effort worthwhile:

> Ms. Nordstrom was very helpful in suggesting, editing, and cautioning me about mistakes I was making. She pointed out, "You've fallen in love with Charlie. A writer should be like an orchestra leader. You're writing for predominantly white readers. Distribute the reader's interest by being fair to all of your characters."

The content of Jackson's first book is fairly predictable. At a time when the only African-American student in suburban Arlington Heights Junior High might be called "Sambo," Charley Moss fights for respect as indicated in the title, *Call Me Charley*. Twelve-year-old Charley, who delivers newspapers, lives in an Arlington Heights garage apartment owned by the Cunninghams. His father is the Cunningham chauffeur and his mother is their cook/housekeeper. At school, Charley gains a part in a play and admission to both a boys' club and a swimming pool.

In *Call Me Charley,* Jackson was writing autobiographically about wanting to be addressed by his own name. He remembered being a table waiter in clubs, hotels, and Great Lake steamers. He would tell patrons his name and ask to be addressed by his name for service. He was hurt since no patron gave him that recognition.

Following publication of *Call Me Charley,* Jackson returned to Ohio to begin work on a sequel, *Anchor Man.* He decided to rent his Columbus home and move with his wife and three-year-old daughter to New York City. His wife became a social worker, and he began work for seventy-five cents an hour at H. Wolfe Book Manufacturing Company. He was promoted to a final reader's job there, and he could read galleys at home, receiving between $200 and $500 for each job.

In 1951, the National Bureau of Economic Research asked Wolfe Company to recommend a technical book reader. Jackson got the chance and stayed for seventeen years. He would rise at 3 or 4 A.M. in order to write before arriving at 9 A.M. at Madison and 39th Street. He completed the "Charley" trilogy for Harper with *Anchor Man* (1947) and *Charley Starts from Scratch* (1958). In the last book, eighteen-year-old Charley is more than six feet tall. Events in both books are based on Jackson's track-team days at Ohio State University.

The National Council of Churches of Christ asked Jackson to write a book about integration in the Protestant church for Sunday school use. (Previously, the council had placed 10,000 copies of *Call Me Charley* in church libraries.) Jackson submitted *Room for Randy,* which was altered by a review committee's criticism and published by the church's Friendship Press in 1957. Jackson was not satisfied with the final rendition and did not keep a copy.

A librarian asked Jackson to write about girls, since they outnumber boy readers. The idea jelled when he overheard a phone conversation about a private school's play. The director asked a friend's daughter to take the role of a maid in the play. *Tessie* (Harper, 1968) shows Tessie Downs, a vulnerable teenage Harlem girl, accepting a scholarship as the only African-American student at Hobbe, an exclusive private school. Tessie barely wins her mother's permission to perform in the school play as a servile character. Judith Jackson, the author's daughter, told her father that racial integration at her private school was not the same as economic integration. He noted: "At spring break, many white families were going to Bermuda or for ski vacations while we struggled to keep our heads above water."

Each year from 1966 to 1968, Jackson was able to spend a couple of months writing full time as a guest at the MacDowell Colony in Peterborough, New Hampshire. The artists' retreat was founded by composer Edward MacDowell in 1907. Jackson spoke about his experience:

> After I had done several books, I was accepted, so I could devote myself to writing. I worked on *Tessie* while I was there.
>
> Each guest has a separate studio. The former occupants of my studio had put their names on a shingle standing on a fireplace shelf. I could see the outstanding people who preceded me. James Baldwin and Edwin Arlington Robinson, the great poet of *Matthias at the Door*, had been previous occupants of my studio.

The 400-acre retreat gives artists in more than forty small studios uninterrupted time during the day to work on their creative projects. So the artists don't have to take a midday break, lunch is delivered to each studio door at noon. "It's 'Cloud Eleven,' and the beautiful countryside is soothing," Jackson said.

Jackson left his "cloud" to write nonfiction, *Black in America, a Fight for Freedom* (Messner, 1971), with Elaine Landau. The author traced its inspiration:

> My mother first bought me books about blacks from door-to-door peddlers. When I was a kid, a common practice in the black community was to pay fifty cents weekly toward the cost of a book. Peddlers never did tell buyers how much it would cost in the end. That's how my mother got me *Famous Blacks in American History*. I remember reading about Crispus Attucks, W. E. B. DuBois, and Robert Abbott, founder of the *Chicago Defender*. It always puzzled me why I could never find Mother's book in my school or public library.
>
> I began reading *The Journal of American History*. There I came across recruiting lists of soldiers from Virginia in the Revolutionary War. I have an accumulation of stories and articles that I've written, some printed in *Crisis*.

Jackson's second nonfiction book began in an unusual way:

> Prior to 1962, black authors had problems getting published. After school integration, publishers saw the need for more books with black characters. At a cocktail party, I met publishers who asked me to pick from a list of famous blacks, living and dead, and write a biography of that person. When I saw Mahalia Jackson's name, I picked her.
>
> I talked to Mahalia Jackson personally. I followed her from concert to concert. She'd long been a favorite of mine. Our backgrounds are similar, for I attended

the Baptist Church, listening to the gospel choir on Sundays. There were always two choirs: one with trained singers and one with more spirit than training.

Based on his research, the author wrote *Make a Joyful Noise Unto the Lord! The Life of Mahalia Jackson, Queen of Gospel Singers* (Crowell, 1974). It is an amazing story of the gospel singer's success, despite minimal encouragement.

Jackson's last two fictional works were in a freer, more humorous style than his earlier creations, a style encouraged by his new Doubleday editor, Patricia Connelly. Jackson commented on his change in style in *Language Arts* (March 1977, p. 339):

> Before doing *The Sickest Don't Always Die the Quickest* and *The Fourteenth Cadillac,* I had worked closely with white editors who were anxious that my books reflect the viewpoint of a white writer writing for white readers. The difference in style between these two and my earlier works was that I told *The Sickest . . .* and *The Fourteenth Cadillac* purely from the viewpoint of a black in a black setting under the supervision of a white editor who happened to have been born in England and had less of a hang-up than Americans about white being right. Miss Patricia Connelly is the name of that kind editor. . . . The difference was Miss Connelly seemed to be unafraid of violating the unwritten law in the juvenile field that all books for children must satisfy the aunts, uncles, and parents who set the tone for what children read.

The Sickest Don't Always Die the Quickest (1971) and its sequel, *The Fourteenth Cadillac* (1972), feature Stonewall Jackson, who is more autobiographical than Charley Moss of earlier days. The books take place in the 1920s in the author's hometown, Columbus, Ohio. In the prequel, Stonewall is twelve years old, and in the sequel, he is seventeen. Jackson portrays memorable characters with apt nicknames, like "Lucifer" to denote Aunt Lucy's hot temper in *The Sickest Don't Die the Quickest.* The nickname "Steeplehead," abbreviated "Steeple," is based on the cranium shape of Stonewall's best friend, a continuous character in both books.

The Fourteenth Cadillac begins with the death of Stonewall's beloved Aunt Hetty. The book's theme is Stonewall's choice of an occupation. He tries to work at Ed Coffin's funeral parlor but is miserable. He joins Steeple at Bolt's horse farm for $5 a week, plus room and board.

The "Stonewall" books show Jackson had at last found an original way of expressing himself.

UPDATE

Jackson, who was among the first to offer children's books that show integration, spent his final years in Boone, North Carolina, as writer-in-residence and lecturer at Appalachian State University. He died on April 14, 1983, in Boone. For more than thirty years, he worked at other jobs and deprived himself of sleep in order to write for young people. His fiction at the end of his career shows he had discovered his own voice in humorous, folksy accounts.

Ezra Jack Keats, author–illustrator (1916–1983)

1970 Interview

Ezra Jack Keats received quite a compliment for his book *The Snowy Day* (Viking, 1962), 1963 Caldecott Medal winner. African-American poet Langston Hughes wrote him a letter, stating that he wished he had grandchildren, so he could give them copies of *The Snowy Day*. Keats discussed his book:

> *The Snowy Day* was the first full-color children's picture book with a black hero, Peter, who doesn't appear through the courtesy of other characters. I became attached to Peter and drew him in other books. After a while, I noticed that he was growing. He grew so big, I drew him with another boy, Archie, for younger children. Peter is like a sympathetic older brother to Archie.

Peter became a continuous character, appearing in two Macmillan books, *Goggles* (1969), a 1970 Caldecott Honor Book, and *Hi, Cat!* (1970), which won the 1970 *Boston Globe-Horn Book* Award. Keats explained where his model came from:

> Long before I ever thought of doing children's books, I found these four photos in *Life* magazine of a boy about three or four years old. The boy's expressive face, his clothes, his gestures captivated me. For years, he was on my walls or tucked away in a drawer. When *The Snowy Day* was finally finished, I asked the magazine's staff when those pictures were published. To my astonishment, I discovered that I had known this little boy for twenty-two years.

Keats was born on March 11, 1916, in a tenement section of Brooklyn, New York, the youngest of three children in a struggling Jewish family. He began to draw at the age of four, though his parents, Polish immigrants, were too poor to buy their children picture books. He never saw a picture book until he was thirty-five years old. He said. "As a child, I didn't write stories, but I was the neighborhood storyteller. I wanted approval badly, so I continued to draw pictures."

The artist's father, Benjamin Keats, a waiter in a Greenwich Village beanery, worried about how his gifted son would make a living. He did, however, support Keats's talent. He'd bring home a tube of paint, claiming that a starving artist exchanged it for a bowl of soup. Keats's father saw how resourceful his son was, stretching muslin over ends of orange crates and substituting mercurochrome for red paint at times. When the boy earned a quarter for making a candy store's sign, his father offered praise. He also took Keats to the Metropolitan Museum of Art where Daumier's painting "Third Class Carriage" hypnotized the boy.

His mother, Augusta Keats, admired her son's interests: "When I was five, my mother would awaken me at dawn so I could see the sunrise, which I later drew." After he painted pictures on the entire top of their enamel kitchen table, his mother refused to wash it off. She covered it with her Friday night tablecloth but displayed it to neighbors.

At the age of seventeen, Keats painted his parents:

> When I asked them to pose, my father wanted to wear a shirt and tie, but I painted him as he was, in his undershirt and work pants. I used house paints and everything I could get my hands on. Those were tough times!

When his father died, Keats identified his body and had to search his wallet. He was moved to find it contained worn newspaper clippings about his awards. His father had been a silent fan. Keats thought about capturing his relationship to his family in a book: "I'm working now on an autobiography for teenagers. I've been talking to a tape for years."

Keats was a track star at Thomas Jefferson High. He won a prize for one of his paintings in the National Scholastic contest, which resulted in a scholarship offer to the Art Students' League. When he was a high school graduate in 1935, in the midst of the Depression, he had to refuse three scholarships to art schools because his parents needed any money he could earn. Keats once supported his whole family by loading melons on a truck for a dollar a day. He became a WPA muralist and a production assistant for "Captain Marvel Adventures" comics.

During World War II, Keats was a camouflage expert in the U.S. Air Force. After the war, he got jobs doing *Collier's* illustrations and in 1948 went to Paris to paint. When he returned to the United States, he exhibited art he had done in Paris and other work at the Associated American Artists Gallery in New York City. He said, "Here artists were given chances to do commercial and institutional advertising or specialized work." Elizabeth Riley, an editor for Crowell, saw his book jacket for an adult novel and asked him to do one for a juvenile book. Next, she interested him in illustrating a novel for young people, Elizabeth C. Lansing's *Jubilant for Sure* (1954).

Since Lansing's setting was Kentucky's Smokey Mountains, Keats went there to sketch. He hitched a ride on a truck, hopping off when he saw a shack, a porch, and a rocker. A four-year-old girl with golden curls came on the porch, and he included her in his sketch. The child's parents liked his drawing and invited him first to eat lunch and then to stay a few days, only if he didn't pay. He sketched for a week:

> I got instructions for my first book: "Do everything in line because it's part of a series, and the lady who drew before, did it in line." I went to the Smokey Mountains, did the book, and then couldn't stop. That's what I've been doing ever since.

For ten years, he illustrated books written by others, always with white characters. In 1960, Crowell issued *My Dog Is Lost!* with his illustrations and Pat Cherr as his coauthor. It features Juanito, from Puerto Rico, and uses Spanish words sporadically. Solo work was next:

> *The Snowy Day* was my first book that was really my own. When I did it, I used a model. I wanted to make very certain that my main character looked like a black boy, not a white child painted black. I wanted to appreciate the unique beauty of every race.
>
> It's my own childhood that I recall in my books, the things I experienced when I was growing up: discovering snow, loving colors, learning to whistle, loneliness, wanting something very badly, running away from home, growing up, and discovering that there are girls.

Keats drew his Caldecott winner with minimal details:

> In *The Snowy Day*, the figure you see walking through the snow is a little abstract shape. I wanted to keep it simple. The hills of snow in pink and blue and yellow are pure shapes with no definitions and no shadows. If you look at *Hi, Cat!* and *Goggles*, you'll see the illustrations are more realistic.

Keats made snowflakes at the end of *The Snowy Day* by cutting patterns out of gum erasers, dipping them in paint, and stamping them on pages. His main artistic effect was through collage, pasting cut or torn paper as he illustrated *The Snowy Day* and most of his later children's books. He created the mother's dress from oilcloth used for lining cupboards. Paper became a sidewalk in *Whistle for Willie* (Viking, 1964), the sequel to *The Snowy Day*. For *Jennie's Hat* (Harper, 1966), Keats added in addition to the usual collage material, dried leaves, old valentines, postcards, paper flowers, bits of old wallpaper, and paper fans. Paper that looked like wood became a fence in *A Letter to Amy* (Harper, 1968).

In a Spring Garden (Dial, 1965) features Keats's illustrations of Japanese haiku gathered by editor Richard Lewis. The Library of Congress selected it as one of its Books of the Year in 1965.

> For *In a Spring Garden,* I made material in a special way. I diluted oil paints that I dropped into a shallow pan of water. It bubbled and floated into interesting patterns. If the results looked right, I gently placed a piece of paper on top. After the paint had time to be absorbed by the paper, I picked it up carefully to see the effect.

In *Whistle for Willie,* the young character Peter becomes dizzy from turning around, so the artist showed this with an agitated sky in a marbleized pattern, tilting his composition up and then down on successive pages. Iran's empress liked this book so much, she invited Keats to be guest at the Second Teheran International Festival of Films for Children in 1966.

John Henry, an American Legend is a popular hero tale that Keats retold for Pantheon in 1965. Children love the picture of the fat baby who becomes a powerful African-American railroad worker and beats the steam drill in a deadly race.

In 1966, Keats designed five UNICEF Christmas cards and produced a book for youths and adults, *God Is in the Mountain* (Holt):

> I wanted to share quotations showing the universality of many religions. I envision a nonestablishment kind of religion. I get letters from older people who read parts of this book to children, and they grasp its ideas. For example, a saying from Kenya is: "Talking with one another is loving one another."

One child thought it took Keats two days to write and illustrate a tale. Keats replied:

> It takes about half to three-quarters of a year. I keep changing the words and the pictures. Sometimes the words or pictures are not good enough. Maybe I can improve the colors or the way the little boy is standing or sitting. I go out on the street, look at children, come back, and think. Sometimes I'm still thinking when the book is being printed, but then it's too late. A book is never finished. It goes on and on.

UPDATE

Keats's fantasy, *The Trip* (Greenwillow, 1978), was a 1979 Children's Choice from the International Reading Association and the Children's Book Council. Among the last books of Keats's career was *Maggie and the Pirate* (Four Winds Press, 1979). Keats picked book topics that interested children internationally. The Japanese translation of his book *Skates* (Watts, 1973) is popular, and the Japanese named a roller-skating rink for him in 1974. His books are available in seventeen languages.

Keats won a Silver Medallion in 1980 from the University of Southern Mississippi. Recognized were thirty-three books that he illustrated, twenty-two of which he also wrote.

Keats died of a heart attack on May 6, 1983; he was sixty-seven. In his memory, UNICEF and the U.S. Board on Books for Young People grant a $5,000 Ezra Jack Keats biennial award to a winning illustrator chosen internationally. Maurice Sendak is among the judges.

E. L. Konigsburg, author–illustrator (1930–)

1983 Interview

Author–illustrator Elaine Lobl Konigsburg explained why her initials are on the byline of her books, all published by Atheneum: "When I submitted my first manuscript, I used the initials E. L., partly because it wasn't important for me to be known as male or female and partly out of admiration for E. B. White," she said.

Her first and second books made history: *Jennifer, Hecate, Macbeth, William McKinley, and Me, Elizabeth* (1967) was a 1968 Newbery Honor Book, and *From the Mixed-Up Files of Mrs. Basil E. Frankweiler* (1967) won the 1968 Newbery Medal. It was the first time a recipient had received both honors in the same year.

Konigsburg was born in New York City on February 10, 1930, to Adolph and Beulah Lobl. She grew up in small Pennsylvania towns, where, judging from her 1968 Newbery acceptance speech, "no one named Jones" was in her classes. She was in Phoenixville until fifth grade, attended William McKinley Elementary in Youngstown, Ohio, and finished high school in Farrell, Pennsylvania, graduating as class valedictorian. Her father housed his family often above his store. She always enjoyed art and extensive reading, including *Mary Poppins* and *The Secret Garden*, books that did not portray her world.

No one in her family had ever gone to a university, and her high school had no guidance department to tell her about scholarships. She worked for a year as a bookkeeper to pay for classes at Carnegie Mellon University, where she majored in organic chemistry. During her freshman year, an English professor helped her get a scholarship so she could stay in college. She graduated in 1952 with honors. She married David Konigsburg, an industrial psychologist, and earned a master's of science degree. College work that strengthened her writing was scant. She reported:

> I did graduate work in chemistry at the University of Pittsburgh. The one course I ever had in writing was freshman composition. I don't think I could have had better training though. I dedicated my book, *Throwing Shadows,* to the only teacher I ever had for writing, "A. Fred Sochatoff, who was there at the beginning, before either of us knew it was a beginning." As a student of science, I was taught to write what I had to say in very straightforward language. I think that's the best training I could get for writing children's literature.

Konigsburg and her husband moved to Jacksonville, Florida, where she taught science in a private girls' school. She began to question her career choice in chemistry. She left teaching before the birth of her first child, Paul, and after the birth of her second child, daughter Laurie, studied painting in local adult education classes. She entered one art contest and won, so when the family moved to New Jersey, she resumed art studies. Her family moved again, this time to Port Chester, New York. When Ross, her third child, entered school, she began to write:

> All the years I had spent growing up in little Pennsylvania mill towns, I would pick up books that promised I would read about a typical family. I read books about children who took naps, and had both patient mothers and maids. I wanted to write something that reflected more my children's lives.

Part of that reflection was diversity. "When we were newcomers in Port Chester, the first person to offer friendship to my daughter was a black child," she recalled. That child became Jennifer in a 1966 book submitted without an agent. She said:

> Naming the book was difficult. That book was written for ten-year-olds, and my oldest son was then ten years old. He had great difficulty summarizing. If I asked him what that book was about, he would have answered much like my title, which I arranged in a rhymical pattern: *Jennifer, Hecate, Macbeth, William McKinley and Me, Elizabeth.* Some of my book titles are almost a paragraph, but children like the rhythm of saying them.

The characters in Konigsburg's first book are outsiders: Jennifer, the only black student in a suburban classroom, and Elizabeth, the new kid on the block.

From the Mixed-Up Files of Mrs. Basil E. Frankweiler, which also won the William Allen White Award, was motivated by three experiences. Konigsburg described them:

> I had read a novel called *A High Wind in Jamaica* . . . [about] children living in [Jamaica] who study in England. On the way over on a ship, pirates . . . capture them. The children become pirates themselves. They go to England and take on the coloration of an English finishing school.
>
> The second thing that happened: I read . . . that a museum bought a statue they thought was carved by Leonardo da Vinci or his teacher, Andrea del Verrocchio, but they bought it for only $225. They knew it was an enormous bargain, regardless of who had sculpted it.
>
> The third thing that happened was we were vacationing in Yellowstone National Park. I said, "Instead of eating in the commissary, I'll buy picnic things: cupcakes, paper plates and napkins, bread, bologna, and chocolate milk." We went to look for a picnic table, but there was none. I found a little clearing in the woods. We spread out on the ground, and the complaints began: "The sun was melting the icing on the cupcakes. The chocolate milk was getting warm. There were ants!"
>
> I knew if my children ever left home, they would never become piratical. The mere veneer of civilization is a crust for them. They would go to a place that is as elegant or more elegant than home. They would go to the Metropolitan Museum of Art, and maybe while they were there, they would solve the mystery of this statue that the museum had bought for $225.

The Newbery winner, partially set in a museum, is the story of Claudia Kincaid, almost twelve, who runs away from home, taking her miserly, younger brother, Jamie, for his money. The two sleep in the Metropolitan Museum of Art for several nights, collecting coins in a fountain where they bathe and standing on toilet seats to elude guards. The children are excited about "Angel," a statue donated by Mrs. Basil E. Frankweiler, and spend their last coins visiting her to learn if Michelangelo carved the statue. The Frankweiler chauffeur drives them home. Konigsburg probed the book's theme:

> I think the primary theme of *The Mixed-Up Files* has to do with suburban living, how we can retain a sense of identity while appearing to fit in where everything is the same. Claudia says she's tired of the sameness of every day. I think all my books are about how we can retain a sense of identity.
>
> I believe there are three things that bother the middle-aged child: What makes me the same as everybody else? How can I fit in? And what makes me different on the inside where it counts?

Konigsburg introduced Michelangelo in her winner of the Newbery Medal and traced Leonardo da Vinci in *The Second Mrs. Giaconda* (1975). Kings wanted da Vinci to do their portraits, but the painter's assistant, Salai, arranged for his master to paint the haunting expression of an unimportant Florentine merchant's second wife: Mona Lisa.

A different kind of book is *A Proud Taste for Scarlet and Miniver* (1973), which concerns Eleanor of Aquitaine. The historical novel begins as a twentieth-century fantasy with Eleanor in heaven nervously tapping her fingers on a cloud, affecting television reception below. She wants to know if her second husband, England's King Henry II, who died fifteen years before her in 1189, gets into heaven. He was due up earlier but had to wait for lawyers to handle his case. While waiting, she converses with other cloud sitters. Konigsburg talked about her subject:

> She lived in the twelfth century and tiptoed into the thirteenth century. She lived at a time when women were considered chattel. Her husband, Henry, kept her in prison for fifteen years in Salisbury. Despite this, she was the essence of women's liberation. I wanted to write about a woman who lived in the Middle Ages at a time when women were viewed as property. She was truly liberated because being liberated is something that happens in your head more than anywhere else.

Konigsburg created black-and-white line drawings that uniquely suited a particular novel. She talked about her 1974 National Book Award nominee, *A Proud Taste for Scarlet and Miniver,* "I drew pictures like miniatures for this book about the Middle Ages."

Another free-spirited Konigsburg character is in *About the B'nai Bagels* (1969). She is Bessie Setzer, the first female manager of a baseball team, the B'nai Bagels. Konigsburg cited the baseball tale's background, based on another family's experience:

> Two brothers were playing basketball for the Port Chester Jewish Center, despite a ruling that brothers were not allowed to play on the same team. I was watching a game.
>
> Peter and his little brother, Steven, were on the same team. Peter was passing the ball to Steven, and little Steven could not get his hands on it. The poor mother was watching in the stands, making all the correct moves for Steven. Finally, she rushed to the court and said, "Peter, leave your poor brother alone!" I thought: *That's my mother in the baseball story!*

Another book about liberation, but for teenagers, is *Father's Arcane Daughter* (1976), which Konigsburg calls fiction based on fact: "I know a situation that I cannot discuss. It has to do with a woman who comes into a home and liberates children from a very wealthy kind of prison in which they were kept." *Father's Arcane Daughter, Throwing Shadows* (1979), and *Journey to an 800 Number* (1982) have no illustrations since they are intended for teenagers.

Konigsburg used other illustrators (Gail E. Haley, Mercer Meyer, Gary Parker, and Laurel Schindelman) for only one book, *Altogether, One at a Time* (1971), a short-story collection. The author explained:

> Each story needed a different style of drawing, so I chose four different illustrators. I'm not as sophisticated as required. Someone called my art, "Mrs. Konigsburg's clumsy drawings," but children seem to relate to them.

Particularly poignant is the second story in *Altogether, One at a Time*, "The Night of the Leonids":

> The story shows the relationship between a grandmother and a grandson. They go to Central Park to see this incident that occurs every thirty-three years. He remarks on how old he will be when it next occurs, and he holds her hand when he thinks about his sixty-three-year-old grandmother in thirty-three years.
>
> My older son made me promise to wake him up to see this magnificent shower of stars. Clouds came, and we didn't get to see the Leonids. I changed myself into a grandmother [in the story] so that his awareness of mortality would be even more pronounced. . . . Some things come to me either as a short story or as a novel. I have never had a short story grow into a novel. A small incident that seems to me to crystallize an experience becomes a short story.

When Konigsburg visits schools, she advises children, "*Finish* your writing with a beginning, middle, and end."

UPDATE

Konigsburg has followed her own advice, having completed more than sixteen books for children. Her adult book is *Talk-Talk, A Children's Book Author Speaks to Grown-ups* (1995). For older readers, she wrote *Up from Jericho Tel* (1986).

In the 1990s, Konigsburg introduced a format that was new to her: two conceptual picture books in color about Samuel Todd, her oldest grandchild. The first picture book is *Samuel Todd's Book of Great Colors* (1990), which shows vegetables, fruit, animals, and children in bright to dull colors. The second picture book, *Samuel Todd's Book of Great Inventions* (1991), includes items like Velcro, a backpack, training wheels, and french fries.

Konigsburg credited her editor, Jean Karl, now deceased, who helped her for more than thirty years on new and old projects.

Karl was a wonderful editor. Some authors submit an outline and a chapter. I choose to finish my work before submission. Some of my work has gone directly from manuscript into typesetting and from typesetting into proof. I told my husband, "That's the adult equivalent of getting an A."

The adult equivalent of an A-plus is winning a second Newbery Medal thirty years after the first. That is what Konigsburg received in 1997 for *The View from Saturday,* identified as a Jean Karl book. It is an unusual story of a sixth-grade Academic Bowl team from the Epiphany, New York, middle school. They defeat sixth-, seventh-, and eighth-graders and become state champions. The participants—Noah, Nadia, Ethan, and Julian—tell their own stories. Binding the four is their teacher, Mrs. Olinski, a paraplegic. Victories of her team, "The Souls," give her self-confidence and help cement the foursome's relationship.

Konigsburg's *Silent to the Bone!* (2000) is for older youths. Two thirteen-year-old boys communicate with flashcards when one is mute for many days after a serious incident. Speech is restored following the solution of a significant mystery.

Joseph Krumgold, author (1908–1980)

1971 Interview

Books generally precede their film version, but film producer–director Joseph Krumgold released the cinemagraphic version of . . . *And Now Miguel* before he wrote his 1954 Newbery Medal–winner. Krumgold's film was released for national showing in 1953, and another version was released in 1966. "By the time I finished writing my children's book, . . . *And Now Miguel* [Crowell, 1953], I was utterly respectful of a whole area of literature that I'd never looked at before and was very stimulated," he said.

A companion book, *Onion John* (Crowell, 1959), brought the writer the 1960 Newbery Medal, making him the first to receive two coveted Newbery Medals. Krumgold was forty-six years old when he got the first medal for his second children's book, and six years later, the second medal for his third book. His first children's book, *Sweeney's Adventure* (Random House, 1942), was written as an afterthought to his film *Adventure in the Bronx* (1941) and sold 30,000 copies. During World War II the U.S. Navy commissioned Krumgold's documentary film, *Tomorrow We Fly,* about a preflight school. It was nominated for an Academy Award.

Krumgold was born on April 9, 1908, in Jersey City, New Jersey, where his father built movie theaters while his brother Jules bought and sold them. His brother Sigmund played an organ for California movies. Joseph Krumgold fished, swam, and skated for sport. At New York University (NYU), he was in Pi Lambda Phi fraternity with future motion picture executives Stanley Kramer, Arthur Lowe, and David Lowe.

Krumgold graduated from NYU before he was twenty years old. He went to Hollywood to learn how to make movies and began by writing Chinese dialog for Lon Chaney's first talking picture. For about twelve years, he wrote and produced screen plays for major studios (including Metro-Goldwyn-Mayer, Paramount, RKO, Columbia, and Republic) and later, for Joseph Krumgold Productions. When he left California, he worked on documentary films that won him first prize at the Venice, Prague, and Edinburgh film festivals. In 1935, Vanguard published Krumgold's first book, *Thanks to Murder*, an adult detective novel that he wrote so he could be considered a writer–producer–director.

Krumgold married Helen Litwin in 1947, and until 1951 the couple spent most of their time in Israel, where he made documentary films. They returned to their homeland, moving into a Greenwich Village apartment. Here he cut and edited his films. The Krumgolds also bought and restored an old Moravian stone farmhouse, Shiloh Farm, in Hope, New Jersey. Krumgold did his writing in this house, beginning with *Onion John,* which he dedicated to his wife. He dedicated . . . *And Now Miguel* to their son, Adam, who was born in 1952.

The film . . . *And Now Miguel* was done for the U.S. Information Service under the direction of anthropologist Margaret Mead. He said:

> One of the purposes of the program was to show that the family in American life, to a considerable extent, continued as an economic and social unit that was highly important. Families ran farms, grocery stores, gasoline stations, things of that sort. The family is a unit of cohesion in this country still.
>
> I was asked to begin with a farm family. I started the search in Oklahoma and went west, looking for them. I pitched up in the valley of the Colorado around Taos with the Chavez family, having found them through the local county agricultural agent. The story of the Chavez family fit the program. I discovered later when I put it into a book that it had a universality that went beyond any governmental program and took on real meaning.

Krumgold revealed that Miguel's film voice was actually that of a female with suitable pitch whose spoken English had Spanish inflection. The book's appeal comes partially from Krumgold's retention of authentic awkward English phrasing in first-person narration. After all, the boy's native language is Spanish.

The book's protagonist, twelve-year-old Miguel Chavez, lives as his ancestors did, on a sheep farm in the small community of Los Córdovas, New Mexico, near Taos. Miguel is a middle child, too old to be always content, like his little brother, Pedro, but not given responsibilities, like his older brother, Gabriel. He prays to his patron saint, San Ysidro, to go with men in his family to the sheep's summer pasture in Sangre de Cristo Mountains. Miguel's prayer is answered, only because his oldest brother, Gabriel, is drafted.

Krumgold was not aloof from his film's subjects. He celebrated saints' days with them at barbecues, basking in dancing and fiddle playing. He spoke about the sheep industry:

> From the inception through the shooting of the picture, I spent some six or seven months with the Chavez family. I thought we would wind up raising sheep more than making a movie half the time. It was a lengthy process, and thank the Lord for that, because I enjoyed every minute of it.
>
> Curiously enough, the sheep industry in itself places great emphasis on the family. Caring for a ewe and a lamb is an economic activity. If a sheep family doesn't stay together, the lamb dies, and the rancher loses money. There was a rather neat corollary between the sheep family and the human family.

After doing the film, Krumgold faced unexpected challenges in writing his book version:

> A children's book editor saw the shooting script and suggested that I write the story as a children's book. I thought it would be an easy way to make money out of what I'd already done. It seemed it could be done fairly quickly.
>
> I soon discovered that one undertakes the writing of a children's book in a serious fashion at one's peril. One soon becomes engrossed in a new problem. The picture and the book are completely different statements. What started out as a simple moneymaking venture became a fascinating search for a whole new kind of literature and storytelling. I now find it's as meaningful as anything I've done.

In his Newbery Award acceptance speech for . . . *And Now Miguel,* Krumgold showed how close he was to the people of Los Córdovas. The village, with rutted roads, is only twenty-three miles from Los Alamos, New Mexico. In Los Alamos, Krumgold said that a boy becomes a man when he gets FBI security clearance. In Los Córdovas, manhood recognition is more serious. Krumgold said:

> It revolved around the theme of a child growing up and being received into his family and into the community as an adult. It's the theme of confirmation. It's celebrated in religions by *bar mitzvahs* or Catholic communions. It's no longer a ritual but it happens.
>
> At that moment, two things are judged: One is the child, whether he is prepared to be an adult, and the other thing is the society that is inducting him. It has to explain itself either through a study of the catechism, the Torah, or taboos, values, and standards by which the community lives.

Krumgold turned next to small-town life in *Onion John* to show how a storekeeper's son, twelve-year-old Andy, resolves his manhood quest. The story takes place in a town called Serenity, but it is actually Belvedere, a town near the author's New Jersey home. One of Andy's friends is an immigrant man, whom Krumgold depicts as unique:

> It is essentially the story of a childlike man. Onion John is his name. He eats onions with great relish, and when he enters a bus, everyone moves back. He is superstitious, tying large rocks on trees to shame apples to grow equally big. The man, who is adopted by a town in Warren County, is being treated with loving kindness in a way that distorts his own values. He is being destroyed by the love of this town.
>
> My publisher and I were worried about libel, so I changed the town's name and the names of the people. Originally, I called everybody by their real names.

Twelve-year-old Andy, who can interpret Onion John's strange language, has a communication problem with his father. Led by Andy's father, Rotary Club members build John a new home, but he cannot handle the electric stove and accidentally starts a fire. In the book, he injures some ribs but recuperates and refuses to live in a reconstructed house, preferring a cave. In actuality, Onion John caused an explosion when he did not know how to use his cooking stove, and injuries led to his death. Townspeople buried him. After publishing *Onion John*, Krumgold was surprised to hear from respectful Belvedere citizens:

> On Christmas Day in the morning, I got a phone call from a very fine gentleman who runs the furniture store. He said, "I've been reading that book you wrote. We've never bought him a headstone." I thought, *The story starts all over. We're going to raise enough money and buy him a headstone, and we're going to have an "Onion John Day."* By God, that's what they did as soon as the frost was off the ground. I was an honored guest at the ceremony and so was the state librarian, Roger McDonough. He came up from Trenton.

Krumgold moved from a small-town setting to a New York City suburb, Crestview, for *Henry 3* (Atheneum, 1967). In this book, Krumgold notes a change in manhood rites:

> *Henry 3* takes place in the early 1960s, a time of the generation gap. The boy is not following in his father's footsteps. He is not taking his place individually in the adult world, but there is a tribing together of youngsters and a rejection of adults. I wrote that story in Rome, and when I came here, that was what was happening. It's my most significant look at this process that started with Miguel. . . . There are days when I think my son, Adam, utterly rejects me.

Although Krumgold spent time abroad, only his picture book has a setting outside the United States. It is *The Most Terrible Turk: A Story of Turkey* (Crowell, 1969). Michael Hampshire's black-and-white drawings effectively portray Uncle Mustafa, an Istanbul porter with a white moustache, and his schoolboy nephew, Ali, whom he is raising.

To Krumgold, writing for children and adults was similar:

> I think it's a highly artificial distinction between writing for adults and children. . . . The book I'm doing now, *The Children's Crusade*, is nonfiction about the year 1212. It's for adults because children would find it dull, perhaps rightly so. This historical analogy is relevant to today's youth.
>
> If you deal with any subject honestly, it's the hardest labor to realize fully the potential of the story you're telling. When you're writing for children, a critical, honest audience, they'll put your book down as soon as they find you're being patronizing, fashionable, or phony.

UPDATE

Krumgold died of a stroke on July 10, 1980, in Hope, New Jersey.

Beth Krush, illustrator (1918–)

Joe Krush, illustrator (1918–)

1972 Interview

"As illustrators, our primary aim has been to communicate with people. We need an extensive background, so we become repositories of knowledge," said Joe Krush, summarizing his work and that of his wife and partner, Beth Krush.

Joe and Beth Krush are best known for their collaborative illustrations in more than 150 books, mainly for children. Most of their fame comes from their drawings in the U.S. editions of the *Borrowers* series, published by Harcourt in 1953:

> Editor Margaret McElderry gave us our most famous assignment. It was to illustrate five books in the American edition of a series starting with *The Borrowers*. This is a children's classic by British author, Mary Norton. The tiny characters, Pod, Homily, and their daughter, Arrietty Clock, live in a miniature world under a grandfather clock. They use an empty spool as a chair and a postage stamp as a portrait. They never steal, only "borrow" from the big house.

Joe and Beth Krush's success as a team is partially due to their varied backgrounds. Joe, who was born on May 11, 1918, in Camden, New Jersey, traces his roots to Polish grandparents who immigrated to the coal mines of Shenandoah, Pennsylvania. He spoke about his father, who knew those mines well.

My father, a Renaissance man, worked as a "breaker boy" in the coal mines when he was only eleven, apprenticed as a tinsmith, and even played brass instruments and the violin as a uniformed bandleader.

In the couple's home in Wayne, Pennsylvania, Joe referred to shelves in the living room that he built for old relics: "In this cubicle, I put Grandfather's planer, a reminder of his woodworking days, and Dad's calipers to recall his machinist trade." Beth hung the powder horn that belonged to one of her ancestors, an American Revolutionary War soldier, and a belt buckle that had belonged to a recruit in the War of 1812. She also displayed her grandfather's 1834 tailor's ledger and her family's key-wound Civil War watch.

Beth, whose maiden name is Henninger, was born on March 31, 1918, in Washington, D.C. She remembered visiting national exhibits and drawing what she saw:

At the Smithsonian, my grandmother would place herself on a bench facing a mammoth painting of the Grand Canyon and let me roam for hours among the dinosaur bones and wax Indians. I always loved to draw, and my hometown supplied me with subject material.

Beth's family moved to Wilkes-Barre, Pennsylvania, when her father, a General Electric lighting engineer, was transferred there to improve mine illumination. Her father agreed to pay for one extra-curricular activity for his thirteen-year-old daughter. She chose to learn from a local artist, James Rutter. "After four years of instruction in portrait painting with oils, I'm good at capturing a likeness," she said.

The couple met at the Philadelphia Museum School of Art. Beth recalled, "This nonacademic institution had great art instructors, like Mary Sweeney, our first-year drawing teacher, a spiritual person, who had us sketch from casts and life models." Beth added, "Art school was a joy after years of being sent to the office for drawing in study hall. I won the girls' prize for illustration and Joe, the boys' award. We also won an assortment of other prizes for watercolor, graphics, and drawing."

Joe recalled:

We students got Benton Spruance to teach a lithography class. And Henry Pitz, a master at drawing trees, was our illustration teacher. Pitz knew Howard Pyle's work. That's why we felt we were descendants of the Brandywine Tradition.

When art school was over, I did free-lance art before enlisting as a World War II private. The army sent me to Engineer's School, and eventually, I ended four years of service as a captain in the Office of Strategic Services [OSS].

> I was among artists, writers, and movie folk working in OSS for the Presentation Department. We were assigned as a secretariat to do all the artwork for the United Nations Conference on International Organization in San Francisco. I did the original drawings for the United Nations seal, which had the U.S. in the foreground. In Nürnberg, Presentation Department members designed the courtroom and arranged for simultaneous translation. We also did the charts showing Nazi bureaucratization. Our office was adjacent to the courtroom, so we could see Göring, Hess, and others on trial.

Beth also remembered the war and the period that followed:

> We opened our first joint studio in Camden. . . . We didn't intend to work together. I drew for children's magazines, and Joe illustrated album covers for RCA. Then we started to help each other meet deadlines, and clients liked the results. Our first job together was to illustrate Courtis-Watter's *Golden Dictionary for Young Readers* [Western, 1965].
>
> When we work together, we discuss staging and incidents to illustrate. Joe does the first composition and perspective sketch. I rework it, adding plants, animals, and people, looking up costumes and interiors. Often, Joe does the final rendering in his own decorative line.
>
> By teaming, we can do the work of three people. I love to research and draw three-dimensional persons or animals. Joe is better with sports, machinery, and lettering. We mainly do line drawings.

In illustrating an approved story, Joe first packs a portfolio with sample pictures to show a publisher's art director. When Harcourt's art director assigned them to illustrate Elizabeth Cooper's *The Fish from Japan* (Harcourt, 1996), Joe arranged the story's words in a galley proof. In a hardbound dummy, the pair distributed the words with a draft of intended art. Later, they received a long press sheet with their printed art which, when folded and cut, produced a finished picture book.

Among the books the couple illustrated for children are Virginia Sorenson's *Miracles on Maple Hill* (Harcourt, 1956), a 1957 Newbery Medal winner; and Beverly Cleary's books published by Morrow: *Fifteen* (1956), *Jean and Johnny* (1959), *Emily's Runaway Imagination* (1961), and *Sister of the Bride* (1963). They also illustrated independently, Beth doing Sally Scott's books, such as *Judy's Summer Adventure* (Harcourt, 1960), and Joe doing Carl Sandburg's *Prairie Town Boy* (Harcourt, 1955).

One of the couple's main joint projects has been renovating their home. In time, it became their studio as well as living quarters. Handyman Joe discussed this undertaking:

> In 1948, we finally found an old, derelict Victorian summerhouse that was built in 1892. It was on two and a half acres atop a hill. The property was called *Kenjockety,* a Native American word meaning "Beyond the Multitude."

I did repairs for about twelve months before we occupied, and many years later, I'm still shoring up and redesigning. When we first moved in 1949, Beth and I ice skated in winter and swam in summer at Martin's Dam across the road. We're lifelong members of the dam's Philadelphia Skating Club and Humane Society, founded in 1718.

Upstairs in this welcoming setting, the couple illustrated such books as John Langstaff's *The Swapping Boy* (Harcourt, 1960) while raising Jay, their red-headed son. Jay was a boy when Langstaff, who was compiling folk music, visited the family home. Langstaff dedicated *Ol' Dan Tucker* (Harcourt, 1963), which Joe Krush illustrated, "For Jay, who knows the beauty of the soar and dip of a toy glider in the air and who let his father leave their model airplane construction long enough to draw these pictures!"

In high school, Jay created a tuba sonata for a sixty-five-piece band. He graduated as a composition major from Eastman School of Music, and he received a master's degree in performance from Northwestern University.

Musical instruments also interest Joe, who rebuilt two violins. He has other interests as well: "I have my ham radio license and build radio-controlled airplanes and boats." He also constructs and flies indoor model airplanes, powered by rubber bands.

UPDATE

In 1996, Joe and Beth Krush updated their earlier interview. He said, "We were paid a flat fee of only $500 in 1953 for illustrating the first *Borrowers* trade book but that went up to $5,000 in 1982 for the last one."

Beth Krush commented:

> Harcourt released the *Borrowers* books in the United States from 1953 until 1982. In that thirty-year span, we communicated with Mary Norton only once.
>
> When our *Borrowers* work was ending, Norton sent a single letter saying she liked our drawings but some things in them were a little too fancy for Homily (the mother) to make. If Norton had told us earlier, we would have gladly arranged changes. I've noticed our counterpart in England, Diana Stanley, drew sparse pictures. Anyway, our art often gets some credit for the American edition's popularity.

In time, Jay, the couple's son, illustrated a juvenile collection of science fiction stories, *Creatures of the Cosmos*, edited by Catherine Cook De Camp (Westminster Press, 1977).

Joe and Beth Krush have taught illustration with the same excitement that inspires their hobbies. Joe instructed mainly at the Philadelphia College of

Art. Beth taught at Moore College of Art and directed their illustration department for twelve years. She also taught a special course, Illustrating for Children.

The couple won the 1980 Drexel Citation from Drexel University and the Free Library of Philadelphia for their contributions to children's literature.

John Langstaff, folksong compiler (1920–)

1978 Interview

John Langstaff, while not an author or illustrator, has played a large role in the field of children's literature. His specialty is compiling that which is already created: in this instance, folk songs. Langstaff, who has compiled at least twenty-five folk-song collections, spoke about his contribution to traditional literature:

> My work differs from most authors because I'm a compiler from many sources and use exactly what I find. In picture books and song collections, I introduce sung stories or traditional literature: adult songs that they pass on to their children. These don't include alphabet songs written especially for children. Ballads are my favorite traditional literature since they're easy to illustrate.

A good example of a ballad is *Frog Went A-Courtin'* (Harcourt, 1955), about a mouse who accepts a frog's wedding proposal, plans the event, and then greets animal guests before the surprise ending. Langstaff explained that, more than four hundred years ago in Scotland, adults told or sang the tale to children. Travelers brought the song to the United States, where children added new verses and sometimes changed the tune. Langstaff studied fifty to sixty variants to choose just one, the melody from the southern Appalachian Mountains. He explained, "When there is more than one variant, I pick the verses that appeal most to children. For *Frog Went A-Courtin'*, I chose a happy ending from Michigan. Usually, the endings are sad."

Feodor Rojankovsky, the 1956 Caldecott winner, colorfully illustrated *Frog Went A-Courtin'*. Langstaff spoke about Rojankovsky and their joint project:

> I didn't know him well. He loved music and played the balalaika. No one drew insects as well as he. My Russian wasn't much, and he didn't speak English too well. As an example, he illustrated the line, "She (the old gray goose) picked up her fiddle and she cut loose!" What he showed was a broken violin string. I caught that error when it was too late.

Langstaff's life has been filled with music, right from the start. He was born in New York City on Christmas Eve 1920, after his parents had led carolers through their Brooklyn Heights neighborhood. At home, his parents entertained singers of carols, madrigals, Bach chorales, and Gilbert & Sullivan.

Langstaff sang his way through childhood. "I did a lot of singing at home with my mother," he recalled. He began his professional life as a boy soprano with the Bretton Woods Boy Singers. "I was given a free education and a lot of training," he recalled. "Later, I wound up in Philadelphia, came to Curtis Institute of Music, and sang at churches to pay expenses." He attended Curtis (1941–1942), Juilliard (1947–1951), and Columbia University (1949–1953). Between his years at Curtis and Juilliard, he served in the U.S. Army Infantry in World War II. He became a first lieutenant and received both the Purple Heart and Gold Star.

As an acclaimed music educator, he led music departments, first at Potomac School in Washington, D.C., and then at Shady Hill School in Cambridge, Massachusetts, spending about fifteen years at each place. He went on to teach music at various colleges.

Langstaff has performed in recitals, concerts, and operas throughout the United States and overseas. He has performed with the New York Philharmonic as well as with the Montreal, National, and Minneapolis symphonies. His media opportunities have been unusual:

- He was host/narrator on "The Lively Art of Picture Books." He gives credit for this popular Weston Woods film to Mort Schindel.

- On an RCA Victor recording for children called "Hello World!" with the Little Orchestra Society, "I did my part, Eleanor Roosevelt played her role, and we never did meet," he said.
- He did a weekly television series entitled "Children Explore Books," on NBC in 1966. He explained, "We taped two programs for fifty-two weeks: pirate stories, and animal or family tales. I read a portion of a book to children, leaving off at a 'cliff-hanger.' They finished reading the book before the next session and, without rehearsing, discussed reactions."
- Also in 1966, NBC-TV invited Langstaff to host a Christmas Eve special, "A Christmas Masque," similar to Christmas Revels. Young Dustin Hoffman acted as the dragon in the mummer's play, "Saint George and the Dragon."
- While performing in Europe, Langstaff accepted a BBC offer to do London "recording sessions, having children sing with me. This led to *Making Music*, a two-month program for six years in which I sang with fifty or sixty children [in a studio], the very thing I tried to start in the United States. The children studied words and notation with me."

Additional recordings for children by Langstaff include: *Singing Games for Children* (His Master's Voice), *American Ballads and Folk Songs* (Tradition), and *Contemporary Ballad Poetry* (Jupiter).

Langstaff has promoted traditional literature with broad audiences and in his own home. Carol, his daughter from his first marriage, is a singer who accompanies herself on a dulcimer. She is also a dancer who has studied with Martha Graham, and an actress. Langstaff dedicated *Frog Went A-Courtin'* to "my Carol, who was the first to give me the fun of singing with children."

Langstaff's second wife, Nancy, is a singer, teacher, and mother of three other Langstaff children: John, Peter, and Deborah. Langstaff dedicated *Hi! Ho! The Rattlin' Bog and Other Folk Songs for Group Singing* (Harcourt, 1969) to child singers, fellow instructors, and his wife, Nancy, "who is both teacher and collaborator."

Carol Langstaff is listed as John Langstaff's coauthor on *Shimmy Shimmy Coke-Ca-Pop! A Collection of City Children's Street Games and Rhymes* (Doubleday, 1973). The book shows how children, aged five to eleven, enjoy aspects of oral tradition. Captured on camera and tape recorder, the subjects were on the sidewalks, stoops, and doorways in Boston, Roxbury, and Cambridge, Massachusetts, and New York City. The book's introduction explains how current games may be tied to past customs.

Jumping rope, an ancient game, began after spring planting when people believed that crops would grow only as high as people could jump. In

Greece, vines took the place of rope, and the Chinese made their "rope" from rubber bands. When Langstaff was compiling the *Shimmy* book, he said, "I was surprised to find how widespread some jump rope rhymes are in this country. In Rapid City, South Dakota, I heard Sioux Indians chanting this same rhyme that I heard in Boston:

Cinderella, dressed in yella
Went downtown to see her fella.
On the way, her girdle busted.
How many fellas were disgusted?
One, two, three, four, five, six!

"Ol' Dan Tucker" has been passed from child to child since the 1800s. Still sung by city children, this favorite song of Abraham Lincoln was composed by the American minstrel showman, Dan Emmett. Langstaff compiled *Ol' Dan Tucker* (Harcourt, 1963) with Joe Krush's jaunty illustrations. Langstaff accepted children's additions to nonsensical "Ol' Dan Tucker," such as:

He combed his hair with a wagon wheel
And had a toothache in his heel.

Urban, suburban, and rural children alike enjoy singing animal rounds, like those in Langstaff's *Sweetly Sings the Donkey* (Atheneum, 1976). He described how to sing the rounds in two, three, or four parts. He suggested recorders and other instruments for accompaniment. Beyond the title song, the book contains notation and words for "The Woodchuck," "Pussycat, Pussycat," and ten other tunes.

Langstaff offered a single song in the book *Soldier, Soldier, Won't You Marry Me?* (Doubleday, 1972). A young girl sings her request for marriage to an armed, musical soldier, but he sings excuses that he needs a different item of clothing per verse, such as a hat, shirt, coat, tie, boots, and gloves. After she buys them, he admits that he can't marry because he has a wife at home.

More ambitious is Langstaff's *Hi! Ho! The Rattlin' Bog and Other Folk Songs for Group Singing* (Harcourt, 1969). Intended for children aged eight to fourteen, the collection has songs from oral tradition and out-of-print books. These include sea chanteys and other work songs; lullabies; question-and-answer songs; folk hymns; counting and riddle songs; jig tunes; historical, dance, ghost, and calypso songs; narrative ballads; laments; multiple-part songs; and chorus songs to be led by a single voice. The songs may be sung with piano or guitar accompaniment. The title song is an old Irish variant of a popular song in Europe, Canada, and the United States. The song begins with a tree to which, in separate verses, is added a limb, branch, nest, egg, and bird.

Langstaff has long been identified with traditional Christmas music. His book *The Season for Singing, American Christmas Songs and Carols* (Doubleday, 1974) reveals that early colonial settlers could not celebrate Christmas with caroling. The Reformation and Puritan suppression drove carols underground, but after the Revolutionary War, Christmas music became evident. Carols that originated in the United States include "It Came upon a Midnight Clear," "O Little Town of Bethlehem," and "We Three Kings of Orient Are." "*Los Reyes de Oriente*" is the Spanish version of the last song, and it appears with "*Aguinaldo*" as Puerto Rican carols. The "Huron Indian Carol" is among other offerings.

Early in his career, Langstaff issued carols in *On Christmas Day in the Morning* (Harcourt, 1959). Langstaff dedicated the book: "For my mother and father who gave us, as little children, the joys of singing Christmas music together as a family." In addition to the title song, he offered three carols adopted in this country from abroad: "Dame, Get Up and Bake Your Pies," "I Saw Three Ships," and "The Friendly Beasts." He wrote that in France, people used to sing the last song while riding to church on a real donkey. Singers may dance to the carols or pantomime them as mummers did generations ago.

In another book, Langstaff offers an old mummer's play, *Saint George and the Dragon* (Atheneum, 1973). The players, known as "mummers," perform standing in a semicircle in simple disguise, like a paper costume. They used to travel and perform in farmyards with carolers. In the play, a dragon kills the champion, Saint George, and the Fool revives him, symbolizing life's triumph over death, light over dark, and spring over winter.

In Cambridge, Langstaff and his daughter, Carol, promote community theatrical productions, the Revels, for families (including children). They sing traditional songs and celebrate the winter solstice, the spring harvest, and the sea. His first successful Revels program was in 1958 in Washington, D.C., when he used traditional and medieval music, dance and drama for a show involving audience singing and dancing with the cast.

Since 1974, Revels, Inc., a nonprofit organization, has expanded across the country. Revels is based on Langstaff's philosophy that there is a commonality among diverse people that includes a need for connectedness and celebration, mainly through musical participation.

Among other efforts, Langstaff has directed and mounted operas for children. These include Benjamin Britten's "Noye's Fludde," Richard Rodney Bennett's "The Midnight Thief," and the medieval "Play of Daniel." Langstaff promotes Youth Audiences, which enables talented persons to perform in schools. He is also on the governing board of the Country Dance Society of America, and is the founder and director of the Folk Song Society.

UPDATE

Reflecting Langstaff's interest in the Revels are several of his latest compilations: *The Christmas Revels Songbook* (Godine, 1985) and *Sally Go Round the Moon and Other Revels, Song, and Singing Games for Young Children* (Revels Publications, 1986).

Langstaff compiled a multicultural juvenile book, *What a Morning! The Christmas Story in Black Spirituals* (Macmillan, 1987). He selected and edited a 1991 juvenile book, *Climbing Jacob's Ladder: Heroes of the Bible in African-American Spirituals* (Maxwell-Macmillan, 1991), illustrated by Ashley Bryan with piano arrangements by John Andrew Ross. This work, a Margaret K. McElderry Book, consists of illustrated musical scores by a dynamic interracial team.

Madeleine L'Engle, author (1918–)

1970 Interview

Photograph by James Phillips

"Never look at the stars and yawn!" proclaimed Madeleine L'Engle, once an actress with Gypsy Rose Lee's dimensions. Her science fiction books for young readers, many of which have received awards, are proof that the author follows her own advice. *A Wrinkle in Time* (Farrar, Straus & Giroux, 1962) won the 1963 Newbery Medal, and it was a Hans Christian Andersen Award runner-up in 1964. It also won the Lewis Carroll Shelf Award and the Sequoyah Children's Book Award in Oklahoma.

Madeleine L'Engle Camp was born on November 29, 1918. Her father, Charles Wadsworth Camp, was a foreign correspondent and author, and her mother, Madeleine Barnett Camp, was a pianist. Her father did not see the baby until she was six months old because he was serving overseas in World War I. Mustard gas, used in the fighting, ruined his lungs. After the war, her father became a music and drama critic, so her parents were busy at night. Their only child ate her supper happily in her room with a book for company.

Madeleine was reading and writing before she entered first grade and enjoyed her first three years in a small private school. During fourth to seventh grades, she attended a girls' private school that emphasized sports. Teachers assumed that because she was a poor athlete, she was dull. At home she wrote stories, drew pictures, and took piano lessons.

In eighth grade, she went to another New York private school. Her homeroom teacher was Margaret Clapp, who later became president of Wellesley

College. In the spring term, her father suffered from the city's air quality, so the family moved to an old chateau in the French Alps. She enrolled in an English boarding school in Switzerland where teachers considered her stupid and gave her a pair of black, laced gym shoes, one with a raised sole to compensate for her slightly shorter left leg. She secretly buried the uncomfortable shoes in the snow.

When she was fourteen, she began four happy years at Ashley Hall in Charleston, South Carolina. She acted in Shakespeare's *Twelfth Night,* and her sophomore class chose her as president. She went to Smith College, and after graduation moved back to New York City, hoping for a theatrical career. She auditioned before Eva LeGallienne, Margaret Webster, and Joseph Schildkraut and became a Broadway understudy. While acting, she wrote her first book, *The Small Rain: A Novel* (Vanguard, 1945) about her Swiss boarding school. She put L'Engle on her byline, not her surname, Camp, since she didn't want to benefit from her father's recognized name as a writer.

The next autumn, while she was general understudy for Chekhov's *Cherry Orchard,* she met actor Hugh Franklin. They married in 1946, and in the next year bought a 1770 farmhouse, which they called Crosswicks, near Goshen, Connecticut. Their daughter Josephine was born in 1948, son Bion in 1952, and in 1956, they adopted Maria, a seven-year-old daughter of close friends who had died. They lived full time at Crosswicks, and they ran Goshen's general store.

In her "Austin Family" books, L'Engle wrote about her own family in an idealized manner, with the fictitious household headed by a country doctor. The series begins chronologically with *Twenty-four Days Before Christmas* (Farrar, Straus & Giroux, 1964). The Austin children are John, ten, Vicky, seven, and Susan, four. Every night in December, they decorate or cook for Christmas. A Christmas Eve blizzard prevents car travel, but Dr. Austin in snowshoes returns from the hospital in time to deliver his son, Rob.

L'Engle's *Meet the Austins* (Vanguard, 1960), an ALA Notable Book, is next in the series's sequence though written first. Starting with this book, the series's narrator is Vicky, now aged twelve. The family invites the orphaned daughter of a friend to their home in a small New England town. L'Engle shared problems in getting *Meet the Austins* published:

> I went through a whole decade when I couldn't sell anything because, believe it or not, I was too realistic. It [*Meet the Austins*] begins with a death, and at that time, children were not to allow that death exists. Well, death does exist. Toynbee said, "We're a sick society because we're afraid to accept death and infinity." Children are far more realistic about it than grown-ups.

In 1959, the Franklins sold their Connecticut store. They took their children on a ten-week camping trip that ended when Hugh Franklin decided to be in a new Broadway play. The family spent summers at Crosswicks but moved back to New York City where Hugh eventually starred as Dr. Charles Tyler in the television program "All My Children." L'Engle was a school librarian and continued writing, her primary occupation. The 1959 camping trip became the basis for the "Austin Family" book, *The Moon by Night* (Farrar, Straus & Giroux, 1963), which won an Austrian State Literary Prize in 1969. The four Austin children are not happy about leaving their large house and moving to a New York City apartment.

In *The Young Unicorns* (Farrar, Straus & Giroux, 1968), Dr. Austin is working for a year on a research project. The family's apartment is above that of a blind twelve-year-old violinist, Emily Gregory. Her seventeen-year-old reader, Josiah ("Dave") Davidson, previously belonged to a street gang whose members want to kill Dave, Emily, and the Austins. L'Engle's book title shows she identified intended victims as young unicorns:

> The unicorn is my symbol of the structure that liberates. It cannot be coerced into being tamed. . . . One of my themes is the particular versus the general. You are particular persons or we're lost!
>
> A summer ago, I was paying a grocery bill with an old check that didn't have the cybernetic salad in the bottom left-hand corner. The check bounced. . . . At Christmas, a friend, Dan, bought something for me . . . and I went to pay him back. . . . When I pulled out one of those old checks, he protested. I asked, "Dan, do you mean my name means absolutely nothing?"
>
> He answered, "Yes."
>
> It was a perfectly awful gray, windy day. I said, "I feel like Emily Bronte today." I took out a check with that magnetic salad on the left-hand side and signed on the right-hand side: Emily Bronte. . . . I now have cancelled checks signed Emily Bronte, Jane Austen, and Elizabeth Barrett Browning.
>
> I think this is really what I am writing about. It is to save each individual human being who is valuable, not as a member of a group or a cause or a party. In art in general, you don't write about general characters but about particular persons.

Canon Tallis, a character who fights evil in *The Young Unicorns*, played that same role in *The Arm of the Starfish* (Farrar, Straus & Giroux, 1965). The book's title refers to Dr. O'Keefe's research in Portugal: taking nerve rings around a starfish's mouth and transplanting them to create a new starfish. O'Keefe regenerated a finger of a girl who had been bitten by a shark. Canon Tallis realizes that regeneration can be abused. Tallis's allies include Joshua Archer from the U.S. Embassy and Rabbi Pinhas. Sixteen-year-old Adam Eddington, Dr. O'Keefe's summer helper, learns who is trustworthy in Portugal, but only after Joshua's death. L'Engle discusses Joshua and the models for two of her characters:

> In *The Arm of the Starfish*, Adam wakes up in the Ritz Hotel in Lisbon. Sitting calmly and watching him in his room is a young man named Joshua. I had no idea why Joshua was there. He made me rewrite the entire book. It's a better book because of him, but I cannot possibly explain why he was there.
>
> My son has never forgiven me for Joshua's death. In fact, it was a long time before he would read anything else that I wrote. I said, "I didn't want Joshua to die either. It just happened."
>
> I never deliberately write about anybody that I know because then you're limited by that person. There are two exceptions. One is the Rob Austin character. That is our youngest child. I simply could not keep him out. The other is the Canon Tallis character in both *Starfish* and *The Young Unicorns*. I certainly had no intention of allowing him in the book.

The Canon Tallis character is based on Canon Edward West, an Episcopal priest in New York City's Cathedral of St. John the Divine, where L'Engle is writer-in-residence. One holiday season, when L'Engle was helping children rehearse for the Christmas pageant, West complained about the children's noise. L'Engle explained that the performance was the only holiday experience for many nonchurch members in the cast. This conversation led to a deep friendship between West and L'Engle.

As for the use of composite characters, L'Engle explained:

> I don't think I can wholly make up a character. I'm drawing on all the people I've ever met. There's always got to be one character with whom I particularly identify. When a book's in first person, that's me. I'm Vicky in *Meet the Austins*. I'm Meg in *A Wrinkle in Time*. In *Starfish*, I identify with Adam and Poly, but it's usually someone awkward, clumsy, and a very slow developer.

L'Engle's realistic novels may be overshadowed by her science fiction, the most popular being *A Wrinkle in Time*. When she wrote it in 1959, a female protagonist was rare in this genre. Its release ended a decade during which no publisher bought her books. L'Engle was depressed as she told why more than thirty publishers in a two-year period didn't accept this book:

> *A Wrinkle in Time* was rejected for two reasons mainly. Quite a few publishers didn't know whether it was for children or grown-ups. It dealt too overtly with the problem of evil in the world. Well, there is evil, and we've got to fight it. If you protect children entirely from death, evil, and people who hate and would

like to hurt them, they have no weapons. They're going to grow up incapable of loving. You cannot love truly, maturely in an unreal world. . . .

L'Engle, who suffered from her book's rejections, took *A Wrinkle in Time* from her agent and gave it to John Farrar of Farrar, Straus. He bought it, not expecting many sales.

A Wrinkle in Time is the story of twelve-year-old Meg Murry who, helped by her young brother, Charles Wallace, and a high school friend, Calvin O'Keefe, uses time travel and extrasensory perception to rescue her physicist father. Her father is doing secret governmental work on *tesseracts,* or wrinkles in time. Three supernatural guardians help the children *tesser* to the planet Camazotz, where an evil brain called IT has imprisoned Meg's father. Here, in front of identical houses, children play with identical rhythm. Sacrificing individuality, the people let IT think for them. Meg breaks IT's spell over her brother by saying that being "alike" and "equal" are not the same.

L'Engle sees Madison Avenue as a counterpart of IT:

Madison Avenue is my scapegoat. I'm frankly convinced that it's run by the powers of darkness. He sits behind his great desk with his horns and his tail, planning the whole thing. Madison Avenue wants you to buy the product. The less particular you are, the less you're able to think for yourself, the more of the product you'll buy.

Madison Avenue has taken the four-letter word, "love," and made it into a three-letter word, "sex." If two men like each other, they're "fags." If two women like each other, they're "lesbians." We're losing friendship. Friendship is a thing that happens between two people who get excited together, eat meals together, or sit in silence together. It's what makes the world go round!

In her 1963 Newbery Award acceptance speech, L'Engle said that Frederic Melcher, originator of Newbery/Caldecott Awards, in one of his last letters, wrote her that he was excited about *A Wrinkle in Time.*

L'Engle is best known for themes in her books:

Many of us repeat our themes. You can always tell a fugue by Bach or a concerto by Rachmaninoff. One of my favorites is emphasis on friendship/love. . . . Without my friends, I couldn't exist because they drag me through everything. If you say to somebody, "I'm willing to be your friend," then you open yourself. You're vulnerable. You can be stabbed. If you won't be a friend, no one can hurt you. . . . You can either be destroyed as a person or you lick your wounds. You pull yourself back on your feet again.

This is one thing young people write me about. I think they're sick and tired of our scrambling for security. They're willing to be vulnerable. They say, "Take me!" That does mean you're going to get hurt. There isn't any way out of it.

L'Engle refuses to be crestfallen about her surroundings. She believes strongly that books for young children should not be depressing:

I don't want to be sentimental because sentimentality always involves lying. It's not quite truthful. Even when you look at all the very, very bad things, as long as a baby is born who can laugh or if I went to bed furious with my husband and we made up, that's enough! It's a realistic hope. When you take all hope away, you might as well dig a hole and climb in.

L'Engle's hopeful books have brought her the Regina Medal and the Kerlan Award. Her words have guided children and adults in more than sixty books, including plays and poetry. Her sparkle and insight have inspired readers for more than five decades.

UPDATE

L'Engle's science fiction book, *A Swiftly Tilting Planet* (Farrar, Straus & Giroux, 1978), received the 1980 American Book Award for Paperback Fiction. A realistic fiction prizewinner is the 1981 Newbery Honor Book, *A Ring of Endless Light,* another "Austin Family" book. In 1988, L'Engle received the Margaret A. Edwards Award of the American Library Association, honoring her contributions for more than five decades as a writer for adolescents. Also in 1981, she received the Smith Medal from Smith College.

In 1980, she published *The Anti-Muffins* (Pilgrim Press), a book set early in Vicky Austin's fourteenth year. The title comes from a club the Austin children started, urging peers not to be like other muffins in a pan and to think independently. L'Engle's *Camilla* (Crowell, 1965; Delacorte, 1981) won the Austrian State Literary Prize in 1971.

Adam Eddington, now eighteen and engaged in dolphin research, is a character in an "Austin Family" book, *A Ring of Endless Light* (Farrar, 1980), a 1981 Newbery Honor Book and winner of readers-choice awards in California and Colorado. Narrator Vicky is almost sixteen when the Austins end their New York City stay. Before returning to Thornhill, they visit the New England island home of maternal Grandfather Eaton. John and Adam get summer jobs at a marine biology station.

Madeleine L'Engle and Hugh Franklin celebrated forty years together before he died of cancer. She described their relationship in an adult book, *Two Part Invention: The Story of a Marriage* (Farrar, Straus & Giroux, 1988).

E. B. Lewis, illustrator (1956–)

1999 Interview

For illustrator E. B. Lewis, what he does is not necessarily work—it's more like a passion. He sometimes gives his art students a primer on passion, telling them, "You know, that thing you can sit down and do for hours? That is passion. That emotion is what an artist needs." He said:

> If you bake a cake, you may put in cinnamon or nutmeg, and you will taste your ingredients. The same is true in a painting or illustration. The artist has to put in his emotion, so the viewer will feel it.

Lewis does both book illustrations and fine art. He uses his initials for his work with books, and his full name, Earl Lewis, for his fine art. He said, "I already had a reputation as a fine artist when I became an illustrator. I decided to keep the two separate, so I developed a literary name, E. B. Lewis."

His triumphs include illustrating two Simon & Schuster prizewinners: Gavin Curtis's *The Bat Boy and His Violin* (1998), a 1999 Coretta Scott King Illustration Honor Book, and Jane and Christopher Kurtz's *Fire on the Mountain* (1994), which won a 1997 Parents' Choice Award. His art in Alice Schertle's *Down the Road* (Harcourt, 1995) helped make it an American Library Association Notable Book.

Lewis was born on December 16, 1956, to Charles E. Lewis, an art handler at the Philadelphia Museum of Art, and Earline Lewis, a homemaker. Lewis described his childhood in "a wonderful community," the Frankford section of northeast Philadelphia:

> I like to tell about my formative years, which were not easy for me. I grew up in a household where education was very important. I was the eldest of five children. As a child, I was seeking attention.
>
> When I was in sixth grade, something traumatic happened. During Career Day, there was a doctor, a lawyer, and a fireman on the stage, and as children, we were allowed to raise our hands and ask questions. Little Charlie raised his hand and said that he wanted to be a doctor. He got plenty of attention, so I, the class clown, raised my hand and said, "I want to be a lawyer." I didn't really want to be a lawyer. I just wanted to outdo Charlie. When I spoke, the whole sixth-grade class laughed. I didn't want them to laugh.
>
> My father used to say, "They're laughing *at* you, not *with* you." That day, it rang true.

Lewis's role model was his uncle Bradley, his mother's brother, who urged Lewis to develop artistic traits that are strong in his family. (Another uncle, Lyles Smith, was an artist at the Philadelphia College of Art.) Bradley Smith, a sculptor who lived in Cherry Hill, New Jersey, directed Saturday morning art classes at Temple University before becoming a full-time professor there. For six years, he would drive from New Jersey every Saturday morning to take Lewis to the classes. "From that point on, my life started to change," Lewis said.

Artistic talent extended to one of Lewis's younger siblings, Russell, who received a four-year art scholarship from the Philadelphia Board of Education to the University of Pittsburgh, and it is showing up in the next generation. Lewis's son Aaron, born in 1986, "is talented in art, much better than I was at his age," Lewis said. His son Joshua, born in 1988, "is not as talented, but he loves to paint and draw and to get his hands into paint. I encourage it all." In 1975, after graduating from Frankford High School, Earl Lewis attended Temple University's Tyler School of Art and discovered watercolor as his medium of choice.

> I graduated from Temple's School of Art in 1979, majoring in art education, graphic design, and illustration. Like others, I didn't want to be the starving artist, so I needed something to fall back on, and art education was that thing. . . . When I graduated from Tyler, I was poorly prepared for the job market. For eight years, I taught. . . . I started to paint, positioning myself on the banks of the Schuylkill or Delaware rivers. I painted all up and down ever-changing South Street.

After leaving Tyler, Lewis learned to enjoy teaching and found what would improve his paintings: "In the beginning of my freelance work, I painted too many details. I was looking for an element to diffuse the detail. Fog became that element. I now get up early in the morning to paint, so I can catch the fog."

Since 1985, Lewis's watercolors have been included in esteemed collections, such as the Pew Charitable Trust. He has exhibited in prestigious galleries nationally, including annual one-man art shows at Philadelphia's Richard Rosenfeld Gallery. He is a member and former officer of the Philadelphia Watercolor Club.

Lewis distinguished the difference between being an illustrator and a fine artist:

> I joke that one makes money and the other does not. It's very much like the difference between classical music and jazz. Because of having to satisfy someone else's problem, you don't really get into the emotional side of the illustration. On the same vein, when you look at the illustration, you're not looking at an individual image as you do with fine art. The book represents a complete package of illustrations and, therefore, it becomes an emotional *body of work* as opposed to one particular image.
>
> When I sit down as a painter, I'm thinking how I'm going to solve the philosophical problem that I set up for myself. But as an illustrator, I'm thinking about how I can best invade this piece of text.

Lewis's professional life changed dramatically for the better in the early 1990s, he recalled. For eight years, he had been painting and teaching in Trenton, New Jersey, at a psychiatric hospital. In 1993, *The Artist's Magazine* featured Lewis in a cover story that was noticed by an agent, Jeff Dwyer:

> Dwyer saw the cover and called me to ask if I wanted to illustrate children's books. I said I wasn't interested at all and that I was a fine artist, not an illustrator. . . .
>
> He answered, "I want you to send me some slides of your work and go to a bookstore. Look up the work of Chris Van Allsburg, Jerry Pinkney, and Barry Moser."
>
> I went and found that some of the country's finest art is being done in children's books today. I rushed back to the phone after a week and told Dwyer, "I'm interested."

Dwyer had already taken the liberty of sending Lewis's slides to nine publishers. Within a few weeks, Lewis had contracts with all nine companies.

He started out with five books, the first of which was Jane Kurtz's *Fire on the Mountain*. The cover shows a sister's love for her younger brother. Lewis told how he prepared the book's Ethiopian setting: "I did my research at the Free Library of Philadelphia in the print department and in the stacks, spending weeks on end." To illustrate Jane and Christopher Kurtz's *Only a Pigeon*

(Simon & Schuster, 1997), Lewis traveled to Ethiopia to do sketches. On his trip, he carried five hundred copies of *Fire on the Mountain*. Residents found the earlier pictures so accurate they thought that he had visited their land before doing them.

His life changed again in 1996 when he bought a home in Folsom, New Jersey, that he had wanted for years:

> I fell in love with the house. I'd been looking at it for about twenty years when I passed it to go to my grandparents, who live beyond it. Every time, I would slow down and say, "I love that house!" When it went on the market, I decided to buy it. It's convenient because it's only thirty minutes from Philadelphia. I'm near the shore, and I have an affinity for water. It's a great location!

Lewis named Alice Schertle's *Down the Road* (Harcourt, 1995) among his preferred books:

> I'm often asked about a favorite of my own books. My answer is: "All of them!" But if I really had to pick a favorite, I'd answer, *Down the Road*. It's a wonderful story, not only about a child's getting responsibility but also about how parents react to so-called spilled milk: the dropping of the eggs. . . . It's a book that I hope will stay in print forever. Being a Notable Book may help.

In 1995, Lewis did the art for Doreen Rappaport's *The New King* (Dial). Being a stickler for authenticity, he had a dressmaker fashion the nineteenth-century clothing from Madagascar that his characters wore. Their clothes were based on pictures from the University of Pennsylvania archives.

Lewis has also traveled in the United States to sketch book settings. While doing two Dial books, he went first to New Orleans to capture that city's architecture for Fatima Shaik's *The Jazz of Our Street* (1998). Then he saw Glen Allan, Mississippi, with Clifton Taulbert, author of *Little Cliff and the Porch People* (1999), before illustrating a tale of neighbors contributing to a sweet potato pie:

> I traveled with Clifton Taulbert to get nuances of the Mississippi Delta community. I grew up in Philadelphia, but I spent summers in Maryland with my great-aunt and great-uncle, and I remember having sweet potato pies cooked on a wood-burning stove.

Lewis carefully selects models. For Gavin Curtis's *The Bat Boy and His Violin,* Lewis used his younger son, Joshua, in a baseball suit.

Joshua ended up as the model because the one who was chosen first did not work out. It should have been Joshua all along. He was delighted! . . . *The Bat Boy and His Violin* won a Coretta Scott King Honor Award in Illustration that I did not even know about five years ago since my interest then was in fine art. It's an incredible honor!

Two mid-1999 books Lewis illustrated had African settings. *The Magic Tree* (Morrow) by T. Obinkaram Echewa is about a Nigerian village orphan boy who feeds on the udara tree's magical fruit. *My Rows and Piles of Coins* (Clarion) is by Tololwa M. Mollel, a Tanzanian Canadian, whose *Big Boy* (Clarion, 1995) Lewis had previously illustrated. The 1999 book concerns a boy with insufficient savings to buy a new bicycle.

Lewis dedicated Mollel's second book to the late Dorothy Briley, a Clarion editor in chief, declaring, "Dorothy was one of the first editors who gave me an opportunity to do books. We developed a friendship though I hadn't known her many years. She influenced my life!"

One book Briley assigned Lewis to illustrate was John Steptoe's *Creativity* (Clarion, 1997), about a friendship between a Puerto Rican and an African-American boy. This story came to Lewis after Steptoe died.

Lewis has said that he does not want to restrict the types of books he illustrates. He told how cautious Little, Brown was in offering him the art assignment for Natasha Anastasia Tarpley's *I Love My Hair!* (1998):

I Love My Hair! is a wonderful book. Little, Brown contacted me and said, "We have a story for you that's unlike your other books. It's whimsical. Can you do whimsical?" I thought about it and said, "Why not accept the challenge?" My first image was of the cornrows that turn into a field of corn.

Lewis said, "In the beginning, my books were about African Americans or people of African descent, but I truly want multicultural stories. I don't want to be pigeonholed." He got his chance with the book *Dirt on Their Skirts* (Dial, 1999). It is about a female, all-white baseball league that Philip Wrigley, who owned the Chicago Cubs, began in 1943 to interest baseball fans during World War II when male players were overseas. The Female League ended in 1953.

Lewis, who has a Web page (www.EBLewis.com), is planning to write and illustrate his own future tales. He said, "I like strong human-interest stories. I've turned down a number of submissions but keep the ones that challenge me."

Lewis added, "I've now completed art for twenty-two books. I'm accepting *great* stories and maintain bookings at least four to five years in advance!"

UPDATE

In 2000, Lewis won the Coretta Scott King Honor Award for Illustration for his art in *My Rows and Piles of Coins*. In 2001, he won the Coretta Scott King Honor Award for *Virgie Goes to School with Us Boys,* written by Elizabeth Fitzgerald Howard (Simon & Schuster, 2000).

Richard Lewis, anthologist (1935–)

1970 Interview

Richard Lewis has traveled around the world to collect poetry and prose from boys and girls. His 1966 compilation, *Miracles: Poems by Children of the English-Speaking World*, a 1966 American Library Association Notable Children's Book, and *Journeys: Prose by Children of the English-Speaking World* (1969) are among his juvenile anthologies published by Simon & Schuster. The Library of Congress selected his anthology *In a Spring Garden* (Dial, 1965) among its books of the year in 1965.

Lewis told some of his many findings about children:

> Children are imagists. They want to share what they see outside and inside themselves. Children's art is an initial form of visualization, a way of reading the world. "Languaging" takes place with words, gestures, and visual presentations. . . . As adults, we need answers. Children are sometimes satisfied with just asking questions. . . . I am interested in children's creativity, especially through writing.

Richard Lewis was born in New York City on May 15, 1935. He graduated from Bard College and attended Mannes College of Music. He planned *Miracles* in 1961, when he was working part-time in scattered locations as a children's teacher of literature and creative writing. He has taught at the Poetry Center of Young Men's Hebrew Association in New York City; the Art Center of Northern New Jersey; Manhattan Country School; and New York City's Walden School. In higher education, he instructed adults at the New School for Social Research, Fordham University, Lesley College, Queens College, Rutgers University, and University of Vermont. He was once an assistant to Henry Simon at Simon & Schuster.

At his Saturday classes in New Jersey, Lewis began to collect children's writings, an inspiration for *Miracles*. With UNESCO assistance, Lewis visited schools and creative centers in eighteen countries in 1964. In *Miracles*, he published nearly two hundred out of three thousand English poems submitted by writers, aged five to thirteen, from Australia, Canada, England, India, Ireland, Kenya, New Zealand, Philippines, Uganda, and the United States. The only copyediting Lewis did was correcting spelling.

The companion volume to *Miracles* is *Journeys: Prose by Children of the English-Speaking World*. Again with UNESCO cooperation, Lewis received prose from boys and girls aged four through fourteen. He selected about 140 entries from 4,500 submissions by young writers in Australia, Canada, Ghana, Great Britain, India, Ireland, New Zealand, and the United States.

Though Lewis said he doesn't like to designate favorites, he found particular pleasure with some *Journeys* entries:

- John R. Sullivan, eight, wrote about beginning with no ending. Lewis appreciated what John implies, "There is not always a beginning and an ending. Despite periods, there is no such thing as the end of a thought, just continuity."
- The anthologist said he did not work "with" but "beside" Rick Rothenberg, nine, who wrote that dew "dies in silence." Lewis said, "Rick was probing silence. He was aware of the weight of silence. We were probing silence together."
- John M., ten, of New Zealand offered "Trees," which compares a tree to an octopus. Lewis interpreted, "The tree is a metaphor for life. The prose is not only about a tree but about John M. and us."

The youngest child Lewis cited was Sally-Anne Fryman, seven, from England. Her eight lines are a run-on sentence linked with "and" used nineteen times, prompting Lewis to comment:

At age seven, language is not institutionalized yet. "And" is pivotal. Playing is an extension of "and." Nobody tells a child how to play, but it is necessary for survival. A child discovers language through play, and language is part of playing. If we called school off, maybe we would learn the innate ability to play.

In addition to his anthologies in the English-speaking world from children, Lewis also collects simple poems by adults that children understand. An example is *The Moment of Wonder: A Collection of Chinese and Japanese Poetry* (Dial, 1964). This contains poems by known and unidentified poets, some writing before the first century, with a timeless sense of wonder. They stress fleeting moments, like blossoms gently falling on dark velvet moss.

Haiku (with seventeen syllables in the original Japanese) are the short text for *In a Spring Garden*. Eight haiku are by the Japanese poet Issa. The verses follow a spring day from an early-morning grasshopper to a nighttime firefly. The book appeals to children because animals are the main subjects, and Ezra Jack Keats captures them in handsome colored illustrations. Lewis narrated this book for a Weston Woods film.

Lewis presented *In a Spring Garden* as a wedding gift to Nancy Adams, his first wife. He had met her and an innovative educator, Sylvia Ashton-Warner, when collecting poems and lecturing at Wellington Training College, a New Zealand teacher-training institution. Later, Ashton-Warner became godmother of their daughter, Amanda, whose younger brother is Sasha.

After a divorce, Lewis married Carol Grock; they have a daughter, Sarah.

Lewis continued multicultural publication, arranging for Dial in 1970 to issue his *Still Waters of the Air: Poems by Three Modern Spanish Poets*, Focusing on Juan Ramon Jiménez, 1958 winner of the Nobel Prize for Literature, Federico García Lorca, and Antonio Machado. The book contains Spanish poems on the left page, and on the facing page, English free-verse translations.

Lewis explained the purpose of his anthologies:

One purpose (of the collections from adults) is to see what we gain from other cultures. . . . My anthologies of children's writing show the degree to which human beings possess creative powers and express what's important to them.

In addition to collecting anthologies and teaching, Lewis has participated in radio and television programs about children's literature in the United States and abroad. He has also recorded albums based on his anthologies. Since 1964, he has guided Touchstone Players, a New York City children's theatrical group that presents dramatizations at Lincoln Center Library, Bank Street College of Education, and its main base, Manhattan Country School. The group has worked with the National Theater for the Deaf, which created a full-length production based on material from Lewis's anthologies, *Miracles* and *Journeys*.

Lewis said, "Children probe the unknown with words. I don't believe the child within us dies."

UPDATE

In 1971, Simon & Schuster released Lewis's *I Breathe a New Song, Poems of the Eskimo,* considered to be the first Eskimo anthology. The book's primitive art is by (Jessie) Oonark, a mother of eight children in Canada's Northwest Territories. The book's title reflects that the Eskimo word for "to make poetry" is the same as "to breathe." This book consists of mainly anonymous poems, called "songs."

A treat is Lewis's *All of You Was Singing* (Atheneum, 1991), with colorful, stylized illustrations by Ed Young. It tells the Aztec myth about how music came to Earth.

Joan M. Lexau
(Joan L. Nodset),
author (1929–)

1973 Interview

When Joan Lexau was a young girl, her mother read to her every night. Eventually, Joan learned to read on her own, and her love of literature made her decide to become a writer when she matured. That she did, becoming the author of more than fifty published books, ranging from picture storybooks to material for "middle-aged" children. Along the way she won a few awards, including the Child Study Association's Book Award for Children for *The Trouble with Terry* (Dial, 1962), and an Arkansas Children's Choice Award, named for Charlie Mae Simon, for *Striped Ice Cream* (Lippincott, 1968).

Joan Lexau was born on March 9, 1929, in St. Paul, Minnesota. Possibly her closest ties were with her brother, Henry, now deceased, who was one year older than she. Their father, Ole, who had emigrated from Norway at age seventeen, was a bridge engineer, newspaper book reviewer, and would-be novelist. Her mother, Anne, worked in a factory before she married.

Lexau spent her first few years in Washington, D.C., where her mother took both children to the Library of Congress because she wanted to read St. Paul's newspapers. The library had an original edition of *Alice in Wonderland*. Though the children were young, their mother read them *Alice*, and they loved it.

Lexau was four years old when her parents divorced and her mother took her two children back to the outskirts of St. Paul. Here was room for baseball, tree climbing, and picking wildflowers in the woods. However, reading always had a high priority:

> Mother had great respect for the printed word, an attitude her two children copied. She once read aloud every night from a children's book with a story for each day of the year. I remember realizing that those funny marks on the paper stood for unvarying words. When I asked Mother what one was, she said, "Buttons," and patiently repeated it.
>
> Finally, in one magic evening, I read a whole book, *The Three Billy Goats Gruff*, borrowed from my first-grade library shelf at Horace Mann School. Then I spent most of my free time reading and decided I would become a writer.

One day, Lexau's brother, Henry, took her on the streetcar to the downtown library. "It was the day the whole world opened for me," she exclaimed. From her father, she received books by Grimm, Andersen, Dickens, and Rawlings. They were a treat for the girl, who found school dull, though her marks were good.

After graduating from Central High School, Lexau took philosophy night courses at the College of St. Thomas in St. Paul. She mainly focused on a variety of jobs, from salesclerk to waitress. In her twenties, she moved to New York City to work in publishing.

After being a magazine advertising production manager and a weekly newspaper reporter, she worked in Harper's children's book department. She fulfilled a childhood ambition to become a writer when Dial published her first book, *Olaf Reads* (1961). The book "came about because I read in *Time*'s 'Miscellany Column' about a first grader who was learning to read," she recalled. "He saw a sign that said, 'Pull.' He pulled and set off a fire alarm!"

After *Olaf Reads* was published, Lexau, who had been working at Harper for four years, decided it was time to focus on her own books, rather than edit those by other writers. "I gave up my job and became a full-time writer, which is very risky. I now work seven days a week and even during vacation to support myself."

Once she no longer had to report to work at 9 A.M., Lexau moved to Otisville, New York, about a hundred miles from New York City by commuter rail line:

> I stay in a noon-whistle village of a thousand people. On Saturday nights, we have a penny social. My home is an old parsonage and a church with a pipe organ. I stay in the parsonage and keep references in the church that was a hundred years old in 1949.
>
> In New York City, I raised tomatoes whose vines climbed up my windows from planters. In Otisville, I have a former parking lot to contend with. I'm try-

ing to remove asphalt topping so I can plant outdoors. In Otisville, I'm enjoying photography, swimming, and biking.

To support herself by writing, Lexau knew she would have to be very productive. Harper published several of her 1963 books, including *Who Took the Farmer's Hat* and *Go Away, Dog.* She explained why these books' by-lines do not read "Lexau":

> I used Joan L. Nodset as a pseudonym when I did these books with controlled vocabularies. My Norwegian father had two last names, Lexau and Nodset. When we needed a pen name, both my brother and I used Nodset. My editor suggested if I wrote two books for children of the same age and sent them to different publishers, this would be acceptable as long as the author's name differs.

Lexau has met many writers but credits Else Minarik, author of *Little Bear* (Harper, 1957), for inspiring her to write for beginning readers. A simple Lexau book at this level is *Crocodile and Hen* (Harper, 1964), a folk tale from Bakongo, Africa, that she retold. In the tale, which can be adapted for puppets, Hen prevents Crocodile from eating her by calling him "Brother," and a friendship develops.

Experiences influence Lexau's work: "When I wrote *José's Christmas Secret* [Dial, 1968], I was in a cold apartment. I tried putting a blanket on the window, but it didn't help." *José's Christmas Secret* begins with a bedroom scene on a freezing December night. A family from Puerto Rico is shivering in New York City. José's father dies of pneumonia soon after his wife and young sons arrive. Ten-year-old José, who sleeps with his seven-year-old brother, Tomás, worries that his widowed mother is cold at night with just a cotton blanket. She insists that her boys, whose mattress is on the floor, use two covers made of wool. José gets an after-school job selling Christmas trees and earns money to give his mother a red woolen blanket for the holiday.

Lexau often writes about a fatherless home where money is scarce. After all, that was what the author experienced in her own life:

> When I was growing up, my mother bought a pint of striped ice cream every month. It wasn't that I liked the combination, but each of us had to have chocolate, vanilla, and strawberry. We ate all three, and one of them we really liked.

Striped Ice Cream (Lippincott, 1968) gets its name from a treat served on the eighth birthday of Becky, the youngest in her six-person, African-American family. Becky, who is used to hand-me-down dresses, gets as a birthday surprise a new dress with the colors of striped ice cream. In *José's Christmas Secret,* the father's absence is due to death. In this story, the father left his fine family since he could not find a job. Lexau said that fans still write her about this story, so they don't find it dated.

In 1971, Lexau wrote about divorce in a nonstandard dialectal book, *Me Day* (Dial).

> My parents were divorced, and I had been wanting to write about divorce. I was inspired when Columbia Broadcasting Corporation Records asked me to write a story for one side of a record. The other side would be a song influencing the story. The song assigned to me was "Feeling Groovy," and I played it over and over. CBC cancelled the project, but I got a book out of it.

Lexau often writes about minorities. In *Benjie* (Dial, 1964), an African-American boy, whose grandmother is raising him, stops with her at a bakery after church. Granny loses her valued earring there, and Benjie finds it in the trash. In a sequel, *Benjie on His Own* (Dial, 1970), the boy is even more heroic when Granny is ill at home, and neighbors respond to his pleas for help.

One of Lexau's best-known books for the intermediate grades is *The Trouble with Terry* (Dial, 1962), winner of the Children's Book Award of the Child Study Association of America. This realistic fiction is roughly based on Lexau's childhood but set in Mississippi. It tells about sibling rivalry between Terry and her older brother, Tommy.

Lexau said her childhood memories of her brother, Henry, are as her champion, not as a competitor:

> Henry made up exciting stories about houses with secret panels and treasure chests, which I and neighborhood children enacted. He also explained strange new concepts to me, such as "abstraction." For most of his life, he read at least one book a day. A finalist on "Quiz Kids," he was very bright, and became managing editor of *The Catholic Digest* in St. Paul. He wound up doing nonfiction, and I, fiction.

Lexau identifies with each of her characters, even animals. In *Millicent's Ghost* (Dial, 1962), she said she identified with both Millicent and the ghost. In writing fiction, Lexau is known for her emotional attachment to poor-but-honest underdogs. She said she borrows another author's words of caution: "When you're writing for children, you have to become a child, and you better be able to get back."

UPDATE

Lexau's dog-training book is *Come! Sit! Stay!* (Franklin Watts, 1984). Also in 1984, she had fun writing two Dial books, *Miss Hap in the Poison Ivy Case* and its sequel, *Miss Hap in the Dogfood Caper.* In 1985, Harper published Lexau's easily read *Don't Be My Valentine,* about two African-American children, Sam and his helper, Amy Lou, in an integrated class. Lexau is proud of the distinguished illustrators who have enhanced her books, such as Aliki, Tomie dePaola, Syd Hoff, and Symeon Shimin.

Lexau's chapter book, *Trouble Will Find You* (Houghton, 1994), a humorous tale about "Diz" Aster and a burglar, was a nominee for the Mystery Writers of America Edgar Award. Her offering for beginning readers on the life cycle of a spider, *The Spider Spins a Web* (Hastings House, 1979), was named an American Library Association Outstanding Science Book. In 1997, Harper reissued *Go Away, Dog.*

In 1995, Lexau's brother, Henry, died. She endured the loss of her only sibling, a "Quiz Kid" applicant, and staunch ally.

Arnold Lobel, author–illustrator (1933–1987)

1973 Interview

Author–illustrator Arnold Lobel smiled as he fingered two of his early Caldecott Honor books: his *Frog and Toad Are Friends* (Harper, 1970) and Cheli Durán Ryan's *Hildilid's Night* (Macmillan, 1971). His illustrations in both picture books merited the honors. A third book, his *Frog and Toad Together* (Harper, 1972), a 1973 Newbery Honor Book, was the first "I Can Read Book" to be recognized for distinguished writing.

> I consider myself an illustrator who also writes. Now I'm a writer with a capital "W." Up until now, I've used my writing as support for my pictures. My editor was telling me, "Now you've got to write a novel."

Though his work is cheerful, Lobel said his background "was rather depressing." Hoping for wealth, his father, a salesman, and his mother, a secretary, went to Los Angeles, where he was born on May 22, 1933. His parents returned with him to Schenectady, New York, and divorced when he was six months old. He was raised by his maternal grandparents, who bought him two pet mice. He enjoyed walking to the public library, picking five books, the maximum allowed, and reading them in the shade of a large tree at home. He was ill during much of third grade and felt isolated from peers until he began to illustrate their stories. Eventually, he ended up studying art at Pratt Institute in New York City. At Pratt, he said, "I did some rather good paintings but decided to specialize in book illustration. I was poor in advertising."

Lobel was directing a Pratt play when he met two fellow students who are now author–illustrators. One was Tomie dePaola, and the other was a Holocaust survivor, Anita Kempler. Following graduation in 1955, Arnold and Anita married and had two children, Adrianne and Adam. Lobel's family struggled in the beginning, living in cramped, low-rent apartments. After doing some advertising, he tried to become an illustrator:

> I went from publisher to publisher with my portfolio. It's often humiliating. I saved Harper for last because it's such a big house. An editor there gave me my first book to illustrate. It was the story of a salmon swimming upstream with sixty-four pages of fish drawings. I don't think she would dare give it to a well-known artist, so she chose this young kid off the street. I nearly fainted. Of course, I was willing to try because I needed the money.
>
> The editor [who later identified herself as Susan Hirschman] asked, "Can you draw a fish?"
>
> I replied, "Of course!" though I'd never drawn a fish in my life. Then I rushed home, drew fish, and got the job.

Lobel lamented how difficult it is for a children's book illustrator to make a living in the beginning:

> Young men or women, who have a family to support, cannot make a living with just one or two books to their credit. They need a backlist. It doesn't happen with children's books, as with adult books, that artists will have an overnight success and make $100,000 on one book.
>
> To build a backlist, it's no good accepting a manuscript you don't respect, because you'll hate the assignment. Sometimes it takes a year to complete, and you'll dread crawling from bed to the drawing table. If you don't like it in the beginning, you'll hate it in the end!

After the fish book, Lobel began to illustrate his own books, thirty-six over the years, and he carefully chose the seventy he illustrated for others. His first original book was *A Zoo for Mister Muster* (Harper, 1962), showing animals leaving their cages to visit Mister Muster, the new assistant zookeeper. Lobel used pen and ink to illustrate his self-written tale and its funny sequel, *A Holiday for Mister Muster* (Harper, 1963). In the sequel, Mister Muster packs a "small" lunch for animals and takes them on a bus to a beach and an amusement park. This book was among *The New York Times* Best Illustrated Books of the Year 1963. Lobel summarized:

> I began *A Zoo for Mister Muster* in 1961. In 1962, '63, and '64, I couldn't look at it because it just seemed terrible to me. Now that it's years later, I look back and

see it has a certain charm about it that I find appealing. If I just live long enough, I'll get to enjoy all of my books again.

Lobel was thrilled with the text for *Hildilid's Night* (Macmillan, 1971), his 1972 Caldecott Honor Book. He rendered magnificent detailed pen-and-ink drawings of an old woman who tries to chase away night and sleeps by day. Black and white is the color scheme until the last three pages when the artist introduced the gold of sunlight. He created a complete first-draft dummy in pencil.

Self-critical Lobel was pleased with his work only after 1970. For books that he wrote and illustrated, he divided his tasks:

> I write first because I'm rather insecure. The pictures are the dessert, so I like to eat the spinach early. . . . The funny parts come easily, but they have sat in my brain for years. They're working in my subconscious level.
>
> I've just written *The Man Who Took the Indoors Out* and *Owl at Home*. I'll illustrate them in a year's time. I'm willing to bet that I won't get any more story ideas until that time has passed. I'm rather like Mother Hubbard. If the cupboard is bare, I can write again.

The Man Who Took the Indoors Out (1974) is a long nonsense poem about Mr. Bellwood Bouse who invites the indoors of his large Victorian house, including sink and stove, to share the outdoors with him. After a year outside, Bouse begs for their return, and they come back, anxious for repairs. Lobel described the book's writing/graphic challenge:

> I like working in verse. I get the same kind of satisfaction from it that someone else would find in doing crossword puzzles. It's quite an elaborate story about a man who decides to ask his furniture out for an airing. Since I'm an Edward Lear fan, I did this in his writing style. It's a graphic effort because there's lots of furniture and architecture. I'll be starting it next month, and I'm bracing myself.

After writing *The Man Who Took the Indoors Out*, Lobel began to conceptualize his book, *Owl at Home* (1975):

> I'm working on a book about an owl who lives at home and is very sedentary. He has contact with things but not another creature. He talks to himself and is quite psychotic.
>
> On successive sheets of tracing paper, I drew the cover of the owl book, beginning with an armchair. I seated the owl in the chair, giving him a robe. I added a table beside the chair with a bowl of pea soup, which is in the story. I added shading to give solidity to the owl. To make him extremely comfortable,

I gave him a footstool. I put a little box around the picture for the cover, adding the title, my name, and an "I Can Read" banner.

These steps are on tracing paper, one atop the other. My whole career rests on the invention of tracing paper. Without it, I could not possibly work.

Editors—including Susan Hirschman, who worked with Lobel at Harper and at Greenwillow—have commented about the high quality of his book dummies that look like "finished art." He enjoys this phase of bookmaking most. Lobel said:

I submit a complete dummy because a picture book is a wedding of story and pictures. I have to see dramatically how the text and pictures work together. Everyone tells me I'm crazy to do such a detailed dummy, but this is part of my insecurity. I want to hurry and get it right.

What's right are Lobel's "Frog and Toad" books. He commented about them:

I don't remember having any experience with frogs and toads in my own childhood, but during a trip to Vermont in the 1960s, my own children would bring frogs and toads into the house. Frogs aren't good in captivity because they won't eat. Toads do, and toads are marvelous pets. Frogs and toads are a good analogy to people: alike in some ways but so different. Incidentally, there's a Frog and Toad Fan Club with membership cards.

The "Frog and Toad" series is part of Harper's "I Can Read" books for beginning readers, limited to black and two colors. I tend to like limited color better than full-color books. I don't use a word list. I have an "I Can Read" mind and use small words in conversation. Book vocabulary is not limited. In *Frog and Toad Together*, I used the word, "avalanche," which couldn't be replaced. It's a good word for children to know.

Each of the "Frog and Toad" books has five short stories. In the first book of the series, *Frog and Toad Are Friends,* Toad is shown as a hibernating creature who wants to end his winter sleep in May. It is April, but Frog merely tears off calendar pages from November through April so he can have Toad's company sooner. This 1970 American Book Award finalist establishes the friendship theme that pervades the series and is so appealing to young readers.

In *Frog and Toad Together,* one tale concerns cookies that Toad shares with Frog. Both eat gluttonously. Frog puts the treat on a high shelf, but he finds he has no willpower to stop eating. Frog finally gives the remaining cookies to hungry birds.

Lobel has created work that departs from the friendship of two creatures, including an "I Can Read Book" such as *Mouse Tails* (Harper, 1972) in which Papa Mouse tells seven tales, one for each of his sons. Particularly humorous is "Very Tall Mouse and Very Short Mouse." The tall mouse sees birds while his friend sees bugs.

The author, remembering mice from his childhood, had bought a single mouse as a pet for his son, Adam, when they lived in a crowded apartment house. Lobel managed to build it an interesting cage with steps, but the monogamous mouse grew fat and lazy. Lobel welcomed mice as a book subject, even drawing Mouse to look like himself.

Different from an I Can Read Book is *On the Day Peter Stuyvesant Sailed into Town* (Harper, 1971), a 1972 Christopher Award winner. It shows Peter Stuyvesant in New Amsterdam complaining about excessive garbage. In poetical form, it traces cleaning and rebuilding a city that Stuyvesant dreams will one day have skyscrapers.

Another distinct early book is *Giant John* (Harper, 1964). Giant brings his mother a bouquet of trees, but she worries since they have no food. He earns gold and returns in time to see his hungry mother eating her shoe. Lobel credited Barbara Borack, his Harper editor at the time, for urging him to correct flaws in that book to make it publishable:

> If a book is in trouble, I stick it in a closet for six months. Then I can see what's wrong and fix it. If I try to change something immediately, it's terrible. I very much want an outside opinion beyond that of my wife and friends. I want an editor to say, "This is good!" or "This is rotten."

Marriage combined the artistic talents of Arnold and Anita Lobel. The two had side-by-side drawing tables in their Brooklyn home's third-floor studio, which was also a lounge for his cat, Orson. The Lobel children are now grown. Adrianne is a set designer in New York City. Adam is a video consultant, photographer, and rock guitarist.

When asked which book gave him the most pleasure, Lobel replied, "You always enjoy the book you're going to be doing *next!*"

UPDATE

In 1977, two Harper editors, Charlotte Zolotow and Pat Allen proposed that Lobel, with a generous advance, do a book on Aesop's fables. After accepting, Lobel studied Aesop's fables and found cruel animals, a far cry from the tenderness of Frog and Toad books. He proposed to write his own fables and did so while housebound with a broken ankle. In full-color paintings, he showed his camel in a tutu and his baboon with a ventilated umbrella. After twenty-one years of artistry, Lobel's original *Fables* brought him the 1981 Caldecott Medal.

In 1982, Anita Lobel won a Caldecott Honor Medal for illustrating her husband's alphabet book, *On Market Street* (Greenwillow, 1981). Her alphabet pictures were similar to drawings she used in a 1977 Children's Book Week poster. The Lobels collaborated for other Greenwillow books. He wrote and she illustrated Greenwillow folktales, such as *How the Rooster Saved the Day* (1977) and *A Treeful of Pigs* (1979), as well as an accumulative tale, *The Rose in My Garden* (1984), an ALA Notable Book.

The Man Who Took the Indoors Out (Harper, 1974) was one of the *New York Times* Best Illustrated Books of the Year. *Owl at Home* (Harper, 1975) became a *Horn Book* Honor Book and was nominated by New Jersey children in 1977 for a Garden State Children's Book Award. *Mouse Tails* was on the *Horn Book* Honor List and won the 1979 Irma Simonton Black Award from Bank Street College of Education.

Lobel published two more Frog and Toad books. *Frog and Toad All Year* (Harper, 1976) finds the amphibious duo in a story for each season. A fifth episode depicts shared friendship at Christmas. The book was a 1977 Christopher Award winner. A funny tale in the fourth book, *Days with Frog and Toad* (Harper, 1979), shows Frog dealing cleverly with an overlarge hat he gives Toad as a birthday present.

For Greenwillow, Arnold Lobel wrote and illustrated *Ming Lo Moves the Mountain* (1982), a folktale about China. From 1983 to 1986, Lobel labored on his last project, *The Random House Book of Mother Goose* (Random House, 1986), 306 nursery rhymes that he selected and illustrated.

In 1985, Arnold Lobel received the University of Southern Mississippi Silver Medallion and in 1986, the Laura Ingalls Wilder Award. Arnold Lobel died on December 4, 1987, in New York City at age fifty-four.

Anita Lobel's *No Pretty Pictures: A Child of War* (Greenwillow, 1998) was a 1998 young people's National Book Award finalist. The book, a Holocaust survivor's tale for readers aged nine to twelve, begins when Anita, barely five years old, faces Nazis in her birthplace, Krakow, Poland, then hides with her younger brother disguised as a girl.

Lois Lowry, author–photographer (1937–)

1990 Interview

When it was time to think about cover art for Lois Lowry's *Number the Stars* (Houghton, 1989), the editors asked the author about how the main character, Annemarie, should look. Lowry handed them a picture of a Swedish child she had photographed, "thinking they would give it to an artist who would be doing a painting." She said, "They preferred my photograph, so I had to get the girl's permission."

Number the Stars also won the 1989 Sidney Taylor Award and in 1990, both the Newbery Medal and the Jewish Book Award. Lowry's *Autumn Street* (Houghton, 1979) was an International Board on Books for Young People Honor Book. *A Summer to Die* (1977) won the 1978 Children's Literature Award of the International Reading Association.

Lowry was born on March 20, 1937, in Honolulu, where her Norwegian father, Robert Hammersberg, was stationed. She reported:

> My father was a career army dentist. When World War II started, he had to go overseas. My mother's family was in Pennsylvania, so we had to travel back there to live in my grandparents' house, and my baby brother was born there. All of that happens in *Autumn Street*, a book I wrote many years later.

In *Autumn Street,* Elizabeth is six and her sister, Jessica, is eight when Gordon, her baby brother, is born at Grandfather's home. Her special friends are an African-American housekeeper, Tatie, and Tatie's grandson, Charles. Lowry spoke about her book, which is largely based on fact:

> The cook/housekeeper was a real person [Fleta Jordan]. . . . Her grandchild was a girl, Gloria. The book was overpopulated by females: my father was gone, and my mother, sister, and I lived with my grandmother. I suddenly realized there are so many girls. I took Gloria and changed her into Charles, but the real little girl was indeed murdered.
>
> That story was autobiographical although the town, Carlisle, was never mentioned. . . . The theme of *Autumn Street* is the loss of innocence. The child has to come to terms with a number of things that really happened. I put them into a smaller time span than actual occurrences, placing them on top of this very innocent child during wartime.

The beautiful prose of *Autumn Street* probes the protagonist's childhood: "When I'm writing, I always think about that kid who lives inside me," Lowry said. "That kid" read before the age of three for two reasons:

> First, before she married, my mother had been a kindergarten teacher, so she was used to small children and books. She was a great reader to my sister and me. My sister was the other reason. When I was three years old, she was six and bringing home her books from school. It was probably my sister who taught me how to read when I was that little.
>
> I went to first grade like other children my age, but I already read well. In those days, they were a little cavalier about saying, "This one knows how to read. Let's put her in another classroom." The next thing I knew, I was in third grade. That means I never learned cursive writing.

The author had close ties with her sister, Helen, who was three years older and was memorialized in Lowry's first book:

> *A Summer to Die* is based on things that actually happened, but it's more fictionalized than *Autumn Street*. My sister . . . died when she was twenty-nine, and I was twenty-six. What I did was keep in mind that I was writing for a particular age group, so I reduced the ages to thirteen and fifteen.

Lowry made use of her knowledge of photography in *A Summer to Die*. She had studied photography in graduate school, thinking it would be an easy way to earn credits. She said, "I loved it, and I was good at it. There was a period of time while writing for magazines that I was a professional photographer. However, I had not been a photographer as a child. I wanted to take that field that I enjoyed and put it into the book."

Lowry tries to have her books appeal to readers in all parts of the country, so she does not always mention exact settings:

> I lived in Maine when I wrote *A Summer to Die*, and I pictured New England. However, I never mentioned the state. The only geographic spot that's mentioned is Portland. You and I know it's Maine, but when a little girl got up to present me the California Young Readers' Medal for this book, she said, "It's set in the northwestern part of the United States," thinking Portland, Oregon. She was so nervous, I didn't jump up and correct her. I thought: *That's okay. It makes the book more generic. It could have happened anywhere.*

An editor encouraged Lowry to write *A Summer to Die*. The author said:

> I had written a short piece in *Redbook* magazine in the winter of 1975 or 1976 . . . about a child and told through the eyes of a child. An editor read that story and contacted me to see if I'd be interested in writing a children's book for Houghton Mifflin. . . . It was so unusual to have an editor approach me and show an interest rather than write a book and start sending it to unknown publishers.
>
> I wrote the story, and they finally agreed to publish it. However, one of the first readers at a lower level hated the story and wrote a report on it that ended with the work, "Yuk!" About five years later, they showed me this first report. Fortunately, other people had read it. They felt terrible because they invited me to write this book. Walter Lorraine is my editor there now.

Lowry's second book, *Find a Stranger, Say Goodbye* (1978), set in Maine, is about seventeen-year-old Natalie Armstrong. As her high school graduation gift, her adoptive parents welcome her search for her birth mother. Natalie learns that a fifteen-year-old unwed student gave birth to her after a one-night tryst with a physician's son, now deceased. Natalie returns home where she discards her biological mother's photograph.

Find a Stranger, Say Goodbye is based on two of Lowry's friends:

> One friend was adopted but had no desire to search for her birth mother. However, another friend, who was adopted when she was five months old, got a letter from her birth mother, a professor in a major university, and met her.
>
> I still get letters from readers who want the story to end in a different way. Many endings were possible.

Anastasia Krupnick (Houghton, 1979) initiated a series that the author has continued. In the initial book, precocious Anastasia is ten years old, has eyeglasses with owl-eyed rims, and lives in Cambridge. Her father is a Harvard literature professor and her mother, a painter. As the book ends, Anastasia names her baby brother, Sam. He is the central figure in at least three books.

Anastasia Again! (Houghton, 1981) won the 1983 American Book Award nomination in the juvenile paperback category, and the New Mexico Readers' Choice Award. Twelve-year-old Anastasia is horrified at her family's decision to move from their city apartment to a suburban house. She changes her mind after she meets neighboring Gertrude Stein; a handsome tennis player, Steve; and those at the Senior Citizens' Drop-in Center.

As the series progresses, Anastasia becomes a teenager who always is embroiled in humorous incidents. Her fans have rewarded her with readers-choice awards in Arkansas, Florida, Indiana, Kentucky, New Jersey, New Mexico, Tennessee, Utah, and Vermont, among other states. Lowry's fan mail comes from many countries and from both boys and girls. The "books have a girl's name on titles, so girls like them, but because they're humorous, boys like them too," she said.

Lowry seems to enjoy writing more than one book about some characters. *Your Move, J.P.!* (Houghton, 1990) introduces twelve-year-old J. P. Tate who, with his ten-year-old sister, Caroline Tate, are scholarship students at a private school. J. P. is lovesick over a student from London, Angela Galsworthy. He can't even concentrate on chess, his obsession. To impress Angela, he pretends to be suffering from a fatal family disease, "framosis," unaware that her father is a genetics specialist. *Your Move, J.P.!* is the prequel to a book that takes place one year later, *The One Hundredth Thing About Caroline* (Houghton, 1985).

In *Switcharound* (Houghton, 1985), Caroline is eleven and J. P. is thirteen when they have a summer visit with their father, Herbie Tate. The father's new family includes a wife, Lillian; a six-year-old son, Poochie; and identical twin girls, Holly and Ivy. Readers-choice awards for *Switcharound* are from Florida, Indiana, Missouri, South Dakota, Tennessee, Texas, Utah, Vermont, and West Virginia.

Equally popular is *Rabble Starkey* (Houghton, 1987), winner of the 1987 *Boston Globe-Horn Book* Award and the 1988 Golden Kite Award, as well as readers-choice awards in Georgia, Indiana, Kentucky, Virginia, and Vermont. This concerns Sweet-Hosanna who runs away, gets married, and has a daughter, Parable, nicknamed "Rabble," when she is fourteen. Lowry expressed her joy in writing *Rabble Starkey*:

> I love the characters. Sweet-Hosanna ran away and married when she was fourteen years old because she liked the fellow's pickup truck. Readers have written me more than once to have Rabble move into Anastasia's neighborhood. That would be interesting, but I have no such plans.
>
> My brother and his wife live in Appalachia, the setting for *Rabble Starkey*. If I say something to my own children, and they don't understand me, they'll question, "I beg your pardon?" My nephews would look at me and ask,

"Ma'am?" It's that slow cadence of speech and basic set of values that we in our fast-paced, sophisticated urban life have lost. I guess that's why I chose to set the book in a small Appalachian town.

Lowry's *Number the Stars* is about ten-year-old Annemarie Johansen and her Jewish friend, Ellen Rosen, in German-occupied Denmark during 1943, and the attempts made to evacuate the country's Jewish residents to Sweden. Lowry discussed her book's title and Resistance heroes:

> The book's title, *Number the Stars*, comes from a Psalm. Of course, Jews had to wear stars during the World War II Nazi regime, but not in Denmark. I modeled one of the characters named Peter after a Resistance leader, a real person who was killed. I saw the graves of such people in Copenhagen.
>
> Because the book was about the relationship of two children, I had the Christian child, whom I named Annemarie, take the Jewish star off of Ellen when Nazis were about to question Ellen, rather than have Ellen do it independently. Purely as a plot device, it adds to tension if one child yanks it off another. . . .
>
> After the book had been printed, my editor cited that maybe I had overused an image of Nazis' high, shiny boots. Then I went to Australia and met a woman who wore the same necklace as on the book's cover, so I asked her about it. She described hiding in Holland when she was two years old. Her Jewish mother had been taken away. Her father was not Jewish. What she recalled was scary boots. On my return, I asked my editor to keep all boot references.

Winning the Newbery Medal was exciting, but Lowry never expected tension connected with a television presentation of her as honoree:

> When the Newbery Committee called me from Chicago in January 1990 to tell me I'd won the Newbery Medal, they asked me to get on a plane that day and go to New York, so I could be on the *Today* television program the next day.
>
> It was snowing outside, but I didn't think about that. I threw some clothes into a suitcase and took the 4 P.M. air shuttle to New York for a supposed one-hour flight. The plane [couldn't land and] circled New York, almost running out of fuel. Finally, it landed on an abandoned airstrip in upstate New York where everyone sat until 11 P.M. I was on this plane for seven hours! . . .To make a long story short, I finally got to my hotel about 2 A.M. They did pick me up [at 6 A.M.], and I got to the *Today* show. While waiting, the studio announced that the space shuttle was going off live, and they had to drop one interview. . . . There I was. There was a French movie actress, and there was a priest, Andrew Greeley, author of sexy novels. Of course, I was the one who got bumped. How could I not?

UPDATE

Lowry did a jacket photograph again for her 1994 Newbery Medal winner, *The Giver* (Houghton, 1993), a futuristic book. The protagonist, Jonas, is in a so-called ideal community without unemployment, war, hunger, prejudice, or turbulent weather. Residents are in a world with no memory, music, color, or love. Elders pick a person's mate and occupation.

With fantasy concluded, Lowry returned to realistic tales. A dog lover, Lowry wrote *Stay! Keeper's Story* (Houghton, 1997), an account of a stray dog's successful search for his frail sister, Wispy. Lowry has written more than twenty-five books for young people, including winners of readers-choice awards in more than fifteen states. She lives with her husband in Cambridge and enjoys her four children, four stepchildren, and their progeny (including dogs).

Patricia MacLachlan, author (1938–)

1989 Interview

Patricia MacLachlan's *Sarah, Plain and Tall* (Harper, 1985) started as a family story about her mother's uncle who had placed an ad for a mail-order bride. It became a best-selling children's book and the 1986 winner of the Newbery Medal, the Scott O'Dell Historical Fiction Award, and the Christopher Award. It was also a Notable Children's Trade Book in the Field of Social Studies, as were two of her other books, *Through Grandpa's Eyes* (Harper, 1980) and *Mama One, Mama Two* (Harper, 1982). Her *Arthur, for the Very First Time* (Harper, 1980) won the 1980 Golden Kite Fiction Award.

In real life, a woman came from Maine to marry the uncle and help raise his children. MacLachlan said:

> My mother loved her. I thought: What a brave and risky thing to do, traveling all the way to the prairie! That's where the story came from. When I decided to write it, my mother was losing her memory to Alzheimer's disease. The reason one writes sometimes is to confront problems. In a way, I was losing my mother. My story is about a family and a mother coming to that family. I was really writing for my mother.

In the book, Sarah Wheaton responds to Jacob Witting's newspaper advertisement for a farmer's wife and mother. She is willing to leave the Maine home she shares with her older brother, William, because he will soon marry. She writes to the Wittings about her cat, Seal, and tells them that she sings.

232

Singing is important to the Witting children. Ten-year-old Anna, the protagonist, remembers her mother singing daily. Caleb can't recall, because his mother died soon after his birth. The Wittings are pleased that Sarah, who says she is "plain and tall," will come for a one-month trial.

MacLachlan cited her Newbery winner's main idea: "The theme is how a family comes about even if the persons are not always blood relatives. I consider some friends to be as dear as family members."

From that prizewinner, MacLachlan gave her favorite sentence:

> My favorite sentence is in a letter from Sarah to the Wittings: "My brother William is a fisherman, and he tells me that when he is in the middle of a fog-bound sea, the water is a color for which there is no name." As a writer, I feel that words are not enough. We cannot hold a world with words. There are spaces and moments in between.

Sarah, Plain and Tall is set in the prairie that the author and her parents knew well:

> My father was born in a sod house in North Dakota where a farm on 2,500 acres is small. My mother grew up in Kansas, and I spent my early years in Wyoming. My father taught school when he was nineteen in a one-room school, riding his horse across the prairie through drifts of snow, getting there early so he could start a fire. . . . When I travel, I carry with me a little bag of prairie dirt with sage to teach me that the place in my books is as important as the people. . . . When I visit the prairie, I feel like I'm home. I've missed the wide, open spaces. It's funny how what we know best stays with us.

Patricia Pritzkau was born on March 3, 1938, in Cheyenne, Wyoming, the only child of Theopolus ("Philo") and Madonna Pritzkau, both teachers. She described how attentive her parents were:

> I did not write in school because my writing did not thrill my teachers. My father had books all over the house, and we acted out stories constantly. It made stories more real than life. . . .
>
> My father came to the University of Connecticut to teach when I was in elementary school, so I grew up in the East. My mother would take me to the library and hold me at the back of my collar on the way home so I could cross streets. I'd read the whole time.

MacLachlan received her bachelor's degree from the University of Connecticut and married a clinical psychologist, Robert ("Bob") MacLachlan in 1962. She taught English at Bennett Junior High in Manchester, Connecticut, from 1963 to 1979. She has lived in Leeds, Massachusetts, for twenty-four years.

Sometimes she is a visiting lecturer in children's literature and does creative writing workshops at Smith College. Her three children include John, a photographer and freelance writer; Jamie, who was a college student majoring in journalism; and Emily, the youngest, who had no career plans then.

MacLachlan has coped with challenges through the years:

> My first book was not published. The mailman and I got to know each other well. If I received a small envelope, I might have had a manuscript accepted. If it were large, my would-be book was being returned.

Pantheon published MacLachlan's picture book, *The Sick Day* (1979), about Emily's father nursing the child's aches and pains. In 1980, Pantheon released *Moon, Stars, Frogs, and Friends* with Tomie dePaola's art. MacLachlan next went to Harper:

> My agent suggested that I send Charlotte Zolotow at Harper my book, *Through Grandpa's Eyes*. It had a certain quality, the young and old together, which Charlotte and I both like. She became my friend and editor ever since.
>
> *Through Grandpa's Eyes* started in response to my father telling me that he was going to sell his house and move closer to the ocean. I thought: *That was my house too,* but I couldn't tell him not to sell. My story's about the people in the house, not just the house. I mention a piece of thinking wood that a nonsighted person could touch. It feels something like a river. I have a piece that I saved.

Through Grandpa's Eyes (Harper, 1980), illustrated by Deborah Kogan Ray, is dedicated, "For my father, Philo, and my son, John, each of whom has taught me to see the world through his eyes." The story shows how young John and his blind grandfather function together. Grandpa and John play their cellos, the boy using music and Grandpa, by memory.

Through Grandpa's Eyes is a "Reading Rainbow" selection. The author gathered information for the book while serving as a board member of a local family agency. That same agency gave her the idea for her 1982 picture book, *Mama One, Mama Two*:

> About a year after I finished that book, I realized I was influenced by my work with a family service agency. I did a series of articles on foster mothers who were wonderful in the love they brought to young children. They were a breed unto themselves! They did a good job, and then the children would be adopted.
>
> When I was little . . . I knew a woman called "Mama Two" by a little boy. This book was the hardest one I ever had to do. The picture books take me the longest to write. People think it's the novels, but in the picture books, the author has to condense, "squish all thinking," as one youngster told me.

Mama One, Mama Two depicts young Maudie's mother (Mama One), so poor and depressed, her social worker, Tom, takes her to a hospital. He drives Maudie to her "for-a-while home" with a kind foster mother, Katherine, who calls herself "Mama Two." Maudie realizes Mama One may return, but until then, Mama Two will be by her side.

Another short book is *Seven Kisses in a Row* (Harper, 1983). When Emma's parents go to an eye doctor's convention, nonconformist Uncle Elliott and pregnant Aunt Evelyn baby-sit for seven-year-old Emma and her big brother, Zachary. Emma teaches the couple to give seven kisses in a row. MacLachlan said:

> *Seven Kisses in a Row* stresses that one can learn from children. My children have taught me a lot. These youngsters try to teach grown relatives how to be good parents. Empowering of children might be the theme, one I often emphasize.

MacLachlan's first novel was *Arthur, for the Very First Time* (1980). Ten-year-old Arthur Rasby suspects his cross mother is pregnant, so he enjoys being with his nonconformist Aunt Elda and Uncle Wrisby. MacLachlan traced Arthur's roots:

> In *Arthur,* my first longer story, I thought my aunt and uncle inspired the grown-ups, but writer Jane Yolen realized it was my parents. Uncle Wrisby's garden of onions and roses was like that of my father who enjoyed the contrast between low roses and tall onions.
>
> *Arthur* has a vignette of Aunt Mag, a mail-order bride. The germ of an idea for a new book often begins in the one before it. My agent, Craig Virden, suggested that a mail-order bride would be good for a book unto itself. This idea developed into *Sarah, Plain and Tall.*

Arthur, for the Very First Time; Sarah, Plain and Tall; and *Unclaimed Treasures* (Harper, 1984) were American Library Association Notable Books. *Unclaimed Treasures,* a 1984 *Boston Globe-Horn Book* honor book, shows eleven-year-old Willa; her twin, Nicolas; her "true love," neighbor Horace; and his unmarried aunts, whom MacLachlan identifies with a special term. "'Unclaimed treasures' are what my mother called unmarried men and women," the author said. "Married or single, you can be 'unclaimed.' You have a life of your own."

Cassie Binegar (Harper, 1982) is named for a fourth grader whose family moved from a large home to a cluttered Maine coastal house. Her father and two older brothers are fishermen, and her mother rents cottages not occupied by relatives. Cassie Binegar longs for orderly space, like her friend Margaret Mary has in a neat home with plastic plants. Cassie complains about her raucous family, but Margaret Mary says that she has only one aunt who wears a tea cozy on her head. Cassie wants to be a writer and secretly hides under a long tablecloth to record conversations.

MacLachlan dedicated *Cassie Binegar*: "For Ann, Dale, and Shulamith— companions through the process." She referred to Ann Turner, Dale Ferguson Cope, and Shulamith Oppenheim, who, along with Jane Yolen, are members of her writer's group. "They very kindly, very gently, criticize each other's work."

MacLachlan dedicated her next book, *The Facts and Fictions of Minna Pratt* (Harper, 1988), "To Nat from Pat." "Nat" is one of her favorite children's authors, Natalie Babbitt, who encourages MacLachlan's writing. *The Facts and Fictions of Minna Pratt*, a 1988 American Library Association Notable Book, again shows a nonconformist, eccentric family, but one that loves music. The author, a cellist who has her vibrato, revealed:

> I started *Minna Pratt* when my daughter and I weren't getting along. My husband said, "You're acting her age, another fifteen-year-old." Now we get along fine. I play the cello, like Minna. I used to play in the back row of a high school orchestra to slow the boys down.

In 1989, MacLachlan was concerned about the brevity of her Newbery winner. "It's because I'm writing a two-hour movie now for the 'Hallmark Hall of Fame,' so unless everyone speaks slowly, it's obvious to me that I have to write the story yet again." Her solution was to add to the story for the telecast.

MacLachlan, who became an author at age thirty-five, regrets not starting earlier. When composing, she reads her copy aloud, weighing each word. Understated prose contributes to her artistry with language. She discussed her approach to writing:

> As a child, I had imaginary conversations with characters, so I begin each work now with a character. I start not knowing how the story will end. In about the middle of a book, I see how it could possibly be resolved. I tell my editors that I was sick on the day they taught plot. It's always the hardest part.
>
> I used to get up early to write, but the older I get and the more books I've written, I think I have less to say, so I write in peaks and valleys. I've used a typewriter and am trying a computer which I might shoot if I had a gun. I like the sound of the typewriter and the carriage going by.

With gentle humor, MacLachlan shows how her characters become more accepting of themselves and even their eccentric families: "My parents accepted diversity, so I do have a lot of tolerance for people's differences," she said.

UPDATE

A gentle picture book, *What You Know First* (1995), has Barry Moser's life-like engravings and MacLachlan's free verse. A little girl mourns having to move with her family from the farm where she was born. She'll take a cottonwood twig, a bag of prairie dirt, and memory of cowboy songs to teach her baby brother.

Three years after her *Minna Pratt* book, MacLachlan released *Journey* (Delacorte, 1991), a book for adolescents. Teenaged readers identify with eleven-year-old Journey and his younger sister, Cat, deserted by their irresponsible single parent, Liddie, and raised by rural grandparents.

Different from Liddie is Julia, a mother who temporarily deserts her baby in MacLachlan's second book for teenagers, *Baby* (Delacorte, 1993). Twelve-year-old Larkin and a friend, Lalo, find a basket with a baby and a note saying that the child, Sophie, is almost a year old, but her mother will return for her. The mother fulfills her promise.

MacLachlan published again with Harper in 1994, continuing *Sarah, Plain and Tall* with *Skylark*. After Papa marries Sarah, their barn burns during a long drought. Sarah brings Anna and Caleb to visit her family in Maine. Rain returns to the prairie, so Papa goes to Maine to take his family home, and they joyously anticipate the birth soon of another Witting child.

Robert McCloskey, illustrator–author (1914–)

1977 Interview

McCloskey (seated) with Carolyn Field and Jaqueline Weiss

Robert McCloskey won his first Caldecott Medal in 1942 for his most famous picture book, *Make Way for Ducklings* (Viking, 1941). "Even my ducks look a little bit like me," he joked. "They looked more like me when I had a crew cut some years ago."

McCloskey, who is known for his homespun humor, was the first person to win two Caldecott Medals. He received his second Caldecott Medal in 1958 for *Time of Wonder* (Viking, 1957). It takes place in Maine, as do his two self-written Caldecott Honor books, *Blueberries for Sal* (Viking, 1948), a 1949 winner, and *One Morning in Maine* (Viking, 1952), a 1953 winner. McCloskey's 1954 Caldecott Honor Medal was for illustrations in *Journey Cake, Ho!* (Viking, 1953), by Ruth Sawyer.

Robert McCloskey was born on September 15, 1914, in Hamilton, Ohio. His grandmother's house in Hamilton had an old-fashioned bathroom, which he drew in the autobiographical *Lentil* (Viking, 1940). "That crazy washstand was there and the bathtub with claws for feet," he said. The artist created a schoolboy, Lentil, and showed him dressed but barefoot, his head on a pillow in a dry bathtub, playing his harmonica.

As a boy, McCloskey studied harmonica, piano, drums, and oboe, and led a harmonica band. He changed his focus to inventions until he drew for his high school paper and yearbook. He even taught a YMCA soap-carving hobby group. His parents supported all his artistic endeavors.

In his senior year, McCloskey entered a woodcut-engraving contest and won a scholarship to Vesper George School of Art in Boston. During the summers, he returned to Hamilton and worked. One summer, when he was a camp counselor, he carved a totem pole. In 1934, he received a commission to carve bas-reliefs for a Hamilton municipal building.

McCloskey studied at the National Academy of Design in New York City, where he won the President's Award for creative work exhibited there and at Tiffany Foundation. While in New York, he called on Viking's editor of children's books, May Massee.

> I would never have done books for children without May Massee. . . . I had drawings I had made, and she liked them. She said, "I don't have anything for you to illustrate now, but I can see from your drawings that you can tell a story. Why don't you go home and write one?" I went home and returned with *Lentil*, my first book.

In 1940, *Lentil*'s publication year, McCloskey married Margaret "Peggy" Durand, a children's librarian. She is the daughter of Ruth Sawyer, author of *Journey Cake, Ho!* and 1937 Newbery Medal winner for *Roller Skates* (Viking, 1936).

McCloskey drew *Journey Cake, Ho!*, which was also an ALA Notable Book, with red-brown brush strokes on a blue-green litho crayon background. He shows Johnny, a bound-out boy released from a farm in hard times. His aged master gives the boy a journey cake, but as Johnny removes the cake from his bag, it runs away. He chases it, and a sheep, pig, cow, horse, and chickens follow him to the farm. He can stay, now that livestock makes survival there possible.

While painting big murals for the Lever Brothers Building in Boston, McCloskey saw ducks in the Boston Public Garden and began to develop his story *Make Way for Ducklings*, which became an American Library Association Notable Book. It shows Mrs. Mallard leading eight ducklings to the garden. Policeman Michael stops traffic so the mallard family can cross in heavy traffic. His humorous art is in sepia on a white background, and his account of his models is hilarious:

> I drew ducks from models. I bought both ducks and ducklings [at Washington Market] and brought them to my New York City studio, so I could draw them. I tried to make them keep still long enough for me to sketch wingspreads. I tried

a number of ways, and the most successful way was to get them drunk on red wine. They loved it! I crawled around on the floor after them with tissues.

The male mallard would chase the others away from the wine dish, so he could have it all to himself. He would get to the point where he could no longer stay on his feet. He'd just stretch out on the floor. When the females came up to drink, he gave them a peck to send them scooting.

Marc Simont [1957 Caldecott winner for illustrating *A Tree Is Nice*] was my apartment mate. He didn't like the duck noises very much. The ducks got up at dawn and started squawking. He was not very appreciative.

McCloskey was proud of his efforts for accuracy in creating *Make Way for Ducklings,* including consulting ornithologist George Sutton. The artist wanted to "put down a line and know that it is right."

I manage to get clippings from all corners of the world about ducks crossing the road. In Copenhagen, they show it on travel posters, postcards, and hand-kerchiefs. When something like that hits the press, I get dozens of photographs. . . . Photos come from as far away as India.

A year after publication of *Make Way for Ducklings* and after submission of *Homer Price* (Viking, 1943), McCloskey received a rush request from Viking concerning art for *Homer Price*:

I got a call from Viking that they needed another illustration, this time of the robbers in bed, to avoid an embarrassing blank spot in the book. There was a considerable time lag before I did that illustration. I had forgotten how many robbers I'd had. The question most children ask in my mail today is: "Why did you put five robbers in the bed in *Homer Price* when there are only four in the story?"

It [the picture with the mistake] is a conversation piece. The Japanese, in their edition, made a change. They couldn't stand the discrepancy. The Japanese edition is very fancy. It comes in a big box and is beautifully printed.

Homer Price, which was named an ALA Notable Book and received the 1947 Pacific Northwest Readers' Choice Award, is one of McCloskey's favorite books. His drawing of Michael Murphy's musical mousetrap is a reminder of boyhood inventions.

One *Homer Price* story is "The Doughnuts," which Weston Woods adapted as a film, featuring McCloskey in mob scenes. In the story, a wealthy woman stops for doughnuts at Uncle Ulysses's coffee shop and learns none are ready. She puts her jewelry on the counter and mixes a big batter. The doughnut machine's stop button breaks, and the shop becomes filled with doughnuts. Finding her diamond bracelet missing, the woman suspects it is in a doughnut and tells customers, so they eagerly buy doughnuts.

Quite often, I get news clips and letters about classes and library groups that have dramatized "The Doughnuts" and other stories of mine. Occasionally, they make models of Ulysses' coffee shop with little doughnuts on the counter represented by dry cereal [in small, circular shape]. They also make soap carvings of my characters.

McCloskey later issued *Homer Price*'s sequel, *Centerburg Tales* (Viking, 1951), short stories set in Centerburg, Ohio. It is the nearest town to Homer's highway home, Shady Rest Tourist Camp. In "Experiment 13," grumpy Dulcy Doomer inherits a greenhouse and seeds labeled "Experiment 13." Dulcy plants thirteen seeds in his greenhouse, giving them fertilizer, water, and plant food. The plants turn out to be ragweed, whose pollen causes sneezing. Ordered to destroy plants, Dulcy charges the town $1,313, threatening to plant seeds annually, but town leaders tax his thousands of seeds. Finally, Homer bakes the seeds in his doughnuts, telling town leaders that a nut can't grow into a nut tree if baked in a cookie. This story with its inferred ending is a fine example of McCloskey's inventive mind.

From 1942 to 1945, during World War II, McCloskey served as a U.S. Army technical sergeant, stationed in Alabama. He drew visual aids, saying in fun: "My greatest contribution to the war effort was inventing a machine to enable short lieutenants to flip over large training charts in high breeze."

After his army discharge, the McCloskeys, including a daughter, Sally, moved near Cape Rosier, Maine, to an island off Penobscot Bay. Their winter home with a swimming pool is in the Virgin Islands, and, he said, "It's high on an island, not nearly as close to the water as in Maine."

McCloskey's wife and daughter are the two human characters in his picture book, *Blueberries for Sal*, an ALA Notable Book and winner of the 1949 Ohioana Book Award. This story takes place on Maine's Blueberry Hill. Young Sal's mother, Peggy, wants to preserve berries for winter, and Mother Bear wants Little Bear to eat berries to grow fat for cold weather. In a mix-up, Sal cannot find her mother and accidentally follows Mother Bear's noises while Little Bear pursues Sal's mother by mistake. The story ends peacefully with proper reunions. The book's illustrations are in black and white, as are the end papers showing Peggy preserving berries in the kitchen with Sal nearby.

The story occurred to me one afternoon when we were all picking blueberries. Peggy was picking them industriously. Sal was picking and eating, ker-plunking blueberries in her pail. I was sitting there with a sketchbook in a dreamy fashion and added the picture of the bear.

The old-fashioned kitchen stove on the end paper of *Blueberries for Sal* is in the kitchen of Ruth Sawyer, Sal's grandmother. It is much more interesting to draw than our modern kitchen stove.

Sal, this time a little older, is central in another picture book, *One Morning in Maine,* winner of a *New York Herald Tribune* 1952 Spring Festival Book Award. She hunts in the sand for the tooth she lost while digging for clams, assisted by her father. McCloskey sketched himself.

> I keep a mirror in my studio at all times and look into it when I'm drawing a hand or foot or an action. Often, I'm my own model . . . [so] it's very common for faces of characters to look like me. James Daugherty's drawings for *Abraham Lincoln* and *Benjamin Franklin* look a little like James Daugherty.

After the McCloskeys' second daughter, Jane, was born in 1948, the family spent a year in Italy. McCloskey had a studio at Rome's American Academy where he learned glass and marble mosaic techniques. He had won the Prix de Rome in 1939 but could not go there until after World War II. McCloskey visited Mexico for two months in 1955, where he learned new artistic skills.

In 1957, McCloskey completed *Time of Wonder,* a result of three years of effort. This, his first full-color picture book, is a watercolor masterpiece. He shows Sal and Jane as children enjoying Maine's sparkling water in both a sailboat and a rowboat. Joy changes to concern as everyone prepares for bad weather. When a hurricane hits, the girls and their mother sing on a sofa while their father tucks dishtowels around windowsills.

In his 1958 Caldecott Medal acceptance speech for *Time of Wonder,* McCloskey urged "teaching of drawing and design to every child, right along with reading and writing." On this occasion, his former apartment mate, Marc Simont, spoke about McCloskey's mechanical ability. He made the family's island home cozy by maintaining electric generators, water pumps, boat engines, and winches.

After *Time of Wonder,* McCloskey created another full-color book, *Burt Dow, Deep-Water Man: A Tale of the Sea in the Classic Tradition* (Viking, 1963). Retired Burt Dow has a leaky dory on his lawn as a flower planter. *Tidely-Idley* is his double-ender, an old boat with a make-and-break engine that he paints in pink, yellow, and salmon with leftover paint. While fishing, he accidentally hooks the tip of a whale's tail. He removes his hook, puts a band-aid on that tail, and obliges when other whales want the same treatment. This story has more fantasy than other McCloskey books, including Burt Dow's experience in the whale's belly and his exit alive. McCloskey gets letters from children and adults about the colorful book:

> I get good response from pupils to *Burt Dow* and from adults who were Burt's friends. He was a real, live neighbor of mine. I own the boat, *Tidely-Idley.* I traded an old gas engine to Burt for the boat. I had to take the boat to my island on a barge, because it was so leaky. I had the boat sitting around here for years,

wondering how I was going to use it in a story until the tale of Burt Dow finally evolved.

I had a letter last week from a class in North Carolina, saying they've just won $50 and spent it on a boat. They were going to move it into their library, upholster it, put in a few pillows, and have it as a special spot in which to read. The library named the boat *Tidely-Idley.*

When Burt died, McCloskey said, "Captain Haskell's brother put up money for a lovely headstone for Burt in the local cemetery. He inscribed the tombstone, 'Burt Dow, Deep-Water Man.'"

In 1974, eleven years after *Burt Dow's* release, McCloskey received the Regina Medal from the Catholic Library Association. In addition to his eight original children's books, he illustrated ten for other authors. Four are in Keith Robertson's "Henry Reed" series.

During the period when Sal and Jane were teenagers, McCloskey's wife photographed him as he sketched them:

Sal is in her flute-playing days, Jane is accompanying her on the piano, and I'm making a drawing of them. My daughters, when they learned that other daughters didn't have to pose for their fathers, sort of went on strike. I had to take advantage of every opportunity to make drawings of them.

McCloskey, who stopped illustrating books in 1970, seems fascinated by a project to create new puppets for animation and adapt them as characters. Whatever his inventive mind pursues, he seems mobile: "I'm fortunate that I can carry my business—illustrating and writing—more or less in my pocket or at least pack it in a small suitcase."

UPDATE

On December 4, 1987, at a 150-year commemoration of the Boston Public Garden, sponsors unveiled a bronze sculpture of a mallard family from *Make Way for Ducklings* and honored McCloskey on a plaque. On July 30, 1992, Raisa Gorbachev and Barbara Bush unveiled the sculpture's replica in Moscow's Novodevichy Park, a second tribute to McCloskey, whose nostalgic, humorous books have become American classics.

Milton Meltzer, author (1915–)

1994 Interview

Milton Meltzer, an outstanding historian and biographer for young people, has written more than a hundred researched books and edited many more. He is especially known for such titles as *Tongue of Flame: The Life of Lydia Maria Child* (Crowell, 1965); *Langston Hughes: A Biography* (Crowell, 1968); *Never to Forget: The Jews of the Holocaust* (Harper, 1976), a Hans Christian Andersen Honor Book; and *All Times, All Peoples: A World History of Slavery* (Harper, 1980). His 1968 and 1976 titles were among his four children's literature finalists for the National Book Award, and his 1980 title was a Christopher Award winner.

"I identify with underdogs because of my own personal history, not having much in life. . . . Being Jewish, I sometimes suffered discrimination and persecution," said Meltzer, who is often considered "champion of the oppressed by book reviewers."

In *Starting from Home: A Writer's Beginnings* (Viking, 1988), Meltzer's autobiography, the historian sketched his parents' Austrian-Jewish roots. His maternal grandfather, Samuel Richter, left the Old World for New York. In 1900, he sent for his oldest daughter, fourteen-year-old Mary, to join him. She became a garment worker and helped him save money so the other eight children and their mother, Rose, could come to the United States in 1905.

At age eighteen, Benjamin Meltzer, Milton's father, left his parents' straw-roofed Austrian farmhouse and never saw his parents again. Benjamin rented a room in the Richters' Bronx flat, where he met Milton's mother, Mary. They married and had a son, Allan, before moving to Worcester, Massachusetts, where Benjamin Meltzer worked as a window cleaner. Milton was born in Worcester on May 8, 1915, and another brother, Marshall, was born five years later.

"I don't recall having a single conversation with my father," Milton Meltzer said. The taciturn man's energy went into work, but he liked Jack Benny on radio. Milton's parents spoke English only at home, because they wanted their sons to develop as Americans. His mother was a homemaker who dressed her sons in self-knitted, fine sweaters.

Meltzer liked school. In junior high, to help the family, he got jobs delivering milk and newspapers, and he worked in a warehouse and a shoe store. He also found time to play tennis, his lifelong sport, and became hooked on public libraries. He confessed, "I think now I got more out of independent reading than out of school studies." Classical High School was an exception in eleventh and twelfth grades with English teacher Anna Shaughnessy, to whom he dedicated his autobiography. Meltzer and a few other students formed The Club, weekly book discussions held at Shaughnessy's home.

In the Depression, Meltzer said, "My family did not 'go broke.' We started broke." His mother tried to peddle hosiery to help, but Meltzer's father wanted to be sole provider. Realizing Meltzer's economic plight, Miss Shaughnessy told him about Columbia University's teacher-training scholarship. In 1932, he not only got a full scholarship but also on-campus housing, and in exchange for food, a job in the college dining room.

Before leaving for college, Meltzer took a date to a drugstore, where he found his father cleaning windows. Shame kept him from introducing his father to his date. Such details make his publisher and fans want his life story continued, but he declines.

At Columbia University, Meltzer majored in English and history, and worked Saturdays in a shoe store for pocket money. He left college as a senior, and stayed in Worcester with his fifty-seven-year-old father, who was dying of cancer. After the funeral, his family moved to New York City.

Meltzer stayed in a cheap Chelsea room and got his rent plus $5.50 every two weeks as relief. He said, "I was on welfare until I got a job. My first job after college was with the Federal Theatre Project. It gave me pay of $23.86 weekly."

The government dismissed him and others, but the Workers Alliance union saved their jobs for three years until 1939. The experience made him value unions and want to learn about labor history. In 1939, an unemployed Meltzer toured the country with friends, learning to drive en route. He saw California migrant camps, later inspiring his biography of an on-site photographer, *Dorothea Lange: Life through the Camera* (Viking, 1985).

Returning to New York, Meltzer met Hilda Balinky, who worked as a model and attended City College at night. The couple married on June 22, 1941.

Soon after the wedding, Meltzer was drafted into World War II. "I was an Army Air Force control tower operator from 1942 to 1945. For over three years, I helped bomber fighters in the states."

After the war, his brother Allan helped Meltzer get Columbia Broadcasting radio work in New York, interviewing veterans. Meltzer left to do public relations, first for Henry Wallace, a 1948 independent presidential candidate, and later, for Pfizer Pharmaceuticals. When Meltzer was forty, his wife told him, "I'll let you out of washing dishes if you write a book." She now claims he writes to avoid dishes.

Meltzer's first book was for adults: *A Pictorial History of the Negroes in America* (Crown, 1956), which he published with Langston Hughes. He said, "I've revised that book six times, twice with Langston, and after his death, with other black scholars. It still sells well, now titled *A Pictorial History of Black Americans.*" He and Langston wrote another book, *Black Magic: A Pictorial History of the Negro in American Entertainment* (Prentice-Hall, 1967). That was followed by *Langston Hughes: A Biography* (Crowell, 1968). Meltzer began the latter with the poet's willing help. Meltzer finished it after Hughes died.

The author had been writing books for adults when his two daughters accosted him at the supper table:

"Why don't you write for us?" they asked. I questioned, "What do you mean, 'for us'?" They replied, "For kids!" I was entranced with that idea.

Since then, with rare exceptions, he has written for a younger audience, feeling that young people are more open than adults to new ideas.

His wife, Hilda, was a counselor at City University of New York before she retired early; she now does adult assertiveness training. The couple have two children, Janie, a florist, and Amy, a clinical psychologist. Amy's husband, Philip McArthur, is also a clinical psychologist; they have two children, Zachary and Benjamin.

Meltzer's grandsons value his biographies, like *Mary MacLeod Bethune, Voice of Black Hope* (Viking, 1988), about an African-American educator who began her own Florida school and became prominent. Meltzer discussed his biography of another female leader, *Tongue of Flame: The Life of Lydia Maria Child* (Crowell, 1965):

In order to do the story of this Massachusetts abolitionist, I got a grant through the University of Massachusetts. For four years, I became a research professor, not a teaching professor, and had a crew of three young Ph.D. candidates helping me. We found 2,600 letters by this remarkable woman!

Meltzer's life stories of Bethune, Child, and Hughes are among his individual biographies that include George Washington, Benjamin Franklin, Thomas Jefferson, Andrew Jackson, Samuel Gridley Howe, Thaddeus Stevens, Henry David Thoreau, Mark Twain, Margaret Sanger, Dorothea Lange, and Betty Friedan. In the books, Meltzer explains how each of these admirable individuals, influenced by their environment, struggled for unpopular causes.

Columbus and the World Around Him (Franklin Watts) was published in 1990. Meltzer said, "Christopher Columbus started the American slave trade. Some argue that Columbus Day is a chance to mourn rather than celebrate. What a mixed bag his accomplishments were!" Ten years before his Columbus book, Meltzer published *All Times, All Peoples: A World History of Slavery* (Harper, 1980), a book with bold black-and-white woodcuts by Leonard Everett Fisher. The author told why he wrote it:

Slavery was a step forward in the development of civilization because in ancient days, war captives were killed, not enslaved. The reason I wrote the book was to overcome the notion among Americans and children in particular that blackness is a badge of slavery. They have no notion whatsoever that people all over the world—black, brown, white, red, and yellow—have been enslaved and in many cases, have enslaved others. Slavery has an ancient lineage. Later, slavery took on racist implications that were used to make the lot of slaves even worse.

Though Meltzer has written about slavery and abolitionists, he may be best known for *Never to Forget: The Jews of the Holocaust* (Harper, 1976). Since young readers are its main intended audience, Meltzer used twenty-seven documentary passages from boys and girls. The book, which is on the international Hans Christian Andersen Honor List, mentions that the United States, then led by President Franklin D. Roosevelt, failed to help victims of the Holocaust.

I think Roosevelt's failure to do anything was politically motivated. What a lot of people who were not alive in the '30s never knew was that anti-Semitism in America was widespread. It dominated the equivalent of the American Nazi Party and many other fascist or semifascist groups. A number of politicians from the South who were in Congress felt the same way. Roosevelt must have believed if he had rescued Jews, he would have lost part of his political support.

Never to Forget also expressed the idea that modern bureaucratization of power helped make Auschwitz possible. He writes, on pages 191–192:

> I've studied the workings of Nazi machinery and machinery in Nazi-occupied Europe (because many other people besides the Germans took part in the persecution and murder of Jews and other minorities). I found persons of every rank in civil and political life were involved in the Holocaust. It took enormous bureaucratic machinery to do that. As in any bureaucracy—big business anywhere—citizens acted like cogs in a wheel without taking an independent stand and refusing to do what, in their consciences, they knew was right.

A companion book to *Never to Forget* is Meltzer's *Rescue: The Story of How Gentiles Saved Jews in the Holocaust* (Harper, 1988):

> Most of my *Rescue* material comes from documentary sources. At the end of World War II, Jewish survivors were held in European camps and interviewed by social workers, many of whom came from America. Records are on microfilm. There are also memoirs from people who have written about themselves.

On a lighter note are Meltzer's popular Harper children's books. One is *The Amazing Potato: A Story in Which the Incas, Conquistadors, Marie Antoinette, Thomas Jefferson, Wars, Famines, Immigrants, and French Fries All Play a Part* (1992). Meltzer told how the book began:

> My wife and I attended a summer session at Cambridge. In their bookstore, I bought a huge book, almost as big as the Manhattan phone directory, on the potato. I could not believe there was that much to say on the lowly potato.

Having done the first book on a vegetable, Meltzer did the second on a mineral: *Gold: The True Story of Why People Search for It, Mine It, Trade It, Steal It, Mint It, Hoard It, Shape it, Wear It, Fight and Kill for It* (1993). He said, "I convinced my publisher, now that I'd done two kingdoms of nature, to let me publish the third on an animal. The third book is on the role of the horse in human history."

Meltzer explained the background for *Cheap Raw Material* (Viking, 1994), a different type of book.

> A lot of kids work in the fast-food trade. It wouldn't be bad if employers didn't violate state and federal child labor laws. Kids work long hours in many fields, sometimes resulting in their death. They give so much energy to their jobs, often to acquire material things, such as a compact disc player or a camcorder, that they can't do justice to their schoolwork. If enough funds were appropriated for

the number of inspectors needed, fewer violations would occur. Now control is minimal.

Meltzer's book topics inspired his documentary films, lasting from twenty minutes to over an hour. He said, "My first three for McGraw-Hill were on *The History of the Negro in America.* James Earl Jones, the great actor, narrated. Today, I'd write a film script for a producer on any topic that interests me."

Although Meltzer has an agent, he finds his own publishers. He said, "My agent handles contracts only. I'm too prolific to use a single publisher. It would be to the disadvantage of a publisher and myself if two or three of my books were issued by the same company during the same year. Their salesmen would compete with one another."

As for preparing his copy, he said:

As a journalist for many years, I learned to type fast to meet deadlines. I began my first book with Langston that way, but now it's better if I slow down and write on a yellow, lined pad. The next morning, I rewrite my copy on a portable, manual typewriter. I make lots of interlinear changes. I have learned that writing is really rewriting. Ann, my typist for thirty years, who can read my scrawl, prepares a final copy for the publisher.

Meltzer has created nonfiction that has won the Jane Addams, Christopher, Thomas Alva Edison, Olive Branch, and Carter G. Woodson awards among other prizes. In *The Black Americans: A History in Their Own Words, 1619–1983* (Crowell, 1984), Meltzer uses words of ex-slaves and modern folk, including leaders, to trace history.

UPDATE

Meltzer completed his kingdoms of nature Harper books—having written previously about a vegetable (potato) and mineral (gold)—in 1995 with a book about an animal (horse) in *Hold Your Horses! A Feedbag Full of Fact & Fable.*

In 1998, Dutton released the author's *Ten Queens: Portraits of Women of Power,* in which he featured some powerful female rulers. Beyond quoting their words, he reproduced paintings of them.

In 1999, Meltzer's *Witches and Witch Hunts* (Scholastic) described fifthteenth- to seventeenth-century executions of thousands who were accused of witchcraft, including men. The mayor of Bamberg, Germany, Johannel Junius, smuggled a letter to his daughter from jail, describing his torture. The witch hunts in Salem, Massachusetts, are also described. Meltzer depicts Hitler's persecution of Jews as a witch hunt. Finally, he cites Joseph McCarthy's witch hunt for communists in the United States in the early 1950s. The book, intended for readers aged nine to fourteen, features a provocative book jacket by Barry Moser.

Milton Meltzer was honored in 2001 with the Laura Ingalls Wilder Award.

Photograph by Bachrach

Eve Merriam, poet–author– playwright (1916–1992)

1974 Interview

When asked if she should be identified as an early feminist, poet Eve Merriam replied, "I hope you call me a humanist. I'm very pro-man as well as being for women." Both genders have enjoyed her enthusiasm for social causes. Her honors include *Collier's* Star Fiction Award for "Make Something Happen," 1949; a grant to write poetic drama for CBS, 1959; *Finding a Poem* (Atheneum, 1970) was a Junior Literary Guild selection; and the National Council of Teachers of English awarded her for excellence in writing children's poetry in 1970.

Eva Moskowitz was born on July 19, 1916, in the Kensington section of Philadelphia. Her parents, Max and Jennie Moskowitz, emigrated from Russia as children and grew up in small Pennsylvania towns. They owned Quality Dress Shops, a small chain of women's clothing stores—the right business for a family with three girls and a boy. Eva acquired her sense of style from this background, and developed an interest in fashion. She was feature editor of *Deb* in 1946 and in 1947, and fashion copy editor for *Glamour* before writing nonfiction, *Figleaf: The Business of Being in Fashion* (Lippincott, 1960).

Eve and her brother, Louis, were close in age, and shared many interests. They made model airplanes, and when they moved to Lincoln Drive, they skated on a little pond created by pouring water into their yard's low area. They read aloud "The Highway Man" and "Ghunga Din." After they went to

Gilbert and Sullivan operettas, she repeated Gilbert's tongue-twisting words. She found puns as much fun as playing jump rope, hop-scotch, or tag.

Her family was fond of books, and as a child, she read *Swiss Family Robinson, Alice in Wonderland*, myths, and fairy tales. She also read *Epaminondas*, and in 1972 got Scholastic to publish a nonracist version, *That Noodle-Head Epaminondas.*

She recalled some childhood stimuli that made her a poet:

> Unlikely as it may seem, when I went to grammar school, we used to read the Psalms in Philadelphia at the beginning of class. I'm not a religious person at all, but I do think the Psalms in the Bible are among the most beautiful poetry in the world. . . . I was brought up on Mother Goose, and I think it was one of the things that helped make me a poet. I had the Psalms for beauty and Mother Goose for bounce and jollity. I think I was very fortunate.

Poetry surrounded the young girl at home as well as in school. She enjoyed seeing love poems her father wrote her mother before marriage. Germantown High School published her serious poems in a weekly newspaper and magazine. She remembered one English teacher there who encouraged her and a Latin teacher who helped her appreciate etymology. Fascinated by words, she was delighted that her high school was on High Street and her birth state's name meant "Penn's woods." She recalled children's concerts:

> I used to go to the children's concerts at the Academy of Music. Schools let us out early on Friday afternoons, so that we could go. We would take the train to town from Germantown. I would stop at the old Chinese wall and buy a package of Root Beer Drops. For a long time, I associated music with Root Beer Drops. It's very strange how one sense goes into another.

After two years at Cornell, she returned to Philadelphia to attend the University of Pennsylvania, where she received her bachelor's degree in 1937. She later did graduate work at the University of Wisconsin and, following her move to New York City, at Columbia University. Soon after she adopted her pen name, Eve Merriam, and felt committed as a poet. In 1946, she won the Yale Younger Poets Prize for a book of poems written by someone under age thirty. She had tried for five years, and finally won when poet Archibald MacLeish was judge.

To make a living, Merriam started as a copywriter, became an editor, conducted a weekly New York City radio series on modern poetry, and wrote a daily verse column for the magazine *PM*. She also wrote documentaries for Columbia Broadcasting System, and was a freelance magazine and book writer/lecturer.

Merriam was then married to writer Leonard C. Lewin, and had two sons, Guy Michel and Dee Michel. A fat cat, Towel, joined the family on trips to their vacation home in Stonington, Connecticut. Merriam was devoted to Manhattan, walking two mornings a week to teach writing courses at the College of the City of New York. She and her husband enjoyed playing a vocabulary-expansion game, "Fictionary," at home with friends:

> You go through the dictionary and pick words whose meaning nobody knows. You make up meanings. It's astonishing and very humbling, because *I* can find many words on any page that I don't know. I like to do that, and I think many writers do. It's the surprise and pleasure of discovering new words.

When her children were young, Merriam wrote picture books. Knopf published two for wordmongers. One was *A Gaggle of Geese* (1960), giving plural names of animals, birds, and fish, like "a down of hares" and "a skulk of foxes." The sequel, *Small Fry* (1965), gave unusual names for animal youngsters, like "joey," a young kangaroo.

Merriam found her best writing time was late in the morning. She often worked on several projects simultaneously and managed by putting notes in different folders.

Because she was a poet, Merriam weighed each word she used. This was fine for poetry, but made prose more difficult for her. Among her earliest prose for children were biographies, beginning with *The Real Book about Franklin D. Roosevelt* (Dobson, 1952). She remembered how her family listened to his "Fireside Chats." Her next children's biography was *The Voice of Liberty: The Story of Emma Lazarus* (Farrar, 1959). She also wrote *The Story of Benjamin Franklin* (Four Winds, 1965):

> I did a biography of Ben Franklin, lovely hometown boy. It was designed for third-grade readers, so I had to be very careful when I was describing the Stamp Act. It was important to do it in terms that could be understood by an eight-year-old.

The writer's prose portrait of Franklin helped her do a poetical tribute to him. It is with six other long poems, each about a different ingenious American, in *Independent Voices* (Atheneum, 1968). Of her poetry writing, she said:

> I think as a poet, I don't even look for it, but there's a certain image I may come to, and I hope there's a freshness about it. I recall my older little boy the first time that he saw snow. We were out in it. I always thought snow was cold. He was rolling in it and tasting it. I realized, of course, that snow is warm. You can play with it and have a wonderful time. Many years later, that evolved into a poem. It's called "A Cliché," and it's in *It Doesn't Always Have to Rhyme*.

Atheneum published her children's poetry collection, *It Doesn't Always Have to Rhyme* (1964), and two others in a trilogy: *There Is No Rhyme for Silver* (1962), her first book of verse for children, and *Catch a Little Rhyme* (1966). Some of her poems for children don't have capital letters or punctuation. She explained why:

> If you don't have a capital letter at the beginning of the line, it isn't jarring. You get a smoother trip, and it's simpler to read actually. . . . It may be just a matter of having breathing pauses when you don't want to imply that the reader should pause for the length of a comma or semicolon.

She has found that children do like poetry. "Quite young children like rhyme: that chime at the end of a line," she said. They also like "internal rhymes" within the same line:

> With any poem where there are inner rhymes or just a beat, readers get more out of it by stressing what there is. Those stops are not arbitrary. If poets don't help with stops, because it's iambic pentameter or it's a regular beat, very often it may be because they want the reader to pause at a word or to think about the next word.

When she begins a poem, Merriam said, she doesn't necessarily know in advance if her audience will be children or adults:

> You can't really slot yourself and say, "Okay, this is for children. This is for grown-ups." . . . All of us are children all our lives. Conversely, children at times are adult in some wise ways. I don't want to be Rousseauist since I don't believe that children are perfect until they are corrupted. I believe that children connect with the world. We can learn from them, and they from us. At times, we can relearn joy from one another.

Merriam did have an intended audience for her collection, *The Inner City Mother Goose* (Simon & Schuster, 1969):

> It's for adults. The book came about because I wanted very much to say something about cities and about what life is like today. I was casting about for a form, and it was strange, almost freaky. I was on the subway, and I've never had this happen to me before or after. It was almost like a comic strip where a light bulb goes on in the head. Lines actually said themselves to me. . . . The first part was Mother Goose.
>
> After thinking about it, I did a lot of research. I found that Mother Goose originally was not a series of verses for children at all. It was sophisticated political and social commentary about eighteenth-century times. Many characters were actual historical figures. It didn't seem to me that I was defaming Mother Goose.

When I wrote *The Inner City Mother Goose,* it never occurred to me that it would be taken for a children's book. It's just astonishing what has happened. It is used in colleges, and it is used in some high schools. I have heard stories of it filtering down to all levels.

Merriam said she once anonymously prevented the sale of *The Inner City Mother Goose* to an eight-year-old, middle-class child. "I may not have done the same if the child had been poor," she said. Children from inner cities understand verses that deal with overcrowded housing, tenements needing repairs, installment buying, garbage strikes, use of clinics, nonrelevant reading books, rat control, and mice in a baby's bureau-drawer bed put on the floor. Primary-grade pupils near a housing project identify with "Hush-a-Bye, Baby." It shows a problem when a project elevator malfunctions, and a baby carriage has to be carried down more than ten floors. These children value a poet who knows their environment. Some enjoy the graphic title of a parody, "$imple $imon."

Merriam herself agreed that all intermediate-grade children, regardless of locale or backgrounds, could relate to selected *Inner City Mother Goose* poems, such as "Pussy Cat, Pussy Cat, Where Have You Been?" It concerns a city hall hearing about cats, but only dogs and rats could attend, a good civics lesson. "I have gotten requests from anthologies and textbooks in the last couple of years to pick up selected poems, so they are being used willy-nilly, but I think that some are inappropriate," she said.

As an example, she pointed to "Inner City," a stage play advertised as a street cantata based on her book. The play opened on Broadway in late 1971. Merriam said, "The show is very sophisticated, and there's rough language in the second act. We've had many from high schools and a couple of junior high busloads" in the audience.

Merriam declared one rule about reading poetry:

Do not read poetry. Only *reread* it. You must give it the courtesy of two readings. The main difference between poetry and prose is that poetry has a built-in rhythm or music. Read it the first time for its sense. Even if it's nonsense, there is a certain kind of logic to the nonsense.

The second time, read it for its music, whether it's alliteration, assonance, whatever it is. Pay the courtesy of two readings. I would urge teachers and librarians when stamping out a book of poetry, to give a little bookmark, "Please read me twice."

To help children learn to read poetry, Merriam visits a number of schools each year. She has spent time as poet-in-residence at schools in Cleveland, other Midwest cities, the East, and was planning a trip to Washington state.

There's no question that when you hear somebody reading poetry aloud, you get more excited about it. . . . Poets can come into schools as teachers' helpers. They can read poetry aloud and perhaps get the children and teachers to be a little less inhibited.

At one school, Merriam worked with a group of mentally challenged readers, from age six to about twelve, whose teacher warned her, "Don't worry if they're restless after ten minutes." Merriam used *Don't Think about a White Bear* (Putnam, 1963) among other books:

I started with poems for the very young from *Don't Think about a White Bear* since they asked for it. Then I read from *Catch a Little Rhyme* the poem about the transistor radio, "Umbilical." What I found when I read it a second time, these big boys of eleven and twelve, who couldn't read, were mouthing the words. They remembered the whole thing! They spent an hour before getting tired.

The teacher came to me at the end of the day and said, "It was a thrilling experience for them." Of course, it was for me too. It seemed there was a breakthrough. We know that rhyme helps.

After that experience, Merriam decided to write a book of poems designed to be read aloud. "I would not limit the vocabulary, so it wouldn't matter if listeners were six, seven, fourteen, fifteen, or sixteen," she said. The end result was her book, *Out Loud* (Atheneum, 1973). "All of its poems are more or less onomatopoeic and are designed for oral reading," she explained. The poems symbolize sounds and show interesting textual arrangement, including "A Left-Handed Poem."

Merriam voiced concern about vocabulary in poetry:

In poetry, where the richness of language must come across, I would never think of being careful with my vocabulary. The poem "Alligator on the Escalator" uses big words, but six-year-olds know "escalator." Look at "television commercial." Those are big words, but two- and three-year-olds know them. I think we have to revise our "cat-sat-on-the-mat" vocabulary according to what children already know.

Merriam is deeply committed to women's rights, and wrote a picture book about sex roles, *Mommies at Work* (Knopf, 1961) as well as children's fiction, *Boys and Girls, Girls and Boys* (Holt, 1972). In 1972, M. Evans published Merriam's second edition of adult poems, *The Double Bed from the Feminine Side*, stressing equality in marriage.

Merriam was married four times. Her last husband was the late Waldo Salt, a screenwriter.

The poet told why her body tingled when she read verses aloud: "I think I was very taken up with the spontaneity of language, the joyfulness in playing around with words, which is very near and dear to me."

UPDATE

In 1976, Merriam's play, *The Club*, showed males (enacted by actresses) in a turn-of-the-century club, telling antifemale jokes. In 1977, *The Club* won ten Obies, including Best Writer for Merriam. In 1981, the National Council of Teachers of English awarded her for excellence in writing children's poetry after citing her previously in 1970. In 1982, Simon & Schuster reissued *The Inner City Mother Goose*. Fun-filled *Blackberry Ink* (Morrow, 1985) won a 1985 Parents' Choice Award.

Merriam's poetry books are distinctive. *The Birthday Cow* (Knopf, 1978) was the poet's first collaboration with her son, Guy Michel, as illustrator. Exuberant from the beginning are what she called "jump-on-the-bed poems" in *You Be Good & I'll Be Night* (Morrow, 1988). A novelty is Merriam's picture/poetry book, *The Hole Story* (Simon & Schuster, 1995), with a hole in the center of pages. It is among several of her poetry collections published posthumously.

During the Jimmy Carter administration, Merriam gave a command performance at the White House, reading part of her play, *Out of Our Father's House*.

Merriam died from liver cancer on April 11, 1992. She is remembered as a versatile writer of many works, including twenty-three poetry books for children and ten for adults. Beyond her own books, numerous anthologies carry selected poetry written by her for young people.

Phyllis Naylor (left) and Jean Karl

Phyllis Reynolds Naylor, author (1933–)

Jean E. Karl, editor–author (1927–2000)

1995 Interview

PHYLLIS REYNOLDS NAYLOR

For author Phyllis Reynolds Naylor, writing for young readers means remembering her thoughts and actions at a particular age. She said, "I see things through my main character's eyes. If I write about a thirteen-year-old, I remember how I felt and talked when I was thirteen. If I do a picture book, I'm a three- or four-year-old."

This technique has served her well. Naylor won the 1992 Newbery Medal for *Shiloh* (Atheneum, 1991) and the 1985 Edgar Award from the Mystery Writers of America for *Night Cry* (Atheneum, 1985). In 1995, she received the Kerlan Award from the University of Michigan for all her books, which now total more than ninety.

Most of Naylor's major characters are not wealthy, a reflection of her own background. She was born on January 4, 1933, during the Depression, in Anderson, Indiana, the second of three children. Her father, a salesman, suffered from a kidney disorder. In her book *Walking through the Dark* (Atheneum, 1976), she recalled her mother "taking in washing" to help support the family, and how her older sister, Norma, insisted on returning neighbors' clean clothes after dark.

Naylor began writing booklets as a child. At age nine, she created a self-illustrated "Manual for Pregnant Women" after her mother told her the facts of life. Naylor was twelve at the time her father's company transferred him to Illinois. When the family moved, Naylor got her own room with a desk, at which she wrote her stories.

In time, Naylor earned an associate's degree from Joliet Junior College in Illinois, worked as a clinical secretary, taught third grade, and still managed to write. "Using the pseudonym P. R. Tedesco, I started a weekly, humorous essay column, 'First Person Singular,'" she said. "Church magazines for teenagers published it for twenty-five years." While she was progressing as a writer, Naylor entered into a relationship that ended tragically:

> I was married very young, when I was eighteen, to a brilliant man at the University of Chicago. Five years later, seemingly overnight, he became paranoid schizophrenic. It was a terrifying experience. We eventually divorced, and he was committed to a state institution. Fifteen years later, I wrote the adult nonfiction, *Crazy Love: An Autobiographical Account of Marriage and Madness* [Morrow, 1977].
>
> Readers responded to my autobiography by saying, "Be glad you had no children." I took this statement one step further and thought, *What if I were a child, a thirteen-year-old boy, Nick, and my father began doing the strange things my husband did when he was mentally ill?*
>
> That was when I wrote the young adult book, *The Keeper* [Atheneum, 1986]. It gives children a better idea of what a classmate might be experiencing that is unknown to them. It applies to any secret that persons feel they must keep hidden from peers, whether it be drug use, alcoholism, or sexual abuse, and for that reason, they're reluctant to invite friends home.

Her tragic experience inspired Naylor to study psychology, and she received a bachelor's degree in that field from American University. For her career, however, she continued to choose writing. Then at age twenty-seven, she married again, this time to Rex Naylor, a speech pathologist. The couple raised their two sons, Jeffrey and Michael, in Bethesda, Maryland.

The family's cats are models for Marco and Polo who leave their sheltered world in her book, *The Grand Escape* (Atheneum, 1993). Feline-loving Naylor identifies with a young fan who sent her this one-sentence letter: "I have two brothers except one is a cat."

Another animal, an abused beagle saved by eleven-year-old Marty Preston, is the subject of Naylor's 1992 Newbery Medal winner, *Shiloh*. The dog is named for the bridge where Marty discovered him. The dog's prototype, Clover, was found and nurtured by friends. When Naylor learned that she had won the Newbery Medal for *Shiloh* and would have to appear on the *Today* show the next day, she turned to her husband and said, "I have twenty-four hours to lose thirty pounds."

As evidence of *Shiloh*'s popularity, a reading class at Alden Elementary School in Millbrook, New York, made Naylor a *Shiloh* quilt. On a white cotton square, each child drew a picture from the story before putting squares in chronological order. Mothers sewed the squares on a green background, including a final square with young artists' names. Naylor said, "Only my grandchildren sleep under the *Shiloh* quilt."

Though *Shiloh* is successful, efforts were made to censor the book:

> The strange thing is that Judd Travers, the tale's villain, lies, cheats, kills deer out of season, and abuses his dogs. However, the criticism I get is that he says two curse words. Parents argue that children imitate what they read, which assumes they'll go home and kick the dog, as Travers did. It underestimates children.

Naylor also was criticized about two issues in her young-adult prizewinner, *A String of Chances* (Atheneum, 1982):

> A father wanted a school to ban the book because the baby didn't have a Christian burial. The parents dig the grave themselves and get inside to spread grass, staying with their dead son as long as possible. It's based on a real incident in a community out west.
>
> Some fundamentalists felt it was all right for the protagonist to disagree with her preaching father as long as she returned to his thinking in the end, but none of this "finding your own truth."

While promoting freedom of expression, Naylor stresses the importance of setting in her books: "Sometimes it gives me a clue to the plot. It tells me about the characters, their names, and what they value. I try to write about places I've seen or know well." Naylor discussed the key role of location in *Send No Blessings* (Atheneum, 1990), a book for young adults:

When I got a National Endowment for the Arts grant, I traveled in West Virginia and went through Hinton where I saw a trailer askew off the main highway. It became the home of my main character, Beth, after I thought: *What if Beth were a teenager and had to get off the school bus here rather than at better homes down the road?* That's the way many of my books begin: "What if?"

"What if?" has led to a quantity of books with more "in the pot on the stove." Her productivity is related to her high degree of discipline. This is obvious as she described her writing practices:

> I'm a morning person. I get up at 6 A.M., go to a swimming pool to deep-water jog, wearing an aqua-jogging belt, and return home to write till I go flat. Sometimes, I get my "second wind" and write at night.
>
> I do my first two drafts in longhand on a clipboard's tablet. When I'm traveling by train to fulfill speaking engagements, I may write all night if I'm in the mood, with no kitty litter to empty and no dishes to wash. I spend the most time on my first and last paragraphs of a book. When I return home, I type my story on the computer.
>
> Before I release any book to the publisher, it runs the gauntlet. First, my husband, Rex, is a severe critic/editor. Then I read every chapter to three other published authors in my critique group. We meet for three hours a week. Critics are sharp enough to cause tears at times. I often rewrite after a critique session, averaging a total of six or seven revisions per book. However, for *Ice*, my 1995 book, I did seventeen drafts, and I wrote *Shiloh*'s first draft at break-neck speed.
>
> After my final draft, I generally send the book to my main Atheneum editor, Jean Karl, who has a knack for seeing the overall as well as details.

In 1985, Atheneum released Naylor's *Night Cry*, a children's kidnapping thriller that epitomizes one of her common themes, coping with fear. This book, honored by the Mystery Writers of America, is dedicated to Jean Karl.

JEAN E. KARL

Jean E. Karl uses a middle initial in her name to distinguish her roles as a writer (initial) and as an editor (no initial). She has written five science fiction books and three nonfiction works, and is best known as an Atheneum editor with her own imprint.

Karl explained how she responds when editing a new manuscript:

> I read it and make notes to myself. Later, I reread it and write more notes, often on the copy. Then I correspond with the author about what's not working for me. The writer knows everything about the book and thinks it's all there but can't see the holes. It's my job to point out holes. Sometimes husbands and critique groups are too close to the creator. It takes someone a little further away to be objective.

Karl was born on July 29, 1927, and has a background similar to Naylor's. As a child, she also cherished books, wrote and illustrated her own booklets, and had stories published in magazines. Karl's were printed in *Story Parade.* Her father was a Depression-era salesman, and she grew up in Illinois.

During the Depression, Karl's parents moved into her paternal grandfather's Chicago house with their only child and three of her aunts. Aunt Anne, a teacher, shared her class library with her niece. Karl enjoyed her years in public school, Thornton Junior College, and Mount Union College in Ohio. She said, "I had lots of literature, history, science, philosophy, and enough education courses to qualify as a teacher. The more an editor or a writer knows, the better."

Before college graduation, Karl wrote fifty publishers asking for a job. She accepted a Scott, Foresman training offer in Chicago and soon helped edit *Dick and Jane* readers.

After Chicago, Karl worked in New York as an Abingdon Press children's editor for five years. In 1961, she started Atheneum's children's department, eventually becoming a vice president before semiretiring in 1985. She was a field editor and lived in Lancaster, Pennsylvania. She explained, "I continue to release Jean Karl books for Atheneum and edit for Naylor as well as fifteen to twenty other authors."

Karl began writing middle-grade science fiction after someone who had heard one of her original "sci-fi" short stories in a speech told her, "Why waste your time as an editor?" Karl reflected:

> We need editors, too. After I finished writing my first book, I didn't know what to do with it. I couldn't publish it myself, and I knew the other editors. It's hard to evaluate your own work. Editors need editors too. I got an agent to submit my book, using a pseudonym. An editor told my agent she'd like to talk to the new author. I had a bad cold, so I called her. She recognized me, but the result was *The Turning Place.*

The Turning Place: Stories of a Future Past was published by Dutton in 1976. Her science fiction books that followed are: *Beloved Benjamin Is Waiting* (Dutton, 1978); *But We Are Not of Earth* (Dutton, 1981); *Strange Tomorrow* (Dutton, 1985); and *The Search for the Ten-Winged Dragon* (Doubleday, 1990). Her nonfiction includes: *From Childhood to Childhood: Children's Books and Their Creators* (J. Day, 1970); *America Alive, a History* (Philomel, 1994); and *How to Write and Sell Children's Picture Books* (Writer's Digest Books, 1994).

> Writer's Digest Books asked me to do *How to Write and Sell Children's Picture Books.* So many books I'd seen on the subject made it seem easy. It isn't easy to

write anything, and picture books may be harder than others. I felt if I exposed difficulties but explained a path to success, I'd accomplish something.

My other 1994 book is *America Alive: A History.* I wrote it at Philomel's invitation. Bookstores were getting requests for American history books at about the fifth-grade reading level. I felt it would be an interesting challenge in a hundred manuscript pages, so I did *America Alive.*"

Known as an editor–author, Karl moved with ease between work on her own manuscripts and assisting other authors. Naylor planned to keep both of them busy, as she explained in her children's book, *How I Came to Be a Writer* (1978): "I'll go on writing because an idea in my head is like a rock in the shoe; I just can't wait to get it out."

UPDATE

In summer, 1997, director Dale Rosenbloom completed directing a film that he wrote, *Shiloh,* based on Naylor's book. The film is a family classic.

In 1997, a book edited by Karl, E. L. Konigsburg's *The View from Saturday,* won the 1997 Newbery Medal. Jean Karl died on March 30, 2000, at a hospital in Lancaster, Pennsylvania, at the age of seventy-two.

Emily Cheney Neville, author (1919–)

1975 Interview

Emily Cheney Neville, who has written five books for Harper, said she doesn't believe in moralizing. She explained, "It's a way to lose a character. The moment the author asserts, 'This is what I believe,' her character is a cardboard illustration who is not able to do what he or she wants to do." Two of her Harper books have won awards: the 1964 Newbery Medal for *It's Like This, Cat* (1963), and the 1966 Jane Addams Children's Book Award for *Berries Goodman* (1965).

Emily Cheney was born on December 19, 1919, in South Manchester, Connecticut. Her mother, Anne Bunce Cheney, a Christian Scientist, gave birth to Emily, her last child, helped by a psychiatrist friend. Emily's father, Howell Cheney, had studied to be a lawyer, but went into the family's silk business after a bout with measles affected his eyes. For thirty years he was on the Manchester Board of Education, and helped start the state's first technical-vocational school.

In *Traveler from a Small Kingdom* (Harper, 1968) and in person, the author described growing up with six brothers and sisters on the Cheney Place (the "Place") in South Manchester:

South Manchester was a company town. The Cheney Silk Mills were the industry of that town. My grandfather had twelve children and his brother had eleven. The area was perhaps the size of a small golf course dotted with ten or fifteen small houses for workers. We did not tend to go out of that boundary much. For some time, I went to school there just with my cousins. I hardly knew any other children until I was ten years old and went to [public] school in seventh grade [at Manchester's Barnard Junior High School].

During the summer, Emily's family visited their mother's former home in Keene Valley, New York, where her mother's family had settled when her great-grandfather, Horace Bushnell, a "climbing cleric," chose to live there in the 1850s.

While growing up, Emily and her sister, Mary, had a governess, Mrs. Goodall, who, along with Emily's parents, read a lot of stories by Mark Twain. Both sides of Emily's family had known Mark Twain when he had lived in Hartford, Connecticut.

In 1931, her mother died of pneumonia, so when Emily was twelve, her father was her only parent. That year, the Depression forced Emily's father to leave the family business. He worked in Hartford and drove his youngest daughter to a girls' day school, but her sister, Mary, went to boarding school. He taught Emily to drive when she could see through (not *over*) the steering wheel. In eighth grade, she transferred to Hartford's Oxford High School, where she enjoyed sports, books, and friends.

Emily graduated from high school at age sixteen and went to Bryn Mawr College. She majored in economics and history, working for pleasure on the college magazine and newspaper. After graduation, her extracurricular college activities led to her first job as copygirl on the New York *Daily News*.

Emily switched to another newspaper, the New York *Mirror*, eventually writing the "Only Human" daily column for a year. She socialized with the chief editorial writer, Glenn T. Neville. In time, she became his wife, raising their five children: Emily Tam, Glenn H., Dessie, Marcy Ann, and Alec. They lived with two large dogs and a cat in a first-floor Manhattan apartment near Gramercy Park. Their vacation home was in Keene Valley. She helped with the parent newspaper of the children's Public School 40 but read aloud to her children only sporadically: "With my (five) kids, I copped out once they reached third grade except now and then."

When her youngest child began school, Neville started writing regularly. She wrote a short story, "Cat and I," which the *Mirror* published on a Sunday without her husband being informed and without her mentioning his name to the editor:

I was trying to write a story to sell to the Sunday *Mirror*, a tabloid newspaper. They ran a short story complete on one page every Sunday. I had sent this editor one previous story, which she was sort of interested in. She asked if I had anything else. I wanted to write a story that had a New York setting.

The Sunday *Mirror* is not highly intellectual. I got started on this story about a kid having an argument with his father, and the kid telling it. This was the first time I wrote anything in first person. . . . I was having a good time writing it (the argument) as dialog, as a funny scene.

I thought: What would they argue about? The father might say, "How great it is to have a dog!" so the kid will want a cat. Okay, I've got a boy, a cat, and a father. . . . What happened to our cat? Two things: like everybody's cat, he got lost, and he jumped out of the car on the parkway.

Neville approached Harper's children's book editor, Ursula Nordstrom, and showed her the published short story, "Cat and I." Nordstrom encouraged Neville to enlarge the story to suit boys aged ten to fourteen, a group that lacked quality fiction. Almost two years were consumed with developing episodes that led to a book, *It's Like This, Cat.* Neville recalled:

Writing the book was really from then on a matter of adding another incident, another location, another person. I had no real plot in mind when I started. The original story depicted a baby-sitter, and a cat jumping out of the family car on a return trip to New York. It was just a short story.

The story progressed in little expansions, chapter by chapter. I "roped in" Inwood Park, downtown, the Fulton Fish Market, and Coney Island. When I got Dave up to ninth grade, as I was trying to think of some things that a kid would do, it was obvious that he would meet some new friends. My children were in school in New York City at that time, and I realized almost all their friends were Jewish. I added a colorful episode involving a Rosh Hashanah celebration.

Some of her book characters are based on people she knows, including the baby-sitter in the cat book. Neville recalled, "I had had a baby-sitter who came to my home who was a real cat nut and a cottage cheese and no-string-beans nut. She eventually began bringing her sick cats when she came to work, and we parted company at that point."

By contrast, Neville introduced a character, Tom, who was not based on a known person. She first cast him as a burglar:

I inserted Tom for the purpose of getting the cat out of the locked cage in the cellar back in chapter two. I realized I didn't know anything about burglars, fortunately, so I changed him into a college student to get on surer ground. I depend very much on knowing about any character, so I put in a college kid because I know what he might think or do.

Neville's persistent revisions finally won over her editor:

I sent my manuscript back to Ursula Nordstrom at Harper's two, three, or four times in the course of the book. Roughly speaking, she said, "It's fine but keep on going. It's not a book yet."

There were some suggestions she made after we'd signed a contract. We got to this word, plot: "You need a little more thread to tie the book together, and this thread appears to be the boy and his father, so simply strengthen this. You began with the boy and his father, so end with the boy and his father." I had previously ended with the boy and Kate with her kitten.

The relationship between Dave and his dad was similar to her ties with her own father. Dave's attachment to his cat in the book was like her childhood affection for her dog, Jump.

"Harder to write than *Cat* was *Berries Goodman*, since there are many more ideas in it, and it's harder to record your treatment of each idea," Neville said. This second book concerns anti-Semitism, and Neville limits her topic:

You can't undertake the whole area of anti-Semitism in a juvenile novel. You've got to pare down to a restricted topic that you can deal with or you get pompous. . . . I played golf occasionally with a friend who sold real estate and hated living in the suburbs with her four children. . . . Her discontent grew out of restrictions understood by real estate agents: "Don't sell north of Broad Street to anyone who is Jewish." It put her in an uncomfortable position, since many of her New York friends were Jewish. I chose to get that situation into *Berries*.

In *Berries Goodman,* Berries moves from New York City to the suburbs and is happy when he meets another outsider in his class, Sidney Fine, a Jewish baseball whiz. While ice-skating, Sidney is knocked unconscious when he accepts a dare from Berries's biased neighbor, Sandra. Afterward, Sidney transfers to another school, but Sidney and Berries stay friendly. Berries's family moves back to Manhattan, and his mother ends her real-estate job. Her disgust stems from being told to restrict home sales to Jews in certain areas.

Berries Goodman has its humorous moments too. An example is when adolescent Berries thought the family's new maid, Mavis Funk, actually intended to bathe him.

On June 30, 1964, when Neville received the Newbery Medal, her husband, Glenn Neville, spoke, praising her as both a mother and writer. He died a year later after suffering a second stroke.

Complimented for believable dialog in her books, Neville expressed reluctance to convert her books into drama or screenplays:

I have thought about it. There's one drawback: plot! You really have to have a tight plot to make a play work. Anybody who tries to make a screen play of one of my books would have to be inventive, inserting some plot where mine is loose. I have thought about it for *Seventeenth Street Gang,* which would make a good screen play, but there are some fuzzy plot areas.

Harper published *Seventeenth Street Gang* in 1966. The story focuses on white youths in Manhattan. A newcomer from Philadelphia, Hollis, earns acceptance on the block, which is near the Nevilles' former Manhattan address.

In 1969, Neville accepted an invitation from St. Louis city schools to be "author in residence." They already used *It's Like This, Cat* in eighth-grade classes. She accepted the challenge to inspire writing in five or six classes a day. An outgrowth of the St. Louis experience was her book, *Garden of Broken Glass* (Delacorte, 1975). This is an urban story with a thirteen-year-old white protagonist, Brian Moody, a seventh-grade student. His father abandoned the family, and his mother is an alcoholic. He finds comfort and inspiration from African Americans who live nearby.

After writing her Delacorte book for young adults, Neville redirected her life. She remembered that her father left law school due to illness. The hero in her 1969 Harper book for young adults, *Fogarty,* is twenty-three-year-old Dan Fogarty, a Temple University graduate who, before he became a teacher, was a would-be playwright and a law school dropout. Law school was on her mind, so she enrolled at Albany Law School.

To her surprise, Neville passed the thirteen-hour New York Bar examination comprised mainly of essay questions, her forte. She lives in Keene Valley, New York, where she practices law. She has found that lawyers and writers use different processes to reach goals. She said, "A lawyer must plot steps toward a goal, think of 'how' to resolve a problem. I think like a fiction writer concerned with motive or 'why' the problem occurred."

Neville diverts her mind from work with sports:

Where I live in the summertime, the water is icy, so if I want to swim, I have to swim in icy water. I get used to it. I don't mind warmer water. Also, I did a lot of fly-fishing with my husband. He made a big thing of it, but I'm not so good. I tied my own flies and caught a few fish. It was what my husband liked to do. We went together, so it was good fun.

The sportswoman mountain climbs in her neighboring Adirondacks. She also likes visiting distant places, to learn about cultures.

Neville counseled aspiring authors to give their characters free rein and to continue sending stories to editors:

Don't give up when you're rejected. I've had stories and books rejected, and so has every author. . . . When I began *It's Like This, Cat,* I just had two or three characters, and I started them talking. I soon saw where they were going.

UPDATE

After returning from Asia in 1985, Neville wrote two Harper books. *The Bridge* (1988) is a picture book about a rural boy, Ben, who, with his dog, Chowder, and his rabbit, Rhubarb, watches the building of a replacement bridge. The simple story suits young children, but the text is for the intermediate grades. Neville's young-adult book, *The China Year* (1991), is about Henrietta "Henri" Rich, a New York teenager who joins her father, a professor, for a year in Beijing and witnesses the 1989 Tiananmen Square protests.

Scott O'Dell, author (1898–1989)

1976 Interview

It was a naturalist's passion that led Scott O'Dell to write *Island of the Blue Dolphins* (Houghton, 1960), the first of twenty-six children's novels, all published by Houghton. O'Dell became ardent when he spoke of "being damn mad at the hunters who came and killed everything [nonhuman] that crept or walked or flew."

His premier children's book won the 1961 Newbery Medal, and three of his other works of historical fiction were Newbery Honor Books: *The King's Fifth* (Houghton, 1966) in 1967; *The Black Pearl* (Houghton, 1967) in 1968; and *Sing Down the Moon* (Houghton, 1970) in 1971. In 1972 he won the international Hans Christian Andersen Medal for all his books.

O'Dell was born on May 23, 1898, a descendant of Sir Walter Scott, in Los Angeles, which was a frontier town then. His father, Bennett Mason, worked for the Union Pacific Railroad and moved his family often. His mother, May Elizabeth Gabriel O'Dell, "read me *Jack and the Beanstalk* every night. If she didn't, she had trouble."

From ages six to nine, O'Dell lived in San Pedro, part of Los Angeles, where he could almost see San Nicolás Island, home of his Newbery winner's protagonist. At school, he was accepted by sons of Portuguese and Italian fishermen. He joined them on Saturdays, digging for cockles and abalones on the beach. His family moved across the bay from San Pedro, to Rattlesnake Island, where their house was on stilts, and the tide came up below. On summer mornings, he and other boys paddled to the sea and back on long separate logs.

He was a good student at Long Beach Polytechnic High School, and enjoyed both the 440-yard dash and water polo. He attended Occidental College, University of Wisconsin, Stanford University, and University of Rome but never received a college degree. His sole interest was in courses to help his future writing career.

After college, he was a cameraman for the film *Ben Hur* in Rome. During World War II, he was in the Air Force in Texas. Returning to California, he wrote for magazines and became the Los Angeles *Daily News* book editor. When his father bought an orange grove near Claremont, California, his son joined him.

For ten years O'Dell wrote books for adults before starting a forty-five-year career writing for young people. The switch "was purely accidental," he said. "I'm delighted that I made the change. I wouldn't go back if I could write as well as Saul Bellow, John Updike, Cheever, Faulkner, and all the rest." One adult book, *Country of the Sun* (Crowell, 1957), an informal history, has a chapter about a small Pacific island off Baja California. Called "Lost Woman of San Nicolás," the chapter tells how a ship took survivors of Aleut and Russian attacks from San Nicolás Island to what is now California in 1835. One woman jumped overboard to return to the island, where her child had been left.

O'Dell's *Island of the Blue Dolphins* changes the above account slightly, having his protagonist go back to tend Ramo, her young brother, who soon dies from a wild dog's bites. She is on the island with no other permanent human beings until 1853. She tames the dog who murdered her brother and calls him Rontu. O'Dell gives a credible account of the woman's rescue after she spent eighteen years alone on the island:

> This is true! She was rescued by the only boat on the Pacific Coast at that time. It was just a thirty-foot boat. They sent it over there to the south Pacific island, a very stormy one. When she was rescued, she went to the Mission of Santa Barbara. She lived there for about two months and died of some mysterious illness. You could be romantic and say that she died of a broken heart, that she longed for her island. It's possible.

A plaque at Mission Santa Barbara commemorates "Juana María, Indian woman abandoned on San Nicolás Island for eighteen years, found by Captain George Nidiver in 1853." She was buried on a nearby hill.

"The plaque did not exist before my book, *Island of the Blue Dolphins,* was written," O'Dell said. "They didn't know anything about her up there.

When the book came out, it did have that effect." The author offered more information about the first boat that brought Karana's people to San Francisco Harbor:

> It sank there two years after its rescue mission, and no one was aboard. It delivered everyone, and then they scattered. For some reason, they went all over southern California. The missionaries were eventually quite interested in what happened to them, because Karana could not speak any of the languages known at the mission. Several Indian dialects were used there. They sent couriers around the West, trying to find survivors taken from the island.
>
> They couldn't find anyone, so she died, not being able to communicate. It was fortunate for me. They could have asked her what she did for eighteen years alone on the island. If she said, "Well, I didn't do much. I knitted a lot of sweaters," I'd be stuck with a female who knitted sweaters for eighteen years.

The person who indirectly influenced O'Dell to write *Island of the Blue Dolphins* was Maud Hart Lovelace, author of the "Betsy-Tacy" children's books.

> During lunch, Maud said, "I have read a book of yours called *Country of the Sun*. In it, you relate a story about a girl who spent eighteen years alone on an island in the Pacific Ocean. Do you know anymore about this girl than you wrote in *Country of the Sun*?"
>
> Instantly, immediately, I knew that she wanted to write this book. I said, "I'm terribly sorry, Maud, but I have already begun that story."
>
> I was so bedizened by this outrageous lie that I told my dear friend that I rushed home, sat down at the typewriter, and began to write. That was the beginning of the story.

O'Dell was also motivated by his view of hunting:

> I thought I might write a letter to the newspaper, and I realized that was ephemeral. Out of this anger, objectively I sat down to do a book that I thought would affect children, particularly girls. I thought that, having read the book and having children of their own, they would do something about this slaughter of innocent animals. That was the reason I wrote the book. That was the motivation.

His agents weren't interested in his book, and in fact turned it down flat. In part, the agents wrote: "We don't think much of this story. Presumably, you want to write it for a girl, but girls only care about themselves and topical things, a little romance, a little mystery, a regular formula. If you're interested (a presumption would be you wouldn't go to all that trouble if you weren't interested), we suggest you change the girl to a boy." O'Dell persevered, helped by Lovelace's support:

> I had faith in the book. Maud Lovelace gave me most of the faith that I had. She said, "It's a good book. Just don't change it. I will make one suggestion. I think she should be a little bit more feminine, not much." So I invented the episode where she makes the cormorant skirt. The novel was finished, and I just dropped in that paragraph. I was very careful throughout the book. I didn't want a feminine girl. I wanted a human being! Her cormorant cape is now in Rome supposedly.

The author found it difficult to name his Newbery winner:

> I had trouble with that title. First, I called it "Karana" after the girl, then "Island of the Dolphins." There's something wrong with that title. The sound is wrong. Then I tried "Island of the Brown Dolphins." That doesn't do it either. They are brown, you know, with white bellies. I fudged a little and called it *Island of the Blue Dolphins.*

Houghton's editor of children's books accepted this future prizewinner the day after receiving the first-person manuscript and has since published all of O'Dell's children's books. Like his other books, it has no inside illustrations. "If you do as a writer what you should do, there is no necessity for illustrations," he said.

O'Dell gave the typescript of his Newbery winner to the Free Library of Philadelphia's Rare Book Department. He added the missing first page in his own handwriting.

His sequel to *Island of the Blue Dolphins* is *Zia* (Houghton, 1976), Karana's fictional niece's name:

> I was very anxious to do it. Children had written, "What happened to Karana?" I thought I should write about it. My publishers fought it. Every time I'd bring it up, which would be every two or three years, the publishers would say, "Write a book, but don't write it about Karana. . . ." So I just crept up on them. They asked me what I was working on, and I'd say, "Go-go girls in New Orleans!" They had to publish it. I guess they like it. I don't know.

In the sequel, Karana's fourteen-year-old niece, Zia, and her eleven-year-old brother, Mando, try to rescue Karana from the island, but wind and waves make them leave. Zia is at Mission Santa Barbara when Karana does arrive.

Speaking different languages impedes communication, but Karana gives Zia her stone necklace before dying.

In 1964, Robert Radnitz produced a Universal Studios film adaptation of *Island of the Blue Dolphins*, starring Celia Kaye as Karana. O'Dell criticized the film:

> I talked to Radnitz, the producer, before he made the picture. I thought he was rather obtuse. I suggested various things and saw rather quickly that he had made up his mind about what he wanted to do. One was to cast the Kaye girl, who had no acting experience, as Karana, because she was very pretty. The girls would envy her, and the boys would fall in love with her. She wasn't an actress. She was a dancer, so she could run up a sand dune very gracefully. . . . She's all gussied up like she's coming to a marshmallow roast. I would have cast the person who played the Aleut girl as Karana. I would have lost my shirt, because children did identify with the filmed Karana.

The film focused on four years, starting when Karana's father is chief. His subchieftain exits by canoe and brings a boat that saves survivors of an Aleut attack. Only Karana stays because her brother was left behind. Both book and film show Karana's reverence for life in nurturing animals and befriending a brief visitor, Tutok, an Aleut girl.

Also on film is O'Dell's *The Black Pearl*, a legend about Ramón Salazar, who dives for pearls in the seaport of La Paz, Baja California. Here Manta Diablo, a giant Manta ray, guards the Pearl of Heaven. When Ramón finds the pearl, he gives it to the church. O'Dell said he found this film version acceptable.

The King's Fifth concerns young sixteenth-century Spaniards who search for the Seven Golden Cities of Cíbola. In New Spain, they cross what is now the Gulf of California into Arizona, New Mexico, the Grand Canyon, Death Valley, and beyond. All is sacrificed to lust for gold.

The third Newbery Honor Book, *Sing Down the Moon*, is set in 1864. After fighting Spanish slavers, Navajos must submit to white soldiers who force them on the Long Walk of three hundred miles to Fort Sumner. A Navaho girl, Bright Morning, marries Tall Boy, who is maimed physically and spiritually. She lives on hope of survival. O'Dell's title, *Sing Down the Moon,* he said, "is a line out of a poem on a Greek theme by Robinson Jeffers. This is a metaphor. Of all the things you can't do, you can't dip up the ocean with a teaspoon, and you can't sing down the moon. Bright Morning hoped that life would be continuous. We know, looking back on what happened to the Navahos, they faced a hopeless task."

Bright Morning differs from O'Dell's liberated female protagonist in a new book, entitled *Carlota*:

This book, *Carlota*, that I have coming out in the spring is based on the life of a girl from the Montero family. She lived in Southern California in about 1846. She had the temerity to ride astride a stallion. If you were a girl then, you rode sidesaddle. She was the scandal of the countryside of Southern California! I've focused on this girl who was raised as a boy by her father. It's sound psychology: if you raise girls as she was raised, they can do as well as boys do. Girls are out of the cage!

In *Carlota*, Don Saturnino trains Carlota to take the place of her dead brother, Carlos. In the Mexican War, she rides with men who ambush Kit Carson and the Yankee army in the Battle of San Pasqual. When she wounds a young soldier, she brings him home to recuperate, a compassionate act in defiance of her father. Carlota demonstrated reverence for life, forgiving her enemy, as Karana forgave Rontu in *Island of the Blue Dolphins*.

When he wrote *Carlota*, O'Dell lived not too far from the ranch setting he described as her home. He moved East since "my wife was managing editor of *Psychology Today*. They moved the magazine from Del Mar, California, to New York. She went, and I went with her." In New York state, he settled on Make Peace Hill in Waccabuc, where he wrote from seven in the morning until noon every day of the week.

O'Dell said he considers writing to be hard work, and the part he enjoys most is research. Before writing *The King's Fifth*, O'Dell followed the trail of the Seven Cities of Cíbola over a thousand miles by boat, automobile, and on foot. He would not write *Sing Down the Moon* until he spent part of 1961 in Navaho country where Arizona, New Mexico, Colorado, and Utah meet. For *The Cruise of the Arctic Star* (Houghton, 1973), a nonfiction book, he traveled the length of the California coast with his wife and two crewmen.

While O'Dell's focus was mostly on historical events, several of his books for young people deal with current problems. For instance, *Child of Fire* (Houghton, 1974) is the story of a sixteen-year-old *macho* Chicano, Manuel Castillo, who jumps in front of a harvesting machine that replaces workers.

O'Dell said, "One reason I preferred to write for young people rather than adults is that children can change easier than adults." He also enjoyed their fan mail. He remembered a boy who fulfilled a class assignment with a three-page letter but got tired in the last paragraph and wrote, "Well, I've gotta go now. Good-bye, you old jerk!"

In jest, O'Dell called himself, "General MacArthur," due to all his medals. Beyond what was previously cited, his awards include the 1976 University of Southern Mississippi Medallion. He won the German Juvenile International Award for *Island of the Blue Dolphins* in 1963, and in 1969 for *The King's Fifth*. For *Island of the Blue Dolphins*, he received a 1960 Rupert Hughes Award, 1961 Southern California Council on Literature for Children and

Young People Notable Book Award, 1962 Hans Christian Andersen Award of Merit, 1963 William Allen White Award, and 1964 Nene Award, the last two being readers-choice honors.

UPDATE

O'Dell's book *Carlota* was published by Houghton in 1977. He continued to collect awards during his career, receiving the Regina Medal in 1978 for all his books. In 1981, he founded the Scott O'Dell Award for Historical Fiction.

To prepare for his last self-written book, *My Name Is Not Angelica* (Houghton, 1989), he talked to descendants of slaves on the islands of St. Thomas and St. John. O'Dell wrote one trilogy: *The Captive* (Houghton, 1979), *The Feathered Serpent* (Houghton, 1981), and *The Amethyst Ring* (Houghton, 1983) about Julián Escobar, a Jesuit seminarian forced to accompany a Spanish conquistador to sixteenth-century Central and South America.

Kathleen, Please Come Home (Houghton, 1978) tells about fifteen-year-old Kathleen whose mother opposes her Mexican boyfriend, an illegal immigrant. *Alexandra* (Houghton, 1984) concerns a young sponge fisher, Alexandra Papadimitrios, in Tarpon Springs, Florida, who learns that a drug dealer is using her family's boat to smuggle cocaine.

On October 15, 1989, Scott O'Dell died of prostate cancer at age ninety-one in Waccabuc. His wife, Elizabeth Hall, completed his last unfinished novel, *Thunder Rolling in the Mountains* (Houghton, 1992).

Katherine Paterson, author (1932–)

1979 Interview

Katherine Paterson (left) with Jaqueline Weiss

"Being able to totally absorb ourself in creation is the thing that distinguishes us from our brothers and sisters, the animals," said storyteller Katherine Paterson. Her awareness of emotional human relations is apparent in her books, edited by Virginia Buckley and published by Crowell.

Paterson created the 1978 Newbery Medal winner, *Bridge to Terabithia* (1977), and a 1977 National Book Award winner for children's literature, *The Master Puppeteer* (1975). In 1979, *The Great Gilly Hopkins* (1978) was a Newbery Honor Book and National Book Award winner for children's literature.

Katherine Womeldorf was born on October 31, 1932, in Qing Jiang in China's Jiangsu Province, where her parents, George and Mary Womeldorf, were Presbyterian missionaries. Her father, who lost his right leg as an ambulance driver in World War I, volunteered as a missionary in China. He and his friend, a Chinese Christian pastor, rode donkeys to bring food and medicine to villagers. Katherine spoke Chinese first but soon became bilingual. During Sino-Japanese Wars, her family moved to Richmond, Virginia, where she enrolled in first grade. Her family returned to China, living in Shanghai's British sector. She did not have many books as a child, but her mother reread Milne stories, and her first poem was published in the school newspaper, "Shanghai American," when she was seven.

277

Katherine's family moved from Asia to the United States and within the United States more than fifteen times before she turned fifteen years old. She described herself on her last U.S. trip as a small, timid eight-year-old, overwhelmed at Calvin H. Wiley School in Winston-Salem, North Carolina:

> I was a weird little kid. I came back to the United States, and you won't believe me, I spoke English with a British accent. I wore clothes out of the missionary barrel, which are not New Bethesda trends. It's from Salvation Army leftovers. I could come from somewhere over there, and children are sort of vague on geography. I could be a Japanese spy as far as my peers were concerned. The only thing I could change was my accent, which I got rid of in three weeks.
>
> I'm a grown-up lady. I move in polite society, and people are very nice to me. But you never lose the child within who did not know how she would be accepted when she moved toward a playground group or who would laugh when she raised her hand in class.

At Wiley School, classmates called Katherine "Jap," but there she acquired an entrenched North Carolina accent. What saved her was being a school library aide. She mended books, handling glue as Jiro later did on the first page of *The Master Puppeteer.*

The future author entered King College in Bristol, Tennessee, graduating in 1954 summa cum laude with a bachelor's degree. The next year, she taught at an elementary school in Lovettsville, Virginia. In 1957, she earned her master's degree at Presbyterian School of Christian Education, where a professor urged her to be a writer. Instead, she became a missionary in Japan from 1957 to 1961 and studied at Naganuma School of Japanese Language, gaining new thoughts and a new tongue.

Returning from Japan, she studied at New York's Union Theological Seminary, where she met a Presbyterian minister, John Barstow Paterson, a Swarthmore College graduate. The couple married in 1962 and had two sons: John Jr. in 1965 and David in 1967. They also adopted two daughters, Lin, born in 1963, and Mary, born in 1968, each of whom joined the family at about age three:

> Lin is Chinese. She was born in Hong Kong. Her Chinese name, *Po Lin,* means "Precious Life." It was given to her in the orphanage. Mary is Apache on one side and Cayawa on the other. Mary's Native American name is *Nah-he-sah-pe-che-a,* which means "A Young Apache Lady."
>
> I have a friend who works in the Bureau of American Indian Affairs. He sent a runner to Will Rodgers Jr. in Oklahoma City to ask for a name from the little old lady who gives names. The name sent back was *Nah-he-sah-pe-che-a.* I asked for something shorter. He said, "The lady gave you a name. You take it!"

Paterson also was a foster parent to two Cambodian boys:

> The reason I wrote a book [*The Great Gilly Hopkins*] about a foster child was because I was a temporary foster mother. I didn't mean to be. It was one of these flukes: because we had adopted, we had already been investigated. We thought it was going to be for two weeks. It turned out to be for two months. What I learned was that I was a terrible foster mother.
>
> Whenever something went wrong, and something went wrong many times every day, I would say to myself, "I can't really handle that, because he's only going to be here a short time." I was treating each child like a Kleenex. There's nothing worse! I created the world's greatest foster mother [Maime Trotter in *The Great Gilly Hopkins*] to make up for my sins.

In the book named for her, eleven-year-old Galadriel "Gilly" Hopkins wants to live with her "beautiful" mother, Courtney. Instead, she joins the household of a fat, almost illiterate guardian, Maime Trotter, and a seven-year-old foster child, William Ernest. Gutsy Gilly schemes to leave Trotter's loving home, but is rejected by her "natural" mother. This book won the 1979 Christopher Award and readers-choice awards in Kansas, New Jersey, Georgia, Iowa, and Massachusetts. The book's theme, Paterson said, is: "Life is tough, but there's nothing like doing well at a tough job, as Trotter has."

Gilly tackles in the United States some of the same problems as the protagonist faces in Japan in *The Sign of the Chrysanthemum* (1973). This book, Paterson's first to be published, is set in twelfth-century Japan's capital and presents thirteen-year-old Muna (which means "No Name"). He searches for the father who left before his birth. His mother is dead, and he knows only that his father, a samurai warrior, has a chrysanthemum tattoo on his shoulder. Paterson discussed her book's theme that emphasizes Muna's maturation:

> He becomes what he is through fire. To fulfill what's there (his potential) is a painful as well as a joyful process. . . . It's a little bit of a parallel between the forging of the sword and the forging of the boy. The essential elements were there all along, but without the fire and water, the sword never is sharpened and is never worthy.

Paterson began her new writing career by composing for the Presbyterian Church. She said, "I discovered with four little children at home, writing was something I could do. I wrote and I wrote and I wrote, and I did not publish."

She took a class on writing for children, and produced *The Sign of the Chrysanthemum*, writing one chapter a week. She discussed how the class helped her: "It imposed a discipline from the outside, but the teacher can't write for you."

Aside from church publications, she had nothing else published for nine years until *The Sign of the Chrysanthemum* in 1973:

> *The Sign of the Chrysanthemum* had been going around for two years when Sandra Jordan saw it. . . . She was, at that time, just out of college and a first reader for Crowell. She took it to Ann Beneduce who decided to take a chance on a book that nobody in his right mind would buy. Who is going to buy a book about twelfth-century Japan for children? The book never went into its second printing until I won the Newbery. She took a chance on it!
>
> Virginia Buckley has been my editor all the way through. It's not fair for my name alone to be on these books because Virginia is such a wise editor. She doesn't ever tell me what to do. She tells me what's wrong and gives me the courage to know that I can do something about it. She's magnificent!

The author described her writing process for a book:

> I have to confess when I start a book, I'm working on my own problems, fears, and anxieties. I start wondering late in the game: This is such a private thing. I don't think anyone else is going to understand it. It's invariably a pleasant surprise. The first person who reads it is my husband, and I think: *At least one other person understands it.* Then I give it to my editor, and if she comprehends it, I have two people. I read it aloud to my children. If they understand, I have some hope that others will. But in the beginning, I'm never quite sure.
>
> It's a very private exercise for me, egotistical in many ways. When you assign noble aims to me, I'm embarrassed because essentially, it's a very selfish process that I'm going through.

Of Nightingales That Weep (Crowell, 1974) is Paterson's second published book, the outgrowth of a telephone call:

> Someone wanted to reach my husband, a pastor. I was trying to remember who the person was, and I thought: *That's the ugliest person I ever saw in my life.* Then I reflected: What would it be like if that were the first thought anyone had about you? How must it be not to relate normally to other people because always you have this barrier that you can do nothing about. We have all these barriers with us of color, class, education, or just physical attributes. In expiation for my sins, I wrote against vanity.

Of Nightingales That Weep, an American Library Association Notable Book, focuses on Takiko, a samurai's vain, musical daughter from age eleven to sixteen. Civil war destroys her easy Japanese feudal life. When she was a beauty, she lived with royalty and secretly loved an enemy spy. The spy rejects her, once her face is accidentally scarred. The only man then who is kind to her is a dwarf potter, Goro, who becomes her husband.

At her husband's request, Paterson wrote *Angels & Other Strangers: Family Christmas Stories* (Crowell, 1978), and he read his congregants a tale each Christmas Eve.

The third book set in Japan, *The Master Puppeteer,* is an Edgar Award winner. It is the story of a young apprentice puppeteer, Jiro, in rioting Osaka. Paterson returned to Japan with her daughter, Lin, and visited the famous Bunraku puppet theater to lend authenticity to her story. She said, "Children question me a lot about the mother [of Jiro] in *The Master Puppeteer.* The thing that worries them is, 'Why is the mother so mean?' Well, *is* she so mean?" The mother, who is starving, takes part in a hunger riot.

In *The Sign of the Chrysanthemum, Of Nightingales That Weep,* and *The Master Puppeteer,* Paterson emphasizes the role of the arts in Japan. This is true of the craftsmanship of Fukuji's sword in the first book, Goro's pottery and Takiko's playing of the *koto* in the second book, and puppets within a theater in the third book. Paterson commented on the intertwining of the arts in Japan:

> The arts are so tied up in Japanese life, you can hardly write a book about Japan without having them.
>
> I think about real caring. When I was visiting Japan, I was able to eat supper at a Japanese friend's house. The vegetables were absolutely marvelous. I asked my friend, "Why are the vegetables so delicious?" She said without a blink, "Because the Japanese farmer loves every vegetable."
>
> It carries over: this kind of caring that makes creativity worthwhile. Of course, in my books, the art is almost a religion, but the protagonists have to combine their creativity with caring for other people before they're through. . . . I can't get them unhooked.

In all of Paterson's books, whether written with a setting abroad or at home, she shows concern for social problems:

> I write out of my own life. I don't set out to write a novel about a social problem. I don't feel qualified to do that, but I think it's significant that when my first three novels were written about Japanese unrest, I was living through the riots of Washington, D.C. I was living in an integrated area one block outside the city of Washington all through the Vietnam demonstrations.
>
> All those things were a part of my life, and I didn't set out to put them consciously in my books. C. S. Lewis said, "The writer cannot be what the man is not." The book can only come out of this woman's life. I don't have any other experience. I'm sure it's related.

Paterson discussed the origin of her Newbery Medal winner, *Bridge to Ter-abithia*:

> It grew out of a friendship my twelve-year-old son, David, had with a girl who was very dear to all of us. She was killed. She was struck by lightning. A kid asked me yesterday about why I didn't put that into the book. Because nobody would believe it! You don't accept that kind of thing.
>
> It was just after I had gone through a cancer operation. So when I started writing the book, thinking I was going through the child's death, of course, what I was doing was facing my own death. It became a difficult thing. It was many days before I could write that chapter. Finally, a friend asked me, "How's the book coming?"
>
> I said, "I can't go through Lisa's death again."
>
> She replied, "It's not *Lisa's* death, Katherine."
>
> So I went home and faced my own death.

Bridge to Terabithia, winner of readers-choice awards in Colorado and Virginia, is an account of ten-year-old Jesse Aarons and his struggling farm family that includes four sisters. Jesse is starting fifth grade when Leslie Burke and her writer parents move next door. Though Jesse and Leslie compete as runners, together they create Terabithia, a secret kingdom in the woods. After Leslie drowns in the swollen creek waters that flood Terabithia, her parents move.

Paterson claims that Jesse Aarons is most like her, compared to other characters in the book. Like Jesse, she was a middle child of five. She was youngest of the older trio and oldest of the younger trio.

> He's scared to death of death. His ideas of death parallel my own absolutely. I didn't get those ideas from anybody else except myself. If you want to know my feelings about death, just read that book. There are no secrets.

Paterson said, "I relate to each of my characters." She told one reader that she is like May Belle:

> I was this scrawny, dumb kid with romantic notions. . . . But I'm other people too. One time, my husband couldn't possibly understand what I was about, so I said, "John, don't you understand? I'm William Ernest" [the foster child in *The Great Gilly Hopkins*].

This champion of the world's "have nots" pays the price of no privacy, saying: "Everybody knows everything about me. It's as though I'm naked in church. If you want to know about me, all you have to do is read my books!"

UPDATE

The Great Gilly Hopkins received the 1980 American Book Award for a children's paperback. In 1981 Paterson won her second Newbery Medal, this time for *Jacob Have I Loved* (Crowell, 1980), a book that explores sibling rivalry. This is a first-person account by hardworking, large-boned Louise whose fraternal twin is pretty, fragile Caroline, a talented singer-pianist. In the Chesapeake Bay, Louise catches crabs, helping her father. Grandmother looks upon Caroline as Jacob, and Louise, as jealous Esau. Paterson imagined how biblical Leah might have felt toward Rachel.

After writing about Japan, Paterson translated a children's tale from Japanese, *The Crane Wife* (Morrow, 1981) by Sumiko Yagawa. She revisited China before writing *Rebels of the Heavenly Kingdom* (1983), one of her first books issued by Dutton. The story is about a fifteen-year-old peasant boy, Wang Lee, rescued from slavery by Mei Lin, a girl with unbound feet. She introduces him to a secret Christian society working to overthrow the hated eighteenth-century Manchu emperor.

In *Park's Quest* (Dutton, 1988), eleven-year-old Parkington "Park" Broughton wants to learn more about his father, who was killed in the Vietnam War. The boy visits his paternal grandparents in rural Virginia where, instead of being welcomed, his newly discovered stepsister, Thanh, taunts him.

Katherine Paterson's talent extends to picture books. In *The Tale of the Mandarin Ducks* (Dutton, 1990), she retells a Japanese folktale, illustrated by Leo and Diane Dillon, about a caged duck who helps his liberators.

Paterson switches from Asia to her own country for *Lyddie* (Dutton, 1991). In 1843, the protagonist, Lyddie Worthen, is thirteen when a bear enters her family's Vermont cabin. She stares him down long enough for her mother, sisters, and brother, Charlie, to flee to the loft, where she joins them. The biennial Honor List of the International Board on Books for Young People (IBBY) included this book from the United States because of its superior writing.

While in Russia for a symposium on children's books, she met a great illustrator, Vladimir Vagin. She wrote *The King's Equal* (HarperCollins, 1992) so Vagin could illustrate this picture book. Vagin also illustrated her book *Celia and the Sweet, Sweet Water* (Clarion, 1998).

Paterson again chooses a Virginia location for *Flip-Flop Girl* (Dutton, 1994). Nine-year-old Vinnie Matthews and her five-year-old brother, Mason, stay with their grandmother, who buys Salvation Army dresses and leather shoes for Vinnie's school clothes.

Paterson wrote *A Sense of Wonder* (Dutton, 1995), an omnibus edition of both *Gates of Excellence* (Nelson, 1981) and *The Spying Heart* (Dutton, 1989) about reading/writing for children.

Paterson's *Jip, His Story* (Dutton, 1996) is a sequel to *Lyddie*, though it is not apparent until the book's end. The story is set in Vermont, where Paterson lives but in earlier years, 1855 and 1856. Jip is abandoned as a toddler after falling off a wagon, and survives on a poor farm where he does chores and helps Put, a caged lunatic. His teacher, Lyddie Worthen, and her Quaker suitor, Luke Stevens, tell Jip about his true parents and help him escape to safety.

Paterson followed her editor in a move from Crowell to Dutton in 1983, and a 1998 move to Clarion. She won the 1998 Hans Christian Andersen Award for superior writing in all her books, which number more than twenty-five. She also won the Regina Medal in 1988 and was the 1997 May Hill Arbuthnot lecturer.

Ann Petry, author (1908–1997)

1975 Interview

"When I was in high school in Old Saybrook, Connecticut, in a town where the majority of the people were white folks, the only mention of black people in history textbooks was slavery," recalled Ann Petry. Her children's books published by Crowell include *The Drugstore Cat* (1949); *Harriet Tubman: Conductor on the Underground Railroad* (1955); *Tituba of Salem Village* (1964), an American Library Association Notable Book; and *Legends of the Saints* (1970).

"We were portrayed as being happy-go-lucky people who were always dancing, playing. We were childlike. . . . I had no way of proving it, but I knew that this was wrong," she said.

Ann Lane was born on October 12, 1908, in the resort town of Old Saybrook. She lived above James' Pharmacy with her father, Peter Clarke, a pharmacist, and her mother, Bertha James Lane. She traced her drugstore ties:

I was in the store since I could walk. All the rules and regulations I knew by heart. I finished high school and went to pharmacy college. I spent three years in a drugstore that we owned in the town of Old Lyme. In the meantime, I was getting increasingly devoted to the man who was to be my husband. I decided that I didn't want any drugstores. I was going to write.

Petry received her pharmacology degree in 1931 from the University of Connecticut, and in 1938 she married George D. Petry and moved with him to

New York City. During her first three years there, she wrote and sold adver-
tisements for *Amsterdam News,* and was woman's page editor of *People's
Voice.* She gave birth to a daughter, Elisabeth Ann Petry, and attended Columbia University with multiple interests:

> I did write some children's plays, not commercially. When I first lived in New
> York City, I was struggling to write short stories. I decided I'd like to write a play.
> In the meantime, I became a member of what was called the American Negro
> Theater. We lived and had our being in a little theater at 131st Street and Sev-
> enth Avenue. We were together for two or three years.
>
> Some who acted became famous, including people like Ruby Dee, Harry Bela-
> fonte, Fred O'Neill, and Helen Morgan. They came out of that grubby theater. I've
> heard people complain about little theaters, but they don't know about what it can
> be like where there are no dressing rooms other than little cubicles. It was fun!

While Petry's first picture storybook, *The Drugstore Cat* (Crowell, 1949), was
partially autobiographical, Susanne Suba's line drawings show white characters, not the author's family. The author commented:

> I wrote that particular book for a reason. We're getting to be an old family. We
> hadn't had any young children in heaven knows how long. My sister had a
> child. In order to celebrate, I had to write a book for her. We had had drugstores,
> and we all were cat lovers. It seemed quite fitting to have this book be about a
> cat who lived in a drugstore. That part was true about a cat thumping down the
> stairs and frightening the burglars. It actually happened!

Petry's next children's book was *Harriet Tubman: Conductor on the Underground Railroad* (Crowell, 1955).

> I wish I could say that it was the result of a considerable amount of thought on
> my part. Actually, it was not. It was a pure accident. Most of what I write is the
> result of an accident. I had been to a book and author luncheon in a Hartford
> department store. . . . I sat next to Harry Commer, who was raised in New York
> state, in Auburn, where Harriet Tubman had lived. During the course of the
> luncheon, he asked me, "Have you ever thought of writing a book about Har-
> riet Tubman?"
>
> After doing research on Tubman, I thought: *Of all the people I've ever heard
> about or encountered, I ought to write about Harriet Tubman.* And it was
> really the result of an accident. If I hadn't been sitting next to him, the chances
> are that book never would have existed.

Petry said, "Much of my book's data about the underground railroad in
Philadelphia came from William Grant Still's diary." Still, whose parents were

born as slaves, was clerk of the Pennsylvania Society for Abolition of Slavery from 1847 to 1861. He later became the society's vice president and later, president. He used his records on former slaves to write a book, *The Underground Railroad* (Porter & Coates, 1872). Petry said:

> I own William Grant Still's diary. It is one of my treasures. At the time I wrote my book, there was really very little interest in that particular period in American history. I have no idea how much his book would sell for today. It was one of the first books I found. You really wouldn't need to do much more research than to use that book. It was so graphic, marvelously written! It was in a little second-hand bookstore in Harlem. I paid ten dollars for it. . . .

Petry was lucky to find this source for her own book, which she wrote mainly for a family member:

> When I did finally decide to write a book about Harriet Tubman, I wrote it specifically for my niece. I wanted her to know that there had existed a woman with the kind of courage Harriet Tubman had, and that this woman had been a slave. To me, in all history, this is the one great American heroine!

While Petry needed little library work to do her Tubman biography, her research was extensive for her second juvenile biography, *Tituba of Salem Village* (Crowell, 1964), an American Library Association Notable Book. Petry said:

> I would rather do the writing than the research. When I go back into another period, I always feel a bit hampered. I don't write freely because I'm always worried that something I'm writing about probably didn't exist at that time. I think it's in *Tituba*, I mentioned that a young man had a pocket, but pockets were not used in that period. It's that kind of little stumbling block that I don't like.

Tituba of Salem Village begins in 1688 in Barbados where John and Tituba Indian, both twenty-nine years old and married, become slaves of Reverend Samuel Parris. He brings them to Boston, and Tituba is a weaver's helper until Parris moves them to Salem Village, where she is accused of being a witch.

Petry credited a New York City library with data she needed for *Tituba of Salem Village:*

> I owe a debt of gratitude to libraries and librarians. As far as *Tituba* is concerned, some of the original documents are in the 42nd Street Library. . . . You say who you are, why you want to see what you want to see, identify yourself, and you think you're in the clear. You go way up in the library to a room where

there is a locked door. They have bars on the doors, and you ring a bell to be admitted. Someone comes to look you over very carefully, and after you present your credentials again, you are permitted to go in.

I think one of the greatest thrills in my life was seeing that document of Tituba's, and here is this cross. Most of the people involved in witchcraft in that period in Salem could not read and write. In most of that material, someone has signed a cross (in lieu of a name). It's heartbreaking! In addition, they didn't know what they were signing because they couldn't read it.

Tituba of Salem Village was followed by another children's book, *Legends of the Saints* (Crowell, 1970). Petry chose ten saints, including Martin de Porres, a black healer and barber-surgeon's apprentice in Peru with a Panamanian mother and a father from Spanish nobility.

Before writing for children, Petry wrote for adults:

My first short story was published in *Crisis,* the official organ of the NAACP. So many things happen by accident. Because it was published, a reader at Houghton Mifflin in Boston saw the story and wrote to ask me if I were working on a novel and if I were, would I submit it for their fellowship award.

I wrote back to say, "No, I am not, but perhaps in another year, I will be," because it never occurred to me to write a novel. It always seemed to me like climbing barehanded up the side of a mountain. That's how *The Street* got started.

Petry received a Houghton Mifflin literary fellowship in 1945 to write her adult novel about life in Harlem, *The Street* (1946). She wrote it while her husband was a World War II serviceman. Houghton published her other adult books, including *Country Place* (1947), a British Book Club selection, and *The Narrows* (1953), both noted for careful structuring. *The Narrows*'s movie rights were purchased by Columbia Pictures. Houghton also published her adult short story collection, *Miss Muriel and Other Stories* (1971). Petry's evaluation was positive:

The novels are translated into many languages and so are my children's biographies. They're still in print. I do think that novelists write better than other people because they know how to make something move. I think all forms of writing support or help each other.

I write since I think it's the only way I can express how I feel about the world, about people. I read somewhere that people who write do it because they're displeased with the world, and they want to play God. They maneuver, manipulate. They create situations they can control. They can't control much of the world. If they write, at least they can control the world of their books.

Petry approached the writing process in an organized way:

I usually begin with people. I have to know how the book is going to end before I start because the whole thing builds to that finale. In the case of *The Street*, I wrote the whole book except the first chapter, and then the first chapter seemed to write itself. It's one of the few things I didn't have to edit. I always do a lot of editing. If you write things, people ought to be able to understand easily what you've written. It's rare that you can write "off the top of your head." That old expression, "Easy writing is cursed hard reading," is true.

Petry talked about her preference to write early in the morning: "At dawn, the day is at its purest, closest to the beginning of things. My mind is clear of all the cobwebby accumulations of the day before." The author works for four hours at a stretch before stopping for tea.

After ten years in New York, she returned to Old Saybrook and moved into a handsome white house with green shutters. Her home had wide lawns on three sides with trees that are hundreds of years old. Here she writes daily in a journal:

People don't remember things well. They can't remember from a month ago and ought to keep a journal. Each person is unique. Each one is different. That uniqueness ought to be recorded somewhere. Unfortunately, I think historians are going to have a devil of a time in another few years because people don't write letters as they once did. Historians, in order to authenticate a particular period, need letters, diaries, or journals.

Some of the most interesting journals were kept during the Civil War when you knew what food cost, what people ate, and had a record of life during that period. To me, probably because I live right now, I think this is one of the most extraordinary times in the world in which to be alive, and there ought to be a record. . . .

There's a collection at Boston University in one of their libraries, the Ann Petry Collection, so if you want to look at my journals and correspondence, it's all there. The letters come from everywhere, all over the world. They still come because there are new editions, some in paperback.

From 1974 to 1975, Petry taught creative writing in Hawaii. She commented on the experience: "Hawaii is so beautiful that it's unbelievable. In spite of all the stories and all the pictures, you don't really have any idea what it is like until you are there. That applies to the people, who are stunning."

At the end of her spring semester writing class, Petry was surprised when she invited questions from students:

I thought they were going to ask me about writing. One brash young man with very athletic shoulders asked, "What does your husband do for a living?"

I replied, "I'll be very happy to answer that question, but I would like to point out you have been conditioned by the culture in which you live, because it would never occur to you to ask a man what his wife did for a living. My husband is a retired advertising executive and used to be in New York City."

Among the advice Petry offers would-be writers is to live with simplicity:

I think everyone should read Thoreau's *Walden* where the message is: "Simplify your life." Even simplify the food you eat. . . . As far as clothing is concerned, I believe one of the greatest things in the world that ever happened is when people began to wear blue jeans. This is a perfectly practical way to dress, inexpensive to maintain. You no longer have to go to dry cleaners.

You keep the shelter as simple as you can. You don't have any extra things around. If you can live where people don't look in your windows, you don't have curtains. If the floor is fairly attractive, you don't have rugs. . . .

You get a job that does not tax your brain. Don't let other people use your brain. . . . You save your head for your own writing. Faulkner wrote *The Sound and the Fury*, I think, in a boiler factory. He was the night watchman. He wasn't using his brain, but he was being paid. You look for jobs like that.

You write, and you write, and you write. And you decide in advance that nothing and nobody is going to stop you, no matter how many rejection slips you get. If this is the way you want to express yourself, you write.

Petry's adult collection of short stories, *Miss Muriel and Other Stories,* shows the survival skills of distinct characters. The last tale, "Doby's Gone," is one most children can understand. It concerns Sue, a six-year-old African-American child in a hostile white community, who sheds an imagined companion, Doby, when she acquires actual friends.

Petry's short stories, each of which have a powerful ending, have been published in numerous magazines, such as *The New Yorker, Redbook, Crisis,* and *Opportunity,* and in anthologies, such as *Black Voices* (New American Library, 1968) and *Stories in Black and White* (Lippincott, 1970). She stated her requirements for good short stories:

You have to be able to create in a very few words a believable character in a situation that the reader can understand, and it has to be done quickly. That is the problem, because in a novel, you can meander. You don't have to stay right on the main road, so to speak.

There is the same difference between a mural which covers a large wall and a miniature which is a tiny painting done maybe on ivory or something like that. To work in that short space is a great challenge.

Petry had plans for her future writing projects. She said, "I always have a five-year plan. I write a novel, a book for children or young people, and then short stories. . . . If I ever get the time, I must write a play, something I've always wanted to do."

UPDATE

In 1994, Petry was inducted into the Connecticut Women's Hall of Fame and received a Distinguished Writer Award. She died on April 28, 1997, near Old Saybrook.

Jerry Pinkney, illustrator (1939–)

Gloria Jean Pinkney, author (1941–)

1997 Interview

JERRY PINKNEY

"The more information I have, the more inventive I can become in my art," concluded Jerry Pinkney, who has received numerous awards, including three Caldecott Honor Medals, four Coretta Scott King Awards, four Society of Illustrators Medals, and a 1992 Drexel University/Free Library of Philadelphia Citation.

Pinkney was born on December 22, 1939, in Philadelphia's Germantown section, the fourth child of six. Their block socialized, so Jerry and his siblings sold neighbors lemonade and barbecued chicken on the sidewalk. His father,

James Pinkney, was a produce vendor for cooperative fruit stores before working independently as a jack-of-all-trades, including carpentry, painting, and wallpapering. His father was the first on his block to buy a car.

Jerry, who started to draw when he was young, realized he'd rather do that than anything else. He thrived on praise from teachers and fellow students. His mother, Williemae Pinkney, encouraged him to be different. "My father had mixed feelings," he said. "He was a little skeptical, having no idea of my potential, but he was instrumental in getting me into art classes."

In junior high, Jerry had a newsstand and, between customers, sketched passersby or displays in a nearby department store. Eyeing the boy's drawing pad, John Liney, who created the "Little Henry" cartoon, invited Jerry to his studio and gave him materials. Jerry realized then that an artist could make a living.

Jerry enrolled in the three-year commercial art course at Dobbins Vocational School instead of going to his neighborhood high school. In vocational school, Jerry studied calligraphy and did perspective drawing in varied media, but in the evenings, he drew from models elsewhere. In his senior year, he met Gloria Jean at Dobbins's Valentine dance.

Also in his senior year, the high school counselor got the most talented white students to complete college scholarship applications. With a push from Jerry, applications were also given to African-American students. His reward was a four-year tuition scholarship to Philadelphia Museum College of Art (PCA). Never before had a member of his family gone to college.

The college required Jerry's first visits to art galleries and museums. A graphic design major, he became artistically more expressionistic, less representational, and realized, "My passion was drawing, painting, and printmaking."

At the start of his third college year, Jerry and Gloria Jean married. When their daughter, Troy, was born, Jerry left college to work for a florist. Jerry concluded about his years of struggle, "It was great discipline. I understood what I had to do and still be creative." Fortunately, a college adjunct professor, Sam Maitin, remembered Jerry and told him about an artistic job at Rustcraft Greeting Card Company in Boston.

As Gloria Jean recalled, "Jerry had not been a college illustration major, and he had only one weekend to prepare a portfolio. He wasn't afraid of taking chances. He boarded a bus with his portfolio for an interview, and got the job."

Jerry, then a card designer with a $10 weekly raise, was the first in his family to leave Philadelphia. After several years at Rustcraft, he worked for two years as a Barker-Black Studio illustrator in Boston. Here, in 1964, he drew pictures for his first children's book, Joyce Arkhurst's *The Adventures of Spider: A West African Folk Tale* (Little, Brown, 1964). He also illustrated his first textbook series, "You Can Spell."

To achieve more creative control, Jerry formed Kaleidoscope Studio with two other illustrators and stayed there for more than two years. Work was limited, so he chose to become independent in his own Jerry Pinkney Studio.

By now, in addition to daughter Troy, the Pinkney family included three sons: Brian, Scott, and Myles. They moved to Boston to participate in the Elma Lewis Center of Afro-American Artists. In Boston, they settled in an old townhouse with Jerry's studio on the fifth floor. Now he had more family time, though he still worked ten to twelve hours daily.

"We encouraged creative freedom in all four children in a workroom with long tables and materials," Jerry recalled. Brian was succeeding his father as an illustrator, so his mother put a small drawing board in a closet that she emptied for Brian.

The family moved again for Jerry to improve his job chances and the quality of their children's education. His timing was good when, in 1970, he brought his family to Croton-on-Hudson, New York. In the early 1970s, publishers were looking for African Americans to illustrate works by African-American writers, and Jerry was there. He began with several publishers, primarily Dial Press, relating well to art director Atha Tehon. In New York, Jerry could enter work in juried shows, meet leading artists, and gain recognition.

As he became prominent, Jerry got government commissions. In 1970, the National Park Service hired him to paint the Nez Perce Reservations and Big Hole, Montana. They also paid for his poster of the George Washington Carver National Monument. For the U.S. Information Agency, he prepared a Jesse Jackson portrait.

In 1978, the U.S. Postal Service commissioned Jerry to design a postage stamp of Harriet Tubman for a Black Heritage series. The series soon grew to include his renditions of Martin Luther King Jr., Benjamin Banneker, Whitney Moore Young Jr., Jackie Robinson, Scott Joplin, Carter G. Woodson, Mary McLeod Bethune, and Sojourner Truth.

In 1982, Jerry was a member of the National Aeronautics and Space Administration's Artist Team for the Space Shuttle Columbia. He said, "I did some small paintings and a large one which is hanging in the Air and Space Museum at Cape Kennedy, Florida. It was extraordinary to be at the launch!"

For Julius Lester's retelling of *The Tales of Uncle Remus* (Dial, 1987) and other books in that series, Jerry drew anthropomorphic animals. He wore baggy pants and acted like various animals while being photographed as a model.

In 1995, the U.S. Department of the Interior commissioned Jerry to do paintings for the Booker T. Washington National Memorial in Tuskegee, Alabama. He spoke about his efforts to be authentic:

I love the idea of doing research. I spent three days on a plantation to gain background for the Tuskegee project and also transferred my findings into illustrations for Alan Schroeder's *Minty: A Story of Young Harriet Tubman* [Dial, 1996]. This story won the Coretta Scott King Award in 1997.

Jerry's other Coretta Scott King Award winners were for illustrating: Valerie Flournoy's *The Patchwork Quilt* (Dial, 1986); Crescent Dragonwood's *Half a Moon and One Whole Star* (Macmillan, 1987); and Patricia C. McKissack's *Mirandy and Brother Wind* (Knopf, 1989). Jerry's Caldecott Honor Books were in 1989 for *Mirandy and Brother Wind*; in 1990 for Robert D. San Souci's *The Talking Eggs* (Dial, 1989); and in 1995 for Julius Lester's *John Henry* (Dial, 1994).

While Jerry generally focused only on illustrating, he adapted and drew *Ricki-Ticki-Tavi* (Dial, 1997), Rudyard Kipling's story about the mongoose.

Jerry told why he works on more than one book at a time:

I work on books in different stages. I may be doing a dummy for one project while researching another. It allows me a little distance from the project. When I get to the finishing stage, I'll work on just one book.

Jerry created the 1994 Children's Book Week poster. He also appeared in "Reading Rainbow" television programs to promote children's literature.

He has been an art professor at the University of Delaware, Pratt Institute, State University of New York at Buffalo, Rhode Island School of Design, and other schools. He has had one-man and collective art shows, joining in Bologna, Bratislava, and Moscow International Book Fairs.

He said of his craft, "My satisfaction comes from the actual marks on the paper, and when it sings, it's magic." He was delighted to illustrate Flournoy's *The Patchwork Quilt,* a Christopher Award–winner:

It was a wonderful challenge for my art to blend with such a soft, warm text. It was one of the first books at that time about a devoted African-American family. Part of the energy and electricity in *The Patchwork Quilt* comes from feelings of love for each other. It reflects the love we have in our own home. . . . Family is very important to us.

GLORIA JEAN PINKNEY

"My goal is to write good, hopeful content for children," said Gloria Jean Pinkney, who offered two Dial books, *Back Home* (1992) and its prequel,

The Sunday Outing (1994), both illustrated by Jerry. Her goal may contradict her present writing: a chapter book about her mother.

Gloria Jean was born on September 5, 1941. Her mother, Ernestine, was a seamstress. She died when Gloria Jean was just eight years old. "My book's working title is 'Best Street in the World.' That was the street I had to leave after Mom died. We changed neighborhoods, and that was another loss. In my two earlier books, I combined fact and fiction. Now I'm trying to write closer to actual events."

Gloria Jean's first published words were not in book form. She researched and wrote legends for a 1973–1976 series of African-American history calendars illustrated by Jerry. They are now collectors' items. She next focused on her own boutique in Croton, New York, where she designed silver jewelry and ladies' millinery, exhibiting hats in Westchester County galleries. Gloria Jean cited:

> My oldest granddaughter, Gloria Nicole, was so funny in my hat shop that I tried to write a story about her. I did this after years of hearing Jerry say, "You should write," because I can tell a good story. I gave my story to Phyllis Fogelman, Dial's editor. She said, "Gloria, you write beautifully. Just put this away. We're not going to reject it, but you have to find your writing voice."
>
> I found my writing voice in Lumberton, North Carolina, where I was born. My first book, *Back Home,* is about my train trip to Lumberton for a family reunion. Uncle Thomas met me at the station, and hearing my uncle talk gave me my writing voice. The last time I heard him was while I was growing up in the rooming house of my great-aunt who was from Lumberton too.

Great-aunt Alma became Gloria Jean's guardian following her mother's death. Raised as a single child, Gloria Jean was motivated to marry a fine person and have her own four children. The author spoke about Alma: "My great-aunt was an older woman who worked very hard. She prayed, 'Oh, Lord, please let me live long enough to see this child marry a good man and make something of herself!' She met and approved of Jerry."

The great-aunt is featured in *The Sunday Outing,* Gloria Jean's second book. In both *Back Home* and *The Sunday Outing,* Gloria Jean's dialog is believable. Her nostalgic style and Jerry's art make the words come alive. For example, in *The Sunday Outing,* Jerry shows tired Alma's heavy gait in orthopedic shoes. Ernestine's mother in the book is accurately portrayed as a seamstress.

To help Jerry in his work, Gloria Jean has located models for characters in the books he illustrates. She herself has served as his model at times, posing for the old woman in Robert D. San Souci's *The Talking Eggs.* Then she found a model who looked just like his drawing. Jerry marvels at his wife's ability to find accurate models, and she explained:

I study people, physically and with regard to personality. It's my habit. I hire the models and costume them for the story. We read the tale to models, and they act out scenes in what we call a "story shoot." Jerry takes photographs with a Polaroid and uses them when he's drawing. He can see details, like the folds in the costumes.

Jerry commented, "Photos make continuity possible throughout a book's thirty-two or forty pages." The "story shoot" promotes interaction between characters, and he can photograph facial expressions.

Jerry creates his nostalgic watercolor art on his home's lower level within view of woods. Meanwhile, Gloria Jean writes in her backyard cottage, fourteen feet square, that she calls "Sunflower." Her grandchildren converted a storage cabin into her snug studio. Gloria Jean spends hours in Sunflower and then goes to schools to inspire compositions by young people. Jerry joins her at times, realizing they are both effective role models.

All four of the Pinkney children use art in some form for their careers. Gloria Jean said: "Our daughter, Troy, is director of child life at Jacobi Hospital in New York City and uses art for healing. Our son, Scott, who lives in Toronto, is creative director and vice president of his own design studio, Mosaic Direct, that does direct advertising."

The book-oriented Pinkney children are the youngest and oldest sons, Myles and Brian. Myles works in television production and is a freelance photographer whose photographs embellish *It's Raining Laughter* (Dial, 1997), a collection of Nikki Grimes's poetry.

Brian has illustrated more than thirty books, mainly with a scratchboard technique, including two by Robert D. San Souci. One was *Sukey and the Mermaid* (Four Winds Press, 1992), and Brian's art made it a 1993 Coretta Scott King Honor Book. The second was *The Faithful Friend* (Simon & Schuster, 1993), and it became a 1994 Caldecott and Coretta Scott King Illustration Honor Book. Brian often illustrates books written by his wife, Andrea Davis Pinkney, a Simon & Schuster senior editor. *Sparrowboy* (Simon & Schuster, 1997), which Brian both wrote and illustrated, won the 1997 *Boston Globe-Horn Book* Award.

"There's a traveling exhibit, 'Meet the Pinkneys,' designed to share information about my family," Gloria Jean said. The exhibit, once funded by the National Endowment for the Humanities and the Iowa Humanities Board, has been in museums in Cedar Rapids, Iowa; Houston, Texas; and Kingston, Jamaica, among other locations.

In addition to their four adult children, Gloria Jean and Jerry have seven grandchildren. The couple draws strength from giving back to the community that celebrates their achievements and those of their family.

UPDATE

Jerry Pinkney was the 1998 illustrator nominee from the United States for a Hans Christian Andersen Award. Called a workaholic, he has illustrated more than eighty children's books and twelve adult books to date, using watercolor, pencil, and colored pencils. In addition, he applied gouache in Julius Lester's *Black Cowboy, Wild Horses: A True Story* (Dial, 1998).

In 1999, Jerry both adapted and drew Andersen's *The Ugly Duckling* (Murrow). He won the Caldecott Honor Medal in 2000 for the book's handsome illustrations. Also in 2000, Brian's art for Kim L. Siegelson's *In the Time of the Drums* (Hyperion, 1999) won the Coretta Scott King Illustration Award.

Keith Robertson, author (1914–1991)

1972 Interview

"It takes me much less time to write an adult murder mystery than to write a children's book," said Keith Robertson, who has authored twenty-seven books, mainly for young people. He is able to make the comparison because, under the pen name of Carlton Keith, he has also written six adult mysteries.

Robertson is best known for his "Henry Reed" juvenile series. His humorous books have won two William Allen White Awards in Kansas, and he received the 1968 New Jersey Author's Award.

Robertson was born on May 9, 1914, in Dows, Iowa, and while he grew up in the Midwest, he never spent two full years in one school until he was a high school sophomore. His father, a merchant, searched in vain for quick prosperity. At home, his older sisters washed dishes while he shoveled snow.

Only his Cherokee first-grade teacher in Oklahoma encouraged his writing and reading since his mathematical ability made other teachers steer him toward engineering or science. He recalled hearing instructors encourage boys to become doctors and telling him it was impractical to write books. Such advice made him postpone his goal to be an author.

While chums played sports, Robertson read books, but he wasn't beyond student pranks. He shut down school one day by putting garlic in the ventilating system. The principal discovered the culprit after smelling garlic's give-away odor on Robertson's penknife.

The author's family lived in Blairsburg, Iowa, during his last couple of high school years. He was one of thirteen in his high school graduation class. Only four went to college, including Robertson. At first he planned to attend Iowa State College in Ames. He didn't have any money, however, so he joined the Navy, became a battleship's radioman, and qualified for Naval Academy Preparatory School. He spent four years as an Annapolis midshipman, earning a bachelor of science degree, but declined a commission.

He worked for a while as a refrigerator engineer in Philadelphia, but when World War II became imminent, Robertson chose a naval commission rather than be drafted. The day following Pearl Harbor, he got orders for destroyer sea duty. He was an officer on destroyers in the Atlantic and Pacific oceans, earned five battle stars, and retired as a Naval Reserve captain.

During all this time, he continued to write. "I planned to write all along," he recalled. "I admit that the Naval Academy seems an unlikely place to go to be a writer, but at the time, I was short of funds. . . . The war came along, so I promptly was called back in, but I had no intention of otherwise returning."

After the war, Robertson sold children's and religious books published by Holt, Rinehart, and Winston. He began to read company books for ten- to fifteen-year-olds, "middle-aged youth," and accidentally discovered his audience. Robertson felt that taking a job as a publisher's representative was one of his brightest career decisions:

> I think the time I spent selling books, going from bookstore to bookstore, was invaluable. Most books are bought by libraries. I probably would have been better off if I had worked in a library and watched what books people check out. I don't know if I'm a little out of date.

While selling books, Robertson met a saleswoman, Elisabeth "Betty" Woodburn, at a Pittsburgh bookstore on his circuit. After his divorce from his first wife, the couple married in 1946, and they had two children, Jeffry and Hope. He also had a daughter, Christina "Christy" Robertson, from his first marriage. His new family moved on the edge of Hopewell, New Jersey, to a small farm named appropriately, Booknoll. By then, Winston had published Robertson's first book, *Ticktock and Jim* (1949), and he became a full-time author. Betty began to sell rare horticultural books, so the couple traveled widely to collect them. He felt lucky to marry someone who valued books and welcomed his writing. From 1958 to 1969, Robertson was president of his family's pottery business, but he continued to write.

As youngsters, the Robertson children always wanted more pets, but they could keep animals only if they took care of them. They acquired peacocks, a black Angus steer, a goat, a pet raccoon, ducks, geese, rabbits, pigeons, six parakeets, a parrot, three pigs, and a crow that talked. Love of animals is evident in Robertson's juvenile books, including *The Dog Next Door* (1950), *The Lonesome Sorrel* (1952), *Outlaws of the Sourland* (1953), *Mascot of the Melroy* (1956), *The Pilgrim Goose* (1956), *The Pinto Deer* (1956), and *If Wishes Were Horses* (1958), all published by Viking. A Robertson horse often strayed from home to scare funeral attendants by peeking in an open church window during eulogies. The animals extended Robertson's sense of humor, which was especially evident in his "Henry Reed" books. The author felt ten- to fifteen-year-old readers, his target, welcomed humorous tales.

Henry Reed, Inc. (Viking, 1958) introduces teenager Henry Harris Reed, a consul's son, who spends his summers in Grover's Corner, New Jersey, with his maternal aunt and uncle. He acquires a beagle, Agony, and earns money with a twelve-year-old neighbor, Midge Glass, selling mushrooms, fish bait, and turtles. The most popular "Henry Reed" book is *Henry Reed's Baby-Sitting Service* (Viking, 1966), in which Henry and Midge focus on helping mothers after a survey reveals a need for sitters. *Henry Reed's Journey* (Viking, 1963) details Henry's cross-country trip with Midge and her parents from California to New Jersey. They start a false gold rush and star in a Hopi Indian float.

Henry Reed's Big Show (Viking, 1970) tells about Henry's and Midge's wild rodeo with an eccentric horse, Galileo. Robertson included a protest march at Princeton University against pollution, explaining: "One daughter is in college now, so the college scene is very close. Of course, we live right near Princeton."

Robertson's model for Henry Reed was not a young boy:

> I always had in mind a female fourth-grade schoolteacher. It seems rather ridiculous, but we had a friend who taught school, and it always seemed that wherever she was, there was trouble. There were all sorts of activity, and things went wrong, not her fault, of course. Just a turmoil!
>
> Obviously, I couldn't write a book about a fourth-grade teacher and have children read it. I converted her into a boy, who was Henry, joined by a girl, Midge. Some incidents resemble what my children did in a similar area of New Jersey. Essentially, Henry is based on a fourth-grade teacher.

Robert McCloskey illustrated the first four "Henry Reed" books. He drew Henry in his own image so humorously that Robertson acknowledged McCloskey's contribution to the series' popularity. Robertson said, "Frequently, an author is disappointed in illustrations, but these were just as I had pictured Henry. I don't think the books would have been nearly as successful if they hadn't had these illustrations. . . . They fit perfectly."

Two "Henry Reed" books brought Robertson the William Allen White Award, a readers-choice prize. The author said:

> The state of Kansas has a very active reading program. Students not only take part in choosing the William Allen White Award winner, but when the award is given, they usually have a dinner. For the dinner, children make place cards or figurines used as centerpieces. The young people get excited about this program!

His wife accompanied the author for the award presentation for *Henry Reed, Inc.,* driving with him to Kansas in a new lavender Oldsmobile. They went to the small town of Caney where he had attended third and fourth grades. The police chief escorted their car behind a uniformed high school band, an honor appreciated by the author.

Robertson got his second William Allen White Award, Pacific Northwest Library Association Award, and Nene Award for *Henry Reed's Baby-Sitting Service.* He said, "The nene is a duck, the state bird of Hawaii. It was almost an endangered species, but it's coming back now."

In the Carson Street Detective Agency mysteries with Neil Lambert and Swede Larson, all published by Viking, Robertson wrote the first story, *The Mystery of Burnt Hill* (1952), in first person; the second story, *Three Stuffed Owls* (1954), in third person; the third story, *The Crow and the Castle* (1957), in first person again; and the fourth story, *The Money Machine* (1964), in third person once more. He was unaware of the error, confiding, "I don't know why I switched. May Massee edited the first book, and Annis Duff edited the others. No child picked up on that, but they often do when I'm wrong."

The detectives, sixteen-year-old Neil Lambert and Swede Larson, live in Belleville, New Jersey. In *The Mystery of Burnt Hill,* Neil and Swede investigate two criminals, becoming involved with a valuable old desk, carrier pigeons, secret-ink messages, and imprisonment in an abandoned mill. The momentum continues in *Three Stuffed Owls* as Neil and Swede search for a man who stole a bicycle but find a football-playing pig, three stuffed owls, and a desperate diamond smuggler.

The Crow and the Castle revolves around the local chess expert, a retired naval officer, Captain Wudge, who drives straddling the centerline. Neil's pet crow flies away with Wudge's antique chess piece, a castle. In *The Money Machine,* Neil and Swede buy a money machine from a mail-order house that sells magic tricks. The Secret Service investigates the boys, but the two youths uncover an actual counterfeiter. This book brought Robertson the 1968 New Jersey Author's Award.

Robertson has received a lot of fan mail concerning the "Henry Reed" books: "I've had one letter from a girl who wrote, 'They don't make boys like Henry anymore.'" For thirty-six years, he corresponded with Robert Bahr,

nurturing his fan until Bahr became a freelance writer. He enjoyed correspondence from fans, even criticism. Robertson said:

> I get interesting letters from readers. On about the third page in *Ice to India,* I
> said that "the carriage jounced up and down on springs." This occurred in about
> 1816. A boy wrote me that carriages didn't have springs then. When I investi-
> gated, I found they didn't. Carriages were suspended by leather thongs, and
> they rocked back and forth on them. When writing about anything historical, I
> have to be very careful of every detail.

Robertson's *Ice to India* (Viking, 1955) has been one of the most popular historical fiction books with boys and girls. It depicts the 1816 voyage of *The
Hope Elizabeth* from Philadelphia to India with a cargo of ice. The captain,
David Mason, has not been to sea in twenty-five years but needs a profitable
voyage to prevent his shipping firm's bankruptcy. His sixteen-year-old
grandson, Nat Mason, is the protagonist. The first mate, Adam Parrish, is a
criminal who has been paid to sabotage the voyage.

Robertson traced the actual background of this unique story:

> *Ice to India* was based on the life of a young man in New England by the
> name of Frederick Tudor. When he was nineteen, he decided it would be a
> wonderful idea to sell ice (from a New England winter) in Cuba and South
> America, so he loaded a ship. Since he didn't pack it very well, the ice melted,
> the ship sank, and some of the people aboard were lost, but this didn't dis-
> courage him. He went back, got a second ship, filled it with ice, and this time
> he succeeded. He sold it, I believe, in Cuba. Eventually, he had a whole string
> of icehouses along the coast, through Central and South America, and made
> a fortune.
>
> Finally, just to prove he could do it, he took a cargo of ice to India. It arrived
> in pretty good shape. He sold it. I don't know what the people of India did with
> it when they got it. No one had refrigerators.

Robertson said he enjoys writing sea stories, both fiction, like *Ice to India,*
and nonfiction, like *The Wreck of the Saginaw* (Viking, 1954). For the second book, he used a paymaster's diary and the *Saginaw*'s penciled log retrieved before its 1870 shipwreck. In the story, five men row fifteen hundred
miles to Hawaii for help while eighty-eight are marooned on a desert island,
and all courageously survive!

The author's interest in sea stories was logical, but he was concerned
about his female readers:

> I spent about seven years at sea, so naturally I'm going to write about it. Most
> girls don't seem to like sea stories. I've had only one or two letters from them,

but if you write a book about horses, about nine out of ten letters will be from girls. Perhaps with the interest in boating, girls may like the sea a bit more. In Russia, it might be different because girls in the armed services go to sea.

Robertson's book that involved the most research time was his *In Search of a Sandhill Crane*. The book is about Link Keller from New Jersey who spends a summer in Michigan's wilderness. His Uncle Albert had loaned him expensive cameras to photograph sandhill cranes, but he learns more than camera skills. Taught by his aunt and a Native American, Charley Horse, he is quiet in the woods without being bored. The author prolonged work on the book:

> I keep finding the research more interesting than the writing. This, of course, is one of the dangers of being an author: that no one sets a timetable for you. The only thing that makes me go to my desk is the grocery bill.

Robertson assumed a pen name to write adult mysteries:

> I wrote for adults under the name Carlton Keith. It's my middle and first names in reverse order. This wasn't an attempt to hide anything. Some smaller libraries order by the author's name, and they might have thought these mysteries were for children. . . .
>
> I've heard that some authors have difficulty arriving at plots. My problem is set-tling down to work. Most of my adult mysteries I put on tape and dictated them entirely. This is very fast, but the revision is time-consuming because when you talk, you use entirely too many words. You cut about every other word.

Robertson advised would-be writers:

> The first difficulty in becoming a writer is supporting yourself until your books finally earn enough money to support you. There is no solution to this except to have a job and write in your spare time. The authors I know have all had to do it. There seems to be no immediate way of getting revenue. At any point in your career, you're liable to work six months on a manuscript that no one wants to publish. I have a file cabinet with half a dozen manuscripts that nobody pub-lished.

Robertson offered high praise for one children's book editor in particular, the late May Massee. She prevented him from making a mistake in the treatment of *Henry Reed's Journey*. He recalled. "I was going to have Midge tell some of the story, but May Massee wouldn't let me. She said that I didn't sound like a girl. I had to rewrite her portion entirely."

After Massee's death, he began a memorial to her, which was displayed in the School of Library Science at Kansas State Teachers College in Emporia. He said, "She was only the second person who was really designated a children's book editor. Prior to that, children's books were sort of a side issue in the main business of publishing. . . . I think she earned more awards than the rest of the editors put together in the children's book field."

UPDATE

In Search of a Sandhill Crane was published in 1973. Since think tanks are common at Princeton, New Jersey, Robertson composed *Henry Reed's Think Tank* (1986), with jacket art by Gail Owens, as the last of his five "Henry Reed" books. Grover's Corner neighbors ask Henry and Midge to help them solve problems of predatory geese and troublesome visiting relatives.

Robertson donated his own manuscripts to the May Massee Memorial before he died of cancer on September 23, 1991, at age seventy-seven. His wife, Betty, a book dealer with thirteen thousand rare volumes, died a year earlier.

Harriet May Savitz, author (1933–)

1983 Interview

To author Harriet May Savitz, wheelchair athletes "are among the few pioneers left in this country." Her books honor these pioneers.

> I have written about the physically challenged. I think it was the first time it was ever done. Publishers felt cautious about putting a wheelchair on the cover of books for young people. They thought readers would believe the books were about sick people. I didn't feel that way. I wasn't writing about sick people at all!

Her books on the physically challenged have brought Savitz honors. *Fly, Wheels, Fly!* (Day, 1971) was a nominee for Vermont's Dorothy Canfield Fisher Children's Book Award. The University of Iowa's Books for Young Adults, 1975–1976, included *The Lionhearted* (Day, 1975) among teenagers' most popular books. In 1979, the National Council of Christians and Jews put *Wheelchair Champions* (Crowell, 1978) on a recommended brotherhood book list. In 1983–1984, *Run, Don't Walk* (Watts, 1979) was a California Young Reader Medal nominee (high school category), based on book circulation.

Harriet Blatstein was born on May 19, 1933, in Newark, New Jersey. After her father, Samuel, lost a thriving produce stand in the Depression, he and his wife, Susan, and their daughter moved to an apartment at the bottom of a

Hackensack, New Jersey, hill with the wealthy at the summit. All students attended the same public school. Students from the wealthy families wore white socks and shoes; Harriet wore brown shoes from a cousin's hand-me-down package. She has one brother, Ira, who is eleven years younger than she is.

Harriet found solace at the public library. At nine, she wrote her first poem, kept by her mother in Harriet's compositions scrapbook. In high school, she majored in business administration, knowing she could not afford college. Her brother, however, earned his doctorate in physics. She did attend noncredit classes in poetry and philosophy at Rutgers's evening school. When she won second prize in a local beauty contest, what she remembered was applause for her performance of her own written material.

After she married Ephraim Savitz, a pharmacist, the couple moved to Pennsylvania. They had two children, a daughter, Beth (named for Beth in *Little Women*), and a son, Steven. Her mother died when her brother was only sixteen years old, so he came to live with his sister's family, and her father helped in Ephraim's pharmacy.

Savitz's only outlet was attending an evening creative writing class at a local high school. She sold several of her assigned interviews to a newspaper for five dollars each and a byline. When her daughter tiptoed into the ocean for the first time, she wrote "Beth Meets the Ocean," selling it for $50 to a city newspaper. She also sold articles about her son's first kindergarten day.

Savitz began to write with her teacher, Maria Caporale Shecktor, who had been a *Holiday* magazine editor. They sold children's poems and short stories to Science Research Associates and Lyons and Carnahan, using restricted vocabulary. Houghton-Mifflin bought one of their poems for an anthology.

In 1965, the coauthors contacted Carolyn W. Field, then Coordinator of Work with Children for the Free Library of Philadelphia. Together they started Philadelphia Children's Reading Round Table to help authors and illustrators of books for young readers.

At one group meeting, Mary Walsh of John Day Company suggested a need for multiethnic, inner-city stories. The coauthors responded with three original short stories, published as *The Moon Is Mine* (Day, 1968). Their second volume was *Peter, and Other Stories* (Day, 1969). At a book autograph party, Walsh introduced Savitz to Charles Blockson, a major African-American historian, whose lapel pin was a wheelchair sports emblem. Blockson told Walsh about wheelchair sports and urged Savitz to write a book on the topic.

Savitz met Edward R. Davenport, a paraplegic basketball player. At age eighteen, he had been standing on a second-floor landing when the floor collapsed. The accident injured his spinal chord. Savitz wrote her first wheel-chair-sports book, *Fly, Wheels, Fly!* (Day, 1970), partially about Davenport's experience:

> I went to a game to see what it was like. I was fascinated enough by the flying wheels to write *Fly, Wheels, Fly!* about wheelchair basketball where athletes fly out of their chairs and fall against walls. It isn't a tender, delicate game. It's a competitive, very rough sport.

Savitz noted wheelchair athletes' initial distrust of her:

> They felt I would come and make "lotsa money." I've never done that. I've demonstrated with them. They made it very tough for me. They waited to see if I would stay with this movement and write the truth about what was happening. I've stayed for over twenty years.

Savitz donates some of her income from sales of her book *Wheelchair Champions: A History of Wheelchair Sports* (Crowell, 1978) to the Pennsylvania Wheelchair Athletic Association. In 1981, the President's Committee for the Handicapped, celebrating the International Year of Disabled Persons, praised her *Wheelchair Champions*. The book deals with wheelchair athletes who participate in football, basketball, track and field, archery, javelin throwing, table tennis, and bowling. Before World War II, paraplegics rarely survived their injuries, so this book begins in the 1940s.

Savitz tries to repay those who led her to exciting action tales:

> For the writer, that's a gift. Where else can I get stories, like one about a woman interviewed for a job who took me along since the boss didn't want to look at a wheelchair? Another tale is about a boy, Cochise, a double amputee, who jumped into the swimming pool at a motor lodge, and others jumped out, re-luctant to look at him. He's a Vietnam veteran.

She incorporated some of the stories she had heard in her second fictional work, *On the Move* (Day, 1973). This focuses on Glen Harris's rehabilitation center and lively young paraplegics, like twenty-one-year-old Carrie, a pampered polio victim; Skip, an aloof Vietnam veteran; Bennie, a knife-wounded paralytic; and Black Diamond, a shut-in who uses a ham radio to contact the outside world.

A female motorcycle accident victim, Rennie, is a heroine in *The Lion-hearted* (Day, 1975). Accepted into Ridge High School, she and a male student, Lee, care for each other, conflicting with his mother's plans for her son.

Perhaps Savitz's most appreciated novel is *Run, Don't Walk* (Watts, 1979), which concerns a high school student, Samantha, who was paralyzed in a diving accident. She won't join activist Johnny Jay in a campaign for accessible school washrooms. She changes her mind about activism, however, after a committee won't let her compete in a marathon. "The theme of *Run, Don't Walk* is the same as the theme of all my books about the physically challenged: go past what is," Savitz said. "Create the dream! I write for young people because adults' minds are closed. I'm working on the next generation."

Savitz assessed the special status of *Run, Don't Walk*:

> Henry Winkler from Paramount Studio picked up the option on the book and made it into a television movie. I was unaware until it was made. Winkler and his consultants were terrific. I was petrified because there are so many possible errors (the words and terms), but he did everything right. . . .
>
> In the book, the main character, Samantha, suffers from a diving accident. There are so many paraplegics in hospitals and "rehab" centers due to failure to mark lake areas: "Shallow water!" I wanted to get that point across. Instead, movie directors had her fall off a horse. The movie, an ABC After-School Special, starred Scott Baio and Toni Kalem.

The movie, an ABC "Afterschool Special," starred Scott Baio and Toni Kalem.

In 1978, Edward R. Davenport, paralyzed from the neck down but with limited use of hands and arms, led a campaign to get Pennsylvania to accept federal funds for 80 percent of costs for wheelchair-accessible Transbuses. Savitz recalled that campaign.

> I will never forget Labor Day weekend of 1978. . . . Angry, Davenport planned to go to Harrisburg, Pennsylvania's capital, in his motorized wheelchair. He thought it would take him a day or two to get there. I was in the car behind him. We covered three to five miles per hour. That was like wagon trains in our country's early days. It took us six, ten-hour days. People threw cash and food for him into the car. They took his picture as if he were a hero, though before, he had been shunned.
>
> He didn't eat or drink during the day since there were no accessible bathrooms along the route. He lost ten pounds. When he came to railroad tracks, he had to cross them in his wheelchair. It rained. We put a raincoat on him. We had to leave at 4 A.M. when fewer trucks were on the road. When Eddie's chair overheated, we had to call the manufacturer in California who said that he had never heard of a quadriplegic in a motorized wheelchair for so many days. . . .
>
> He arrived in Harrisburg as if he were a grand politician back from a tour. Results were mixed. Davenport spoke to the State Transportation Commission. The physically challenged got some buses, but they are being taken away. The bus situation is all right when times are good, but not in a recession.

I wrote a short story about this: "The Wheelchair Express." I guess the reason I can't get it published is where the physically challenged are concerned, there's a quota system. They haven't "had enough" since there will never be enough.

The author's help brought her a prized possession, a 1979 plaque reading: To Harriet May Savitz in grateful recognition of her support of wheelchair sports in writing as well as in deed. Presented by the Pennsylvania Wheelchair Athletic Association and the 1979 Games Committee.

Starting in 1981, Savitz published only in paperback, attracting more readers. New American Library issued four books, commencing with *Wait Until Tomorrow,* whose roots Savitz traced:

This book is about my father. He had a laryngectomy [at age seventy] and refused to talk for about a year. He cut himself off from others. He wrote notes and left them all over his house. My daughter, who was living with him, ripped the notes, telling him, "If you have anything to say, speak to me." They had a fight. He took his electronic larynx (a small machine held at his throat), and his first words were to tell her off. That was part of the book I lived with.

The other part was a young man who was trying to commit suicide at a home where I was staying at the shore, and his family asked me to find them a mental health professional in a clinic.

I saw this young man, who was about sixteen, trying to kill himself, and my father in his seventies, trying to talk without his vocal chords. I put them both in one book. I dedicated it to my father and to Carolyn Field who read the first draft and told me, "Give it more!" I had just written the book, about 40,000 words, and I took Carolyn's advice. I rewrote it.

The title, *Wait Until Tomorrow,* comes from a counselor's advice to those wanting to commit suicide because by tomorrow, such intentions might change.

New American Library issued Savitz's *If You Can't Be the Sun, Be a Star* (1982). After someone in school steals her ski jacket, Candy Miller tries to improve her high school. The book's title comes from Douglas Malloch's poem, "Be the Best of Whatever You Are," which is Candy's goal.

In 1983, Signet published *Come Back, Mr. Magic.* Savitz told why she wrote it:

That came about through a tragedy. A young therapist (Norman Constantine) was hit in a hit-and-run accident and left in a coma. He was still in a coma (when he died twelve years later). I was overcome by this situation. My book dedication to him ends, "Awake, sweet Prince!"

We all hoped that would happen, but also, I wanted to bring out the work of the physical, recreational, and occupational therapists who help the physically challenged. Young people have written me to ask how they can help the physically challenged, and these are the professions.

The book's title derives from Norman Constantine, nicknamed "Mr. Magic" before his accident, because his hobby was a magic act.

UPDATE

In 1981, The Pennsylvania School Librarians' Association named Savitz an Outstanding Pennsylvania Author.

Savitz wrote *Summer's End* (New Amsterdam, 1984) when she and her husband, who had retired, moved to Bradley Beach, New Jersey. She experienced Hurricane Gertrude at the shore, and portrayed it in *Summer's End*. This romantic novel features Ali Templeton, a recent high school graduate and female police dispatcher, and Jay Hansky, a seventeen-year-old son of two Holocaust survivors.

Four Scholastic paperbacks by Savitz, mainly featuring animals, include *Swimmer* (1986), about Skip and his dog friend, Swimmer, who enjoy the ocean together; *The Cats Nobody Wanted* (1989), featuring Mrs. Beasley, who feeds stray cats until she becomes ill and gets help from a child, Frankie; and *The Bullies and Me* (1991), a story of a sixth grader, Allan, who is lonely after moving to Ocean View.

The last Scholastic paperback is *A Girl's Best Friend* (1995), which traces blind, twelve-year-old Laurie Moss, whose constant companion is her dog, Jessie. The aging animal becomes ill and needs expensive medicine that his owners cannot afford. Laurie helps pay for the dog's medicine by working in a bicycle shop. In the year this book was available, more than 85,000 copies were sold. In 1996, Savitz wrote Norman Constantine's biography, *Remembering Norm: A Victim's Story* (Dorrance).

Savitz, now a widow and grandmother, contributes to newspapers, including *Chicken Soup for the Golden Soul,* and national magazines, such as *Mature Years*. She has created twenty-two published books, mainly for young people. Her manuscripts are part of the de Grummond Children's Literature Collection at the University of Southern Mississippi. Her new concern is about pollution of "her lifelong friend," the Atlantic Ocean.

Letta Schatz, author (1926–)

1969 Interview

Letta Schatz is an author in the United States known mainly for her books about Nigeria, including *Taiwo and Her Twin* (1964) and *Bola and the Oba's Drummers* (1967), both issued by McGraw-Hill. *Bola and the Oba's Drummers* featured illustrations by Tom Feelings, his first work for a major publisher. She said she was delighted with his tempera pictures.

Letta was born in New York City on July 12, 1926, the only child of a garment worker, Sophie Saroff.

Schatz's concern about female education is deep. She learned how her mother, Sophie, struggled for schooling in another part of the world, Ukraine, in the early twentieth century. Schatz's Grandmother Basya rented the main room of her small village house to a teacher so her daughter, Sophie, could be present during lessons. Later, a Kiev man observed the class and encouraged Sophie's educational pursuit. Sophie, joined by several girl-friends whom she influenced, took exams and got accepted into public school despite quotas on Jewish students, females especially. The girls continued in school until they were fourteen or fifteen, stopping before *gymnasium* (high school/junior college).

Hoping to continue her education, Sophie accepted money from her sister in the United States to come to New York City. Sophie supported herself in the garment trades and went to night school to learn bookkeeping. She wanted to become a doctor, but that goal eluded her. Instead, she married,

312

became Sophie Saroff, and gave birth to Letta. The father left when Letta was three years old and died when she was thirteen. Sophie transferred her own burning desire for an education to her only child.

Letta received her bachelor of science degree on a full academic-achievement scholarship from the University of Chicago, did graduate work at Bank Street College of Education, and received her master's degree in education from Temple University. She has been a preschool and elementary teacher as well as a reading specialist. She now supervises University of Pennsylvania student teachers.

She married Sayre Schatz, an economist who taught at Lincoln University and was an economics professor at Temple University. He went to Ibadan, Nigeria, in 1961–1965 on a Ford Foundation Grant. Letta and their children, Judy and Benjamin, accompanied him.

In Nigeria, Letta was a volunteer English teacher in primary schools, including one in a village much like Olarunda, the setting for *Taiwo and Her Twin*. The tale revolves around a bright child, Taiwo, who has always accompanied her twin brother, Kehinde. She wants more than anything else to go to school with him. Her parents have five children and little money to buy books or uniforms. Moreover, no woman in the family has ever attended school, and her father sees no need for her to go. When the turkey of the village chief, or Bale, gets lost, Taiwo finds it and uses her wits by feeding it until adults catch it. Influenced by the Bale's praise for Taiwo, her father lets her go to school. Schatz said that the Nigerian Association of University Women, which was surveying educational opportunities for females in secondary schools, awakened her interest in the problem and influenced her to write *Taiwo and Her Twin*.

Schatz benefited from the Writer's Laboratory, led by Irma Simonton Black, at Bank Street College in New York City. She attended for five years before publishing. She dedicated *A Rhinoceros? Preposterous!* (Steck-Vaughn, 1965) "To Claudia Lewis and Irma Black and all the other Bank Streeters who set my pencil on its path." This picture book is about a boy who wants a bigger pet than goldfish or gerbils and settles for a puppy.

Schatz's first published work was another picture book, *When Will My Birthday Be?* (McGraw-Hill, 1962). It develops the concept of a year's passage from one birthday to another. The 1964 British edition contains *sledge*, rather than "sled," and *ice lolly*, instead of "popsicle."

Schatz's other chapter book is *Bola and the Oba's Drummer*, which again takes place in Nigeria. When he goes to a market town, Bola, a village boy, is impressed with the Royal Drummers. The drums command the mighty King, the Oba, to dance. Bola learns to play the Gudugudu drum, so the Head Drummer lets Bola play when the Oba dances on New Year's Day. The

Head Drummer promises Bola free lessons and lets him keep a *Kanango* drum, which he earned while playing for the Oba. Bola's father accepts the generous offer, showing pride in his son.

Schatz, who first wrote *Bola and the Oba's Drummer* as a picture book, expanded it to a chapter book at the publisher's request. She said she once saw at a festival two six-year-old sons of the Head Royal Drummer who knew they would follow their father's occupation.

"When the Bale or head man of this village died, my interest in talking drums was born," she said. Schatz attended his Christian funeral in a church. Then mourners followed drummers down the street to his family's compound. The talking drums called specific people to dance. The Bale's fourteen-year-old daughter, Alice, escorted Schatz, her teacher, and explained what was happening. Schatz later gathered information on drumming from an authoritative king, Oba Timi of Edi, who wanted to preserve traditional Yoruba music.

Schatz's 1967 book, *Whiskers, My Cat,* is a long poem in picture book format, illustrated by Paul Galdone. It is based on the writer's observances as an owner of at least thirteen cats.

Schatz next retold African folk tales that she found at the University of Ibadan in anthropological accounts. *The Extraordinary Tug of War* (Follett, 1968) portrays Hare, a trickster, getting Hippopotamus and Elephant to tug against each other, showing brain winning over brawn.

Follett published Schatz's retelling of another folk tale from Africa, *Never Empty* (1969). In this tale, Hare finds a magic spoon that gives his family food. When Hare leaves, Elephant visits Hare's children and feasts on what the spoon prepares. He is so greedy, he even swallows most of the spoon.

UPDATE

Though Brer Rabbit and Spider Anansi are folk tale heroes in other parts of Africa, the Nigerian hero is Tortoise. Schatz presents one Tortoise story in *The Trouble of Kings: Two Tales from Africa* (Ginn, 1971). In "Tortoise Crowns the Elephant," Schatz tells about a king's promise to let his daughter marry any creature who traps huge, destructive Elephant. Trickster Tortoise completes the task and marries the princess.

The only tale set in Africa that Schatz wrote while in the United States was *Banji's Magic Wheel* (Follett, 1975), illustrated by Ann Grifalconi. The story concerns a Nigerian boy, Banji, who is so late fulfilling errands that he asks Tayo, a senior brother in his compound, to help him. Tayo offers a magic wheel, which Banji starts with a stick, but the boy has to keep up with it. Later, when Tayo needs refreshment, he sends Banji to the market. Since other children are using the magic wheel, Banji runs without its help and is so fleet, he knows he no longer needs it.

In the 1990s, Schatz field-tested *Taiwo and Her Twin* in a fourth-grade public school class with splendid results. "I think *Taiwo and Her Twin* is a feminist book that states problems girls still face today, including in our own country," Schatz said. She would like to see McGraw-Hill reissue the book.

Schatz's 1997 literary undertaking was as editor of an adult book. However, her "first love" is working with children. She confided, "A good deal of my time, heart, and enthusiasm over the years has been directed to helping children become expressive, fluent writers."

Maurice Sendak, illustrator–author (1928–)

1977 Interview

Contrary to popular views, Maurice Sendak, who recalls his emotions when he was young, admitted that specific memories of growing up are limited: "I don't remember my childhood. I remember my feelings with just three or four mental pictures of my childhood."

Sendak won many prizes illustrating what some consider to be his childhood emotions. He received the 1964 Caldecott Medal for his book, *Where the Wild Things Are* (Harper, 1963), which is also an International Board on Books for Young People (IBBY) Honor Book. He illustrated six Caldecott Honor Books: Ruth Krauss's *A Very Special House* (1954); Sesyle Joslin's *What Do You Say, Dear?* (1959); Janice May Udry's *The Moon Jumpers* (1960); Else Holmelund Minarik's *Little Bear's Visit* (1962); Charlotte Zolotow's *Mr. Rabbit and the Lovely Present* (1963); and his own *In the Night Kitchen* (1971), all published by Harper.

Maurice Bernard Sendak was born on June 10, 1928, in Brooklyn, New York, the third child of Philip and Sarah Sendak. Both of his siblings were fond of books, and shared this fondness with Maurice. Natalie, who was nine years older than he, celebrated his ninth birthday by giving him his first book, Mark Twain's *The Prince and the Pauper*. It was printed on fine paper, "smelled good," and had a laminated cover. Natalie took him to the library on Fridays to get books for Sabbath reading. Among his favorites were

Robert Louis Stevenson's *A Child's Garden of Verses* and Bret Harte's short story "The Luck of Roaring Camp."

"My parents came from Poland just before the first world war," he recalled. All three Sendak children were born in Brooklyn. He said he stayed there "until I crossed the Brooklyn Bridge, the 'Great Divide.' I moved to New York City where I stayed all my life until I came to Connecticut in 1972."

His brother, Jack, who was five years older than Maurice, wrote books, and Maurice illustrated them. This was Maurice's main hobby when he was kept indoors after a bout of childhood pneumonia. His mother worried about Maurice's health, so he represents her as a protective moon in many of his pictures.

Maurice and his brother collaborated on creating booklets. Their first was "They Were Inseparable," a story about a dying brother who jumps from a hospital's window with his sister, as the two proclaim, "We are inseparable!"

At about age nine, Maurice Sendak began to write and draw his own books. He knew early that his life work would be as an illustrator. He said his main inspiration came from his father, a dressmaker. "My father was a superb, spontaneous storyteller," he said.

Mathematics was Sendak's nemesis at Lafayette High School, which he attended from 1941 to 1945. He was a self-taught artist there, copying the styles of such illustrators as George Cruikshank, Wilhelm Busch, and Boutet de Monvel. At fifteen, Sendak had an after-school job with All American Comics, drawing backgrounds for "Mutt and Jeff."

During his last two high school years, Sendak illustrated *The Snow Queen, The Wind in the Willows*, and self-bound editions of *The Happy Prince, The Luck of Roaring Camp, The Little Match Girl*, and his version of *Peter and the Wolf*, but they were not published. After high school graduation, he carried a business card, "Maurice Sendak, Illustrator," and showed his pictures to New York children's book editors who were encouraging but gave him no commissions.

In 1947, Whittlesey House issued his illustrations for *Atomics for the Millions*, an adult book by Maxwell E. Eidinoff and coauthored by Hyman Ruchlis, his high school teacher who liked his artistic style. The artist earned his living then by making shop-window fairy-tale characters of papier-mâché.

In 1948, the Sendak brothers showed the celebrated Manhattan toy store, F.A.O. Schwarz, their animated wooden toys decorated by Maurice. The company rejected the toys but gave Maurice a window-display job. Occupied by day, Sendak took evening classes at the Art Students' League, where he especially liked John Groth's instruction.

Illustrator Leonard Weisgard, who admired Sendak's displays at Schwarz, recommended him for a picture-book commission with the United Synagogue

Commission on Jewish Education. The commission agreed, provided Weisgard was "art consultant." He taught Sendak how to do preseparated art for *Good Shabos, Everybody,* published in 1951.

Since Sendak was reluctant to show his portfolio to publishers again, two Schwarz employees arranged secretly for Harper's children's book editor, Ursula Nordstrom, to see his work. She immediately gave Maurice, then twenty-one years old, an assignment to illustrate Marcel Ayme's *The Wonderful Farm* (1950). In time, Sendak became an artist for children's books only. In 1952, Nordstrom let him illustrate Ruth Krauss's *A Hole Is to Dig,* including a final picture of a boy's buttocks labeled "The End." Sendak credits Krauss with most of her book's layout ideas since she was experienced. Her husband, Crockett Johnson, creator of "Barnaby" comics, gave Sendak a recommended reading list, including books by Dostoyevsky, Melville, and Kafka.

In 1956, Nordstrom issued the first book that Sendak wrote and illustrated, *Kenny's Window.* It is about young, introverted Kenny and his dream garden. A year later, Sendak wrote his second book, *Very Far Away,* in which Martin, a more aggressive, sulking personality, goes to an imaginary, distant place when his mother ignores his questions.

Nordstrom thought Sendak was a cooperative genius, one who cheerfully made needed corrections. He trusted her above all others:

> We've been together for over twenty-five years. Everything I've written, she has edited. I can't imagine not working with Ursula. We now have a kind of instinct about each other's work. Every time she helps me, there's the same good feeling.

Encouraged by Nordstrom, Sendak had a common theme in his books:

> To simplify it, perhaps it's all right to be a child. It's all right to defy your parents. It's all right to get angry. It's all right to be alive and enjoy yourself! It wasn't correct when I was a child. There aren't many ways you can get even about your childhood when you grow up.

Sendak considers two of his prizewinners to be part of a series because each protagonist acts instantly without parental guidance. The first is *Where the Wild Things Are,* which concerns small Max whose mother sends him to bed for misbehaving. He imagines sailing in a wolf suit to a land of monsters that Sendak says were modeled after "half-feared, half-detested" Brooklyn relatives. He becomes the monsters' king before returning home for supper.

The second book, *In the Night Kitchen,* shows altered New York City features, like a subway train made of bread. Sendak interpreted:

It was a book that was in my head for a long time. All my books have been in my head for a long time. I'm just a very slow worker in getting them finished. It takes years and years.

There was a Sunshine Bakers' advertisement, "We Bake While You Sleep," which seemed to be so typical of adults to do wonderful things while children were excluded. This book was about a child who stays up to see what's going on in the kitchen at night.

The book was an homage to New York City. I knew I would be leaving shortly, and I wanted to say a grandiose farewell to my home. There were any number of feelings that went into it.

Dummies for these two books and those for his *Nutshell Library* (Harper, 1962) are at Philadelphia's Rosenbach Museum along with three thousand of his original artworks. The four boxed *Nutshell* books are so small, they are easy for young children to hold. The claim is that anyone with a birth certificate should own a set. *Nutshell Library* includes an alphabet book, *Alligators All Around*; a counting book, *One Was Johnny*; a book about months, *Chicken Soup with Rice*; and *Pierre*, a cautionary tale. Sendak credited the writer who influenced that book:

Herman Melville is my god so far as writing is concerned. I couldn't call my work *Moby Dick*. That would be rather fatuous. There's *Pierre*. Then I had to get something that rhymed with his name, and that was: "I don't care."

I've never intended that so many of my characters look like me as a child, and I'm sorry they do. I'm depressed about that. I don't want to look like Pierre or Chicken Soup, but I suppose I do because I draw them.

Sendak acknowledged borrowing ideas from other writers:

George MacDonald was a writer who had a large influence on my life in terms of how one forms a fairy tale: the qualities in a fairy tale; the various levels in a fairy tale; or the reverberations (surface, middle, and bottom part). He showed in a very brief work how dense you can make a story for a child.

One can jump to Kafka for stylistic help. There are a number of my books with "lifts" from Dostoyevsky.

One of Sendak's favorite characters was Rosie from his third self-written book, *The Sign on Rosie's Door* (Harper, 1960). He sketched Rosie when he was about eighteen and she was about eight or nine. He said, "The real Rosie, back in the '40s when I observed her from my apartment window, literally picked the garbage can for some of the things she wore. I drew her in one of her better gowns, presumably from her mother's wardrobe."

Later, Sendak did the scenario, lyrics, pictures, and directed "Maurice Sendak's Really Rosie: Starring the Nutshell Kids," which aired on CBS-TV in 1974. He described the experience:

> It was both wonderful and arduous! It was a new medium for me, transforming the book into film. The two forms are very different. I had to do many drawings and resee Rosie from scratch in terms of how she walked, sat, and talked. It was fun!
>
> The scenario was mine. That was like having to recreate a whole new book. I went back over the file that I kept on Rosie, her experiences and language. The whole episode of Chicken Soup's death, which she pretended was her grand-mother's death, was very funny.

When Sendak lived in Greenwich Village, Jennie, his Sealyham terrier, ap-peared in most of his books. She is the dog that Max chases with a fork in *Where the Wild Things Are*. After Jennie died of cancer, Sendak honored her in *Higglety Pigglety Pop!: Or, There Must Be More to Life* (Harper, 1967):

> I was stuck with the actual verse, so the dog had to swallow a mop. Jennie, being the kind of dog she was, would have eaten anything. She consumed quantities of drawing ink and drawing pens, so I didn't think a mop would faze her. You really can't get along with a mop inside you, so she had to dispel it, for want of a better word.

Sendak's dog companions have been a golden retriever, Io, and German shepherds, Erda and Aggie, after he moved to a seven-acre farm in Ridge-field, Connecticut. He used Aggie as a nickname for Erda's son, realizing, "You can't go around calling your dog, Agamemnon." Aggie is a character in *Some Swell Pup: Or Are You Sure You Want a Dog?* (Farrar, 1976), a Sendak collaboration with dog trainer Matthew Margolis. After the passing of Erda and Aggie, Sendak got Runge, another German shepherd.

Sendak also has a Manhattan apartment, and has taught art at Parson's School of Design in Manhattan.

In 1976, Sendak illustrated the last children's book, *Fly by Night* (Farrar), that Randall Jarrell wrote before his death. Sendak drew an eight-year-old boy flying naked in a dream. In the book's only double-spread picture, he drew himself as a baby in his mother's arms:

> If I do insert images as private and personal as that, there has to be a reason. Otherwise, it's just an ego trip. In Randall Jarrell's book, I felt deeply the book was about yearning for mother or yearning for parents who weren't immedi-ately there when children desperately need a kind of affection. *Fly by Night* has

an extraordinary yearning quality about it. It took a long time for me to be able to illustrate that book.

Of course, part of the problem was that Jarrell was dead, and I missed working with him. He was a remarkable person. He was one of the few writers I've known who had coherent, creative things to say about the pictures. When I did do the picture of my mother there, it was because I was missing my mother as much as he was missing the mother in the story. I felt there was a good reason for using my mother's picture. I had never done it before.

Sendak is proud that no authors have objected to his artistic treatment in their books. Most contemporaries are delighted with his results. Else Holmelund Minarik must have known that "Little Bear" characters he drew in Victorian dress with human emotions were so endearing, they helped sustain her series.

Sendak said he tries to consult authors, "only if they're consultable":

Occasionally, they like to work very closely with me, as Ruth Krauss did. There was no one else quite like Ruth. Else Minarik was timid. She thought the illustrations were my job, but I stayed in touch with her and showed her everything I did. Jarrell was much like Ruth Krauss. Some are really very indifferent to the process. They finish with their part of the book, saying: "Now you have it, and you do your job!"

Sendak described how he starts a new book:

I begin with an emotional feeling, almost memories more than ideas, certain needs that have to be expressed. The first step is to find words to embody them. Pictures are as far away at that stage as possible. Then the pictures start coming like Polaroid!

I've always said this about my work and my feelings about my profession. I'm really turned on by words. Otherwise, I could be a painter. I can't be a painter because I have to read in order to see pictures!

Unfortunately, many fine books are now out of print, so Sendak's view of the publishing world today is timely:

It's a prejudiced view, and I'm not so involved in it. I don't think quality has improved in writing, illustrating, or production. Certainly not in production because it's so costly to reproduce, and there are so few good printers around to do it. Let them really retrench and stop publishing for a while so we can review our backlist. We have superb books from the past that are no longer around. It's idealistic. It's not going to happen. I think too many books are published thoughtlessly that are very expensive. This is true in all publishing, not only for children.

The one genre that Sendak favors is fantasy, stating in his Caldecott acceptance speech, "And it is through fantasy that children achieve catharsis." He feels the power of imagination (fantasy) elevates childhood.

Strange as it may seem, Sendak doesn't target his illustrations to children. He said, "I don't illustrate for adults, but I don't illustrate for children either. I don't make these categories in my mind. I'm not conscious of any audience while I'm working. I'm only desperately in need of satisfying myself as an artist and hoping other people will like it."

UPDATE

In 1981, Sendak's "Rosie" sang Carole King's songs in a lively off-Broadway production, "Really Rosie," staged by a children's theater company, The Night Kitchen. Sendak founded the company with Arthur Yorinks, author–playwright and librettist, who wrote the 1987 Caldecott winner, *Hey, Al* (Farrar, 1986), illustrated by Richard Egielski.

The Night Kitchen productions had tryouts at the State University of New York at Purchase, where the nonprofit company was invited to establish residency. Sendak, artistic director, and Yorinks, associate director, coproduced their material with theater and opera companies nationally and internationally.

Sendak's *Outside Over There* (Harper, 1982), which Sendak considers the third in his series that started with *Where the Wild Things Are,* was named a Caldecott Honor Book. The protagonist is Ida, who travels to Outside Over There to recover her baby sister, who had been kidnapped by goblins. *Outside Over There* is about Maurice Sendak's childhood when his sister, Natalie, took care of him after his mother went to work. He dimly remembered the grape arbor in Brooklyn where Natalie wheeled his carriage. Natalie told him about the actual arbor only after seeing the finished book.

Sendak often listens to music while working. He played Mozart while doing *Outside Over There* and even drew Mozart performing in a cottage along a stream as Ida and her baby sister pass.

In the 1980s, Sendak was ballet and opera designer of Mozart's "The Magic Flute," Tchaikovsky's "The Nutcracker Suite," and short operas based on Sendak's fantasies, *Higglety Pigglety Pop!* and *Where the Wild Things Are.* He wrote the librettos for some operatic adaptations of his books. He got involved in opera when Frank Corsaro, a leading American opera director, asked Sendak to design sets and costumes for the Houston Grand Opera's rendition of "The Magic Flute."

In 1985, Farrar released Sendak's *The Cunning Little Vixen*, a Czech children's story about the brutal, often beautiful world of a clever vixen and her cruel human acquaintances. Sendak's book illustrations are based on his work as costume designer for the New York City Opera Company's 1983 production of Leos Janucek's opera, "The Cunning Little Vixen."

In the 1980s, Sendak persuaded his father to dictate in Yiddish a juvenile book, *In Grandpa's House* (Harper, 1985). This is a fictionalized account of his father's boyhood in a Jewish *shtetl* or village. His father's family, who remained in Poland, all died during the Holocaust. Included in the book is a children's fairy tale with magical creatures that Philip remembered from his own father and that Maurice illustrated. It is a story within a story, all translated from Yiddish by Seymour Barofsky.

Sendak illustrated in watercolor the Grimm brothers' previously unpublished *Dear Mili* (Farrar, 1988). The tale is in the form of a letter in 1816 to a child, Mili, whose mother protects her only daughter from war by sending her into the woods. In 1988, Farrar also released Sendak's writings on children's literature, titled *Caldecott & Co.*

Sendak illustrated Iona and Peter Opie's children's folklore, *I Saw Esau: The Schoolchild's Pocket Book* (Candlewick, 1992), with small views of brawling imps in men's top hats and tailcoats and women's mobcaps and empire-waist gowns. In contrast to his humorous art, his frontispiece realistically shows publisher, artist, and editors.

In 1993 Sendak illustrated the Mother Goose rhyme *We Are All in the Dumps with Jack and Guy* (Farrar), interpreting homeless urban children as caregivers of each other. When Philadelphia's Please Touch Museum held a 1995 three-dimensional exhibit of Sendak characters, the artist memorialized his brother, Jack, who died that year. In 1997, fans saw Sendak's sets and costumes in performances of Humperdinck's opera, "Hansel and Gretel."

In 1999 Harper issued James Marshall's *Swine Lake* with Sendak's illustrations. Marshall died before illustrating the tale, so Sendak fulfilled the task. The text features a mangy wolf who stumbles when performing "Swine Lake" with the Boarshoi Ballet at New Hamsterdam Theater. Pigs are everywhere, but the wolf doesn't eat them. On the second night, he leaps on stage to dance, and newspapers give him good reviews.

In 2000 Sendak, Robert Sabuda, David Carter, Tor Lokvig, and others created *Brooklyn Pops Up* (Simon & Schuster). It is a marvelous pop-up book about Brooklyn, including a three-dimensional Brooklyn Bridge, and was published in conjunction with the Brooklyn Public Library and the Movable Book Society. Sendak's involvement shows his interest in new book formats.

For five decades, Sendak, a master humorist, has illustrated more than eighty books that have sold millions of copies in multiple languages. He won the 1983 Laura Ingalls Wilder Award, the 1990 first Empire State Award for

Excellence in Literature for Young People, and is the only illustrator from the United States to date to win the international Hans Christian Andersen Children's Book Prize for his entire work!

Unfortunately, Ursula Nordstrom died on October 11, 1988, after generously handpicking choice books for Sendak to illustrate. She similarly helped advance the careers of others who were talented.

Elizabeth George Speare, author (1908–1994)

1974 Interview

"It's people who get me started, and it's people who prompt my interest in history," stated Elizabeth George Speare, an author who won the Newbery Medal twice: in 1959 for her best-known work, *The Witch of Blackbird Pond* (Houghton, 1958), and in 1962 for *The Bronze Bow* (Houghton, 1961). Among other honors, both books achieved placement on the International Board on Books for Young People (IBBY) Honor List. *The Witch of Blackbird Pond* was then the most widely sold Newbery Medal winner.

Elizabeth George was born on November 21, 1908, and lived in Melrose, Massachusetts. It was easy for her to write about colonial times since "New Englanders and the countryside have not changed much in three hundred years," she said. She and her only brother had a happy childhood, enriched by extended family.

After a year at Smith College in Massachusetts, she attended Boston University, receiving her bachelor's degree in 1930 and her master's degree in 1932. She taught English at high schools in Rockland and Auburn, Massachusetts before marrying Alden Speare, an engineer, in 1936. The couple moved to Connecticut where they raised their children, Alden Jr. and Mary Elizabeth. When the children were in junior high, Speare focused on writing, her first love. She spoke about her childhood efforts:

> I have a brown notebook at home with my first novel. When I was eight years old, I illustrated it with pictures cut out of magazines and pasted in the book. I

think it was modeled after the *Bobbsey Twins* because I started out with *Dorothy Twin in the Country* and *Dorothy Twin at Boarding School.* I didn't get very far.

Elizabeth and a female cousin were enthusiastic writers of stories who spent time at family reunions in a quiet nook, sharing their compositions. When the two visited as college students, they continued to listen to each other's writing.

As an adult, Speare began publishing in magazines. She had always intended to write, but "I took a long time getting under way." Her first published article was on family skiing, and *Better Homes and Gardens* accepted it. She invited her husband, an industrial engineer, to do a homemaker's time-and-motion study, and she published results with her own account in *Woman's Day.*

Speare independently found her correct "fit" in an *American Heritage* article about Abby and Julia Smith, two sisters in Colonial Glastonbury, Connecticut, who lost their land and cows after they refused to pay taxes. A January 7, 1958, televised adaptation was "Abby, Julia and the Cows." The sisters retrieved the land.

Speare explained why she, never a history enthusiast, began to write historical fiction:

> I really wasn't interested in history, as I remember, all through my school years. I think what started me on my first historical fiction was a story in "The Rivers of America" series about the captivity of Susannah Johnson, which was one of the famous Indian captivities in Massachusetts. I later recorded this as *Calico Captive.*
>
> I thought it would make a wonderful story for girls like myself, who enjoyed reading. I looked up the original little volume that contained Susannah's *Narrative of the Captivity of Mrs. Johnson,* which was first published in 1807. While Susannah was a marvelous character, I was fascinated by her younger sister, Miriam Willard, who was captured with her.

Speare set her story, *Calico Captive* (Houghton, 1957), in Charlestown, New Hampshire, in 1754, during the brink of the French and Indian War. In a raid on the fort, Indians captured James and Susanna Johnson and their children, Sylvanus, Susanna, and Polly, as well as Mrs. Johnson's teenage sister, Miriam Willard. The captors took their hostages to Montreal, where French residents paid a ransom for them. When she was seventy, Mrs. Johnson wrote her narrative, but Speare imagined Miriam Willard's adventures. Miriam learns to earn a living as a dressmaker and secures passage back to New England for her and her family before marrying a minister.

Miriam Willard and the heroine of Speare's *The Witch of Blackbird Pond,* Kit Tyler, both reject wealthy suitors in pursuit of true love. Speare revealed the origin of her first Newbery Medal winner:

> There's a wonderful series of books on colonial America written by Alice Morse Earle that's a gold mine for anyone who wants to write on that period. In *Child Life in Colonial Days* [Macmillan, 1899], I found a little story about a ten-year-old girl who came from Barbados to study, which was common in those days. She lived with her grandmother in Boston, and she was very hoity-toity. She brought with her a number of trunks and a personal maid. She wrote home, complaining about her grandmother not letting her have wine and beer with her meals. She was very unhappy. Her grandmother wouldn't buy her a new muff.
>
> It suddenly occurred to me that I would make this girl a little older and send her, not to Boston, which, of course, was the center of civilization in America. I'd send her to a Puritan outpost, such as where I was living: Wethersfield, Connecticut.

Speare depicts her heroine from Barbados in 1687 as free-spirited, sixteen-year-old Kit Tyler. A spoiled Kit arrives at the home of her Puritan uncle, Matthew Wood, with seven trunks, but in time she changes completely. Eventually, she appreciates Nat Eaton, the *Dolphin*'s handsome first mate. The two befriend Hannah Tupper, an aged woman ostracized by Puritans because she is a Quaker. Hannah projects love to those who courageously visit her dwelling beside Blackbird Pond. Witch-hunters burn Hannah's home, and her friends force her to escape. The witch-hunters accuse Kit of guilt by association, putting her on trial for her life.

Two witch-hunters, Goodman and Goodwife Cruff, accuse Kit of bewitching their daughter, Prudence. But Prudence says that Kit has been teaching her to read, and she proves it by reading from the Bible. Her father is so proud, he drops charges against Kit.

Speare gave her interpretation of *The Witch of Blackbird Pond*:

> The theme is Kit's being a misfit and gradually coming to understand the Puritans. I was fascinated by the Quaker history, which I brought in with Hannah Tupper. Then, of course, there was preparation for the Revolution. Although this was almost a hundred years before, the colonists were already thinking about oppression. . . .
>
> *The Witch* is one of my books which is accepted because it has an independent heroine. Most of my characters are orphans, so they have more control over their lives than do young people today. I write about challenging times when people had to rise to circumstances.

A character symbolic of Puritanism in *The Witch of Blackbird Pond* is Matthew Wood, and Speare said he was patterned after recognizable individuals:

> I've known old New England men like that. I've known the harshness of one whose daughter cried bitterly when she was forced to break her engagement because her fiancé in their small town pulled a Halloween prank. The fiancé took a selectman's wagon and put it in someone else's yard. That was one side of Matthew Wood, but then there was the other side. That was strong, reliable, fair, and just in an emergency.

Librarian Carolyn Field chaired the Newbery Committee when *The Witch of Blackbird Pond* won unanimously on the first ballot, a rare event. Field revealed, "Thereafter, we discussed books at our Midwinter American Library Association Meeting and balloted afterwards."

Speare's other Newbery winner, *The Bronze Bow*, is set in the Holy Land:

> My biblical book . . . is an outgrowth of my teaching Sunday school. The whole period seemed so amorphous to me and my students. It could have been yesterday or prehistoric times. . . . The characters and personalities seemed too vague. . . . I tried to make them into human beings. I started out with that purpose. . . .
>
> I probably was writing previously with heroines for girl readers because I was such a great reader myself. In *The Bronze Bow*, I started with a heroine, Thacia, and then I realized I was writing about a period in which girls were completely subservient. My heroine wasn't going to get out and see much of the action herself. It was going to be completely off stage, so I switched to a male protagonist.

In *The Bronze Bow*, protagonist Daniel Bar Jamin changes from a young zealot who wants to avenge his father's and uncle's crucifixions to an individual who realizes that "only love could bend the bow of bronze" (p. 252). He is influenced by the actions of Jesus, for no words are exchanged between them. In her Newbery acceptance speech for this book, Speare's last sentence was: "Those of us who have found Love and Honor and Duty to be a sure foundation must somehow find words which have the ring of truth."

Speare next wrote *Child Life in New England, 1790–1840* for Old Sturbridge Village, Massachusetts, in 1961. Random House commissioned her nonfiction *Life in Colonial America* (1963) as part of its Landmark Series, which, she stressed, is "about people still." Houghton published her only adult novel, *The Prospering* (1967), about a girl merely mentioned in the history of Stockbridge, Massachusetts. Through the girl's eyes, Speare shows the founding of that town.

"While readers of historical fiction learn about heroes and heroines who fight injustice," Speare said, "writers have to be aware of possible stumbling blocks when composing such fiction":

> The main pitfall in historical writing that I've encountered in my own work and in the work of friends who've asked me to read novels they've written is that of getting too caught up with history. The writer has to omit what is extraneous and has nothing to do with the plot.
>
> I've been quite rigid with myself about that. Unless I've found a double reason for every bit of history, I did not include it. Editor Annis Duff has said, "Historical writing is like an iceberg. Most of the research doesn't show, but it's there." I only draw upon the part that contributes to plot or character. Unless it serves that double purpose, I tried not to use it.

Speare discussed how she organized her writing tasks, from the research stage to the finished product:

> Of course, research comes first. That's the fascinating, fun part. I can spend indefinite hours poking around in libraries and finding all the various pieces that are perhaps going to fit together and perhaps not. That can take hours.
>
> For *The Bronze Bow*, it took a great deal of time because I knew nothing about ancient Palestine, nothing whatsoever. I read histories, including that of Josephus, and travel books. I had never been to the Holy Land. Research can take many months, maybe more than a year.
>
> Eventually, the time comes when you have to start writing, and that is a task. I write usually three times through. The first time's the hardest. After that, the rewrites are pure fun. I write at the typewriter. I outline previous to writing with large holes, but I have to know where I'm going. Sometimes, I'm not so sure I'll know how to get there. Serialized chapters would paralyze me.

Speare's perfectionism is obvious in her publications. Her characters are memorable because they have inner grit to cope with problems.

UPDATE

Twenty-two years after her last work of juvenile fiction, Speare created *The Sign of the Beaver* (Houghton, 1983), a 1984 Newbery Honor Book. While reading a history of Maine, Speare came across the story of a boy who survived for months in a cabin, aided only by an Indian friend. Speare introduced Matt Hallowell, almost thirteen, who leaves Quincy, Massachusetts, with his father, for the Maine territory. They claim a plot near the Penobscot River, build a log cabin, and plant corn. The father returns for the rest of the family, and Matt stays behind. During the long months that follow, Matt is helped by Indians with the sign of the beaver. *The Sign of the Beaver* received the Scott O'Dell Award for Historical Fiction. Because of its sensitivity, it also won the Christopher Award.

Speare died of an aortic aneurysm on November 15, 1994, in Tucson, Arizona. Five years earlier, she had received the Laura Ingalls Wilder Award for a distinguished and enduring contribution to children's literature. This award honors all her books, an array short in quantity and long in quality.

Jerry Spinelli, author (1941–)

Eileen Spinelli, poet–author (1942–)

1992 Interview

JERRY SPINELLI

Jerry Spinelli referred to a photograph of himself at age twelve and said, "I was suited for a Norristown Little League All-Stars game. I wanted to be a Yankee shortstop." Instead, he grew up to write about a twelve-year-old orphaned baseball hero in his 1991 Newbery Medal winner, *Maniac Magee* (Little, Brown, 1990).

When Jerry won the 1990 *Boston Globe-Horn Book* Award for *Maniac Magee*, observers said the victory cancelled his chance for a Newbery Medal, but Jerry proved them wrong.

Jerry was born on February 1, 1941. In his growing-up years, he was accustomed to winning, being a sports hero, and being popular:

> In junior high, I was quarterback of the football team, shortstop of the baseball team, a guard on the basketball team, class president, homeroom president, king of the ninth-grade prom, and my girlfriend was the queen. Oh, and I was the valedictorian!

Jerry's self-confidence increased further in high school as a result of an experience that made him want to be a writer. He recalled:

> There was a big football game that my Norristown High School won, defeating a team that hadn't lost in three years. The town went crazy. While others were blaring horns, I went home and wrote a poem. I gave it to my father, and it appeared in the *Times-Herald* two or three days later. Next thing I know, I'm famous. Everyone's patting me on the back, and I'm thinking, *I'm going to be a writer.*

Jerry worked toward his career goal by graduating from Gettysburg College and attending the Writing Seminars at Johns Hopkins University. He taught briefly at Temple University but found instructing gave him little time for writing.

He worked for Chilton in Radnor, Pennsylvania, editing a trade magazine, *Product Design and Development.* He wore corduroy pants and a plaid shirt to work, stayed in his windowless, tiny, computerized office on the fifth floor, never socialized, and never got a raise. For twenty-three years, he wrote from 11:30 A.M. until 1:30 P.M., the beginning of the first lunch shift until the end of the second one.

He once went to work without a chicken lunch because he found at home only chicken bones in his brown paper bag. He knew one of the household's six children was guilty, but he didn't know who. The incident drove him to write a story from a young person's view, inspiring *Space Station Seventh Grade* (Little, Brown, 1982). Agent Ray Lincoln, who accepted the book after reading three chapters, advertised it to editors of juvenile works. John Keller at Little, Brown published it and his other books until 1991, when Simon & Schuster played that role. Knopf and HarperCollins are now his main publishers.

Jerry is partial to his first printed story, *Space Station Seventh Grade.* It depicts lively thirteen-year-old Jason Herkimer, who adjusts to life with a stepfather and weekend visits with his father. At school, he works on a space station but is suspended for a moose call in the auditorium during a trombonist's solo. In track, he beats Marceline McAllister. Their relationship continues in ninth grade with Marceline demanding more equal treatment in the sequel, *Jason and Marceline* (Little, Brown 1986). Adolescents favor earthy language in the first book and references to awakening sexuality in the sequel.

Stroudsburg Middle School Library took *Space Station Seventh Grade* off the shelf because of the realistic bathroom talk by thirteen-year-old characters. Jerry, who first wrote the book for adults, noted that his publisher made few changes in a youth's edition, but parents censor the author.

Several of Jerry's books are related. In *Dump Days* (Little, Brown 1988), Jerry mentions mean old Mr. Finsterwald, a *Maniac Magee* character, and alludes to Maniac, though not by name. In both *Dump Days* and *The Bathwater Gang* (Little, Brown, 1990), he refers to the large Pickwell family. They are included in *Maniac Magee* as a white family who is generous about feeding strangers of all races.

Jerry found it difficult to write *Maniac Magee,* though he knew he wanted to tell "about a kid who was a hero to others." His first longhand composition praised "a mini-superman," so he put the manuscript aside. "They say Maniac was born in a dump," the book's first words, seemed to come out of nowhere, and he wrote easily thereafter.

He was surprised when, on January 14, 1991 at 12:30 A.M., he received a phone call from the Newbery selection committee telling him that *Maniac Magee* won the medal. Unfortunately, Gulf War news cancelled his appearance on the *Today* television show. His Newbery acceptance speech seemed easy to write and deliver to a 1,500-person audience in Atlanta's Ritz-Carlton ballroom. Jerry concluded, "Greater than the event itself has been the windfall afterwards."

As part of his "windfall," Jerry made many public appearances, having been on the road ninety days one year. He has spoken in distant Sri Lanka and received an award in Hawaii. Of course, his book sales have leaped.

Little, Brown issued 60,000 more copies of *Maniac Magee* after Jerry won the Newbery Medal. His readers mail him well-worn, sloppy-soled sneakers, the trademark of his legendary runner. Though Maniac is white, Jerry patterned him after an African-American friend in a Catholic orphanage near Bristol. The hyperactive boy ran everywhere: three miles for a hoagie, free for orphans, and six miles each way to the nearest movie theater.

The model for *Maniac Magee*'s Amanda Beale was a girl in sixth grade from upstate New York. A librarian introduced her to Jerry, who recalled:

She loved books and had her own home library. She enjoyed reading, but every day she found more of her books ruined by siblings and pets. What to do about it? She came up with an interesting solution. She always brought her entire library of beloved books back and forth to school in a suitcase. I gave her my address and made her promise to write me, but she hasn't. I wonder if she knows she became Amanda Beale in *Maniac Magee*.

When Jerry described the thumb of Amanda's mother as she iced a cake, he revealed whose thumb had impressed him as a child:

> I remembered the brown fingers and thumb of my mother's dentist, Dr. Winters, as he probed inside my mouth. He was the first dentist I ever met. I must have been jealous of the attention Mother was getting, so he propped me up in the dental chair to examine my teeth.

Jerry considered his own baseball coach's stop ball to be like that received by Maniac from his elderly coach/friend Grayson, a groundskeeper at Elmwood Zoo:

> Skag Cottman was the coach's name when I was a member of the Norristown Brick Company Knee-High Baseball Team. He was and still is a legend today in Norristown. He would tell us that the stop ball was coming, and it was all we could do to make contact with it. No one ever hit it out of the infield.

While Skag's actual stop ball remained a challenge, Maniac returned the fictional ones pitched by Grayson. The legendary hero also untied knots, as he demonstrated with children's shoelaces and the much more difficult, highly original Cobble's Knot.

Maniac Magee is heavily concerned with race relations. Two neglected white boys, Russell and Piper, drag Maniac to their home. It is actually "Fort" McNab, a private West End house of filthy, cursing racists who are buttressing their property against African Americans. Jerry explained why he included the stereotyped McNabs:

> Racial prejudice north of the Mason-Dixon line can be carried to extremes. The extent to which racists indulge themselves seems almost cartoonish and absurd. I have actually known someone who bought a steel door to guard his home against what he imagined would be raids.

The bigots seem concentrated on the West End of Two Mills, a fictitious town inspired by Jerry's birthplace, Norristown, Pennsylvania. A landmark is the Elmwood Park Zoo, where Maniac spends homeless nights in the buffalo pen or in the crude baseball equipment room near the band shell. Finally rescuing Maniac from his zoo home are two African-American youths: Amanda Beale and Maniac's former foe, Mars Bar, now mollified and dubbed "Snickers" by Amanda.

Jerry said that *Maniac Magee*'s short chapters and constantly running hero quickened the pace of his book, which he dedicated to his agent and her husband, Ray and Jerry Lincoln. The author sold film rights, but did not write the movie script. He stated firmly, "There will be no sequel to *Maniac*."

Questioned about his book's theme, Jerry's answer partially applies to all his books:

> The theme is childhood recollected. We recall everything as being grander and more mythic than reality. What we considered frightening may have been a little thing. I didn't think of myself as writing about homelessness, a current topic in newspapers today. I was just writing about a boy who didn't have a family and a home.

Jerry, who said he writes "*about* kids, not *for* kids," said he is aware of a broader audience. He does not focus on elite characters, and when talking to young people, prefers casual clothes. His informal windbreaker appeals to fans like Brooke Jacobs, who wrote him, "When you came to our school, I thought I'd see a big, tall man in a suit looking rich. When I saw you, I got very relaxed."

Jerry's informal style masks his achievements. His *Maniac Magee* won the Carolyn W. Field Award from the Pennsylvania Library Association in 1991. In a National Council of Teachers of English survey, his name appears as a "Leading Author for Young Adults in North America and Great Britain."

Jerry and his wife, Eileen, a fellow writer, help edit each other's work. Jerry found it difficult only once, when they collaborated on an unpublished short story, "The Owl Who Didn't Give a Hoot about Christmas."

EILEEN SPINELLI

While Jerry writes mainly for middle-school readers, Eileen targets her poetry, picture books, and chapter books for a much younger audience. In 1990, Eileen's story/poem "Mannerly Moose" won $1,000 in the *Highlights for Children* fiction contest. Her picture book *Somebody Loves You, Mr. Hatch* (Bradbury, 1991) won the 1992 Christopher Award.

Eileen was born on August 16, 1942, and grew up in Philadelphia. Her father, Joseph Mesi, was an engineer. She recalled a childhood event that might have discouraged a less determined person: "In second grade, my teacher read my composition as an example of the worst in the class, and I've been writing ever since."

Eileen published her first poem when she was eighteen. She began to write for children in 1979 and even taught creative writing, using the public library extensively.

More than five hundred of her poems have been published in magazines and newspapers. Her first book of published verse was *The Giggle and Cry Book* (Stemmer House, 1981), illustrated by Lisa Atherton.

Eileen has written beginning chapter books and picture books. Paul Yalowitz illustrated her picture book about a lonely bachelor learning to relate to others, *Somebody Loves You, Mr. Hatch*. One of her best-known picture storybooks is *Thanksgiving at the Tappletons'* (Addison-Wesley, 1982), illustrated by Maryann Cocca-Leffler. The author remembered:

> When I was a little girl, my father was out of work one Thanksgiving. We couldn't afford turkey, so my mother made meat loaf. We still had all the family in, a nice tablecloth, candles, and a festive mood. As I got older, all the other turkey Thanksgivings blurred, but this one stuck in my head.

When Eileen isn't writing or gardening, she fulfills family and humanitarian tasks. Formerly, she gave hospice care to the dying, explaining: "When I was young, I was always interested in the work of Elisabeth Kübler-Ross. I heard about the hospice program and joined because I wanted to make a difference."

Jerry referred to his book, *There's a Girl in My Hammerlock* (Simon & Schuster, 1991) when he acknowledged his wife's empathic qualities: "She's the model for Maisie's understanding mother in my book. In fact, she's the model for all of my sensitive characters."

Eileen met Jerry at Chilton "where he was the editor, and I was the lowly clerk." That romantic meeting rekindled the creativity of both, who progressed from writing totally alone to writing separately but with a spouse's support.

UPDATE

Jerry Spinelli wrote *Crash* (Knopf, 1996) because he wanted to include his home state's Penn Relays in a book. John "Crash" Coogan, a broad-shouldered football jock, has been making fun of puny Penn Webb for years. When Crash matures, he helps Penn, his competitor, win the single spot to enter the Penn Relays, and they become best friends.

Following *Crash*, Jerry wrote *Wringer* (HarperCollins, 1997) about Palmer LaRue, who is expected to be a wringer, as his father had been, wringing the necks of pigeons who do not die from gunshots during the town's annual shooting on Pigeon Day. Palmer refuses to join the brutality and manages to save his own pigeon pet, "Nipper." *Wringer* won the Carolyn W. Field Award from the Pennsylvania Library Association in 1998, and it was also a 1998 Newbery Honor Book.

Jerry's autobiography about his first sixteen years is *Knots in My Yo-Yo String: The Autobiography of a Kid* (Knopf, 1998). What is memorable in this young athlete's nostalgic account is how sports bridged the racial gap in Norristown.

In 2000, Knopf issued Jerry's *Stargirl,* about a tenth-grade nonconformist, Susan Caraway, who calls herself "Stargirl." She serenades others on their birthdays and is popular at first, but is shunned when she cheers for both the home team and the opposition at school sports events.

In 1995, Eileen released *Naptime, Laptime* (Scholastic), illustrated by Melissa Sweet, for lap-snuggled youngsters. In 1996, repose was still a central theme in her bedtime poems, *Where Is the Night Train Going?* (Boyds Mills Press), with illustrations by Cyd Moore.

Paul Yalowitz drew pictures for Eileen's storybook, *Boy, Can He Dance!* (Four Winds Press, 1993). It depicts a hotel chef's son, Tony, who dances away from his father's kitchen tasks, but succeeds as a hotel show performer.

Among Eileen's most recent picture books is *When Mama Comes Home from Work* (Simon & Schuster, 1998), illustrated by Jane Dyer. The book concerns a mother with a job and her relationship to her child. A counterbalance is Eileen's *Night Shift Daddy* (Hyperion, 2000), with art by Melissa Iwai, in which a father shares bedtime rituals with his daughter before going to work. Another book published in 2000, *Song for the Whooping Crane* (Eerdmans), illustrated by Elsa Warnick, is Eileen's celebration in free verse of an endangered bird.

John Steptoe, illustrator–author (1950–1989)

1975 Interview

John Steptoe, celebrated mainly as an artist, was a very young author when *Stevie* (Harper, 1969), his American Library Association Notable Book, was published. He said, "I met my first editor, Harper's Ursula Nordstrom, when I was seventeen, and two years later, my book, *Stevie*, came out. I never thought of myself as a writer, but it turned out well, and I've been writing and illustrating ever since."

Steptoe was born on September 14, 1950, in Brooklyn's St. John's Hospital. His father, John, a transit worker, and mother, Elesteen, owned two Brooklyn brownstone houses. While other children were playing outdoor sports in his Bedford-Stuyvesant neighborhood, Steptoe preferred staying home to paint and draw. "I didn't like to read, and no one read books to me. I would always do a lot of thinking alone."

From 1964 to 1967, Steptoe attended New York High School of Art and Design, and during that same period, an afternoon art program sponsored by the Harlem Youth Opportunity Act. He left high school three months before graduating. "I wasn't very comfortable at that high school," he said. "It's mainly a vocational high school for commercial artists. . . . I quit home and school when I was sixteen and ran off to Camden. I saw Philadelphia on my own."

In 1968, John Torres enlisted Steptoe for an eight-week summer program at Vermont Academy, funded by a Ford Foundation grant. Torres let Steptoe use his own studio and noticed other students entering. He found that

Steptoe was teaching them. Torres got Philip Dubois, another instructor, to look inside the studio too.

When Dubois asked Steptoe about his art goals, the young artist replied, "I want to create books for black children."

Steptoe began to realize his objective: "To get me a job, I took my portfolio to Madison Avenue where I found my work was appealing to children." Using contact names from a high school teacher, Burman Burris, Steptoe saw Ursula Nordstrom, Harper Junior Book's editor in chief. She urged him to write as well as illustrate the book that became *Stevie*. The Vermont Academy instructor, Dubois, let Steptoe use an apartment over his horse stables when the school's program ended, and that was *Stevie*'s birthplace.

Stevie, reprinted in *Life*, made Steptoe known. Its language and characters appeal to an African-American audience. White readers are drawn to it because of a universal topic: children's rivalry.

Stevie is a Harper book about inner-city life, and so are Steptoe's next two books, *Uptown* (1970) and *Train Ride* (1971). *Uptown* occurs in Harlem's Mount Morris Park where two chums, John and Dennis, question what they will do as grown-ups. *Train Ride,* which was a 1971 *New York Times* Outstanding Book, shows Charles taking his neighborhood friends on a free train ride from Brooklyn to Times Square and back again where home spankings await them. "In these three books, I was identifying myself as a black man," Steptoe said.

Birthday (Holt, 1972) was Steptoe's vehicle for praising African roots by showing an imaginary farm Utopia, incorporating traditional African design motifs in his art. His protagonist, Javaka, marks his eighth birthday as the firstborn child of the Yoruba community, who celebrate with him.

Steptoe explained his illustration techniques:

I illustrated *Stevie* with magic marker and pastels. In *Uptown* and some other books, I used acrylics. I do underpainting. It starts out with no light and then light builds up. Underpainting has lasted through much of my career as an artist. I work to size and don't do color separations.

Some observers think that Steptoe outlined his characters, but the dark lines were actually part of the underpainting that he retained. In his latest books, he eliminated underpainting and made characters airier, less stocky and somber, showing artistic growth.

Steptoe described the MacDowell Colony in Peterborough, New Hampshire, where he won fellowships for part of 1972–1974:

There's a colony of composers, writers, and painters. I was given a studio. My lunch was brought to me at noon. There's a dining hall where I ate dinner with others. Usually, fellowships last for two months. When I was there once, I was doing *My Special Best Words.*

Steptoe's *My Special Best Words* (Viking, 1974) was his first book about his daughter, Bweela, then three years old, and his son, Javaka, then one year old, whom he was raising as a single parent in Peterborough, New Hampshire. He revealed the sources of their names: "Bweela is a name that came to me in a dream and has a pleasant sound. Javaka was a friend's name that I used before in my book, *Birthday.*" Steptoe colored faces and bodies green, red, purple, blue, and brown, depending on the characters' moods, but he painted them more realistically than in earlier books. In his book jacket, he told why he included bathroom training in the book:

> The honesty of the language in the book comes from my direct relations with my children. It is our family's language—almost our code. Very simply, natural functions exist, and they merit (at the least) an honest portrayal.

As a writer, Steptoe often wrote about friends and families:

> It takes me two or three months to think about a book I'm going to do and half a day to write it down if it's simple. I become all the characters in my book. After I've got the manuscript and contract approved, within six months, I may have finished the art if it's an easy book. . . . I love to change and grow.

Steptoe wrote and illustrated at least eleven of his own books, and he illustrated at least five books for other authors. He illustrated Lucille B. Clifton's *All Us Come Cross the Water* (Holt, 1972), and won the 1975 *Boston Globe-Horn Book* Honor Book Award for illustrating Eloise Greenfield's *She Come Bringing Me That Little Baby Girl* (Lippincott, 1974).

UPDATE

In 1978, *Stevie* received the Lewis Carroll Shelf Award and the Society of Illustrators Gold Medal. In 1982, he won the Coretta Scott King Award for illustrating Birago Diop's *Mother Crocodile,* translated and adapted by Rosa Guy (Delacorte, 1981).

For Lothrop, he created two Caldecott Honor Books based on folk tales. The 1985 recipient, *The Story of Jumping Mouse: A Native American Legend* (1984), contains detailed pencil drawings. The book tells a story of a young mouse that becomes Jumping Mouse, thanks to Magic Frog, who helps him achieve his goal of reaching the far-off land.

The multicolored 1988 Caldecott Honor Book, *Mufaro's Beautiful Daughters* (Lothrop, 1987), was also a Notable Children's Trade Book in the Field of Social Studies and won the 1988 Coretta Scott King Illustration Award. This Cinderella story was inspired by an African folk tale and dedicated to the children of South Africa. Steptoe's daughter, Bweela, at age sixteen, modeled for both sisters; his mother, for the queen mother; and his nephew, Antoine, for the boy in the forest.

Among the books he has illustrated for others are two Lothrop books by Arnold Adoff, *OUTside/INside: Poems* (1981) and *All the Colors of the Race: Poems* (1982).

He did a young adult book, *Marcia* (Viking, 1976), with only four illustrations and much text. The book, dedicated to his sister, Marcia, shows a fifteen-year-old who is afraid she will lose her boyfriend if she does not have intercourse with him. She agrees to have sex after she gets her mother to take her to a physician for safe-sex measures.

Steptoe showed writing ability when he provided the text alone for the book, *Creativity* (Clarion, 1997), illustrated in watercolor by E. B. Lewis. An African-American student, Charles, helps a Puerto Rican boy, Hector, adjust to mainland life.

A sequel to *My Special Best Words* was Steptoe's *Daddy Is a Monster . . . Sometimes* (Lippincott, 1980), which takes place in New York City. Six years passed since his first book, and Steptoe showed only a remnant of underpainting in his portrayals of his seven-year-old son and nine-year-old daughter, colored in muted tones. He painted himself realistically and as the monster "in the scary movies" that they envision when he disciplines them.

In 1989, he won another fellowship for the MacDowell Colony. On August 28, 1989, when he was only thirty-nine years old, Steptoe died of complications from AIDS. In 1995, the American Library Association honored his skills by incorporating his name in the Coretta Scott King/John Steptoe Award for New Talent.

John Steptoe's son, Javaka, graduated from Cooper Union College. He collected twelve poems by various writers that complimented fathers and illustrated them for his book, *In Daddy's Arms I Am Tall* (Lee & Low, 1997). An American Library Association Notable Book, the collection won the 1998 Coretta Scott King Illustration Award.

John Rowe Townsend, author (1922–)

1975 Interview

Following the old advice to authors that one should write about what one knows, author John Rowe Townsend incorporates the areas of England he knows best as settings for his prizewinning juvenile books. He said, "I was born in Leeds, England, and worked for a good many years in Manchester, both of these being northern industrial cities. . . . I'm from West Yorkshire, and I love it very dearly."

His books have won numerous honors. He was nominated twice for England's Carnegie Medal, and two of his books were placed on the honors list: *Hell's Edge* (Lothrop, 1963) in 1963 and *The Intruder* (Lippincott, 1969) in 1969, the year he also won the Silver Pen in England. In the United States, *The Intruder* won the 1970 Mystery Writers of America Edgar Award, and *The Islanders* (Lippincott, 1981) received the 1981 Christopher Award.

Townsend explained two British awards:

The Carnegie Award [for writing] and the Greenaway [for illustration] were established in 1936 and 1955, respectively. I think the Carnegie was in reciprocation for the fact that the American award (for writing) was named for the eighteenth-century English publisher, John Newbery. I suppose the British Library Association wanted to name their award for an American, Andrew Carnegie, who was responsible for a good deal of benefaction to libraries. We do have other awards but not as many as you have in the United States.

Townsend was born on May 10, 1922. His father, George, and mother, Gladys, met at Yorkshire Copper Works, where he was a clerk and she was a secretary. After they married, they lived in a row of adjacent brick houses, close to John Townsend's maternal Grandpa Page. His mother visited her father often, holding her son's hand and wheeling his sister, Lois, who was four years younger, in a stroller.

At age five, John Townsend, an early reader, knew he wanted to become a writer. He read school library books, and at age eight wrote his first children's book, *The Crew's Boat,* showing the influence of Stevenson's *Treasure Island.*

In elementary school, John Townsend was a star pupil. At age eleven, he went to Leeds Grammar School on a scholarship (his father had Parkinson's disease and had retired on a very small pension). He hid notices of school trips since his parents couldn't pay for them. Although he was a top student, he could not afford college, even if he had a scholarship. For three years, he worked in Inland Revenue's income-tax department, and then was accepted by the Royal Air Force to decode ciphers for two years during World War II. After assignments in Egypt and Palestine, he was sent to Florence, Italy, where he studied literature and art.

He returned to England in 1946, enrolled at Cambridge's Emanuel College, and in 1947 married Vera Lancaster. He had met her in a walking club when he worked for Inland Revenue. The couple lived at Cambridge with a modest government grant and two bicycles. He majored in English, learning not to read *about* books but to enjoy books themselves.

Townsend chose journalism as a career after his experience as chief editor of his campus newspaper. He received his bachelor's degree in 1949, and that same year started working for the *Manchester Guardian.* He worked for three years as assistant editor, then picture editor, and later was in charge of a weekly international edition. He received his master's degree in 1954, and eventually became children's book-review editor at the *Guardian,* which sponsors the Guardian Award:

> We try to catch writers who have not won other awards and are going to cover themselves with glory. One thing I'm rather pleased about is that the first recognition Richard Adams had for *Watership Down* was by winning the Guardian Award. I don't kid myself by thinking *Watership Down* would not have reached the stars without the Guardian Award. I think it would have gone into the stratosphere regardless.

After reviewing children's books, Townsend felt he should write some. When he planned his own books, he learned about another Englishman,

John Townsend, who had written two for children. To avoid confusion, he added his middle name, creating the byline John Rowe Townsend.

The author's main objection to children's books in England was that too many showed rich children with nannies. Not enough portrayed the poor that he encountered on an assignment:

> I had to do a series of articles for the National Society for the Prevention of Cruelty to Children. This involved going on "rounds" with several uniformed inspectors on the back streets of London and Manchester. In some ways, it was a traumatic experience. I learned I didn't know anything about real poverty. While I grew up in a poor home financially, it was rich in everything that really mattered.
>
> For the first time, I was introduced to the fact that there were children who grew up in poor homes spiritually. Nobody cared about whether the children had proper meals to eat or clothes to wear. Nobody cared if they went to school in the morning, and nobody talked to them except to shout at them. This affected me deeply indeed. In the city of Manchester, England, about two hundred children are deserted by their parents every year. I would imagine major industrial cities elsewhere in England and, for all I know, in America, could produce similarly horrifying statistics.

He had read about a mother who had abandoned her four children, only to return and bring the family together again. It influenced his first book, *Trouble in the Jungle* (Lippincott, 1961; *Gumble's Yard* as published in England). The Jungle is an inner-city district in England, and Townsend wrote three related books about children from such a setting. *Trouble in the Jungle* tells the story of abandoned children, the Thompsons, who move into the Jungle's derelict warehouse.

Townsend's sequel is *Goodbye to the Jungle* (Lippincott, 1965; *Widdershins Crescent* as published in England). Before the Jungle's slum clearance, the Thompsons move to a housing project, Westwood Estate. Doris's respectability quest leads her to buy furniture at Widdowson's that she can't afford. When Walter is imprisoned for arson at Widdowson's warehouse, Kevin has to quit school to support his folks, an outcome the author anticipated:

> I knew more about Walter and Doris than when I wrote *Trouble in the Jungle*. I knew when they got to the housing project, if Walter had to go six miles to work, he'd never get to work, and if he had to go just as far to the nearest pub, he'd find a way.

Townsend spoke of problems related to his honest portrayals: "Walter and Doris obviously are not married, so a BBC reporter accused me of writing children's books that are sordid. Children under difficult circumstances are not sordid at all."

Townsend made a trilogy of his Jungle books by adding *Pirate's Island* (Lippincott, 1968), which briefly mentions Walter Thompson. *Pirate's Island* shows fat, twelve-year-old Gordon Dobbs, a butcher's son, whose only friend, thin, nine-year-old Sheila Woodrow, always wears a tattered dress. They try to escape the Jungle by searching for a pirate's island.

Hell's Edge was Townsend's first young-adult book, a novelty in England, where the assumption was that young people mature at age thirteen and then move to adult books. *Hell's Edge* is about a teenager, Amaryllis (Ril) Terry, who, with her professor father, moves to an industrial community in northern England. Her cousin, Norman Clough, helps her find a letter in a library from deceased George Withishall, giving some of his estate to the town.

Another young-adult work is *The Intruder*, which concerns Sonny from the Jungle. He goes to an English village, trying to swindle eighty-year-old Ernest Haithwaite out of his Cottontree House. He convinces Ernest that he is a long-lost nephew and tries to get rid of Ernest's fifteen-year-old grandson. When *The Intruder* received the 1970 Mystery Writers of America Edgar Award and the *Boston Globe-Horn Book* Award, Townsend was delighted: "Those are American awards. It surprised me very much. I didn't realize I was a writer of mysteries until the Edgar."

Following *The Intruder*, Townsend created *Goodnight, Prof, Love* (Lippincott, 1970; *The Runaways* as published in England). The tale introduces sixteen-year-old Graham Hollis, a middle-class youth from a stodgy, English Midlands town. Graham refuses to go on vacation with his parents and moves to a working-class setting where he becomes involved with Lynn Smith, an eighteen-year-old waitress.

Townsend's next book was *The Summer People* (Lippincott, 1972), which takes place in 1939 in an English village that is crumbling into the sea. The families of sixteen-year-old Philip Martin and Sylvia Pilling think they are the perfect couple. They wander down the beach to meet another girl and boy and secretly fall in love with dates their parents would consider less "suitable."

Townsend varies his pace, commenting on his unusual *Noah's Castle* (Lippincott, 1975):

> The principal character is a father who is certain his family is going to be all right despite an economic catastrophe, outrageous inflation, and armies of unemployed. He has stockpiled his basement and is going to have to face a siege.
>
> *Noah's Castle* is a fitting name for the Mortimers' huge, new house that the six family members occupy at the father's request. He keeps the basement door

locked, windows barred, and prohibits visitors. His son, Barry Mortimer, feels guilt, knowing that his father is an illegal hoarder. This becomes a tense survival story, not only for the family, but also for a starving country.

Townsend and his wife, Vera, were married for twenty-five years before she died in 1973 after a long illness. They had two daughters and a son. He now lives in Cambridge, and is a close friend of Jill Paton Walsh, another author for young people in England. Townsend has chaired the group of Children's Writers in the British Society of Authors. He has taught and lectured in the United States, Australia, Japan, and England. His books, many of which are American Library Association Notable Books, are translated into at least twelve languages.

UPDATE

Since 1978, Townsend has been among visiting faculty yearly at the Center for Children's Literature in Boston's Simmons College. He used the Jungle setting again, though without the Thompson family, when he wrote *Dan Alone* (Lippincott, 1983). Eleven-year-old Dan Lunn runs away from his ill grandfather's house because he doesn't want to go to a children's home. He hides in the Jungle, meets a young female survivor, Olive, and moves into quarters where thieves get him to beg and sing for a living.

Townsend has written more than twenty realistic books on varied topics for children and young adults. A book that approaches fantasy is *The Persuading Stick* (Lothrop, 1986). Sarah Casson, a quiet young English girl, finds an eight-inch stick that seems to give her power and confidence. Using the stick as a wand, Sarah tries to prevent a family tragedy. An island is the setting for Townsend's *The Fortunate Isles* (Lippincott, 1989; *The Golden Journey* as published in England). Two friends search for a living God who can curb their war-prone king.

Townsend's adult nonfiction includes books listed with Scarecrow Press's latest publication dates: *John Newbery and His Books* (1994) and *Written for Children: An Outline of English-Language Children's Literature* (1996). This sixth U.S. edition, an updated history with an extensive bibliography, discusses the best children's books through 1994 in Britain and the United States.

Elizabeth Borton de Treviño, author (1904–)

1977 Interview

For children's author Elizabeth Borton de Treviño, what started as a news-paper assignment in Mexico turned into a life-changing event. She said, "I was sent to Mexico by my newspaper to interview personages in the cultural life of the country: Carlos Chávez in music, Diego Rivera in painting, and Mariano Azuela in literature. I married the first Mexican I set eyes on when I crossed the border, and I've been here ever since." Along the way, she won a 1966 Newbery Medal for *I, Juan de Pareja* (Farrar, Strauss & Giroux, 1965).

Elizabeth Borton was born on September 2, 1904, the oldest child of Fred Borton, an attorney, and his wife, Carrie Borton, in Bakersville, California. One of her father's clients, Don Emilio Castro, branded a heifer to honor her birth. She recalled being deeply interested in Spanish culture from a young age:

I was born in California where there's still a strong influence of Spain and Mex-ico. Both my father and mother were native Californians. Our family doctor was a Mexican (George Carlos Sabichi).

I feel the United States is now becoming almost bilingual through the tremen-dous number of people of Hispanic origin in our country. I personally think that it's a great thing to have educational and many other cultural events in both lan-guages. Whenever there is a confrontation of two cultures, each one is enriched by the other. We're going to experience in the near future a great surge of bilin-gual or Hispanic and English writers who will come from this new *ambiente* [environment].

As a child, Elizabeth Borton played the violin. Her father bought her two violins and opened a music-store account for her, so she could buy a record per week. At dinner, the father kept portable encyclopedias on his left and a dictionary on his right. The children often referred to these sources during dinner conversations.

After learning Spanish in high school, she took more advanced courses at Stanford University, where she got her degree in Latin American history. She also enrolled in a noncredit course in playwriting and won recognition by following the professor's Writing Rule Number One: "Keep trying!"

Elizabeth next studied violin at the Boston Conservatory of Music. While there, she had to earn money: "I went to work for a newspaper in Boston [the *Boston Herald*] and got my first byline after an interview in Spanish." She reported on the dancer, "La Argentina," and later, the pianist, José Iturbi. Among her English interviewees were Eleanor Roosevelt and actors she met when the newspaper sent her to Hollywood.

Because of her actor interviews, Page and Company commissioned her first children's book, *Pollyanna in Hollywood* (1931). She was to continue the "Pollyanna" series begun by the late Eleanor Parker. The series emphasized "The Glad Game," seeing something positive in each disappointment. In time, Page commissioned five "Pollyanna" books and two "Little Cousin" selections, *Our Little Aztec Cousin of Long Ago* (1934) and *Our Little Ethiopian Cousin* (1935).

During the Depression, when she was allowed only half-days of work, the writer went home to California. She told her father that she wanted to write books, so he rented a small office for her with a typewriter, table, and chair. He paid her a small salary to work all weekdays from nine to five with an hour for lunch. He told her to do what other would-be novelists seldom do: finish her books!

In 1931, the *Boston Herald* recalled her as a full-time reporter, and three years later sent her to Mexico to interview President Cárdenas and other leaders. At the border, she met a contact from the Monterrey Chamber of Commerce: Luis Treviño Gómez, whose family had lived in the United States during part of the Mexican Revolution. The two fell in love and married fifteen months later. She adjusted to life in Mexico:

> Ever so many people ask me about that, but I didn't know I had adjusted until it took place. I thought that was the way marriages were, that you just fought things out until you came to a level place. I had a tremendous ally and defender in my mother-in-law, an adorable person.
>
> A funny thing happened to me. In all my years of studying Spanish, I never learned the intimate [verb form] with the result that I always addressed my husband as "Your Mercy." This was considered to be very respectful on my part!

The couple rented a Monterrey house with barred windows and an inner patio. The violinist made friends with Nella Siller, a former Boston cellist, and a local pianist, Esperanza Esparza, forming the Trio Clásico Femenino, known privately as "Petticoat Trio." Her cat, Policarpo, was a guest at their rehearsals, but wider audiences paid to engage them.

Treviño reported weekly Monterrey news for *Laredo Times* and occasionally for *Time* magazine. In 1953, with the help of her agent, Virginia Rice, she launched her book career, beginning with adult books about her life in Mexico.

Treviño's family moved to San Angel near Mexico City. She said, "I was first violinist for six years with the Vivaldi Chamber Orchestra and did a lot of radio work." In 1947, she served as secretary to Carlos Chávez, Mexico's most famous composer. Another job was with the Mexican Tourist Department, which enabled her to travel throughout Mexico, giving her ample story content.

Treviño began to write about the people who lived in various periods of Mexican history. Her first Mexican children's story was *A Carpet of Flowers* (Crowell, 1955) about Huamantla's people who come from the Puebla region on December 12, Our Lady of Guadalupe Day. Their destiny is outside Mexico City: the Basilica of Our Lady of Guadalupe. On the cathedral's floor they place a beautifully designed carpet of newly cut flowers. A blind Indian boy, who grew pansies for the floral eyes of the carpet's Virgin, miraculously recovers his eyesight.

Her second children's story is *Nacar, the White Deer* (Farrar, Strauss & Giroux, 1963). She had read that a galleon, the *Manila,* traveled yearly in the seventeenth century between Asia and New Spain (now Mexico). This ship held an albino deer with a gold collar, a gift for the king. In her story, the deer's keeper dies en route to New Spain. When the viceroy sees how weak the deer, named Nacar, is, he lets a boy herder, Lalo, care for him though the boy has been mute from shock. Lalo accompanies Nacar to Spain, and their bond becomes so strong, when Nacar's life is threatened, speechless Lalo utters words that save the animal.

Treviño began to write for children after she had two sons. Her older son, Luis Frederico, is a painter. Her younger son, Enrique Ricardo, is a lawyer and teaches at several universities near Mexico City. She enjoys sharing music appreciation with her family and said: "Both of my sons love music. Enrique is a very fine cellist. My husband was a pianist."

The artistic son once told Treviño a story from his Spanish painting teacher about a slave that belonged to Spain's great artist, Velásquez. Treviño went to Spain to do research on the Moorish slave, Juan de Pareja. Seventeenth-century laws did not allow slaves to paint, so he had to study secretly until Velásquez freed him and hired him as an assistant. The author wrote the story as a first-person account, *I, Juan de Pareja,* and is proud that "this Newbery winner appears in many languages, including Afrikaans used in South Africa."

Though she is a resident of Mexico, Treviño is eligible for the Newbery Medal:

> I am a citizen of the United States. I've always taken great pains to keep my passport valid. After all, I have two sons who should remember and appreciate their heritage through me as well as the very rich heritage through their father.

I, Juan de Pareja arouses interest in a painting by Velásquez, *Portrait of Juan de Pareja,* which the Metropolitan Museum of Art in New York City formerly owned. The portrait shows a sturdy man with dark eyes, hair, moustache, and short beard. He is wearing a dark jacket that has a broad white collar and full sleeves.

A self-portrait of Velásquez is featured on the dust jacket of *I, Juan de Pareja.* The painting, exhibited in Madrid's Museo del Prado, is in a dim portion of his large oil painting, *Las Meninas (The Family of Philip IV).* The painting is significant because it shows Velásquez with the Cross of Santiago, a sign of knighthood, on his doublet. He received the award after his death, the time when the king may have had Pareja add the cross to the painting, as shown on the back of the book's dustjacket. Treviño also wrote a romantic story about Velásquez's daughter, who is seen in his painting *Lady with a Fan.*

Treviño discouraged suggestions that the publisher add prints of these paintings in her book:

> I'm sure people would love them, because they very much enhance the story, but I have always attempted to keep down the prices of my books. With each new print, you raise the price tremendously, and I would rather more people had access to my books than actually saw the prints. At the same time, children might be tempted to look up reproductions of those paintings. Anything you discover for yourself is valuable.

The author also had to be content with sometimes seeing reproductions of paintings rather than the actual works:

> When I was in Spain, I saw one portrait of Pareja in the Museo del Prado that was since sold, and there are others in private collections that I was not able to see. I saw reproductions of them in Spanish books about collections. Even the one of Pareja, which was bought by the Metropolitan, is now in a private collection. Unfortunately, many of the great paintings of the world are still in private hands.

Treviño had limited documentation from Velásquez with which to embellish her story:

> Painters are laconic. They talk through their brushes. Only one quotation we know for sure came from Velásquez: "I would rather be first in painting something ugly than twentieth in painting something beautiful." You must immediately understand that all his painting transcends the subject matter. For example, he painted portraits of two of the dwarfs of the court. . . . Something shines through in them. They move the viewer and are very beautiful, because undoubtedly Velásquez was a psychologist, whether he knew it or not. He saw what was inside, as well as outside, and he knew how to paint it.

The author found her own way to write a biography with few primary resources concerning Velásquez and Pareja:

> I think the first thing is to cultivate all you can of a feeling of empathy, of getting into the shoes and inside the skin of another person, feeling what he must have felt, and seeing what he must have seen.
>
> I often write in first person, because it helps the reader to visualize himself inside another skin. If the painter has written little, a biographer, beyond knowing a few dates, must merely surmise something from the paintings. In the case of other biographies, you judge character and feelings of your subject through that person's work.

Treviño's books show her unusual thematic approach:

> The theme in *I, Juan de Pareja* is the same as in every book I have written. The theme is love. I feel that love is the motor that animates us all. It's the cure of everything ill. It's the rescue of the hurt and bewildered, and there are still enormous fields in which we must learn to love. I personally feel that this is why we are here on Earth: to learn to love. When I discover an example of this, I like to write about it. Certainly the marvelous relationship between Juan de Pareja and Velásquez can only be described by that word, love, although it was friendship between two men of different races. . . . I would say that second to love in all my books, I would put compassion, because people have to open their hearts to every living thing and to each other.

Readers are curious about why Treviño dedicated *I, Juan de Pareja* to her agent, Virginia Rice, rather than to a family member. The author commented:

> Virginia Rice is much, much more than an agent. She was a very dear and devoted friend, and a staunch supporter of everything I wanted to do. *I, Juan de Pareja* had been offered twice before when nobody wanted to print it. She was

behind me all the time. Besides, I've dedicated other books to members of my family.

When *I, Juan de Pareja* won the Newbery, she sent me a telegram: "Hooray, we've won the Newbery! I went downstairs and bought a chocolate bar and ate it." This was her celebration!

While Treviño was in Spain gathering information for *I, Juan de Pareja*, she researched *Casilda of the Rising Moon* (Farrar, Strauss & Giroux, 1967), a tale of Saint Casilda in eleventh-century Spain. She was born a princess, daughter of a Moorish king who fought Christians to hold Toledo. Casilda makes mercy visits at night to help Christian prisoners in her father's castle dungeon. She becomes Christian and leaves her luxurious life to serve those who are ill.

Casilda preceded *Turi's Poppa* (Farrar, Strauss & Giroux, 1968) by one year. Based on fact, *Turi's Poppa* concerns Turi Hubay, a boy in Hungary, whose Gypsy mother died of tuberculosis. Turi's father, who is in debt from trying to save his wife, receives a letter from Cremona, Italy, inviting him to lead the Institute of Violin Making, a school where he had trained. Father and son walk across Hungary and Yugoslavia into Italy.

Here Is Mexico (Farrar, Strauss & Giroux, 1970), which is nonfiction, touches on Mexico's early civilizations, the conquistador period, and the world's first great land revolution to the present. She adds the taste, smells, and feelings of Mexico. Next, the author offered young people fantasy, *Beyond the Gates of Hercules* (Farrar, Strauss & Giroux, 1971), named for Plato's words about the lost continent of Atlantis. Treviño focused on the island, Poseidon, where she creates six children in a leading family, the Archers, who tend the sacred saffron flower. All are doomed when the sea drowns them.

Just as Treviño's older son inspired *I, Juan de Pareja*, her younger son, Enrique helped her with *Juárez, Man of Law* (Farrar, Strauss & Giroux, 1974): "He guided my study and got me a fine bibliography in Spanish," she said. The nonfiction book tells the story of a Zapotec Indian who was born into poverty in 1806, became Mexico's Supreme Court president, and eventually Mexico's president. His presidency was interrupted for three years by the reign of French-supported Maximilian and Carlota. In the United States, President Lincoln recognized the Juárez government.

In the late 1960s, Treviño began to work on her books in her Mexican ranch-style home with a terrace, lush garden, and oval swimming pool, all surrounded by a high wall and only two blocks from the Cuernavaca city market. Here she has graciously received enthusiasts of children's literature and has played chamber music.

UPDATE

Treviño and her son, Enrique Borton, endorsed Manuel Figueroa's *Yo, Juan de Pareja* in the *School Library Journal* (May 1997, p. 154). The book is the Spanish version of the 1966 Newbery Medal winner.

Voigt (far right) with Jaqueline Weiss and Carolyn Field

Cynthia Voigt, author (1942–)

1988 Interview

Reviewers have praised author Cynthia Voigt's strong sense of place and rich characterizations as her greatest strengths. For her, character delineation is like "pulling out a thin piece of torte. It's that narrow sliver from which I intuit outwards. I think that's why most of my characters are absolutely different."

"I enjoy interweaving plots of books in a series," Voigt shared. Her best-known books are the "Tillerman Family" series. *Homecoming* (Atheneum, 1981), the first book, was a 1981 Notable Children's Trade Book in the Field of Social Studies and an American Book Award nominee. The second book, *Dicey's Song* (Atheneum, 1982), won the 1983 Newbery Medal, and the third, *A Solitary Blue* (Atheneum, 1983), was a 1984 Newbery Honor Book. The fourth book, *The Runner* (Atheneum, 1985), won the 1988 (Dutch) Silver Pencil Award. Beyond this series, her individual books have also won recognition, including *The Callender Papers* (Atheneum, 1983), which earned the Mystery Writers of America Edgar Award, and *Izzy, Willy-Nilly* (Atheneum, 1986), which received the 1990 California Young Readers' Award.

"Writing is important in my life, Voigt said. "When I'm not writing, I tend to screw up in everything else. I get grouchy."

Cynthia Irving was born on February 25, 1942, in Boston, and grew up in a small Connecticut town, the second of five children; she has two sisters close to her in age and twin brothers who are thirteen years younger. *The Secret Garden* was the first book she selected from her grandmother's ample library. As a good reader in fourth grade, she complained about few available young adult books, so she read adult classics by Tolstoy and Shakespeare.

Her family encouraged her independence, sending her to Dana Hall Boarding School in Wellesley, Massachusetts. Later, she enrolled at Smith College in Northampton, Massachusetts, hoping to become a writer. After college, she worked for a year as a New York advertising agency secretary. In 1964, she moved with her first husband to Santa Fe, New Mexico, and became a teacher. "Within six months, I was certified," she recalled. "I vowed I would never teach when I left Smith, and yet, the minute I walked into a classroom, I loved it."

Cynthia taught high school English from 1965 to 1967 in Glen Burnie, Maryland. In 1972 she moved to Annapolis with her baby daughter, Jessica, and she and her first husband divorced. Once she was single again, she began to write for an hour at the end of each day.

She taught for about twenty years at the Key School, a small, private elementary and secondary institution in Annapolis. She instructed English in second, fifth, and seventh grades, and required book reports in the last two grades. She began to read children's literature herself, discovering: "It inspired me with writing ideas, a new 'country' for me to explore!"

In 1974, Cynthia married Walter Voigt, who taught Latin, Greek, and ancient history at the Key School. She was a full-time teacher and still wrote for an hour a day until she became pregnant. Then she taught part-time and wrote more until her son Peter, nicknamed "Duffle," was born.

Voigt told how she got her first book published in 1981:

> I sent the first three chapters of *Homecoming* to five publishers, and only one, Atheneum, responded positively, though the editor thought it was too long.
>
> What did the other four write? One had moved without leaving a forwarding address. One didn't read Xerox copies. One replied, "It's much too long, so I'd like to see something else you've done." The last one commented, "Yes, you can write for children, but this doesn't have too much plot," and I thought: *This is the best plot I've ever cooked up!*

Voigt was prompted to write *Homecoming* after a visit to a supermarket. She said, "I pulled in next to a car where children were waiting. As I went through the store's electric eye, I worried: What would happen if no one ever came back for those children?" Buoyed by that question, Voigt reported:

> I wrote an outline, then a chapter, revised my outline, typed a second chapter, and revised the outline again. I planned a book that was half its present length with the children's long Connecticut walk down Route 1 ending at Bridgeport. In the midst of writing, the grandmother popped up out of my typewriter, and I could actually hear what she was saying. Then I thought: Okay, I can take the children as far as Crisfield, Maryland, to meet Gram.

The author identified with both Dicey, the oldest girl, and her eccentric grandmother: "Gram and Dicey, her oldest granddaughter, have similar character traits. They are mirror images of each other. . . . Gram's advice to Dicey, 'Reach out, hold on, and let go!' is the structural basis for the second work in the series, *Dicey's Song* [Atheneum, 1982]." In this book, the children's mother dies, so Gram adopts her grandchildren. Voigt told how *Dicey's Song* and *Homecoming* are linked:

> I think of *Dicey's Song* as the next part of *Homecoming*. It's the one book I didn't have to rewrite. When I sent the manuscript to Atheneum, my covering letter said, "I don't know if you will want this, but I think you will enjoy it."

In 1983, after Voigt received the news that *Dicey's Song* won the Newbery Medal, she and her family went for a celebration dinner at a local restaurant. Her son, Duffie, then five years old, told "Oma," his paternal grandmother, "We're going to Chicago now to win the Blueberry Medal."

The coveted first medal was followed by a second triumph. The third "Tillerman Family" book, *A Solitary Blue,* which traces the childhood of Dicey's boyfriend, Jeff Greene, became a 1984 Newbery Honor Book. In it, a male offers stability. The author stated, "In *A Solitary Blue,* Jeff's mother, Melody, deserts him at the age of seven to care for the world's 'needy.' Jeff's father, the professor, is the reliable parent. It's important not to generalize that women are the only ones who hang on," she said.

Another fine male is Liza's younger brother, Samuel or "Bullet," who is seventeen and eighteen in *The Runner.* Voigt tells why she values Bullet:

> What Bullet has is integrity. A London newspaper said, "The track star is admirable but not a good role model." My reply is, "Here is the most noble character I've ever made up." It's true that Bullet is a definite loner. He's partially autobiographical since half of me is a hermit who feels, "If I could be quiet and solitary, I could really write a lot." The other half enjoys family life.

In *The Runner*, Frank Verricker, the father of Liza's four children, tells Bullet that he offered to marry Liza when she was pregnant and give her half of his merchant seaman's wages. Liza refused. "Frank's not a good candidate for marriage," Voigt said to explain Liza's decision. "Moreover, what Liza's seen of marriage in her parents' home is not exemplary. Liza does love Frank, but loving a man doesn't mean you ought to marry him."

Voigt provokes thought in her "Tillerman Family" books, with the major theme centered on responsibility toward each other. The author proclaimed this theme "defensible" in all the books of the series. The fifth book, *Come a Stranger* (Atheneum, 1986), focuses on Mina Smiths, an African-American girlfriend whom Dicey includes in her inner circle. The sixth "Tillerman Family" book, *Sons from Afar* (Macmillan, 1987), depicts Dicey's brothers at ages sixteen and twelve. They find their father's seedy Baltimore cohorts as they explore their paternal background.

"I love this family!" Voigt said. "There is one more book that I've planned from the beginning but haven't revealed yet."

Other Voigt books include *Tell Me If the Lovers Are Losers* (Atheneum, 1982) and *Izzy, Willy-Nilly*. Some librarians have argued that *Izzy, Willy-Nilly* shows a villain, Marco, who is not punished for a terrible act. He is drunk when he drives a teenaged girl, Izzy, and causes a car accident in which she loses her leg.

While most of Voigt's books are for young adults, one that she advocates for children is *Building Blocks* (Atheneum, 1984):

> It's a quiet, time-travel fantasy that permits the protagonist to visit the past and meet his father as a child. This idea would make a good writing assignment [for my classes] but one can't teach one's own books. It's too tacky!

Voigt's family consists of her husband, Walter, who critiques her manuscripts; her daughter, Jessica, a manuscript reader; son, Duffle; and a dog, Rosie, subject of Voigt's only picture book, *Stories about Rosie* (Macmillan, 1986).

UPDATE

In 1989, Voigt released her seventh and final "Tillerman Family" book, *Seventeen Against the Dealer* (Macmillan, 1989). Here twenty-one-year-old Dicey becomes so involved in her boat-building business, she almost loses those closest to her. She trusts the wrong adult in this trying period before she agrees to marry Jeff Greene.

Inspired by local scenery, the author used Maine as her setting for *Tree by Leaf* (Atheneum, 1988), which focuses on a twelve-year-old girl after World War I. Voigt also wrote a Maine mystery, *The Vandemark Mummy* (Atheneum, 1991).

Voigt's writing in Maine and Maryland has resulted in deserving citations for the total body of her books. In 1989, the Assembly on Literature for Adolescents of the National Council of Teachers of English (ALAN) gave her its award. In 1995 she received the Margaret A. Edwards Award from American Library Association's Young Adult Library Services Association.

Lynd Ward, illustrator
(1905–1985)

May McNeer, author (1902–1994)

1974 Interview

LYND WARD

To celebrate Lynd Ward's 1953 Caldecott Medal for *The Biggest Bear,* his publisher, Houghton, gave him a very unusual Christmas gift: a bearskin-covered copy of his prizewinner. He said, "This was probably the most limited edition in the world, only two copies, one for me and one for the publisher. It's the only book that's ever interested our dog and requires moth treatment just like a fur coat. My wife [author May McNeer] brushes off any dandruff."

Beside his Caldecott Medal, Ward received a Caldecott Honor Medal for gouache illustrations in Stewart Holbrook's *America's Ethan Allen*

(Houghton, 1949). He also illustrated two Newbery Medal recipients: Elizabeth Coatsworth's 1931 winner, *The Cat Who Went to Heaven* (Macmillan, 1930), and Esther Forbes's 1944 winner, *Johnny Tremain: A Novel for Old and Young* (Houghton, 1943). He won the Lewis Carroll Shelf Award and the *Boston Globe-Horn Book* Award in 1973 for his wordless children's book, *The Silver Pony* (Houghton, 1973).

Ward was born on June 26, 1905 in Chicago. He was a sickly baby, so his parents tried an unusual cure. They bought Canadian frontier land and moved to a log cabin on Lonely Lake for the summer, returning to Chicago in October with their two children in good health. The pattern was repeated over many summers.

One picture from Lonely Lake was indelibly impressed on Ward's mind: the sight of three-hundred-pound Mrs. Bass, who loved trout fishing, being rowed from her Lonely Lake summer camp by a puny farm boy. (In his Caldecott acceptance speech, Ward alluded to the woman as a bear.) She sat heavily in the stern, and the boy rode high in the prow, much like the pictured bear and lad in *The Biggest Bear*. "I drew all the pictures in opaque watercolor before writing a single sentence, then added a minimum of words to hold it together," he said.

The Biggest Bear tells how a farmer's son, Johnny Orchard, made a pet of a bear cub that grew so big, the boy had to take it back to the woods. The bear always returned until he fell into the zookeeper's trap. The animal wound up at a zoo where food was plentiful, and Johnny was a visitor.

Ward is a perfectionist. As McNeer noted when she wrote the Caldecott Committee about her husband: "When he was doing *The Biggest Bear*, he discarded the first ten finished drawings and did them over. One drawing he did over six times." He thought of becoming an artist as early as first grade when he learned that "Ward" was "Draw" spelled backward.

Ward's father, a Methodist minister, felt called to help the poor, so he accepted Northwestern University Settlement House as his first assignment. He taught his family to identify with those who lived "back of the yards."

Ward continued to pursue his artistic interests and graduated as an art major from Columbia University's Teachers College. He married a fellow student, May McNeer. "The night of our wedding, we went to Germany for a year," May McNeer remembered. "In Leipzig at the National Academy for Graphic Arts, my husband studied wood engraving, etching, and lithography because in 1926, he couldn't get training in the United States in these techniques."

Ward explained lithography:

In the nineteenth century, an artist happened to discover rare Bavarian limestone. Part of it absorbed only water and another part, only grease. Water and grease don't mix. On a level surface of the grease-receptive part, he drew with a crayon, applied a roller with greasy ink to the picture, and pressed to print the picture on paper. Then he cleaned the stone for another color in the same picture or for a new print. Today, a lithographic picture is transferred to a metal plate for offset printing in a high-speed press.

Besides being a master lithographer, Ward excelled at wood engraving. He did wood engraving prints to illustrate May McNeer's early book for young people, *Waif Maid* (Macmillan, 1930). His wood-engraving exhibit is on display at the Smithsonian, and his prints are in permanent collections of the Library of Congress and the Metropolitan Museum of Art.

Ward's wordless, first adult novel in woodcuts is *God's Man* (Cape & Smith, 1929; World, 1966). The book argues that creative talent (like that of Keats, Shelley, van Gogh, and so on) may be traded for a short life. Ward did a total of six wordless adult woodcut novels, the first without words published in the United States. Their combined 743 illustrations are in *Storyteller Without Words: The Wood Engravings of Lynd Ward* (Abrams, 1974).

In 1973, Ward told a children's story, *The Silver Pony* (Houghton), only with opaque watercolor pictures. The book's eighty pictures show a Midwestern farm boy fantasizing six experiences atop a winged pony. On his own farm, the boy finally gets a real pony he can love. "I've used a sponge instead of brush marks for an interesting effect in the pony's wings," Ward said.

Another of Ward's juvenile books, *Nic of the Woods* (Houghton, 1965), has minimal words. Nic is Davey Woods's city dog. The Woods family takes him to their rustic summer camp, but they leave him behind to go boating. He runs away, is fearful in the forest, and returns before the family goes home.

As an artist, Ward did a casein painting for a National Park Service traveling exhibit on the Battle of Morris Creek in North Carolina, noting, "If Loyalists had won this battle, the War for Independence might have ended differently."

The artist–illustrator said he likes to work without models, relying on a prodigious memory. His black-and-white portraits from McNeer's *Armed with Courage* (Abingdon, 1957) adorn the Free Library of Philadelphia's main building. He chose a variety of media, including mezzotints (prints made from metal engravings) to illustrate four other McNeer books. He tried colored inks combined with casein for *Martin Luther* (Abingdon, 1953). He used oil on gesso for *America's Paul Revere* (Houghton, 1946) and casein in wet varnish for *America's Robert E. Lee* (Houghton, 1951). For a book on one of his favorite authors, *America's Mark Twain* (Houghton, 1962), he described his art process:

> On the black-and-white portions, I rendered with a small watercolor brush a line as fine as can be done with pen and ink, but I have the advantage of easily filling

in larger dark areas. Rather than use transparent watercolor, I favor opaque watercolor because I can hide what's underneath.

Ward created four-color lithographs "to give a full-color effect" in two of McNeer's Farrar books, *The Mexican Story* (1953) and *The Canadian Story* (1958). Identifying Cortez's picture in *The Mexican Story*, Ward showed scorn for his subject:

> Cortez, the conqueror of Mexico, the destroyer of the Aztec civilization, a man remembered in Mexico only by the fact that the Mexicans in all these hundreds of years have refused to have a single statue to Cortez anywhere in their land!

Ward's prolific work was the result of long hours. He generally labored from nine in the morning until midnight, seven days a week. He once threw away a whole set of book drawings, three months of toil, because it did not meet his high standards, he said. As another example of his perfectionism, McNeer shared: "He enjoyed building stone fireplaces, which never emitted smoke, and walls or walks, but he wouldn't come to meals as long as wet mortar lasted. He labored by moon or lantern light while his recipe for cement mix got larger and larger." For fun, he did carpentry, played an accordion by ear, and sang folk songs.

He illustrated more than two hundred books for children and adults, and was president of the Society of American Graphic Artists for six years. He was New Jersey Artist of the Year in 1963, and six years later won the Rutger's University Award. In 1973, he and May McNeer received the University of Southern Mississippi Silver Medallion for their combined work.

MAY MCNEER

May McNeer's writing of *Armed with Courage* (Houghton, 1957) brought her the Thomas Alva Edison Society Award for developing character in children. Translators have rendered four of her books in Burmese, Arabic, Greek, and several languages of India. She explained her interest in children's historical nonfiction and fiction:

> I've always loved history. I started reading history when I was a little girl. I practically lived in a large bookcase. That was my home, I think. I welcome the scent of library stacks. For me, the past is fresh with each new book. I find it difficult to bring myself up to date.

McNeer was born in 1902 in Tampa, Florida. Her aunt and mother, identical twins, raised her and moved throughout the southeast. She chose her career early, being only eleven when her first story appeared in a Washington, D.C., newspaper. She attended the University of Georgia and graduated from Columbia's School of Journalism in 1926 after meeting a fellow student, Lynd Ward, on a "blind date." In 1926 and 1927, they honeymooned in Germany where he studied, and she learned "to cook on a monster of a tile stove."

Ward and McNeer, who have been married for fifty-nine years, have two daughters, Nanda Ward Haynes, an author, and Robin Savage, a book designer, and four grandchildren. The family still summers at Canada's Lonely Lake.

In a studio on Lambs Lane in Cresskill, New Jersey, Lynd Ward illustrated books by many, including those by daughter Nanda and his wife. A studio corner houses McNeer's typewriter desk, but elsewhere, her husband's materials overflow. In the studio, a local drama group rehearsed and stored props. McNeer must have been able to concentrate on writing despite rehearsals. Her first book was published in 1929. She writes for children of all ages, from preschoolers to adolescents.

For older children, McNeer said she especially enjoys creating nonfiction that is half text and half pictures:

> We got the publisher's permission in advance for such projects and planned carefully to be comprehensive with regard to sexes, races, and religions. I prepared the text and Lynd, the pictures.

Examples of their comprehensive joint work are Abingdon's collective biographies that McNeer wrote for readers of age twelve and beyond: *Armed with Courage* (1957), which includes life accounts of Florence Nightingale, George Washington Carver, Jane Addams, Mahatma Gandhi, and Albert Schweitzer; and *Give Me Freedom* (1964), which covers William Penn, Thomas Paine, Elizabeth Cady Stanton, Marian Anderson, and Albert Einstein.

Farrar published two books for readers who are ten and older, *The Mexican Story* (1953) and *The Canadian Story* (1958). They show Ward's colorful art and McNeer's text about historical figures and interesting places.

The McNeer/Ward team also created single Houghton biographies, such as *America's Abraham Lincoln* (1957) and *America's Mark Twain*. For five years before arranging the first publication, the couple read extensively about Lincoln and visited places associated with him, such as New Salem and Springfield, Illinois, and Washington, D.C. Then Houghton commissioned McNeer to write both books and Ward to illustrate them.

After writing so much nonfiction, McNeer decided to write historical fiction. *Stranger in the Pines* (1971), intended for readers who are ten to fourteen years old, is set in New Jersey in 1830. This was a time when there was no war. Following discovery of bog iron in streams, residents started furnace towns. Bog iron was used to make weapons for the American Revolution. The prototype for her hero was the African-American physician Dr. Micah Jenkins, who often treated patients with herbs.

For readers who are fourteen years old and beyond, McNeer explained the background of her historical fiction, *Bloomsday for Maggie* (unpublished at the time of the interview):

> My publisher has to see finished copy before agreeing to print my fiction. I don't want a contract in advance because I don't want a deadline. It makes me nervous. My latest book, which I rewrote at least five times, required new research because it takes place in 1925–1926, the boom time in Florida land deals. Before I got my journalism degree, I worked on a Florida newspaper in the summers.

Bloomsday for Maggie refers to the time in Magnolia "Maggie" Murphy's life when she is planting seeds for the future since the present yields no fruit. She expects to write some front-page articles as her "fruit" when she volunteers at the *Baghdad Trumpet* in fictional Baghdad, Florida. Instead, she works in an old closet, and editors restrict her to society news, counting roses in bridal bouquets. She uses the ladies' page to reveal scandals with bitter results.

UPDATE

Houghton published McNeer's *Bloomsday for Maggie* in 1976.

On June 18, 1985, Ward died in the couple's home in Reston, Virginia. He had Alzheimer's disease. McNeer died from stroke complications on July 11, 1994, in Reston. One of the last awards she received with her husband was the 1975 Regina Medal from the Catholic Library Association.

David Wiesner, illustrator–author (1956–)

Dorothy Briley, editor (1934–1998)

1998 Interview

DAVID WIESNER

For illustrator–author David Wiesner, some stories are better said with few or no words at all. Others agree with him. He won the 1992 Caldecott Medal for *Tuesday* (Clarion, 1991), a book with minimal words, and his wordless *Free Fall* (Lothrop, 1988) was named a 1989 Caldecott Honor Book. He said:

> I always liked to tell stories, mainly with pictures, like comic books. I went to Rhode Island School of Design. My roommate, Michael Hayes, told me about a

book he'd seen in Carnegie-Mellon Library, *Madman's Drum*. Lynd Ward did it in the thirties in woodcuts but without words, and he later set a precedent when he drew a wordless children's book, *The Silver Pony* [Houghton, 1973].

Wiesner discussed the genesis of his picture storybook, *Free Fall*:

> One professor made a particular assignment: metamorphosis. We were to respond any way we thought. I've always had an interest in images that mutate and change. Since childhood, I've liked M. C. Escher's work: flat graphic images reforming into other shapes. Using paper that was ten feet long and forty inches high, I worked on oranges that broke into sections, then transformed into golden fish in water. Several professors, including David Macaulay, said, "You could do more with this idea."

Macaulay won the 1991 Caldecott Medal for *Black and White* (Houghton, 1990). Three years later, Wiesner's *Free Fall* became a 1993 Caldecott Honor Book. His story begins with a sleeping boy, tucked under a checked blanket, who had been looking at a book of maps. During a long dream sequence, blanket squares change into an overhead view of land plots that become a chessboard entry to a castle with a royal dragon. The beast alters into books containing maps that lead the boy back to bed.

Before working with watercolor, Wiesner created a dummy for *Free Fall* using charcoal pencil. The dummy, presented in folding panels, "like an accordion," is what won him a contract from Lothrop's editor in chief Dorothy Briley.

Panel size is limited when Wiesner plans his work. He said:

> I generally work close to book size. I'm governed by the size of scanners that break down colors for the printing process. Scanners tend to be twenty-four inches long, and my work is often twenty-two inches wide. I'd like to work much larger.

Wiesner's *Hurricane* (Clarion, 1990), which *School Library Journal* named among the best books of 1990, tells about a childhood incident. Wiesner pictures the adventures he and his brother, George, had in their yard after a hurricane toppled a tall elm. "When it came down, we could actually walk on the treetop. All too soon, the fallen tree became sawed logs."

Wiesner was born on February 5, 1956, the youngest of five children, and grew up in Bridgewater, New Jersey. His father, George, a chemical plant research manager, and his mother, Julia, a homemaker, encouraged his artistic talent and that of his oldest sister, Carol, and brother, George. They also fostered musical interests of all their children.

When a classroom teacher read a book and showed illustrations, Wiesner said he would create pictures in his mind. He watched "You Are an Artist," Jon Gnagy's televised art lessons, his first formal exposure to techniques. He bought Gnagy's instructional books, practicing what the expert advised. Wiesner said art lessons would have been a mistake for him, adding:

> I'm glad I didn't have private art lessons. It let me develop my own vision and style without possibly running into someone who might try to impose these on me. I know there are new things going on in schools today. This is something parents have to figure out for themselves.

In junior high, Renaissance and surrealistic paintings influenced Wiesner's style. In high school, Wiesner developed "Slop, the Wonderpig," a hero inspired by comic books. He also created his own film, "The Saga of Butchula," about a milquetoast who becomes a vampire and conquers bullies.

Planning for college, Wiesner applied to and was accepted by five art schools. He told why he never regretted his choice of Rhode Island School of Design (RISD):

> I tried all media there, particularly oils. It was a struggle, but I developed a certain level of proficiency. Eventually, I went back to watercolor, which is what I did all through grade school and high school. In coming back to watercolor, I found I brought more to it.

While Wiesner was at RISD, Trina Schart Hyman, who was then art director for the children's magazine *Cricket,* came to his campus. He accepted her offer to design a magazine cover.

After earning his bachelor's degree in fine arts, Wiesner moved to Brooklyn and began to illustrate books by other authors. He and his wife, Kim Kahng, a medical surgeon, survived a home fire that destroyed much of Wiesner's art, but he began anew. The couple now has two children: a one-year-old daughter, Jamie, and a six-year-old son, Kevin, whose colored-pen drawing of flowers was posted on his bedroom door.

Wiesner acknowledged his wife's assistance in writing the story for his first original picture book, an English fairy tale retold as *The Loathsome Dragon* (Putnam, 1987):

> When I decided I wanted to do this book, I began working on the illustrations. I wanted to continue with the pictures since I didn't have much experience as a

writer. Kim would check my progress. One day, she took the manuscript with her and returned the next morning with it rewritten, saying, "Here, see how this works!" She did a great job. The editor was thrilled, and we became the book's coauthors.

The Loathsome Dragon won the 1987 Redbook Children's Picturebook Award. The tale is about an evil witch who traps her beautiful stepdaughter in a dragon's body until the girl gains freedom.

Wiesner did his second *Cricket* cover in March 1989. Because the magazine contained an article on frogs, he chose to draw frogs flying on lily pads. Wiesner later expanded on this theme for *Tuesday*. Reflecting on his sky-filled frogs and later, pigs, Wiesner confessed, "It's the kind of animal story I've really wanted to do!"

In 1992, Wiesner showed celestial views of enormous vegetables when Clarion released his *June 29, 1999*. For her science class, a third-grade pupil, Holly Evans, attaches vegetable seedlings to orange balloons and lets them fly away. Landing on earth are giant broccoli, turnips, peppers, parsnips, and so on. Wiesner's alliterative allusions include, "Lima beans loom over Levittown."

In addition to his own books, Wiesner has done art for about twenty-five books by other authors. He illustrated Eve Bunting's *The Night of the Gargoyles* (Clarion, 1994) on such a large scale, he had to use a special scanner. Jane Yolen's *Neptune Rising* (Philomel, 1982) has a Wiesner jacket. He contrasted his artistic treatments in the Yolen and Bunting books:

> For Yolen, I did the inside pictures with brush and turpentine, using powdered graphite. They are painted with pencil and with dry brush when the turpentine has dried. In place of graphite, I used pastel for Bunting's book.

Wiesner illustrated *E.T.: The Book of the Green Planet* (Putnam, 1982), by William Kotzwinkle, based on Steven Spielberg's tale. "It was interesting working on a character that's so well known, conceiving his parents, home planet, and pet," Wiesner said.

Wiesner spoke about the special way he collaborated in illustrating *Firebrat* (Knopf, 1988) by Nancy Willard, who won the 1982 Newbery Medal for *A Visit to William Blake's Inn: Poems for Innocent and Experienced Travelers* (Harcourt, 1981):

> Willard's editor, Barbara Lucas, saw a time-consuming poster I did for an exhibition and asked Nancy Willard, "Do you think you can write a book to go with his poster?" She did just that. It was the opposite of the way I generally work.

He also did the jackets for two books by Lawrence Yep, *Rainbow People* (Harper, 1989) and *Tongues of Jade* (Harper, 1989). "Larry's a wonderful writer, and I responded to his work," Wiesner said. "He is one of the few people who inspired my book jackets. I've drawn many for others that were okay. Larry's work brought out good images for me."

More recently, Wiesner, who loved the fantastic in Stanley Kubrick's film *2001: A Space Odyssey,* complied with electronic experts' offer to write and design his own CD-ROM. *The Day the World Broke* is for viewers aged nine and older. His setting is the middle of Earth. Mechanimals, descendants of dinosaurs, live here, controlling Earth's land, air, fire, and water. Viewers make choices during the interactive compact disc, but the ending is fixed.

Originally, he presented some of his CD-ROM ideas as a proposed picture book to editor Dorothy Briley. When he realized it was too long for a picture book, he was versatile, adapting it to another medium.

DOROTHY BRILEY

Dorothy Briley, Clarion's editor in chief, was born on September 8, 1934, and was raised on a farm about thirty miles from Nashville, Tennessee. Her father, a chemist, and her mother, a homemaker, raised her with two younger brothers who still live in Tennessee.

Briley attended Middleton State Teachers' College in Murphfreesboro, Tennessee, where she trained to teach science and English. She pursued a book-publishing career, however, starting with five years in Nashville as a copy editor for Abingdon Press, a Methodist publishing house.

When Abingdon's children's book editor in New York City left, Briley went to New York, promoting liaison between Nashville and New York Abingdon offices. She said: "I succeeded in getting rid of my southern accent, because I was tired of having to repeat myself. If I ordered coffee, the waitress would reply, 'Say that again, honey.'"

After a year, Briley went to Viking as a copy editor for children's books.

My experience at Viking was *the* most influential of my career. Editor May Massee had just retired, and I had access to her files. It was an education, working with Annis Duff as editor and later, Velma Varner. My pay was the minimum wage of $2.15 per hour. From Viking, I went for a year to Dutton as children's book associate editor under Leanna Deadrick. Next, I started with Lippincott's New York office and commuted to Philadelphia monthly. I stayed for ten years as associate editor under Jeanne Vestal and replaced her as editor. I left when Harper, with plenty of editors of children's books, bought Lippincott.

I went to Lothrop, Lee, and Shepherd (part of Morrow) for ten years as editor in chief. My last switch was to Clarion (part of Houghton) as editor in chief and publisher. I've been there for eight years and going strong!

As she moved through the six publishing houses, Briley learned her job "from the ground floor up," becoming a leading editor of children's books. She also served as president of U.S. Board on Books for Young People. "I really enjoy the international aspect of that organization and see books from many perspectives," she said. She also relished encouraging talented book creators:

I'm working with Beverly Brodsky to publish the Golem story until we finally get it right. *Golem* by Clarion's David Wizniewski won the Caldecott Medal in 1997. Brodsky did it about fifteen or twenty years ago, and it was a Caldecott Honor Book, so *Golem* keeps getting medals. Nina Bawden is another good friend and novelist that I'm fond of publishing. And then, there's David Wiesner. He's always a pleasant surprise.

In addition to those mentioned, Briley published books of many other prizewinners, such as Toshi Maruki, 1983 Batchelder winner for *Hiroshima no pika* (Lee and Shepard, 1980); Russell Freedman, 1988 Newbery Medal recipient for *Lincoln: A Photobiography* (Clarion, 1987); and Karen Cushman, 1996 Newbery Medal winner for *The Midwife's Apprentice* (Houghton, 1995).

Briley was at Lothrop when Wiesner met her, and he followed her to Clarion. She spoke about his work:

I really liked his *Free Fall* dummy. It was so detailed! *Tuesday* was popular, selling 35,000 copies even before it became a Caldecott winner. It's fun! It's pleasant to look at. Sometimes books are so sophisticated in their art style, they're 'off putting' to very young children. It's an easy book to hand to a child.

UPDATE

Dorothy Briley died of a heart attack in New York City on May 25, 1998, at age sixty-three.

Jane Yolen, author (1939–)

John Schoenherr, illustrator (1935–)

1991 Interview

JANE YOLEN

Jane Yolen, a gifted poet and storyteller, seems to be able to write in rhyme just about any time:

> On an American Intellectual History exam at Smith College, I wrote in rhyme. The professor was walking up and down the aisles as proctor for the exam. He suddenly looked over and realized I was writing in rhyme. He was so fascinated, he forgot to watch the other people. Whether they cheated or not, I don't know. I got an A-plus for grace under fire, though I actually deserved a C.

Creative to her core, Yolen found it easier to write in verse at times than in prose. The prolific author has signed a contract for her two-hundredth book in a list mainly for young people. She wrote *The Emperor and the Kite* (World Publishing Company, 1967), illustrated by Ed Young, a 1968 Caldecott Honor Book and a Lewis Carroll Shelf Award winner. Also winning the Carroll Award was *The Girl Who Loved the Wind* (Crowell, 1972). Her literary folk tale collection, *The Girl Who Cried Flowers and Other Tales* (Crowell, 1974), was a 1975 National Book Award nominee. Another literary folk tale, *The Seeing Stick* (Crowell, 1977), won the 1978 Christopher Award. Her book *The Devil's Arithmetic* (Viking, 1988), a Holocaust story, won awards from the Jewish Book Council and the Association of

Jewish Libraries. She has also received many readers-choice awards for her books.

Yolen was born in New York City on February 11, 1939, and was raised in a culturally rich environment. Her mother, Elizabeth Berlin Yolen, a social worker, wrote crossword puzzles. Her father, Will Hyatt Yolen, a journalist and a descendant of Russian storytellers, wrote two books, edited five, and composed both plays and radio scripts. Both parents read to their daughter early, and she taught herself to read before starting school. She was a precocious writer: "I was a writer from the time I learned to write." She composed her first grade's vegetable musical, performing as a carrot and ending in a salad finale.

Yolen entered Hunter High School, a school for gifted girls, after passing a sixth-grade qualifying test. It was there that she wrote her first two books. After her family moved to Westport, Connecticut, Yolen attended Staples High, where she won the school's English prize and toured with the choir. She received a bachelor's degree in 1960 from Smith College in Massachusetts, hoping to be a journalist. Instead, she moved to New York City to work for publishers. In 1962, she became Alfred A. Knopf's assistant editor of juvenile books. On her twenty-second birthday, she learned that McKay would publish her *Pirates in Petticoats* (1963), nonfiction about female pirates.

In 1962 Yolen married David Stemple, now a computer science professor at the University of Massachusetts, Amherst. The couple camped in Europe in 1965, returning for the birth of their first child, Heidi.

Yolen's *The Emperor and the Kite*, a literary folk tale, depicts a tiny princess who attaches food to a kite to reach her father in a tower prison. She later ties a rope to the kite, which her father grabs and descends to safety.

Yolen dedicated *The Emperor and the Kite*, "To my father, who is king of the kite fliers and for my little princess, Heidi Elisabet." She said, "My father merited the dedication since he had been the world's champion kite flyer who won his championship in 1959 at the Hunting Palace of the Maharaja of Barrackpore near Calcutta, India." Her father wrote *The Young Sportsman's Guide to Kite Flying* and *The Complete Book of Kites and Kite Flying*. The *Guinness Book of World Records* cited him for keeping a kite aloft for 179 hours with a team's help.

All three of Yolen's children inherited her creativity. Her daughter, Heidi Piatt, a probation officer in Fort Lauderdale, Florida, and mother of Maddison Jane Piatt, has collaborated on a book with Yolen. Yolen's second child, Adam Stemple, is a musician. He arranges all of his mother's music and has written one music book alone and four with her. She has had two musical plays produced and has written most of an opera libretto. Yolen's youngest son, Jason Stemple, received a graphic arts degree, studied for a business degree, and works on photographic poetry books with his mother.

While many book creators work with background tunes, Yolen cannot listen to music as she writes because its rhythm influences her. She reads all of her material aloud, requiring it to satisfy the ear as well as the eye. Anything Scottish has special appeal to the author, who has a second home in Fife, Scotland. Yolen's musical score, "The Grey Selchie of Sule Skerrie," is at the end of *Greyling* (World Publishing Company, 1968). It is a literary folk tale about a childless fisherman and his wife who raise a selchie, Greyling, as their son. In myths from the Scottish islands of Shetland, a selchie is a seal in the ocean and a human on land. After rescuing the fisherman from turbulent storm waters, Greyling elects to stay in the sea as a seal.

Ed Young illustrated *The Girl Who Loved the Wind*, using watercolor/collage to suggest Persia. This is the story of Princess Danina, protected by her merchant father, who finds her walled palace imprisoning. She accepts the wind's challenge to leave and discover the real world.

Another land, ancient Greece, is the setting for Yolen's title story in a collection, *The Girl Who Cried Flowers and Other Tales*. The story concerns Olivia, who provides bouquets for villagers by shedding tears that turn into flowers, even though her husband, Panos, forbids such sadness. Another sensitive literary folk tale, *The Seeing Stick*, is a free-verse tale that traces how blind Princess Hwei Ming in ancient China learned to "see" with her fingers on a carved seeing stick. Illustrations by Remy Charlip and Demetra Maraslis are black and white in the beginning when the princess lives in darkness, and switch to color when she begins to "see." Yolen discussed reader reaction:

> I still find people coming up who say that the last line made them cry. In fact, someone from my writers' group [with Patricia MacLachlan, Ann Turner, Sulamith Oppenheim, and Zane Kotter] asked, "Is the old man blind?" I replied, "Yes, of course." Then I added the last line and threaded that idea throughout the book.

Yolen discussed another tearful line in her literary folk tale, "The Boy Who Sang for Death" from *The Dream Weaver* (Collins, 1979). The author referred to Karl's fine singing voice as his gift:

> The boy says, "Any gift I have I would surely give to get my mother back." When I wrote it, I didn't have anyone in mind. I was in my kitchen alone one day and started crying when I realized this was a reference to my mother who had died eight years earlier [of lung cancer].

For her family and others, Yolen wrote a Holocaust story, *The Devil's Arithmetic* (Viking, 1988). In this fantasy, thirteen-year-old Hannah opens the door for Elijah during a Passover *seder* (ceremonial dinner) and finds herself in a Polish Jewish village during the 1940s. Her name there is Chaya, the Hebrew word for "life." What she experiences is life threatening as Nazi soldiers take her and her family to a death camp. "This book was translated into German in Vienna, Austria and won an award from German children," Yolen said. "That is significant!"

The Devil's Arithmetic helped bring Yolen the 1988 Kerlan Award for "singular achievements in the creation of children's literature." In New York state and Nebraska, her satire concerning a Victorian British pig detective-butler, *Piggins*, won readers-choice awards. She also welcomed Garden State's Children's Book Award for *Commander Toad in Space* (Coward, 1980), part of a free-verse science fiction series sprinkled with puns. "Children want to see if they can solve the mystery before Piggins does," Yolen said. "I do more revisions for my short fiction and poetry (ten to thirty revisions) than for my novels. I make them look simple."

For young adults, Delacorte published Yolen's science fiction "Pit Dragon" trilogy: *Dragon's Blood* (1982), *Heart's Blood* (1984), and *A Sending of Dragons* (1987).

Yolen thinks her main strengths are her style and inventive stories, though she wishes she had more intricate plots, and she considers her characterizations as weak.

Yolen taught children's literature for six years at Smith College. She is now a Harcourt Brace & Company editor with her own imprint. That does not guarantee acceptance of her own manuscripts, and for them, she uses many other publishers:

I have twenty publishers because no one house wants to publish eight of mine per year. I prefer to finish a novel before I get a contract, and the same with a picture book to see how it molds itself. After revisions are approved, the editor will look for an illustrator.

People think you're working only when you're at your typewriter, computer, or drawing board. So much is headwork. I'm thinking about a book all the time. I work from about 7 A.M. until noon. Then I take a break, walk or do errands, and in the afternoon, I edit from 2 to 5 P.M. I can do my editing when my brain doesn't work, but not my writing.

With candor, Yolen discussed rejections:

I have drawers full of rejections. Just because you're successful, you can't stop striving for improvement. Two weeks ago, I had a picture book rejected. It doesn't mean that someone else won't pick it up. *Owl Moon* was turned down by two publishers.

Yolen convinced Philomel to publish *Owl Moon*. The book's original Pa was her husband, a rugged West Virginia former mountaineer, and the girl in the book was her daughter, Heidi. Yolen knows how much the pictures contributed to *Owl Moon*'s success, so she praised John Schoenherr, its illustrator.

JOHN SCHOENHERR

Philomel's editor, Patricia Gauch, coaxed John Schoenherr, the wildlife painter, to return to illustrating, without color separation and with no need to travel. She offered him *Owl Moon* by a fellow nature enthusiast, Jane Yolen, and it brought him the 1988 Caldecott Medal.

Schoenherr's self-written and illustrated children's book *The Barn* (Little, Brown, 1968) was an ALA Notable Book. He has mainly illustrated children's books by other authors, including two Newbery Honor Books: Sterling North's *Rascal* (Dutton, 1964) and Miska Miles's *Annie and the Old One* (Little, Brown, 1972). He was the artist for Jean Craighead George's 1973 Newbery Medal winner, *Julie of the Wolves* (Harper, 1973). He won a 1965 World Science Fiction Award as best science fiction artist of the year and a silver rocket ship, two feet tall, a Hugo Award, for illustrating Frank Herbert's *Dune* (Putnam, 1965), adult science fiction.

Schoenherr was born on July 5, 1935 in New York City, and spoke only German in his early years. His father was German and his mother, Hungarian. As a child, to communicate with neighbors he once drew with chalk on a cellar door. He learned English when he was older than three while his mother practiced it, her fifth language, by reading him color comics.

For his eighth birthday, his parents gave him a small set of oil paints. Later, after he visited art museums, he discovered the American Museum of Natural History, which provided artists with chairs, so he sat as he drew habitat groups. It was at this museum that spelunkers met, and a few years later, he began his hobby of exploring caves. Also at this museum, he learned about the Art Students League of New York and from age thirteen began attending classes.

Stuyvesant High School was a challenge for him. The school did not offer art, so he focused on biology. "I almost became a biologist but found that I enjoyed drawing specimens more than dissecting them," he said. His first published art was in Stuyvesant High's 1952 yearbook, the *Indicator*.

He next attended Brooklyn's Pratt Institute, earning a bachelor's degree in fine arts. He enjoyed photography but failed one subject, nature drawing. When school ended, he tried to earn a living as a freelance illustrator of covers for paperbacks and science fiction magazines.

He acquired a snake, and a potential girlfriend, Judy Gray, who not only came to see the snake but also went spelunking with him, a girl "too good to lose," he said. She even backpacked in the Adirondacks on their 1960 honeymoon. They tented on a western trip where he photographed bison. Their bonuses were indoor plumbing at home and a daughter, Jennifer.

"The first book I illustrated was assigned since the preferred artist was too busy," Schoenherr said. Based on his Bronx Zoo art, Dutton offered Schoenherr a chance to illustrate Sterling North's classic about a raccoon, *Rascal.* His main model was a pillow covered with a raccoon skin, but he also did zoo sketches. Black-and-white pictures of Rascal show the animal as Sterling's constant companion when the boy is eleven until beyond his twelfth birthday. Rascal leaves in 1919 when he hears a potential mate's call.

Little, Brown liked *Rascal*'s pictures and hired Schoenherr to illustrate *Mississippi Possum* (1965) by Miska Miles. This book shows an African-American farm family, the Jacksons. Their daughter, Rose Mary, lets an opossum sit on her shoulder. A zookeeper found a wild opossum and brought it to Schoenherr as a model. The artist made a cage for the animal, but he gave it away after completing drawings.

The Schoenherrs bought an 1865 farmhouse in Stockton, New Jersey, close enough to New York City for the artist to commute several times weekly. On the house's screened porch was a playpen for a new family member, son Ian, a future illustrator. Schoenherr rebuilt a barn on his property as a studio. There he illustrated books, such as Walt Morey's tale of a bear, *Gentle Ben* (Dutton, 1963).

Into a neighbor's abandoned barn, part of which dated from the 1780s, Schoenherr trailed a skunk and found its enemy, a great horned owl with no sense of smell. Then he wrote *The Barn* (Little Brown, 1968), with black-and-white illustrations.

By 1978, Schoenherr had illustrated nine more of Miles's books featuring a bear, beaver, bobcat, cat, dog, fox, otter, rabbit, and rat. When wild animals were Miles's subject, Schoenherr drew them wild, made tense from reaction to human beings.

Schoenherr enjoyed exciting paid travel, such as a National Park Service commission to paint bears in the Great Smokies. The artist photographed elusive bears, which he later painted, integrating them into his water-colored forest scenes. On another trip, he was official artist of a tour to Arecibo, Puerto Rico, and he painted the cave where the Camuy River flows. He even received a commission to paint wildlife in Iran for a month. He and Judy hiked miles in the Elburz Mountains, stalking leopards, wild goats, and boars. He once returned from a trip and saw a bear in his own backyard.

He later went to Alaska to study and photograph Kodiak bears at close range as they caught and ate red salmon. He found a brown bear on a pumice beach with a smoking volcano in the background. After returning home, he painted this scene, one that delighted a gallery.

For the next seven years, Schoenherr worked only on large gallery paintings, often in oils. His gallery art included an acrylic, *Otter,* rendered with realistic fur from an Adirondack model, and *Fatherly Pride,* an oil painting of Canada geese parents, the male spreading his wings to protect his three goslings. Photographs of Schoenherr's paintings and those of eleven other artists are in *From the Wild: Portfolios of North America's Finest Wildlife Artists* (Northword Press, 1987).

Obviously successful, Schoenherr acknowledged some rejections: "A gallery may return my painting, saying, 'It's not saleable.' Though I get a contract before illustrating a book, I revise my work more than the art director demands, so I do the rejecting at times."

On an upbeat note, he mentioned *Owl Moon,* which he dedicated to his granddaughter, Nyssa Hargrave, Jennifer's child. For the first time, he could work in full color, and he chose pen with watercolor on d'Arches paper. His wife suggested he enliven wintry scenes by showing hiding animals, which he did. He also added dramatic shadows on the snow. Remembering the joy of sharing outdoor experiences with his own children, Schoenherr agreed with Yolen's realistic attitude toward the wild. He shared details about *Owl Moon:*

> The opening page shows my house and my neighbor's barn in winter. A father and his six-year-old daughter walked throughout the woods with me one Sunday afternoon before I did the illustrations. After all, the main interest of the story is in the feelings of the little girl. I was quite surprised when this book won the 1988 Caldecott Medal.

Philomel was also surprised and rushed a printing of 50,000 more copies of *Owl Moon.* Schoenherr became popular overnight after receiving the Caldecott Medal, and had to delay more artwork to make public appearances. He acquiesced when Philomel's editor encouraged him to write and illustrate his own books again.

Using the excuse that he needed to mention a second grandchild, Emily, in a book dedication, Schoenherr created a picture storybook in watercolor about his favorite animal, *Bear* (Philomel, 1991). He first traveled to the Alaskan Peninsula to study the coastal species. The text is sad because a young bear's mother is gone, and he must learn to catch fresh salmon to avoid starvation. In the abrupt ending, the cub has become a mature bear who has "forgotten his mother." Schoenherr concluded:

> It's about a season in the life of a bear. It's not a given that bears will have a happy life. They have to work for it. Even though they're probably the largest,

most powerful carnivores I've drawn, their lives are still "touch and go." They're not born with the ability to survive. They need to learn.

In illustration and text, Schoenherr, who has illustrated more than seventy books, shows deep respect for animals, small and large, in challenging environments. He said he identifies with prehistoric artists who drew on cave walls their memorials to favorite or feared animals.

UPDATE

Yolen won the 1992 Regina Medal for all her books.

In 1996 Yolen and her daughter, Heidi Piatt, published *Meet the Monsters* (Walker), a monster guidebook. Yolen also wrote a memorial after the death of her kite-flying father, *Grandad Bill's Song* (Philomel, 1994). Her lyrical rhymes give relatives' answers to the grandson's question, "What did you do on the day Grandad died?"

In 1995, Yolen wrote *And Twelve Chinese Acrobats* (Philomel), fiction based on fact, about Wolf (her father's real name) and his older brother, Lou, in old Russia. Lou runs away from a Kiev military school and brings home twelve Chinese acrobats. They later return to Moscow, looking for a circus, and Lou goes to America, hoping to bring his family here.

Schoenherr shifted his setting and focus from bears to feature a gosling in a pond in another self-written Philomel picture storybook, *Rebel* (1995). Unlike his brothers and sisters, a newly hatched gosling swims away from them, waddling into dangers in the pond and dark forest.

Appendix
Children's Book Awards

THE JOHN NEWBERY MEDAL

This U.S. medal is named for an eighteenth-century British publisher and bookseller. The award is announced each January by the Association for Library Service to Children, a division of the American Library Association. The group judges which book showed the most distinguished writing for children in the previous year. The author must be a U.S. citizen, and the book must be published in the United States.

1922 *The Story of Mankind* by Hendrik Willem van Loon (Liveright)
1923 *The Voyages of Doctor Dolittle* by Hugh Lofting (Lippincott)
1924 *The Dark Frigate* by Charles Boardman Hawes (Little, Brown)
1925 *Tales from Silver Lands* by Charles J. Finger (Doubleday)
1926 *Shen of the Sea* by Arthur Bowie Chrisman (Dutton)
1927 *Smoky the Cowhorse* by Will James (Scribner)
1928 *Gay-Neck: The Story of a Pigeon* by Dhan Gopal Mukerji (Dutton)
1929 *The Trumpeter of Krakow* by Eric P. Kelly (Macmillan)
1930 *Hitty: Her First Hundred Years* by Rachel Field (Macmillan)
1931 *The Cat Who Went to Heaven* by Elizabeth Coatsworth (Macmillan)
1932 *Waterless Mountain* by Laura Adams Armer (Longmans, Green)
1933 *Young Fu of the Upper Yangtze* by Elizabeth Foreman Lewis (Winston)
1934 *Invincible Louisa* by Cornelia Meigs (Little, Brown)
1935 *Dobry* by Monica Shannon (Viking)
1936 *Caddie Woodlawn* by Carol Ryrie Brink (Macmillan)
1937 *Roller Skates* by Ruth Sawyer (Viking)
1938 *The White Stag* by Kate Seredy (Viking)
1939 *Thimble Summer* by Elizabeth Enright (Farrar)
1940 *Daniel Boone* by James H. Daugherty (Viking)
1941 *Call It Courage* by Armstrong Sperry (Macmillan)

1942 *The Matchlock Gun* by Walter D. Edmonds (Dodd)

1943 *Adam of the Road* by Elizabeth Janet Gray (Viking)

1944 *Johnny Tremain* by Esther Forbes (Houghton)

1945 *Rabbit Hill* by Robert Lawson (Viking)

1946 *Strawberry Girl* by Lois Lenski (Viking)

1947 *Miss Hickory* by Carolyn Sherwin Bailey (Viking)

1948 *The Twenty-One Balloons* by William Pène du Bois (Viking)

1949 *King of the Wind* by Marguerite Henry (Rand McNally)

1950 *The Door in the Wall* by Marguerite de Angeli (Doubleday)

1951 *Amos Fortune, Free Man* by Elizabeth Yates (Dutton)

1952 *Ginger Pye* by Eleanor Estes (Harcourt)

1953 *Secret of the Andes* by Ann Nolan Clark (Viking)

1954 *. . . And Now Miguel* by Joseph Krumgold (Crowell)

1955 *The Wheel on the School* by Meindert DeJong (Harper)

1956 *Carry On, Mr. Bowditch* by Jean Lee Latham (Houghton)

1957 *Miracles on Maple Hill* by Virginia Sorensen (Harcourt)

1958 *Rifles for Watie* by Harold Keith (Crowell)

1959 *The Witch of Blackbird Pond* by Elizabeth George Speare (Houghton)

1960 *Onion John* by Joseph Krumgold (Crowell)

1961 *Island of the Blue Dolphins* by Scott O'Dell (Houghton)

1962 *The Bronze Bow* by Elizabeth George Speare (Houghton)

1963 *A Wrinkle in Time* by Madeleine L'Engle (Farrar)

1964 *It's Like This, Cat* by Emily Neville (Harper)

1965 *Shadow of a Bull* by Maia Wojciechowska (Atheneum)

1966 *I, Juan de Pareja* by Elizabeth Borton de Treviño (Farrar)

1967 *Up a Road Slowly* by Irene Hunt (Follett)

1968 *From the Mixed-Up Files of Mrs. Basil E. Frankweiler* by E. L. Konigsburg (Atheneum)

1969 *The High King* by Lloyd Alexander (Holt)

1970 *Sounder* by William H. Armstrong (Harper)

1971 *Summer of the Swans* by Betsy Byars (Viking)

1972 *Mrs. Frisby and the Rats of NIMH* by Robert C. O'Brien (Atheneum)

1973 *Julie of the Wolves* by Jean Craighead George (Harper)

1974 *The Slave Dancer* by Paula Fox (Bradbury)

1975 *M. C. Higgins the Great* by Virginia Hamilton (Macmillan)

1976 *The Grey King* by Susan Cooper (Atheneum)

1977 *Roll of Thunder, Hear My Cry* by Mildred D. Taylor (Dial)

1978 *Bridge to Terabithia* by Katherine Paterson (Crowell)

1979 *The Westing Game* by Ellen Raskin (Dutton)

1980 *A Gathering of Days: A New England Girl's Journal 1830–32* by Joan Blos (Scribner)

1981 *Jacob Have I Loved* by Katherine Paterson (Crowell)

1982 *A Visit to William Blake's Inn: Poems for Innocent and Experienced Travelers* by Nancy Willard (Harcourt)

1983 *Dicey's Song* by Cynthia Voigt (Atheneum)

1984 *Dear Mr. Henshaw* by Beverly Cleary (Morrow)

1985 *The Hero and the Crown* by Robin McKinley (Greenwillow)

1986 *Sarah, Plain and Tall* by Patricia MacLachlan (Harper)

1987 *The Whipping Boy* by Sid Fleischman (Greenwillow)

1988 *Lincoln: A Photobiography* by Russell Freedman (Clarion)

1989 *Joyful Noise: Poems for Two Voices* by Paul Fleischman (Harper)

1990 *Number the Stars* by Lois Lowry (Houghton)

1991 *Maniac Magee* by Jerry Spinelli (Little, Brown)

1992 *Shiloh* by Phyllis Reynolds Naylor (Atheneum)

1993 *Missing May* by Cynthia Rylant (Orchard)

1994 *The Giver* by Lois Lowry (Houghton)

1995 *Walk Two Moons* by Sharon Creech (Harper)

1996 *The Midwife's Apprentice* by Karen Cushman (Houghton)

1997 *The View from Saturday* by E. L. Konigsburg (Atheneum)

1998 *Out of the Dust* by Karen Hesse (Scholastic)

1999 *Holes* by Louis Sachar (Farrar)

2000 *Bud, Not Buddy* by Christopher Paul Curtis (Delacorte)

2001 *A Year Down Yonder* by Richard Peck (Dial)

THE RANDOLPH CALDECOTT MEDAL

This U.S. medal is named for a nineteenth-century British illustrator of children's books. It is for the illustrator of the most distinguished picture book for children in the previous year and is chosen by a committee of the Association for Library Service to Children, a division of the American Library Association.

A single listing indicates that the book was written and illustrated by the same person.

1938 *Animals of the Bible, a Picture Book,* illustrated by Dorothy O. Lathrop, text by Helen Dean Fish (Lippincott)

1939 *Mei Li* by Thomas Handforth (Doubleday)

1940 *Abraham Lincoln* by Ingri and Edgar Parin d'Aulaire (Doubleday)

1941 *They Were Strong and Good* by Robert Lawson (Doubleday)

1942 *Make Way for Ducklings* by Robert McCloskey (Viking)

1943 *The Little House* by Virginia Lee Burton (Houghton)

1944 *Many Moons,* illustrated by Louis Slobodkin, text by James Thurber (Harcourt)

1945 *Prayer for a Child,* illustrated by Elizabeth Orton Jones, text by Rachel Field (Macmillan)

1946 *The Rooster Crows* by Maud and Miska Petersham (Macmillan)

1947 *The Little Island,* illustrated by Leonard Weisgard, text by Golden Mac-Donald (Doubleday)

1948 *White Snow, Bright Snow,* illustrated by Roger Duvoisin, text by Alvin Tresselt (Lothrop)

1949 *The Big Snow* by Berta and Elmer Hader (Macmillan)

1950 *Song of the Swallows* by Leo Politi (Scribner)

1951 *The Egg Tree* by Katherine Milhous (Scribner)

1952 *Finders Keepers,* illustrated by Nicolas Mordvinoff, text by William Lipkind (Harcourt)

1953 *The Biggest Bear* by Lynd Ward (Houghton)

1954 *Madeline's Rescue* by Ludwig Bemelmans (Viking)

1955 *Cinderella,* illustrated by Marcia Brown, text by Charles Perrault (Harper)

1956 *Frog Went A-Courtin',* illustrated by Feodor Rojankovsky, text by John Langstaff (Harcourt)

1957 *A Tree Is Nice,* illustrated by Marc Simont, text by Janice May Udry (Harper)

1958 *Time of Wonder* by Robert McCloskey (Viking)

1959 *Chanticleer and the Fox* by Barbara Cooney (Crowell)

1960 *Nine Days to Christmas* by Marie Hall Ets and Aurora Labastida (Viking)

1961 *Baboushka and the Three Kings,* illustrated by Nicolas Sidjakov, text by Ruth Robbins (Parnassus)

1962 *Once a Mouse* by Marcia Brown (Scribner)

1963 *The Snowy Day* by Ezra Jack Keats (Viking)

1964 *Where the Wild Things Are* by Maurice Sendak (Harper)

1965 *May I Bring a Friend?,* illustrated by Beni Montresor, text by Beatrice Schenk de Regniers (Atheneum)

1966 *Always Room for One More,* illustrated by Nonny Hogrogian, text by Sorche Nic Leodhas (Holt)

1967 *Sam, Bangs & Moonshine* by Evaline Ness (Holt)

1968 *Drummer Hoff,* illustrated by Ed Emberley, text by Barbara Emberley (Prentice-Hall)

1969 *The Fool of the World and the Flying Ship,* illustrated by Uri Shulevitz, text by Arthur Ransome (Farrar)

1970 *Sylvester and the Magic Pebble* by William Steig (Simon & Schuster)

1971 *A Story, a Story* by Gail E. Haley (Atheneum)

1972 *One Fine Day* by Nonny Hogrogian (Macmillan)

1973 *The Funny Little Woman,* illustrated by Blair Lent, text by Arlene Mosel (Dutton)

1974 *Duffy and the Devil,* illustrated by Margot Zemach, text by Harve Zemach (Dutton)

1975 *Arrow to the Sun* by Gerald McDermott (Viking)

1976 *Why Mosquitos Buzz in People's Ears,* illustrated by Leo and Diane Dillon, text by Verna Aardema (Dial)

1977 *Ashanti to Zulu: African Traditions,* illustrated by Leo and Diane Dillon, text by Margaret Musgrove (Dial)

1978 *Noah's Ark* by Peter Spier (Doubleday)

1979 *The Girl Who Loved Wild Horses* by Paul Gobel (Bradbury)

1980 *Ox-Cart Man,* illustrated by Barbara Cooney, text by Donald Hall (Viking)

1981 *Fables* by Arnold Lobel (Harper)

1982 *Jumanji* by Chris Van Allsburg (Houghton)

1983 *Shadow,* illustrated by Marcia Brown, text by Blaise Cendrars (Scribner)

1984 *The Glorious Flight: Across the Channel with Louis Blériot, July 25, 1909* by Alice and Martin Provensen (Viking)

1985 *Saint George and the Dragon,* illustrated by Trina Schart Hyman, text by Margaret Hodges (Little, Brown)

1986 *The Polar Express* by Chris Van Allsburg (Houghton)

1987 *Hey, Al,* illustrated by Richard Egielski, text by Arthur Yorinks (Farrar)

1988 *Owl Moon,* illustrated by John Schoenherr, text by Jane Yolen (Philomel)

1989 *Song and Dance Man,* illustrated by Stephen Gammell, text by Karen Ackerman (Knopf)

1990 *Lon Po Po: A Red-Riding Hood Story from China* by Ed Young (Philomel)

1991 *Black and White* by David Macaulay (Houghton)

1992 *Tuesday* by David Wiesner (Clarion)

1993 *Mirette on the High Wire* by Emily Arnold McCully (Putnam)

1994 *Grandfather's Journey* by Allen Say (Houghton)

1995 *Smoky Night,* illustrated by David Diaz, text by Eve Bunting (Harcourt)

1996 *Officer Buckle and Gloria* by Peggy Rathmann (Putnam)

1997 *Golem* by David Wizniewski (Clarion)

1998 *Rapunzel* by Paul Zelinsky (Dutton)

1999 *Snowflake Bentley,* illustrated by Mary Azarian, text by Jacqueline Briggs Martin (Houghton)

2000 *Joseph Had a Little Overcoat* by Simms Taback (Viking)

2001 *So You Want to Be President?,* illustrated by David Small, text by Judith St. George (Philomel)

CORETTA SCOTT KING AWARD

Since 1970, the American Library Association's Social Responsibilities Roundtable has annually recognized an author and, since 1974, an illustrator, both of African descent, whose book of the previous year promotes the "American dream." The January award honors Coretta Scott King, who continues the work of Dr. Martin Luther King Jr. for peace and brotherhood. A new author or illustrator of African descent may apply for a Coretta Scott King/John Steptoe New Talent Award that may be won a single time.

1970 Lillie Patterson for *Martin Luther King, Jr.: Man of Peace* (Garrard)

1971 Charlemae Rollins for *Black Troubadour: Langston Hughes* (Rand)

1972 Elton C. Fax for *17 Black Artists* (Dodd)

1973 *I Never Had It Made: An Autobiography* (of Jackie Robinson), told to Alfred Duckett (Putnam)

1974 Author: Sharon Bell Mathis for *Ray Charles* (Crowell). Illustrator: George Ford for *Ray Charles*

1975 Author: Dorothy Robinson for *The Legend of Africania* (Johnson), and its illustrator, Herbert Temple

1976 Author: Pearl Bailey for *Duey's Tale* (Harcourt). No illustrator

1977 Author: James Haskins for *The Story of Stevie Wonder* (Lothrop). No illustrator

1978 Author: Eloise Greenfield for *Africa Dream* (Crowell), and its illustrator, Carole Bayard

1979 Author: Ossie Davis for *Escape to Freedom: A Play about Young Frederick Douglass* (Viking). Illustrator: Tom Feelings for Nikki Grimes's *Something on My Mind* (Dial)

1980 Author: Walter Dean Myers for *The Young Landlords* (Viking). Illustrator: Carole Bayard for Camille Yarbrough's *Cornrows* (Coward)

1981 Author: Sidney Poitier for *This Life* (Knopf). Illustrator: Ashley Bryan for *Beat the Story-Drum, Pum-Pum* (Atheneum)

1982 Author: Mildred D. Taylor for *Let the Circle Be Unbroken* (Dial). Illustrator: John Steptoe for translator/adaptor Rosa Guy's *Mother Crocodile: An Uncle Amadou Tale from Senegal* (Delacorte)

1983 Author: Virginia Hamilton for *Sweet Whispers, Brother Rush* (Philomel). Illustrator: Peter Mugabane for his book *Black Child* (Knopf)

1984 Author: Lucille Clifton for *Everett Anderson's Goodbye* (Holt). Illustrator: Pat Cummings for Mildred Pitts Walter's *My Mama Needs Me* (Lothrop). Special Citation: Coretta Scott King, compiler, *The Words of Martin Luther King, Jr.* (Newmarket Press)

1985 Author: Walter Dean Myers for *Motown and Didi* (Viking). No illustrator

1986 Author: Virginia Hamilton for *The People Could Fly: American Black Folktales* (Knopf). Illustrator: Jerry Pinkney for Valerie Flournoy's *The Patchwork Quilt* (Dial)

1987 Author: Mildred Pitts Walter for *Justin and the Best Biscuits in the World* (Lothrop). Illustrator: Jerry Pinkney for Crescent Dragonwagon's *Half a Moon and One Whole Star* (Macmillan)

1988 Author: Mildred D. Taylor for *The Friendship* (Dial). Illustrator: John Steptoe for his book *Mufaro's Beautiful Daughters: An African Tale* (Lothrop)

1989 Author: Walter Dean Myers for *Fallen Angels* (Scholastic). Illustrator: Jerry Pinkney for Patricia C. McKissack's *Mirandy and Brother Wind* (Knopf)

1990 Author: Patricia C. and Fredrick L. McKissack for *A Long Hard Journey: The Story of the Pullman Porter* (Walker). Illustrator: Jan Spivey Gilchrist for Eloise Greenfield's *Nathaniel Talking* (Black Butterfly Press)

1991 Author: Mildred D. Taylor for *The Road to Memphis* (Dial). Illustrators: Leo and Diane Dillon for Leontyne Price's *Aida* (Harcourt)

1992 Author: Walter Dean Myers for *Now Is Your Time! The African-American Struggle for Freedom* (Harper). Illustrator: Faith Ringgold for *Tar Beach* (Crown)

1993 Author: Patricia C. McKissack for *The Dark-Thirty: Southern Tales of the Supernatural* (Knopf). Illustrator: Kathleen Atkins Smith for David A. Anderson's retelling of *The Origin of Life on Earth: An African Creation Myth* (Sights)

1994 Author: Angela Johnson for *Toning the Sweep* (Orchard). Illustrator: Tom Feelings for *Soul Looks Back in Wonder* (Dial)

1995 Author: Patricia C. and Fredrick L. McKissack for *Christmas in the Big House, Christmas in the Quarters* (Scholastic). Illustrator: James E. Ransome for James Weldon Johnson's *The Creation* (Holiday House)

1996 Author: Virginia Hamilton for *Her Stories* (Scholastic). Illustrator: Tom Feelings for *The Middle Passage: White Ships/Black Cargo* (Dial)

1997 Author: Walter Dean Myers for *SLAM* (Scholastic). Illustrator: Jerry Pinkney for Alan Schroeder's *Minty: A Story of Young Harriet Tubman* (Dial)

1998 Author: Sharon M. Draper for *Forged by Fire* (Atheneum). Illustrator: Javaka Steptoe for *In Daddy's Arms I Am Tall: African Americans Celebrating Fathers* (various poets) (Lee & Low)

1999 Author: Angela Johnson for *Heaven* (Simon & Schuster). Illustrator: Michele Wood for Toyomi Igus's *i see the rhythm* (Children's Book Press)

2000 Author: Christopher Paul Curtis for *Bud, Not Buddy* (Delacorte). Illustrator: Brian Pinkney for Kim L. Siegelson's *In the Time of the Drums* (Jump at the Sun/Hyperion Books for Children)

2001 Author: Jacqueline Woodson for *Miracle's Boys* (Putnam). Illustrator: Bryan Collier for *Uptown* (Henry Holt)

PURA BELPRÉ AWARD

This American Library Association award was named for the first Latina children's librarian in the New York Public Library. The Belpré Awards are chosen by a joint committee of the Association for Library Service to Children, a division of the American Library Association and REFORMA (National Association to Promote Library Services to the Spanish Speaking). Since 1996, the biennial award has been given to a Latino/Latina author and illustrator whose work affirms Latino culture. Belpré Award Honor Books are available.

1996 Author: Judith Ortiz Cofer for *An Island Like You: Stories of the Barrio* (Orchard, 1995). Illustrator: Susan Guevara for *Chato's Kitchen* by Gary Soto (Putnam, 1995)

1998 Author: Victor Martinez for *Parrot in the Oven: mi vida* (HarperCollins, 1996). Illustrator: Stephanie Garcia for *Snapshots from the Wedding* by Gary Soto (Putnam, 1997)

2000 Author: Alma Flor Ada for *Under the Royal Palms: A Childhood in Cuba* (Atheneum, 1998). Illustrator: Carmen Lomas Garza for *Magic Windows* (Children's Book Press, 1999)

Index

388   *Index*

About the Author

Jaqueline Shachter Weiss was born and raised in Corpus Christi, Texas. After studying at the National University of Mexico in Mexico City, she received her B.A. from the University of Texas and both her M.S. and Ed.D. from the University of Pennsylvania.

Dr. Weiss has taught children's literature at Temple University and Lincoln University. At Temple, she often had children's book creators professionally videotaped in thirty-minute interviews with her students in the studio. Other institutions requested the videos from 3023 DeKalb Blvd., Norristown, PA 19401, so the ongoing *Profiles in Literature* series began. A grant from the Public Committee for the Humanities in Pennsylvania helped support video production by Dr. Weiss, a former Temple University Creativity Award nominee and now associate professor emerita. For video information, fax Dr. Jaqueline Weiss at (610) 279-5460 or email at jackiesweiss@aol.com.

Her previous books include two for adults, and she is sole author of *Prizewinning Books for Children* (Lexington Books, D.C. Heath, 1983). With Carolyn W. Field, she wrote *Values in Selected Children's Books of Fiction and Fantasy* (Library Professional Publications, 1987), winner of the Helen Keating Ott Award from the Church and Synagogue Library Association.

Her children's book, with Eartha Kitt's audiocassette narration, is *Young Brer Rabbit and Other Trickster Tales from the Americas* (Stemmer House, 1985), a Notable Children's Book in the Field of Social Studies. She translated the tales she found in Central and South America from standard and dialectal Spanish, Portuguese, and French. The foreword is by Anne Pellowski, formerly with UNICEF.

Articles about the author's interviews with key creators of children's books in thirty countries in Europe, Asia, the Middle East, and South America have been published in *Bookbird, Journal of Reading, School Library Journal,* and publications of the U.S. Board on Books for Young People, as well as the International Reading Association.